TEACHING AND MEDIA:
A SYSTEMATIC APPROACH

Don Jay Flagg

TEACHING AND MEDIA

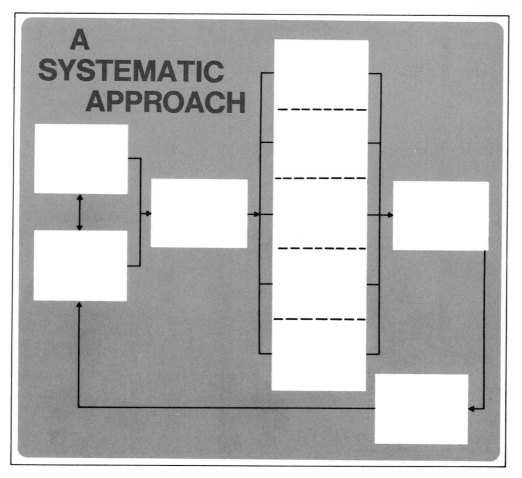

A SYSTEMATIC APPROACH

VERNON S. GERLACH
ARIZONA STATE UNIVERSITY

DONALD P. ELY
SYRACUSE UNIVERSITY

PRENTICE-HALL, INC., Englewood Cliffs, New Jersey

Library of Congress Catalog Card Number: 71-138476

Printed in the United States of America

13-891333-1

Prentice-Hall International, Inc., *London*
Prentice-Hall of Australia, Pty. Ltd., *Sydney*
Prentice-Hall of Canada, Ltd., *Toronto*
Prentice-Hall of India Private Limited, *New Delhi*
Prentice-Hall of Japan, Inc., *Tokyo*

Current printing (last digit):   10   9   8   7   6   5   4

PICTURE CREDITS

The 15 chapter opening montages are the creations of John Okladek. Credits for background photographs in the montages are included in the following sequence. CHAPTER ONE: 6–7, courtesy Ampex Corporation; 35, courtesy Dr. Carl H. Hendershot. CHAPTER TWO: 40–41, Esther Bubley, courtesy NEA. CHAPTER THREE: 76–77, background *and* foreground, James E. Sunnucks, courtesy NEA. CHAPTER FOUR: 86–87, George S. Zimbel, courtesy Educational Facilities Laboratories. CHAPTER FIVE: 108–109, courtesy Viewlex, Inc. CHAPTER SIX: 126–127, courtesy Educational Facilities Laboratories. CHAPTER SEVEN: 146–147, courtesy Viewlex, Inc. CHAPTER EIGHT: 158–159, courtesy Ampex Corporation. CHAPTER NINE: 170–171, James E. Sunnucks, courtesy NEA. CHAPTER TEN: 188–189, courtesy Ampex Corporation. CHAPTER ELEVEN: 204–205, courtesy Educational Facilities Laboratories. CHAPTER TWELVE: 230–231, George S. Zimbel, courtesy Educational Facilities Laboratories; 240, 269, Rondal Partridge, courtesy Educational Facilities Laboratories; 241, 251, 253, 259, 260, George S. Zimbel, courtesy Educational Facilities Laboratories; 252, 255, 256, James E. Sunnucks, courtesy NEA; 254, courtesy Viewlex, Inc.; 257, 258, Carl Cronbach, Syracuse University Photopress; 262, 264, courtesy Tele-Norm Corporation; 263, courtesy Chester Electronic Laboratories, Inc.; 267, courtesy General Electric Company. CHAPTER THIRTEEN: 278–279, Esther Bubley, courtesy NEA. CHAPTER FOURTEEN: 304–305, Esther Bubley, courtesy NEA. CHAPTER FIFTEEN: 320–321, left to right, courtesy Standard Projector and Equipment Co.—Viewlex, Inc.—Ampex Corporation—North American Philips Co., Inc.—Audio-Visual Products, Division of Bell & Howell Co.; 326, courtesy General Electric Company; 334, Ben Spiegel, courtesy NEA; 335, courtesy Hudson Photographic Industries, Educational Products Division; 336 both, courtesy Viewlex, Inc.; 338 both, courtesy Standard Projector and Equipment Co.; 339, courtesy Eastman Kodak Co.; 340, 366, 367 top, Carl Cronbach, Syracuse University Photopress; 345, 347, 348 top, courtesy Technicolor; 346, courtesy Audio-Visual Products, Division of Bell & Howell Co.; 348 bottom, 357, 381 bottom, Esther Bubley, courtesy NEA; 356 bottom, courtesy Charles Beseler Co.; 358, James E. Sunnucks, courtesy NEA; 359, courtesy Advance Products, Inc.; 367 bottom, Jack Stock, courtesy Seal, Inc.; 372, from *The East: Geographic Backgrounds to U.S. History*, by H. V. B. Kline, Jr., H. C. Mavrinac, and Ted C. Soens, © 1967 by Prentice-Hall, Inc.; 382, courtesy North American Philips Co., Inc.; 387, 389, courtesy Ampex Corporation.

CONTENTS

PREFACE

There is probably no single book that treats *all* of the variables which collectively constitute good teaching. In fact, we are quite certain that many of the components of good teaching have never been described. This book is an attempt to identify and to describe in detail several elements of teaching which have been useful to good teachers in the past and appear to be of continuing value. It is intended for both pre-service and in-service teachers.

The best way to learn the purpose of this book is to read the statement of objectives at the beginning of each chapter. Underlying these objectives, however, is an attempt to relate the selection and use of instructional media to teaching objectives in a systematic fashion.

The basic rationale behind our efforts is that teaching must be designed on the basis of what it is that the learner is to do . . . or produce . . . or become. If media are to be used to facilitate teaching and learning, they must be selected and used because they have a facilitating potential. But the role of media is only one aspect of the total design of instruction. Many variables have to be considered, and some of them are beyond the scope of this volume. By employing a systematic approach, we have tried to point out and usefully organize the diversity of the elements in the teaching-learning process. Further details regarding some of these elements must be sought out in other references, and as an aid to this, suggestions for further readings are given at the ends of Parts Two, Three, and Four.

The description of media characteristics has been placed at the end of the book in Part Five. The reason for a separate section is simple: we are convinced that professors who teach the course in which this text is used can demonstrate the various media far better than any book can. The Media Facts section, therefore, is a reference guide intended for use by students as a complement to the demonstrations and laboratory work which are a part of every good course in which instructional media are emphasized. The reference by itself is of little value; it must be used in conjunction with the actual media as a first-hand experience.

The authors divided the labor of writing this book in various ways, most of which defy description. Essentially, Chapters 1, 11, 12, 13, and the Media Facts section are the responsibility of Professor Ely; Chapters 2 through 10, 14, the media–subject area matrix, and the *Teacher's Manual* are the responsibility of Professor Gerlach.

The authors appreciate the assistance of:

John S. Covell and Prentice-Hall, Inc.—as capable and patient an editor and publisher as any author could hope to find;

Francis Atkinson, David Cram, Jerrold Kemp, Howard Sullivan, Desmond Wedberg, and Paul Witt—scholarly and critical readers of parts or all of the manuscript;

Lee Barclay, Nellie Bertrand, Robert Covel, Kenneth Fawson, Steve Kilgore, John Mezger, Sanford Orr, Joan Simmons, and Thomas Sweet—graduate students who are the real authors of the *Teacher's Manual*;

Mrs. Sharon Cosner and Mrs. Jean Gilman—careful and dedicated typists;

hundreds of students at Syracuse University and Arizona State University who used this text in varying stages of completion since 1966.

Above all, each author acknowledges a deep debt to his wife and children, who understood—and cared.

TEACHING AND MEDIA:
A SYSTEMATIC APPROACH

INTRODUCTION

THE TEACHER AS A COORDINATOR OF LEARNING RESOURCES

System . . . a complex unity formed of many often diverse parts subject to a common plan or serving a common purpose . . . an aggregation or assemblage of objects joined in regular interaction or interdependence.*

This book casts the teaching-learning process into a new scheme known as a *systematic approach to teaching and learning.* It will provide the teacher with a framework for the design of instruction and give the learner a roadmap for his educational process. The content is a blend of the science of learning and the art of teaching that focuses on the learner, the definition of objectives, instructional design, the proper selection of media, and the teacher as a coordinator of the entire process. For the learner the ideas contained in this book provide a declaration of independence —independence to learn as an individual regardless of the group size, and independence to learn at a rate which is commensurate with one's abilities and time.

This book is designed for the teacher who intends to be different, for the teacher who will not mimic the methods of former teachers but will begin to use contemporary resources in a systematic fashion. In the past, it has been sufficient to add a unit or a course in audiovisual materials to the teacher preparation program in order to insure an innovative dimension to the education curriculum. This approach is no longer adequate. Instructional media must now be considered as an integral aspect of the total design of instruction and not as an appendage.

The shift from simple tool competencies, such as operating audiovisual equipment and making transparencies for the overhead projector, to systematic planning for instruction is now evident. While the authors acknowledge and discuss the full range of instructional media in this book, it is always in relation to learning objectives in the instructional system. This book relates media selection and use to objectives as systematic planning is analyzed.

The basic premise behind the writing of this book is that media can be selected best and used most creatively when they are chosen on the basis of their potential for implementing specific objectives. Unless objectives are clearly defined first, selection of media is a chance matter. Unless objectives are related to the larger concept of instructional design, they stand alone. We are thus calling for a system-

Webster's Third New International Dictionary (Springfield, Mass.: G. & C. Merriam, 1966), p. 2322.

atic design of instruction, with clearly stated objectives, and a selection of media based on their potential for implementing those objectives.

The design of this book should, in itself, be an illustration of the systematic approach to instruction. It is organized as an instructional system. Media does not dominate but rather permeates all aspects of instructional design. Illustrations are used only where they will help to implement a specific objective, not as embellishment.

The reader should be an active participant in the programmed exercises which are integral parts of each chapter. You should attempt to answer each exercise immediately as a check on your mastery of the information presented and discussed to that point. An answer, or several alternative answers, will appear immediately following the question. It is helpful to cover the answer with your hand or a piece of paper, or at least to pause and think of your own answer before reading on. Of course you can read the answer immediately without attempting to make a response of your own, but that takes some of the challenge out of reading and lessens your active participation in the learning process. The questions are intended to help you to move along profitably in the book. Some of them will be a check on your comprehension of the previous section, while others will demand new kinds of answers in an attempt to lead you into the next section. In any case, view the question and answer exercises as a vital part of the learning process. The answers provided can be instant feedback to you regarding the response you have just made. These answers take the place of a teacher who might otherwise be there to confirm or correct your answers. Be an active learner by using every exercise!

The organization of the book is a kind of roadmap which should help you to discover where you have been and where you are going. Part One is an orientation to the systematic approach to instruction and the changing role of the teacher who will operate within such a system. The fact that the teacher is rapidly becoming a coordinator of learning resources rather than a dispenser of information is an essential concept for understanding the systematic approach to instruction in the schools of today and tomorrow.

Part Two discusses instructional design. It focuses on a taxonomy of instructional objectives: to identify, to name, to describe, to order, and to construct. Lesser emphasis is placed on the development of skills and the building of attitudes. Media-oriented examples of learning and teaching incidents appear throughout the discussions of objectives. This focus on learning places the emphasis at the heart of the educational process. The media then assume an appropriate role as mediators of the process. The emphasis on learning objectives also permits a more rigorous inspection of media alternatives, thus leading to a more pragmatic approach to the selection of an instructional medium.

Arranging the variables for optimum teaching and learning is the emphasis of Part Three. In this section our systematic approach is continued with an analysis of the specific strategies and techniques which can be employed. The organization of groups, the allocation of time and of learning spaces, and the selection of instructional resources follow. These factors lead to an assessment of the learner's performance. All of these variables must be considered in the design of instruction.

Part Four is an analytical look at assessment and evaluation in the teaching-learning process. This section is related to each previous chapter and raises such questions as: "Has learning taken place? If so, how do we know it? What factors have contributed to the learning?"

Although this book is about media in the process of teaching and learning, media does not dominate its content. Part Five is devoted to media facts. Since readers may be familiar with many of the media discussed in this book, the first four parts of the text are reserved for discussion of instructional design while Part Five is devoted to factual information about media. Each section of Part Five introduces one instructional medium and provides: its definition, characteristics, advantages and disadvantages, suggestions for uses, and sources. Pertinent illustrations are used to provide additional information as appropriate. This part should be used as a reference section. As you discover a particular type of equipment or medium with which you are unfamiliar, you should turn to the section in which it is described. In this way the main body of the text is not interrupted with information which may be irrelevant to the topic at hand.

The purpose of this book is to suggest a plan for the design of instruction which begins with objectives and organizes components of the process in a systematic fashion. It assumes that instructional media are integral elements of the process. If the purpose is achieved, you should be prepared to help children learn and to gain satisfaction from the outcomes you observe.

PART ONE

TEACHING AND SYSTEMS

Part One will introduce you to the central organizing concept underlying this book —a systematic approach to instruction. It will identify and name the system's components and describe their characteristics, and help you to begin to use this ordered, sequential process to construct your own instructional system, given the content.

An initial discussion of the changing role of the teacher leads to a brief consideration of the content prerequisites for instructional design and the need for establishing clearly defined goals. A detailed analysis of the ten elements that must operate within the teaching-learning system constitutes the major subject matter of Part One.

This part concludes with a case study of the systematic approach to show you how the model works at a practical level, how the teaching-learning process can be analyzed using the model, and what specific guidance it can offer in your development as a coordinator of learning experiences.

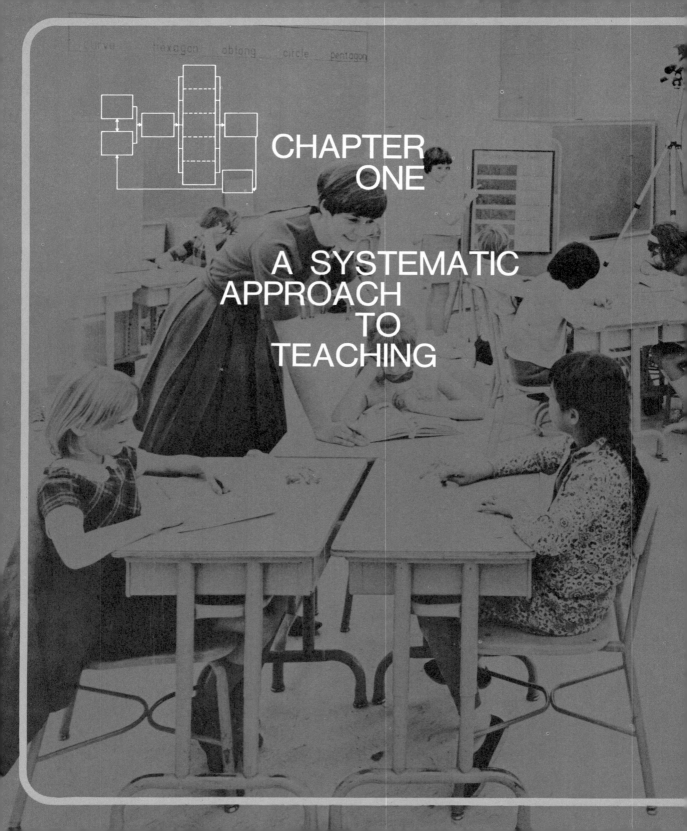

CHAPTER ONE

A SYSTEMATIC APPROACH TO TEACHING

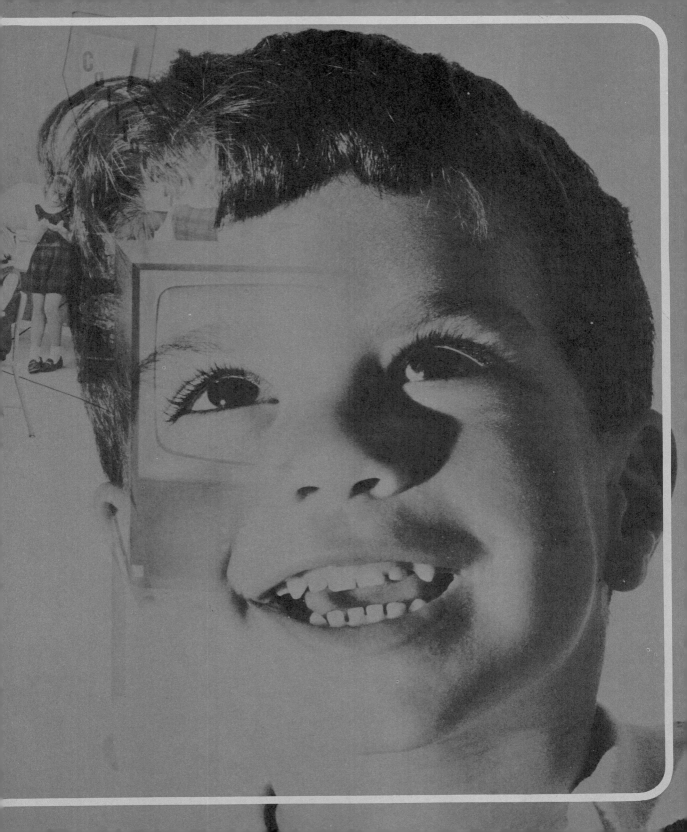

WHEN YOU HAVE MASTERED THE CONTENT OF THIS CHAPTER, YOU SHOULD BE ABLE TO:

1. IDENTIFY the components of a systematic approach to teaching and learning.

2. NAME the components of the instructional system described.

3. DESCRIBE characteristics and at least one example of each component of the instructional system.

4. ORDER the components of the instructional system in the sequential manner that is followed in this chapter.

5. CONSTRUCT an instructional system, given the content.

INTRODUCTION

One of the most common conceptions of the role of a teacher is that of a giver of information, perhaps because most of the instruction on the elementary and secondary levels, and in higher education, traditionally has involved the presentation of information. The process begins with the teacher, who has been the prime source of wisdom. (Placement of the teacher in the front of the room perpetuates the tradition of teacher dominance.) If all goes well the process ends with the student, who has often been a passive receiver. Teaching has been described by a not-too-kind critic as the transmission of the material from an instructor's notebook to a student's notebook, by-passing the minds of both.

However, the teacher's role is changing. As new resources for learning become available, many of which are designed for individual use, new options for instruction are offered. New concepts such as teaching in teams, individually prescribed instruction, and automated learning compel educators to vary groupings of students. New buildings and facilities are being built to include television, electronic learning laboratories, computer terminals, and dial-access retrieval systems. This increases the number of alternatives that the teacher has in the choice of learning spaces in which to accomplish defined learning outcomes. New concerns for the individual learner and new ways of presenting information must be considered if we are to create an effective design for instruction.

The teacher is rapidly becoming a director, or facilitator, of learning experiences. As the conductor uses the various sections of his orchestra to produce a brilliant performance of a symphony, so the teacher calls upon the spectrum of resources available to provide the conditions which will help pupils to reach their objectives. As the artist groups tiles of various shapes and colors to form a mosaic, so the teacher organizes students in many kinds of groups to achieve specific learning goals.

The changes surrounding us in today's society make teaching a more exciting profession than it has ever been. Some of the benefits which are already being realized by professional teachers are the opportunity to work closely with other professionals, the promise of relief from mundane chores through the use of clerical assistants and new instructional equipment, and the freedom to design an instructional program for the children who are to be taught.

But the new excitement of the profession is not without its price. Changing curriculum patterns and more stringent teacher certification standards demand new competence in subject matter. However, it is not sufficient for today's teachers merely to be competent in a major subject field; they must above all be able to define instructional goals in very precise terms.

Prerequisites to Instructional Design

If a teacher is to play the role of a learning coordinator successfully in today's schools, he must possess the basic knowledge and concepts of a subject matter field, and he must know what he wants to teach, that is, he must be able to select content. (The mastery of subject matter, though an absolute necessity for a teacher, lies outside the scope of this book. No single book can possibly deal adequately with all subject areas.)

The selection of content is ultimately the responsibility of individual teachers. They look to state and local syllabi, new curricula in the disciplines, advice from colleagues, departmental chairmen and supervisors, and personal experience in the field for guidance in the selection of content.

Definition of Objectives

To define objectives is to describe specific skills that students should be able to display under defined conditions at a designated time. The specificity of these objectives does not eliminate the need for long range objectives. For the purpose of this book the larger long range objectives are called *goals*. If we can accept the need for goals as a starting point, then we can concentrate on objectives which encompass a much briefer time span incorporating smaller segments of content. For example, a goal might be "to converse in French" while an objective might be "to be able to exchange greetings in French with the teacher at the end of the class period." To clarify the objective further, the specific greeting phrases are named and the standards for acceptable performance are agreed upon. The teaching strategies described in this book are based on the assumption that the objectives can be and should be stated. The characteristics of well-written objectives are discussed in Chapters 2 to 10.

A SYSTEMATIC APPROACH TO INSTRUCTION

Armed with content and objectives, the teacher must assume the directorship of learning and develop a plan, or system, for reaching the defined goals. The procedure is similar in nature to determining plays in a football game, creating a public relations campaign to sell a product, or planning a family vacation trip. In each of these instances someone must do planning which includes identifying elements and recognizing the interrelationships which exist so that a specified goal can be reached at a specified time. In other words, we are dealing with a comprehensive *system* in which all elements are related to each other; all elements contribute to a common goal. A change in one element may cause a change in other elements or in the system itself. A change in one element may even result in a change in the goal, or objective. Take, for example, the planning of the family vacation trip.

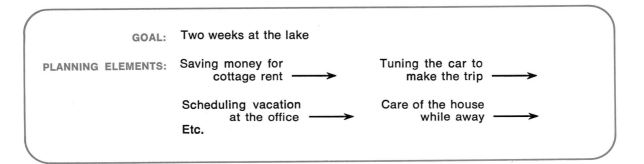

GOAL: Two weeks at the lake

PLANNING ELEMENTS:
Saving money for cottage rent ⟶   Tuning the car to make the trip ⟶

Scheduling vacation at the office ⟶   Care of the house while away ⟶
Etc.

Before the vacation begins, the family car is badly damaged when it is struck by a motorist driving without insurance. The cost of repairs is higher than was budgeted for the tune-up. In fact, it is so high that it seems wise to buy a new car. This means that some of the money budgeted for the vacation must be reallocated.

What effect might this accident have on the goal? It could mean that the vacation must be reduced to one week or that a less expensive vacation must be substituted. Perhaps the vacation would have to be cancelled.

Mr. George, an eighth grade language arts teacher, wants his pupils to criticize their own public speaking performances. His analysis of the goal and plan might follow the lines of reasoning shown in the accompanying diagram.

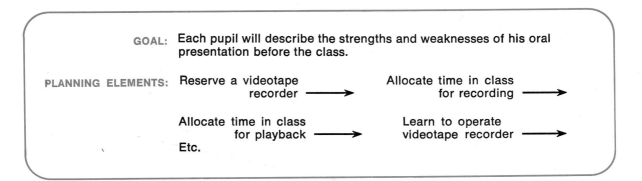

GOAL: Each pupil will describe the strengths and weaknesses of his oral presentation before the class.

PLANNING ELEMENTS:
Reserve a videotape recorder ⟶   Allocate time in class for recording ⟶

Allocate time in class for playback ⟶   Learn to operate videotape recorder ⟶
Etc.

When Mr. George calls the Instructional Materials Center to reserve a videotape recorder, he discovers they are all in use at the times he needs one, but one unit is out for repair and may be returned on time for his use. What effect will the lack of a videotape recorder have on the objective?

It could mean that the public speaking unit must be postponed until a videotape recorder is available. An audio tape recorder might be substituted, but elements of facial expression and gesture could not be effectively included in the self-criticism.

This illustration highlights the necessity of careful attention to defining one's goal as well as to planning how to reach that goal. Both the goal defining and the planning are absolutely essential to good teaching. The entire concept of a systematic approach to instruction is based on this assumption, and it is necessary to keep this in mind as we examine the parts of the system.

There are ten elements that must operate within the system:

1. specification of *objectives* and
2. selection of *content*,
3. the assessment of *entering behaviors*,
4. the *strategy* which will be employed,
5. the organization of students into *groups*,
6. the allocation of *time*,
7. the allocation of learning *spaces*, and
8. the selection of appropriate learning *resources*.

Once the design of the previous elements has been established,

9. the evaluation of teacher and learner *performance* follows, with
10. an analysis of *feedback* by the teacher and the learner.

Each of the elements in the model is discussed and illustrated below.

The model on the facing page is an attempt to portray graphically an instructional system. It is a guideline—a road map—and should be used as a checklist in planning for teaching. It shows the major components of the total teaching-learning system, even though it does not portray the fine details of each component. It does show the relationship of one element to another, and it offers a sequential pattern which can be followed in developing a plan for teaching.

A *model* is a description or an analogy used to visualize, in simplified fashion, something which is not easily observed. When a model is used without constraint it can serve as a powerful aid to a teacher. A model tends to be static even when the process for which it stands is dynamic. The model arrests the action, as does a photograph, but we must remember that the teaching-learning process is one of continuous action.

THE SYSTEMATIC APPROACH—AN ANALYSIS

As this model begins, the teacher specifies behaviors in terms of what the learners should be able to do at certain points along the instructional continuum. He selects content which will help the pupil attain these objectives.

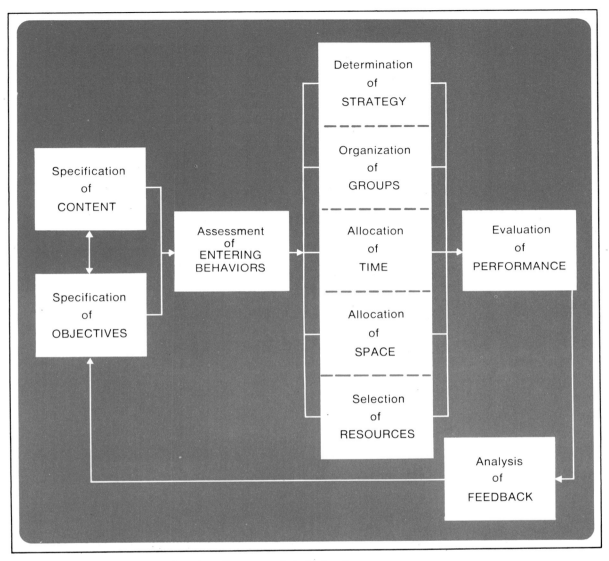

A systematic approach to instruction.

Content specification will vary from subject to subject, from school to school, from grade to grade, and from class to class. This element is not within the scope of this book. Objectives are much more central. The formulation of objectives is discussed in some detail in Chapters 2 to 10. The next element of the system is the assessment of entering behaviors.

Assessment of Entering Behaviors

A professor once began his course by giving the final examination which he had used in the same course the previous term. Much to his surprise, more than half the class passed the examination! The students either knew a considerable amount of the course content or were adept at taking examinations—perhaps both! Another possibility is that the test was a badly constructed multiple-choice exam—one with "slanted" questions and obvious answers. Teachers need to know what each student brings to the course as it begins. Unless the teacher knows the extent and sophistication of the students' knowledge, he must plan his course for an "average" student. Educational psychologists have written about "individual differences" for many decades, but until recently not much has been done about these differences. There are a number of ways of analyzing individual differences.

Use of available records The student's cumulative record probably shows the results of several standardized tests which he has taken. Intelligence tests reveal general information about the student's ability to reason, to verbalize, and to use quantitative data. This information coupled with the data from personality scales provides a general indication

Measurement of entering behaviors in an instructional system.

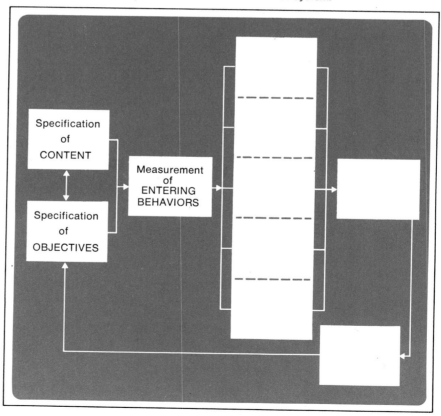

of a student's potential. His grades show performance in courses over his school career. Any information concerning a student's potential or his past performance may be useful.

Teacher-designed pretests   The teacher will probably want to design a pretest to determine the student's achievement in the subject to be pursued. This screening device might indicate a student's ability to define basic terms in the subject area. The ability to describe basic concepts will also be tested. The fundamental question which must be answered prior to formal instruction is, "To what extent has the student learned the terms, concepts, and skills which are part of this course?" It is good practice to organize the course in units and to administer a pretest before each unit. This procedure serves as a check on previous learnings as well as a guide for the teacher and the student in planning future learning experiences.

Determination of Strategy and Technique

The term "instructional strategies" is often used in place of the more traditional term, method. A *strategy* is the teacher's approach to using information, selecting resources, and defining the role of the students. It includes specific practices used to accomplish a teaching objective. *Method*, in the instructional sense, is defined as a systematic plan for presenting information. We are concerned here with two kinds of strategy: the expository approach and the inquiry approach.

Expository approach   Exposition, the more traditional approach, is one in which the teacher presents information to the student. The sources of information most frequently used are the textbook and other reference materials, audiovisual materials, and the personal experience of the teacher. A teacher usually stands before a class to present the information, and students are expected to process this information in the same manner as presented by the teacher. The most frequently used technique is the lecture; but discussion, motion pictures, and student reports are also used. Discussions are expository whenever the teacher uses them to direct students to a predetermined goal. Students are usually examined and evaluated on their ability to identify people, events, dates, and formulas and to repeat, at least in substance, the information originally transmitted.

Inquiry approach   In the inquiry (or discovery) mode, the teacher assumes the role of facilitator of learning experiences and arranges conditions in such a manner that students raise questions about a topic or event. For example, a fifth grade science teacher might demonstrate the arrangement of iron filings around a magnetic field using an overhead projector so that all might see. He asks his class to raise questions without providing any background information except the demonstration itself. He answers questions with "yes" and "no" responses. The conditions for inquiry are thus established. The resources for finding the answers or solutions are factual information and raw data which have not been organized in any particular fashion. Examples of resources are textbooks, documents, statistical data, documentary films or slides, tape recordings, or passages from publications pertaining to the topic. The students raise questions about the content of the materials and attempt to organize this information. The students are active participants as they develop hypotheses which are later tested by use of additional data; eventually generalizations may be formulated.

In planning for teaching we should remember that the expository approach and the inquiry approach each has its own place. Often these approaches overlap. For example, in presenting information to a large group, the teacher is usually most efficient using the expository approach with objectives established, materials carefully selected and organized, information presented clearly through lecture and audiovisual techniques, and evaluation based on the objectives. In independent study, students often follow an expository pattern in learning terminology, formulas, new words, and principles through tapes, workbooks, and programmed instruc-

Determination of strategy.

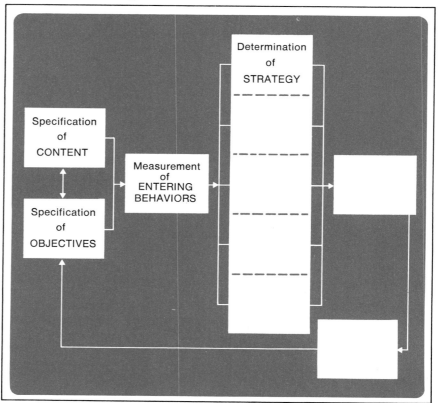

tional materials. In small group discussions, however, the teacher may elect to use an inquiry approach by showing a brief documentary film as the springboard for raising questions, pointing directions and stimulating further research. Both expository and inquiry methods are valid for providing conditions in which students can learn. Each should be considered when one makes decisions about strategy.

Technique This means the procedures and practices used to accomplish teaching objectives, regardless of approach. Examples of techniques are lecture, discussion, audiovisual presentations, and verbal and written reports prepared by students. Teachers will vary their techniques according to the teaching objectives and the resources available. Frequently a variety of techniques will be employed to reach an objective. No one technique is always better than another, but one technique may be superior to others for a specific goal. For example, a teacher who wants a learner to describe the quality of Robert Frost's poetry might select a recording of the poet reading his own works rather than have students read the same poem from an anthology of Frost's works. A teacher who wants students to draw inference about the causes for the growth of cities might use statistical data showing population growth, maps of an area, and a list of transportation developments with the pertinent dates. Once the instructional approach is determined, the teacher must select the techniques which will be most effective in helping the learners reach the stated objectives.

Organization of Students into Groups

There is no inherent magic in any particular number of people learning together. The objectives determine group size. Objectives have been stated and refined; content selection has been made; criteria of satisfactory performance have been identified; and entering behavior has been measured. Now we must answer three basic questions:

1. Which objectives can be reached by the learner on his own?
2. Which objectives can be achieved through interaction among the learners themselves?
3. Which objectives can be achieved through formal presentation by the teacher and through interaction between the learner and the teacher?

Answers to these questions will force decisions about the method to be followed, the strategies to be used, the space and time required and the resources to be selected.

When objectives become the touchstone for organizing groups of students, many variations from the normal groups of 25 to 30 pupils per class begin to occur. One of the early advocates of deviation from the standard class size and time period is J. Lloyd Trump, who recommends a division of the secondary school day into approximately 40 percent for large group instruction, 20 percent for small discussion groups, and 40 percent for independent study.[1] Trump holds that a major barrier to learning is the

[1] J. Lloyd Trump, *Images of the Future* (Washington: National Association of Secondary School Principals, N.E.A.), 1959.

lock-step scheduling of classes, since this does not allow for the independent pursuit of knowledge. He acknowledges the need for formal presentation of information by a teacher, but he suggests that the size of the receiving group might well be 80, 100, or 125 students, since group size is not a major factor when information is presented. The need to discuss is often the most urgent need in education but traditional classes are often so large that discussion, if it occurs at all, is limited to a few outspoken members of the group. Small groups of 12 to 18 students are recommended whenever there is a need for exchanging ideas and probing specific topics in depth. Independent study permits students to seek information from a full spectrum of resources: books, periodicals, tape recordings, slides, motion pictures, programmed materials, and other media.

In his attempt to break with tradition, Trump developed a new type of lock-step. There may be certain content fields where more than 40 percent time allocation for formal presentation may be required, or there may be certain objectives which require 50 percent face-to-face discussion, for example, most learning objectives in a speech class would require exten-

Organization of students into groups.

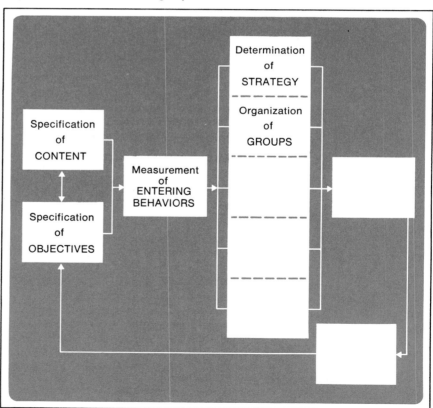

sive small group interaction. The organization of groups will vary as the learning objectives vary.

Another limitation of the Trump plan is the disregard for the learning style of the individual student. Some students may reach a given learning objective efficiently through independent study, while others may reach it most efficiently through formal oral presentations. Some students might need a tutor nearby for guidance at difficult times.

More recent developments in group organization for learning have centered on continuous progress programs and Individually Prescribed Instruction (IPI). Each of these programs is carefully designed for individuals, beginning with objectives which are shared with the students. As a student moves along toward the objectives, he is provided with materials just as rapidly as he is able to master each segment of the program. The full range of audiovisual media is used where appropriate. From time to time students come together in groups, but the primary orientation is toward individual study. The Laboratory School at Brigham Young University became a continuous progress school in the early 1960's. Individually Prescribed Instruction has been developed at the Learning Research and Development Center at the University of Pittsburgh.

The focus of Individually Prescribed Instruction is on the rate at which students proceed through a carefully sequenced series of behaviorally defined objectives for each subject. The provision for differences in rate of learning involves more than permitting each pupil to work as fast as he can. It also involves the determination of how much exposure to content is required so that an individual pupil will achieve mastery of that content. It involves individual prescriptions for each student in the program at each step in the learning sequence.

Allocation of Time

The determination of strategies and techniques to be used in the various groups forces a decision concerning time utilization. The plan for use of time will vary according to subject matter, defined objectives, space availability, administrative patterns, and the abilities and interests of the students. Frequently the best determinant of time allocation is the teacher's analysis of the three questions above (in the discussion of organization of groups). In some areas it may be best to spend the bulk of the time in large groups for formal presentation of information. In other fields, such as the laboratory sciences, much of the time may be devoted to independent study. The teaching plan should take into account the estimated time for each type of activity. No teacher should feel bound by any formula for allocating time; rather, he should analyze the objectives and space availability before making the time estimate. However, sometimes there is very little that the teacher can decide about time allocation. In such cases, he must ask, "How can I best attain the objectives with the time constraints imposed on me? What grouping, what space utilization, what teaching strategy, what resources are most compatible with the time allocation patterns that I must use?"

For example, some schools still maintain a standard 40 or 50 minute time

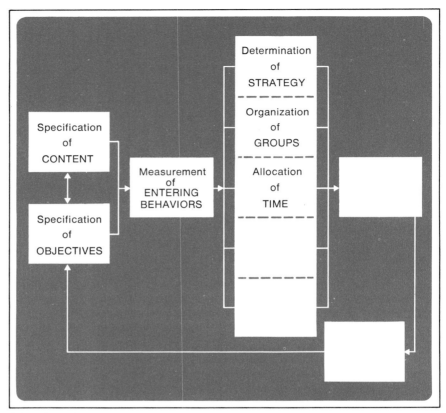

Allocation of time.

period which minimizes the opportunity for allocating time in constantly varying blocks. When bells control the movements of students according to an established schedule, individual teachers are thwarted in their attempts to allocate time efficiently. Still the teacher has the option of organizing the class period to provide for formal presentations for the entire class, for small group discussion periods, and for independent study —all within the limits of the bell schedule. The bells may somewhat hinder the implementation of a flexible approach, but the creative teacher will work around this limitation and provide varied time blocks appropriate to the size of his groups.

Allocation of Learning Spaces

Many classes are taught in classrooms equipped with 30 to 40 student desks, a teacher's desk, and built-in teaching tools such as a chalkboard and a bulletin board. Traditionally, the desks are arranged row by row with the teacher's desk at the front of the room as a focal point. Because of tradition, many teachers uncritically accept this type of arrangement as an excellent one for the expository approach using the lecture technique. Projected audiovisual materials are typically used in this kind of learning space, and discussions can also be carried on in this type of environment. But this traditional arrangement is only one possibility.

Large group spaces   With the new emphasis on groups of various sizes, several classes often join for formal presentations in large groups of 60 to 300, depending upon the subject matter and the grade level. This, of course, usually necessitates a move from the regular classroom to a larger instructional space. Some newer schools have folding or movable walls between classrooms. When the walls are retracted, two or more regular classrooms are instantly combined into a single large-group instructional space. Most new schools are including spaces for large group instruction. Older schools improvise by using the cafeteria, auditorium, or other spaces which are not heavily scheduled and which can accommodate larger groups.

Small group spaces   Movable partitions not only make possible the creation of large group instructional space; they also make possible the conversion of a standard classroom to several small spaces in a minimum of time. However, small group spaces do not require movable walls; they do not even require extensive renovation of the classroom. It is often possible to assign several small groups to areas within the room, even to carry on work in its own area or corner. Since most of the classroom furniture today is movable, such small groups can be arranged easily. In some cases schools use portable partitions to help create some visual isolation of separate groups within a room. However, visual materials usually present a minimum source of distraction to other groups if each group is actively occupied with its own tasks. When the group needs audio materials, the students can use headsets to avoid disturbance which would be caused by sound from a loudspeaker.

Independent study spaces   Within the standard classroom students can carry on independent study activities. In these classrooms students work independently at their desks regardless of the over-all room arrangements. However, educators are beginning to realize the desirability of independent study spaces, especially when audio and visual materials are needed for individual rather than group instruction. A 20th century adaptation of the medieval monk's carrel is seen in new schools and in renovated spaces of older buildings. The semi-isolation provided by the carrel permits each student to pursue topics of interest in privacy. Given the choice of working at a conventional student desk, at a table with other students, or in a carrel, many students will select the carrel. Libraries are beginning to provide the option of a carrel or the traditional work table. Some carrels are being placed along the walls in existing classrooms. These highly desirable spaces belong in all classrooms, old and new.

Determination of space allocations   Given the alternatives of large spaces, small spaces, and independent study spaces, the teacher must

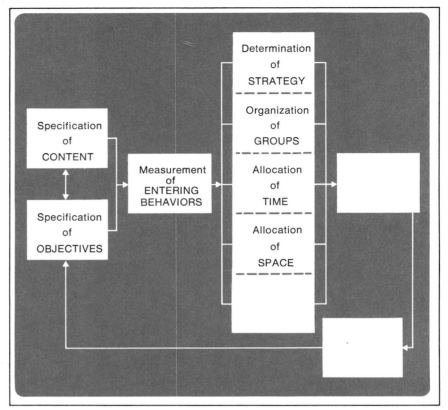

Allocation of space.

consider the three important questions mentioned earlier, for in the final analysis, the allocation of learning spaces must be based on learning objectives.

1. Which of the objectives can be reached by the learner on his own? (Students will be allowed to use independent study spaces to pursue these goals by himself.)
2. Which objectives can be reached through interaction among the learners? (Students will be directed to groups which can be arranged within the classroom itself or to small rooms where interaction activities can take place. The teacher may rotate from group to group or if a team teaching approach is being used, members of the team may be assigned to specific groups.)
3. Which objectives can be achieved best through formal presentation by the teacher and through interaction between the learner and the teacher? (Students will meet in one large group or will join with other classes for listening and observing.)

Greater efficiency and effectiveness are possible in the teaching-learning process once the teacher begins to group learners in relation to the objectives being sought. No longer must a pupil's learning be inhibited because his class is always assembled with the same teacher from early morning until late afternoon, day after day.

Selection of Appropriate Instructional Materials

The teacher is the most important element in the spectrum of instructional resources. The inviting character of an array of instructional devices should not overwhelm the teacher, nor should the availability of materials ever be the sole cause for their use. Prior determination of objectives based on the selection of content is a minimum requisite for selection of instructional material. The teacher will have assessed the pupils' entering behaviors; he will have selected the approach and the techniques appropriate to the objectives and will have made decisions about the group size and the time to be spent with a particular technique. When we consider the full range of instructional media available to the teacher, we should understand that these media will be selected in terms of *responses* desired by the teacher from the learners, not in terms of stimuli alone. Once an objective is defined behaviorally, we can begin the selection of an instructional medium.

The teacher, as a coordinator of learning resources, has a wide variety of materials from which to choose. Notice that the term *learning* resources is used rather than "teaching" or "instructional" resources. These materials do not become teaching or learning resources until the teacher provides a context for their use. These resources can be classified into five general categories:

1. real materials and people,
2. visual materials for projection,
3. audio materials,
4. printed materials, and
5. display materials.

Real materials and people Beginning with the teacher and his associates, the professional staff within the building become resource people. The librarian, the art and music teachers, and other specialists are available for assistance. So are teachers of other subjects or grades who have unique talents or interests in addition to their primary competencies. The community is an ever-present and valuable teaching resource. Individual specialists, from the service station attendant to the neurosurgeon, can bring their talents to the school. Many of the specialists are parents with children in the school who would be honored to contribute their specialized knowledge to the school. In addition to bringing resource people to the school building it is often possible to bring the students to the community through field trips or school journeys. If time and funds were not a persistent limitation, it is conceivable that a large portion of the school curriculum could be built around the resources within the community.

It is possible to bring real objects and to perform "live" demonstrations in the classroom setting with actual materials.   The teacher of earth science who gives each student a piece of limestone is providing the raw material from which concepts are later formed.   There is a sense of drama when the third grade teacher brings an incubator to class for the children to observe the process of an egg hatching.

It is a paradox that these simple resources have always been available, but teachers often have neglected such treasures in favor of an abstract approach.   There is nothing new nor particularly unusual about using resource people, community resources, and real objects and demonstrations, but these media have been neglected over the years.   The creative teacher does not need to depend upon elaborate equipment and large budgets to provide excellent instruction.

Visual materials for projection   When the term "audiovisual materials" is used, it brings to mind the range of media which are projected on a screen.   In some schools audiovisual equipment can be found in every classroom.   More frequently, projectors are distributed from a central

Selection of resources.

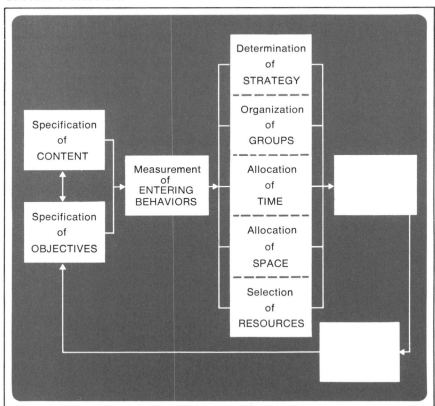

point such as an instructional materials center, an audiovisual center, or a library. Teachers can obtain the equipment by reserving it for a particular hour or day. More and more equipment will be placed in single classrooms as teachers begin to use this equipment many times each day.

Overhead projectors, filmstrip projectors, slide projectors, and opaque projectors are the most common devices for showing static materials. Motion pictures and television are used to show motion. Motion pictures are available in silent and sound both 8mm and 16mm. The videotape recorder (VTR) is assuming some of the functions of the motion picture camera and projectors. Low cost units make the acquisition of this equipment possible for many individual school buildings. The advantages of immediate replay, reusable tapes, and portability have stimulated the use of the videotape recorder.

The materials which can be used with each type of projector can be created by the teacher or obtained from a library, producer, or distributor. The decision to produce new materials for oneself or to select existing materials is dependent upon the objectives which the learners will be expected to attain. The selection of media appropriate for given objectives will involve decisions about content selection, group size, approach and techniques, and time allocation. It is more than a routine task. The selection and evaluation of media will be discussed in Chapters 2 to 10 as specific learning objectives are discussed.

Audio materials Motion pictures and television have audio characteristics, of course, but there is a separate category of materials classified as audio. These include the voice of the teacher (or other persons serving as information sources), radio, disc recordings, and tape recordings. The most frequently used audio medium is the voice of the teacher, yet it is often accepted as a "given" without much thought regarding its creative use. Most disc recordings are commercial pressings of music, drama, historic events, and the voices of famous persons. These are often a part of the school library. On the other hand, tape recordings are frequently the product of local talent within the school. Students, teachers, and groups of students record and play back music, speech, foreign languages, and short plays for the purpose of analysis and interpretation. When there is value in a student's hearing his own voice, one should use locally produced tape recordings in the classroom. Audio tapes are available commercially with content similar to that available on disc recordings. The low cost of tape in cassettes and the availability of recorders which are both portable and simple to operate make this medium almost universally available. Some states and school systems have provided a tapes-for-teaching service which permits individual schools to send "blank" tapes to a central point for duplication from a master tape.

Printed materials While this category contains some of the most traditional and frequently used learning resources, it also includes newer media such as published programmed instructional materials and locally duplicated items.

Workbooks and programmed instructional materials must be used by individuals. For this reason, one copy is usually given to each student. Both workbooks and programmed textbooks (or materials) are usually expendable since they are used by individual students who are required to write in the book. Some workbooks and programs are reusable. These materials belong in the classroom where individuals and small groups can use them. Some programmed materials may be housed in the library when they are used for remedial or advanced study and are not generally required for use in the classroom at all times.

Frequently the audio and visual materials designed and produced by the teacher are the most useful and productive teaching media. The increasing availability of the duplicators and copying machines in every school building permits teachers to write, draw, and type information quickly and inexpensively for use by a large group of students. The possibility of rapid corrections, use of color, and minimum preparation time make the spirit duplicator a particularly versatile tool for providing printed materials to all students.

Display materials Almost every classroom has a chalkboard and bulletin board. Some classrooms have permanent maps and globes. Teachers can easily construct flannelboards or feltboards, charts, and dioramas. All of these media are displayed for students to observe, but certain observations are incidental, such as looking at a bulletin board or a diorama, while other observations are for the purpose of seeking information. Teachers do use chalkboards, flannel or feltboards, maps, globes, and charts as integral parts of the instructional plan. In any case, whether these instructional materials are always available or are used on occasion for specific purposes, whether they are commercially made or teacher made, whether they are used for incidental observation or for formal presentation, they are among the most readily accessible and least expensive learning resources.

This brief survey of learning resources is a catalog of alternatives available to each teacher as he prepares to design his instructional program. Each medium is discussed at greater length in Part Five, Media Facts. There is no one instructional medium which is categorically better than another. The use of each must stem from its ability to contribute to the attainment of the learner's objectives.

Evaluation of Performance

Performance is the interaction between the teacher and the learner, between the learner and other learners, or between the learner and an instructional medium. It is during the performance that the stimuli are presented and responses are made. Performance is the act of teaching, the act of learning. Performance cannot be contained by time, although evaluation does occur at many points during the performance. Learning may occur in an instant as the student identifies a paramecium through the microscope for the first time, or it may be a cumulative sequence which leads the eighth grade history student to describe, in his own words, the events leading to World War I.

Performance is the focal point of learning. All of the effort that has gone into the formulation of objectives, the selection of content, and the assessment of entering behaviors gains significance or becomes nonsignificant as the performance is evaluated. The performance in which we are most interested is that which occurs after the organization of groups, the determination of strategy, the allocation of time and space, and the selection of resources. This performance by the learner is the *denouement* of the system; it is the point at which he confronts the content and begins to move toward the defined objectives. Glaser describes this component of the learning process:

> . . . instruction begins with the student's entering repertoire and ends with the terminal repertoire. . . . During the interval between these two points, instructional manipulations and learning experiences take place in the course of which the student emits responses which guide him toward the terminal behavior. . . . This process is facilitated by determining, for various stages of learning, the subject-matter stimuli, e.g., words, paragraphs, symbols, formuli, etc. to which the student

Evaluation of performance.

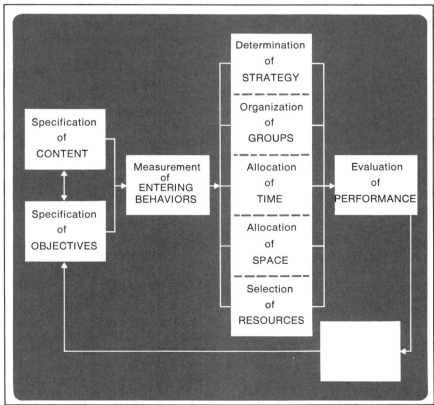

must respond and the kind of response required to each of these, e.g., solving problems, writing, building something, etc. . . .[2]

It is during the performance that certain aspects of behavioral development occur: motivation, practice, reasoning, transfer, reinforcement, and guidance of the learning activity.[3] It is only through a conscious evaluation of the performance that these behaviors can be measured.

Evaluation of performance is one of the last elements of the model of our instructional system, but it is one of the first concerns of a teacher. Once the objectives have been defined and a statement of expected terminal behavior has been written, both the teacher and the learner have a guide for planning and performance.

In its most useful form, the evaluation is a simple "yes" or "no" answer to the question: "Has the terminal behavior been manifested at the level specified, under the conditions stated?"

For example, one of the terminal behaviors for a fourth grader in a social studies unit is "to identify lines of longitude and latitude and to name the three major great circles of the Earth, given a standard classroom globe." The standard of performance is "without error." The evaluation begins by asking a pupil to come to the globe and to point to a line which represents longitude and one which represents latitude and to name the three great circles as he points to each one. The evaluation may be done by the teacher, by other pupils, or by the pupil himself if he can use another globe or map marked with the proper designations to confirm the correctness of his responses.

Some objectives are simple to evaluate. If they are cognitive, observable, and measureable, there is no difficulty. However, there are other objectives which are much more complex and not easily evaluated. How does one assess the qualities of good citizenship, a task often stated as an objective of the social studies? Many of the types of objectives which are discussed in this book lend themselves to precise evaluation. Other types of objectives are very difficult or impossible to evaluate.

Glaser points out that there are two primary assessments which are made at this point:

> One is to provide information about a *student's present behavior*; measurement for this purpose is primarily designed to discriminate between individuals. The second use is to provide information about the *instructional techniques* which produced that behavior; measurement for this purpose is designed to discriminate between instructional methods.[4]

Analysis of Feedback

The concept of feedback comes from the field of cybernetics. It was first used in electronics to account for completion of an electrical circuit.

---

[2]Robert Glaser, *Training Research and Education*. (New York: John Wiley & Sons, 1965), pp. 9–10.
[3]Glaser, *Training Research and Education*, pp. 9–10.
[4]Glaser, *Training Research and Education*, p. 19.

Feedback, in this sense, implies a confirmation of correctness. If an electronic impulse reaches a terminal point, the feedback to the origination point would indicate, "Yes, the impulse arrived here just as it was sent." Or if the transmission was inaccurate, "No, something went wrong. The impulse has not arrived here as it was sent." One of the very best examples of feedback is the thermostat which controls room temperatures. The thermostat is "set" for a particular temperature, and as long as that temperature is maintained, the heating or cooling equipment is not required. When the room temperature deviates from the desired temperature, the feedback mechanism relays this "information" to the control (furnace or air conditioner). The control then pumps heat or cooling to the room until the desired temperature is reached. At that point the thermostat "tells" the control to stop.

An example of feedback is found in a situation where a teacher presents information. The students look puzzled, bewildered, confused. The teacher, noticing this change, backtracks and tries a simple explanation. The puzzled, bewildered, confused looks on the students disappear, and the teacher proceeds to his next point.

Feedback.

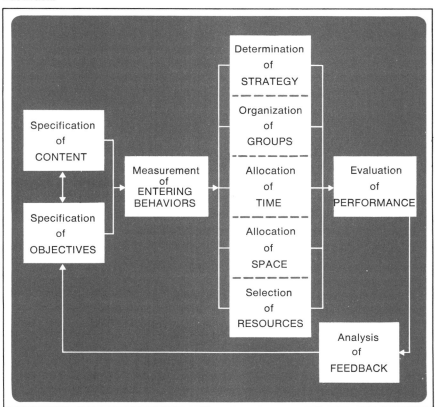

The term is useful in an instructional system since it implies an evaluation of the product (terminal behavior) in direct relation to the original objective. Ideally, the terminal behavior and the original statement of objectives should be congruent. If feedback is to be useful, objectives must include the conditions under which the behavior should occur and a criterion level of acceptable performance. If the terminal behavior is "to identify a peninsula on a map that shows peninsulas, islands, isthmuses, straits, and gulfs," the conditions and standards of performance must be given as well. Thus the further qualification must be added: "on a test to be administered at the end of the map study unit. No errors will be allowed." The feedback in this case would be the pupil's identification (or nonidentification) of a peninsula on the examination.

It is important for feedback to occur as soon as possible after a response is made. Not only is the feedback to the teacher valuable, but the teacher's feedback to the pupil is supporting. If the pupil's response is correct, the teacher should confirm it. Research indicates clearly that such practice facilitates learning. Delay in feedback decreases its effect. Programmed instruction illustrates one of the best applications of these principles. The student knows immediately whether his response is correct. In some experimental classrooms, a student response system permits students to respond to questions raised by the teacher. Correct responses are flashed on a screen immediately after the response has been registered by a counting device. The student sees the correct response and knows which answer is correct. He does not have to wait for his paper to be corrected. The feedback is almost instantaneous.

How does the model work? How can the teaching-learning process be analyzed using the model? What guidance does the model offer? Here is an example.

THE SYSTEMATIC APPROACH—A CASE STUDY

Specification of Content and Objectives (Elements 1 and 2)

The twelfth grade teachers in Central High School have become increasingly concerned about the quality of students' writing in all subjects. Some of the basic skills of punctuation, capitalization, and word usage are weak or lacking. Since about 60 percent of a graduating class normally goes to college, and since the deficiency in writing ability has caused difficulty for some of the former graduates during their freshman college year, the faculty decided to institute a remedial writing skills program. They agreed that the program would be successful if each student who needed the remedial work could write an original two-page statement with two errors or less per page. Errors were defined as mistakes in punctuation, capitalization, and spelling, and as usage that deviated from the rules contained in the textbook used in eleventh grade English. The writing exercise which would be used to measure attainment of the objective would be untimed and unsupervised.

1   The objective has been determined by the faculty. What is it?[5]

  .   .   .   .   .   .

1   *To reduce the difficulty that students from Central High School experience in English classes during their freshman college year.*

2   Reduction of the difficulty is related to competence in a subject area, or content. To what content is the problem related?

  .   .   .   .   .   .

2   *Punctuation, capitalization, spelling, and usage in original written compositions.*

3   What competence should students in the remedial program demonstrate at the conclusion of the remedial program? That is, what level of performance, or standard, do the teachers expect the students to attain?

  .   .   .   .   .   .

3   *The ability to write an original two-page composition containing no more than two errors per page.*

4   Under what conditions should this performance occur?

  .   .   .   .   .   .

4   *The writing is to be untimed and unsupervised.*

5   Summarize in two words the elements in this example.

  .   .   .   .   .   .

5   *Objective; content.*

Assessment of Entering Behavior (Element 3)

Entering behavior refers to prerequisites. Before a student can spell words orally, he must possess the ability to name the letters of the alphabet. A student who is learning to find quotients for long division problems must possess entering behaviors which include, among others, the ability to subtract and multiply.

Additional data were obtained by reviewing the verbal aptitude scores of those students who had already taken the College Entrance Examination Board tests. An analysis of grades in English classes and anecdotal records from the students' cumulative record folders were used to identify the students who needed remedial work. The reason for this analysis was

---

[5]This exercise, and those that appear in the following pages and chapters, are an attempt to build in your participation as a reader and to make it active rather than passive. You should try to answer each exercise immediately as a check on your mastery of information at that point. An answer or several alternative answers will appear immediately following the question. It may be helpful to cover up the answer; of course, you can read the answer immediately without attempting a response of your own, but that takes some of the challenge out of reading.

to discover, as accurately as possible, the current ability and achievement level of each student so that appropriate instruction could be designed for those who required it and those who did not require it could be spared the boredom and waste of time caused by unneeded instruction. This procedure enabled the staff to identify the target group for remedial instruction.

6 Before designing the instruction, the faculty measured something. This measuring is an illustration of the third element in the process. What is this element?

• • • • • •

6 *The third element is* specifying the entering behavior *of the learners. Entering behavior includes such concepts as readiness, aptitude, and achievement level. (In some instances an interest inventory may be administered to determine students' entering behavior—or sometimes motor ability may be assessed.)*

7 Name the three elements illustrated thus far.

• • • • • •

7 *Objective; content; entering behavior.*

Once the remedial group had been identified, and the level of achievement ascertained, the faculty proceeded to the next steps of the instructional system. These elements are so closely related that it is difficult to separate them and to state their order, since one decision affects all other components. The order of the next five components of the model is not fixed. Many occur simultaneously, one element coming before another at one time and after it another time.

Determination of Strategy (Element 4)

In determining the primary instructional strategy to be followed, the teachers unanimously agreed that something other than straightforward exposition was needed at this point. If students taught by expository methods have not learned fundamental writing skills by the senior year of high school, then a new method should be used. An inquiry approach did not seem to afford sufficient opportunity for providing the specific guidance which the situation required. They compromised on a guided inquiry approach, in which each student receives a copy of the objectives and a statement of the expected goal or objective or terminal behavior. The student knows that he may request the examination at any time he feels he is ready to demonstrate the attainment of a defined objective.

8 Why was each student given a copy of the objective and the statement of expected terminal behavior?

• • • • • •

8 *This strategy provides specific directions for each student so that he knows exactly what is expected.*

9   Does the student receive instruction about how to reach the terminal behavior?

      •   •   •   •   •   •

9   *No, he is only told what is expected of him, but not how to reach the objective.*

10   What is this strategy called?

      •   •   •   •   •   •

10   *This strategy is referred to as inquiry, or guided inquiry. Some educational authors use the term discovery or inductive learning.*

11   Which elements of the system have been discussed thus far?

      •   •   •   •   •   •

11   *See the diagram below for a presentation of the answer in flow-chart form.*

System components discussed thus far (answer 11).

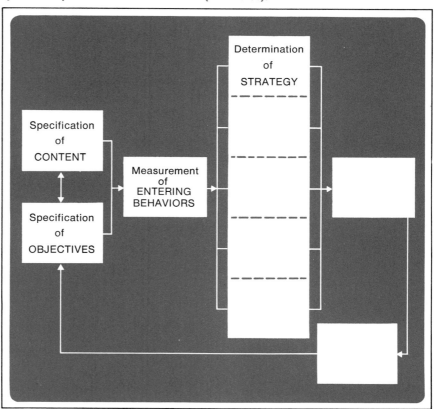

Organization of Groups (Element 5)

The assessment of the students' entering behavior indicated that out of a class of 122 there were 24 who were in serious need of help. Another 61 were in less serious trouble but could profit from additional assistance. The faculty decided to organize those who needed the most help into three groups of eight students each. Two groups would meet one half hour before school two mornings per week, and one group would meet one afternoon per week for one hour. The groups were organized so that individuals would feel that there were others who had the same problem. They were able to discuss common problems among themselves and yet have the guidance of a teacher available. All teachers were given the names of the 61 who had modest problems. The teachers decided that these students should be given remedial aid in the regular classes. These students were helped individually as they submitted their written assignments in each course. Most of the students had at least one unassigned period (study hall) during the day, and the special help was given then.

Allocation of Time (Element 6)

Time allocation is a function of the organization of groups and the selection of method and technique. The difficulty of scheduling remedial work during the school year after school schedules had been fixed necessitated the scheduling of early morning and late afternoon sessions. The impossibility of setting up special groups for the 61 who needed minimal help dictated the need for various time allocations, namely, independent study periods where the time could be spent to meet individual needs in the best ways possible.

12   Why was time allocated as it was?

•   •   •   •   •   •

12   *Time was allocated differently for each large group. For those requiring intensive remedial work, before and after school hours were selected as the only mutually available time for groups to meet. The others, who did not meet as a group, were treated individually as a part of the regular teaching schedule.*

Allocation of Spaces (Element 7)

In this case study, the allocation of learning *spaces* is a relatively simple problem. When the groups meet together before and after school, an area in the teacher's regular classroom is used. Most of the learner's performance will take place independently. Therefore, a desk in the classroom, a carrel or table in the library, or a comfortable working area at home are possible spaces for learning.

13   What factors govern the decision regarding space for learning?

•   •   •   •   •   •

13   *Decisions regarding allocation of space are based on availability of space, the task to be performed, the size of the group, and the resources to be used.*

Selection of Resources (Element 8)

In the case under discussion, the selection of *resources* is limited by the approach selected: remedial instruction.   One instructional medium frequently used for remedial work is programmed instruction.   Programmed instruction permits an individual student to move at his own rate of speed with immediate feedback for each response made.   What are the programs available for remedial instruction in English writing skills which are appropriate for high school seniors?   A comprehensive listing of programmed instruction resources is found in Carl H. Hendershot's *Programmed Learning: A Bibliography of Programs and Presentation Devices.*[6]   Listings in English writing skills are shown in the accompanying figure.

Title, Author, Publisher	No. of Frames	Grade Level	Price	Comments
English 2600 (Revised) - J. Blumenthal (HARCOURT)	2632	9-10	$ 4.00 cloth $ 3.00 paper	need. Test booklets & teacher's manuals provided. Additional copies of test booklets, $.80 each.
English 3200 - J. Blumenthal (HARCOURT)	3208	10-12	$ 4.60 cloth $ 3.60 paper	
Language Arts, CT-3010 (FIELD)	30 min per wheel	24 study wheels	$ 4.25	Cyclo-teacher Learning Aid required. See Section B.
Supplementary Language Arts Cycles, CT-3011 (FIELD)	"	12 study wheels	$ 3.00	" "
English I 58310-3 - Bierman (CENTRAL)	500	6th-9th	$ 2.95	
English II 58310-4 - Bierman (CENTRAL)	500	"	$ 2.95	
Programmed English - M. W. Sullivan (MACMILLAN) Test Booklet Manual	1783	7-12	$ 5.80 $ .80 $ 1.44	Kiver cover binding. A synthesis of structural, formal, & semantic approaches. Suitable to & including college remedial.
Business English, A Gregg Text-Kit in Continuing Education - Reed (McGRAW)	30-60	Kit Adult	$ 4.50	September, 1966.
ENGLISH - GRAMMAR				
Programmed Grammar: Parts of Speech and Sentence Patterns - M. Sullivan (McGRAW)	240pp		$ 2.50 soft	$4.95 cloth ed.
English Review Manual: A Program for Self-Instruction - J. Gowen (McGRAW)	297pp	Coll	$ 2.95 soft	Instructor's manual. $4.95 cloth ed.
Word-Picture Program (BELL) Set 1 Nouns; Everyday Things Set 2 Verbs; Action Words Set 3 Basic Concepts	200 cards "		$ 35.00 $ 35.00 $ 35.00	Bell & Howell Language Master required. " " " "
English Language - M. Doyle & E. Lothamer (CTB) Verbs, Modifiers & Pronouns - Series C-D	220	5-6	$ 1.00	Auxiliary & irregular verb forms.
Verbs, Number & Case - Series E-F	200	7-8	$ 1.00	Tenses, passive verbs, past & present participle, gerund.
Capitalization - Series C-D	220	5-6	$ 1.00	Rules and functions, names, places.
Capitalization - Series E-F	200	7-8	$ 1.00	Practice in various uses of capitals.

A - 29

A page from Hendershot's *Bibliography*.

English 3200[7] was selected, after review by the English faculty, because it is designed to teach eleventh and twelfth graders to use a specified

[6]Carl H. Hendershot. *Programmed Learning: A Bibliography of Programs and Presentation Devices* (University City, Michigan: the Author, 1967).
[7]Joseph C. Blumenthal, *English 3200* (New York: Harcourt, Brace and World, 1964).

vocabulary correctly, and to use specified words and constructions properly.

14 What element of the system model has been discussed?

•   •   •   •   •   •

14 The eighth element, selection of resources.

Evaluation of Performance (Element 9)

First of all, *evaluation* is the measure or the testing of the degree to which the student has attained the objectives. Once the design is established, the *performance* component can be started. It is extremely profitable at this time to tell the students *why* they have been selected for this special assistance. Sharing the objectives and expected terminal behaviors will immediately give direction to the students. For optimum success, there ought to be no secrets between the teacher and the learner.

One student, exposed to this approach for the first time, remarked, "I wish all teachers would realize that the name of the game is *learning*, and not *guess where we're going*." Each pupil knows what group he is in and what the instructional approach will be; each understands what the time commitment will be and that programmed instruction will be used. He knows (or is shown) how to use programmed instruction, and he knows when he can present himself for testing. Most important of all, he knows how to determine whether he has reached the objectives which have been defined. In this case, self-evaluation is built into the performance.

Some students take their programs home while others use them during the school day. They are given short range goals and are asked to come back when they feel these goals have been reached. They meet individually with the teacher as help is required and with the group, as scheduled, to discuss common problems and for group assessment of progress.

15 How did the evaluation phase function?

•   •   •   •   •   •

15 One of the basic characteristics of programmed instruction is an immediate feedback regarding each response. Therefore, each student using programmed instruction was able to evaluate his own program. With the objectives and a statement of expected terminal behavior, the student has a reference point to measure progress. The teacher also served as an evaluator. These evaluative procedures are closely related to feedback.

Analysis of Feedback (Element 10)

This phase in the cycle may occur at any time. It is not tied to units, weeks, months, or semesters. The students know where they are going (since objectives have been defined), how to get there (since resources have been provided), and when they have arrived (since responses are immediately confirmed). Furthermore, the students know that they can present themselves for examination whenever they feel they are ready to demonstrate the specified competency. The teacher helps each student to confirm that he has acquired the terminal behavior. The process of evaluation is a use of *feedback* to measure the degree to which terminal behavior attained by the individual meets the description of the desired behavior as it was defined in the objective. In the case of the remedial English program, the evaluation was made by observing whether each student wrote an original two-page statement with no more than two errors per page. Other kinds of evaluation include an analysis of the student's writing as he progresses through the program; use of a writing skills test, or some other standardized or locally-made test as a post-test; and the writing performance in normal class activity in science and social studies.

16 What are the final two elements in the systematic model?

· · · · · · ·

16 You should have answered evaluation of performance and analysis of feedback. Check with the complete diagram on page 29 to verify your answers.

This is one example of how an instructional system functions. It has many variations, depending upon the objectives, the nature of the student population, the facilities and resources available, and the ability of the teacher to inaugurate a new approach. The model of the instructional system is a guide, not a formula. Though there may be details concerning specific problems and decisions to be made which are not accounted for in the model, all the elements of the system are there for you to use. There are opportunities in every step for creative deviation from the model, but no major steps in the teaching-learning process are omitted.

17 Look at the completed model on page 29. Where does *feedback* terminate?

· · · · · · ·

17 At the beginning of the systematic model—at the specification of content and objectives.

18 What happens now?

· · · · · · ·

18 The feedback information is used as a measure of the degree to which the objectives have been reached. If the objectives have been attained, the feedback will confirm this fact. If not, the feedback will indicate the extent to which the objectives have been reached. If the feedback indicates that the objective has not been adequately reached the system recycles and changes in each component are considered.

SUMMARY

The teacher of today is more often a coordinator of learning experiences than a presenter of information. To design appropriate experiences, the teacher must first state the objective, describe the conditions under which the behavior required in that objective should occur, and then select the content which is to be learned. Other elements of the systematic approach to teaching and learning include the measurement of entering behavior; the provision for students to learn independently or in large or small groups; the determination of the strategy to be employed (expository, inquiry, or both); the techniques which will be used; the space and time required; and the selection of resources which will help to accomplish the defined tasks. A plan to use feedback for evaluation must be included.

PART TWO
DESIGNING INSTRUCTION

"Would you tell me, please, which way I ought to go from here?"
"That depends a good deal on where you want to get to."
*Alice in Wonderland**

Part Two is the foundation upon which media selection and use are based. It focuses on a classification scheme of instructional objectives.

Writing objectives is the initial stage of this approach. For the purposes of our analysis, we assume that the content of learning has been specified, since objectives cannot be adequately stated apart from content. In fact, these two are so closely related in the teaching-learning process that they must be treated together.

The only useful objectives are those that describe the ultimate actions, skills, or products of the learner. Objectives such as these are called *behavioral* objectives. The following nine chapters are concerned with behavioral objectives that are representative of those commonly dealt with in elementary and secondary schools. Since the statement of objectives is so fundamental to our approach, we demonstrate how to use a specific classification scheme that will help teachers to select or write them precisely.

Further, the selection of appropriate instructional media for implementing objectives is also presented, with opportunities for the reader to apply principles of media selection to specific behavioral objectives. The process of assessing entering behaviors is discussed as an integral part of specifying objectives.

*Lewis Carroll, *Alice's Adventures in Wonderland*, Macmillan Classics Series (New York: Macmillan, 1963). p. 59.

CHAPTER
TWO

THE ROLE OF
OBJECTIVES
IN
SCHOOL LEARNING

W HEN YOU HAVE MASTERED THE CONTENT OF THIS CHAPTER, YOU SHOULD BE ABLE TO:

1. IDENTIFY examples of learning, given descriptions of situations in which learning has taken place and situations in which it has not.

2. NAME two types of learning (either acquisition or extension), given descriptive anecdotes illustrating each.

3. NAME three classes of learning (cognitive, affective, or psychomotor), given descriptive anecdotes illustrating each.

4. IDENTIFY objectives that meet the four criteria for good objectives, given statements of objectives which are acceptable and statements which are not.

5. NAME the four criteria for acceptable statements of objectives.

6. IDENTIFY pairs of events which are functionally related, given a description of the two events.

7. IDENTIFY examples of the proper application of the media selection rule, given anecdotes describing either proper or improper application of the rule.

Education is concerned with schools, students, teachers, and materials. The concept of education presented in this book is based upon two assumptions about schools, students, and teachers:

1. Students attend school to learn.
2. Schools employ teachers to facilitate this learning.

THE LEARNING PROCESS

The Nature of Learning

What is learning? To begin with, learning must somehow be related to behavior. Behavior refers to any observable act. Sometimes by implication it refers to a product which results from an act, as when a child speaks, manifesting verbal behavior, or when he writes an essay demonstrating motor behavior in the movement of his arm and fingers as he moves his pen across the paper. The essay is a product of this movement; we can refer to the essay as an example of verbal behavior. In this case the verbal behavior is a written product, a series of written words. Someone may repair a radio or swing a golf club; these are behaviors. Someone may cry or blush or tremble; these, too, are behaviors. A child may circle what he considers the correct answers on a science test; the circling is an example of behavior. In school situations, however, we are usually interested only in the product of this circling behavior, namely his score on the science test. This score is more important than how he makes the circles. For the sake of brevity, it is quite common to refer to his achieving a test score as behavior. Likewise, products such as the solution to an arithmetic problem or a bookshelf made in the shop class are referred to as manifestations of behavior. *Behavior is an observable act or an observable product which is a result of an act or acts.*

Schools are concerned with behavior in two contexts. First, a student may develop the ability to make a new response, to do something he has not done before, to behave differently. One example of this type of behavioral change is found in every beginning foreign language class. Pupils sooner or later begin saying words which they never uttered before. When the boy in the French class first utters "*la femme*," he is making a new response, doing something he has not done before, or behaving differently. We infer that he has learned because we observe him, or, more precisely, we observe his behavior or response.

Secondly, schools are concerned with a student's using existing responses or behavior in a new context. Consider the first grade reading teacher who is teaching the words "look" and "run." Undoubtedly every one of the first graders could speak these words long before he entered first grade. This teacher's problem, unlike the French teacher's, is to enable the learner to say "look" whenever he sees the letters *l o o k* and to say "run" whenever he sees the written or printed three-letter symbol *r u n*. The reading teacher is concerned with bringing an existing response or behavior under the control of a new condition or stimulus.

Types of Learning

Acquisition and extension   The first kind of learning—the kind that involves a new behavior or a new response—is called *acquisition*. The learner *acquires* a new response. The second type is called *extension*. The conditions or stimuli which control a behavior or response are *extended* so that a new condition or stimulus elicits a previously existing behavior or response.

Both acquisition and extension are examples of a change in behavior. In the context of the examples and definitions just given, it is possible to use an extremely simple definition for learning: we infer that a pupil has learned when we observe a change in behavior. To oversimplify, *learning is a change in behavior.*

Two words of caution are in order at this point. "Change in behavior" must be interpreted as either acquisition or extension, as defined above. As I write the manuscript for this book, I come to the end of a page. I put my pencil down, tear the sheet of paper from my tablet, and add it to the stack on the corner of my desk. I have just manifested a change in behavior. I stopped writing and did something else. This, however, is not the meaning of "change in behavior" as used here. It requires only a casual observation for one to conclude that this example involved neither acquisition nor extension. Second, learning is not the actual behavior. Rather, learning is an inference which the *teacher* makes on the basis of the behavior. It is a judgment which a neutral or objective outsider makes because of something that he sees a learner do. A pupil who cannot spell cat, mat, and sat is given instruction. After the instruction he spells the three words correctly. I observe the change: acquisition. I cannot look inside the learner's head to see whether he has learned. I merely infer that he has learned. I make a judgment (on the basis of the change in behavior which I observe to have taken place).

In summary, "learning is a change in behavior" will function satisfactorily as a definition if we remember that learning may be one of two types (acquisition and extension) and that learning is an inference drawn by the teacher (as opposed to something that takes place inside the pupil).[1]

---

[1] We are not saying that nothing takes place inside the pupil. We *are* saying that it is not necessary for the teacher to know this in order to decide whether a student has learned.

We said that learning is a *change* in behavior. If on Friday a fifth grader spelled correctly all 25 of the words assigned for a given week, would it be permissible to say that the student had *learned* the spelling words? Perhaps it would, because one might safely assume that he did not know how to spell these words at birth. Consequently, a change in behavior has taken place. He has moved from a zero performance (and this is inferred, not observed) on the spelling of these words to a 100 percent performance. But if we were to answer the question "Has he learned to spell any of these words in fifth grade?" we would need more evidence. We would need to know whether a *change* in behavior has taken place. The simplest method of discovering whether learning has taken place would be to compare his performance on this word list at the beginning of the school year with his present performance.

Check your grasp of this concept by answering the following questions. Then compare your answer with the answer immediately following the question.

1   At the beginning of the school year, Sue spelled the names of all 50 states correctly. She does so again in November. She does so once again in May. Which of the following statements is or are correct? (You may choose several, one, or none.)

    a.   Sue learned to spell the words in fourth grade.
    b.   Sue learned to spell the words in fifth grade.
    c.   Sue learned to spell the words sometime from September to November (inclusive) in fifth grade.
    d.   Sue learned to spell the words sometime from September to May (inclusive) in fifth grade.

       •   •   •   •   •   •

1   *None. In order to state when Sue learned to spell these words we must know when she most recently spelled fewer than 50 correctly. If she spelled 49 correctly in April of her fourth grade, we could say that she finally completed her learning between April and September. Or, if she could spell none of these words correctly in March of her second grade we could say that she learned to spell the names of the 50 states between that March and September of her fifth grade.*

2   Sally, a high school senior, was able to name in a semester examination the composition and its composer when she was given excerpts from ten different 19th century symphonies. She had named the symphonies and their composers correctly in the beginning of the semester. May we say that Sally has learned anything? Why, or why not?

       •   •   •   •   •   •

2   *No. Her behavior, as manifested by her ability to name the compositions and their composers with no errors, has not changed. The observable behavior in this case is a product: a perfect score on the musical identification test. There is no change in the product, so there is no change in behavior. No change in behavior is the same as no learning.*

3 Tommy could not tie his shoes a week ago. Now he can. Is it proper to say that Tommy learned anything? Why, or why not?

. . . . . .

3 *Yes. Since there is an observable change in behavior, it is proper to say that Tommy has learned something.*

4 What kind of behavior is this, acquisition or extension?

. . . . . .

4 *We don't know. If Tommy had never tied anything before, or (at the very least) if he had never tied anything with a bow, it would be safe to call this acquisition. If, however, he had learned to tie boxes or bundles with a bow and now began to tie his shoes with the same kind of bow, we would refer to it as extension.*

Cognitive learning There are many kinds of learning. Students learn to distinguish one color from another, to name parts of speech, to order events chronologically, to state rules, to apply rules, and to do many other similar tasks. These tasks are examples of what is frequently called *knowledge*. Some writers use the term "cognitive" to describe these kinds of tasks. *Cognitive* means pertaining to the recall or recognition of knowledge and the development of intellectual abilities and skills. Most school learning falls into the cognitive category.

Psychomotor learning Students also learn to write in manuscript letters and in cursive letters, they learn to color with crayons, to cut with scissors, to operate a sewing machine, to type, to pole vault, and to perform many other similar tasks. These kinds of tasks are referred to as *skills* by some writers. Others call them "motor" or "psychomotor" tasks. In most classrooms, only a small portion of the time is devoted to psychomotor learning. *Psychomotor* means pertaining to the manipulative or motor-skill area.

Affective learning Finally, pupils learn to agree, to share, to cooperate, to be polite. These kinds of behaviors are evidence of *attitudes*. Attitudes are sometimes referred to as belonging to the "affective" domain. The affective domain is concerned primarily with behaviors that are related to the emotions. Educational books and journals talk a great deal about the importance of the affective domain, but generally they provide few or no specific directions for teaching attitudes. Behaviors which belong to the affective domain are difficult to define, and consequently it is difficult to specify how to teach them. *Affective* means pertaining to interests, attitudes, and values, and the development of appreciations and adequate adjustment.

Check your ability to name the three kinds of learning by answering the following questions and then comparing your answers with those given below.

5   A child acquires new knowledge: he can factor equations which he could not do a year ago. This is an example of learning which belongs to what domain?

6   Suzy holds the door open for her classmates; she picks up litter from the floor even if it isn't hers. She did not do these kinds of things last semester. Her attitudes have undergone a change. This kind of learning belongs to what domain?

7   Paul can kick field goals with 75 percent accuracy from the 25 yard line. Last month his accuracy from the same place was only 50 percent. This is an example of what kind of learning?

• • • • • • •

5   *Cognitive.*

6   *Affective.*

7   *Psychomotor.*

8   Jim selects only nonfiction books in the field of political science. He never selects light fiction. What type of behavior is Jim manifesting?

• • • • • •

8   *We don't know. If he is a librarian's aide working for the social studies faculty, it's possible that he is manifesting a cognitive behavior, since it is apparent that he can discriminate between political science books and light fiction books. However, if this anecdote is a report of Jim's voluntary reading habits, it could be indicative of affective behavior, since we could infer on the basis of his actions that he appreciates or enjoys the literature in the political science field.*

9   Dave intercepted two passes in last week's football game. Last year he didn't even try out for the team. This kind of behavior belongs to what domain?

• • • • • •

9   *Most likely psychomotor. We assume that he could not intercept passes last year and that he can now. However, someone may argue that the affective domain cannot be ruled out. It certainly is possible that Dave's presence on the team and his intercepting the passes are evidence of a change in attitude toward football. More will be said about this in Chapter 9. For the present it is sufficient to remember that one rarely encounters "pure" forms of behavior in real life.*

THE TEACHER AND THE LEARNING PROCESS

What is the function of a teacher in the learning process? Certainly much learning takes place in the absence of a school teacher. Children learn to walk, to ride bicycles, to play baseball, to swim, without a school teacher. A child learns to identify his home, to distinguish his overshoes from his brother's, to state his name and address, to apply the rule about washing his hands before eating to situations in widely varying times and places. He learns to say "thank you" under appropriate conditions, and he learns to share his toys with his playmates. These and thousands of other behaviors are acquired before he experiences his first meeting with a school teacher.

Children do learn without teachers. Some things could not be learned any faster if the child had a teacher. For example, nearly any child who burns his hand when he touches a hot light bulb learns almost immediately to refrain from this kind of behavior in the future. It is improbable that a teacher could speed up this learning process.

There are many other things, however, which a child will never learn unless someone teaches him carefully and painstakingly. This teaching may be done by anyone—by teachers, by playmates, by the announcer on TV, by parents, by siblings. Many children can write their names before entering school. Almost without exception such children have been instructed by a parent or an older brother or sister for a long time before this learning task is completed.

The teacher's task is to facilitate learning. He is to establish conditions which make it probable that learning will occur within a reasonable period of time. The teacher does this in many different ways. The purpose of this book is to increase the probability that the reader will use effectively the best available means for facilitating student learning.

A major task of the teacher who wants to facilitate learning is to arrange the environment of students. He may do this by taking them on a field trip; he may bring an insect collection into the classroom for the pupils to observe and classify; he may display a picture and a news clipping on the bulletin board in order to lead the students to read something. Teachers who do these things are altering the students' environment in order to facilitate learning.

The teacher may facilitate learning by producing and using original instructional materials. The teacher writes or draws things on chalkboards to facilitate students' learning; he duplicates outline maps to help children locate and name places; he constructs graphs or charts to help learners interpret data.

The teacher also selects and utilizes existing materials. He shows a motion picture to help students learn to identify types of cells; he uses a tape recording to provide a standard for the choral group to imitate; he uses a television program to enable his class to learn to speak a second language.

The teacher arranges and re-arranges the learners' environment in an effort to provide conditions which will facilitate learning. Sometimes there is one optimum condition for a given task and a given learner. The teacher's task is to discover what this condition is and to establish this condition. Sometimes the teacher may be unable to discover what a single optimum condition of learning is. In such cases he ought to have a strategy for making a "good guess," and he must know how to read the signals, if they occur, that indicate that his guess is or is not working. This book presents a strategy for doing these things.

Whatever else a teacher may do in a school environment, his most important function is an instructional one. The teacher performs his instructional function when he arranges the environment to provide optimum conditions of learning for the pupil.

How does the teacher perform his instructional function? There are four steps:

1. The desired objective must be stated in terms which describe an observable act or product of the learner.
2. A means for attaining the desired objective must be chosen.
3. The results of using the selected means must be evaluated.
4. A functional (or cause and effect) relationship between the means and the objective must be demonstrated.

OBJECTIVES—THEIR NATURE AND FUNCTION

Characteristics of Good Objectives

In this book the term *objective* is used to describe an outcome, a goal, a purpose, or any of the other terms used to describe the end result of successful instruction. An instructional objective is simply a *description* of the changed behavior or product which indicates that learning has taken place. These are examples taken from such instructional objectives:

1. to factor quadratic equations
2. to spell the names of the 50 states correctly
3. to tie one's shoestring in a bow knot
4. to pick up litter from the floor
5. to kick field goals from the 25 yard line with 75 percent or greater accuracy

One of the distinguishing characteristics of this kind of objective is that it reduces ambiguity to a minimum. Such objectives are not subject to many different interpretations. Some writers refer to objectives of this type as *behavioral* objectives. Others use the term *operationally-stated* objectives (that is, the objective is stated in terms of the operations or procedures employed by the learner). It makes little difference what name one uses. It is important that the behavior or the product in which one is interested be well-defined. Since this is the type of objective which we find useful in teaching, we will simply use the term "good" or "useful" to refer to such well-defined objectives.

A good objective exhibits four distinguishing characteristics:

1. It describes something which the *learner* does or produces.
2. It states a *behavior or a product* of the learner's behavior.
3. It states the *conditions* under which the behavior is to occur.
4. It states the *standard* which defines whether or not the objective has been attained.

A learner behavior   In many teachers' manuals and curriculum guides, objectives are stated in a form that uses the infinitive form of the verb, e.g., *to name* the senators from our state.   To make certain that such an objective is stated in terms of the learners' behavior, you can apply a simple test: substitute "the learners" for "to."   Thus, *"to* name the senators from our state" becomes *"the learners* name the senators from our state."   A useful instructional objective must be stated in terms of the learners' behavior.   Ask yourself the question "Who?"   If the answer is "the learner," the objective meets the first criterion.

There are thousands of objectives that cannot pass this simple test. A glance at many curriculum guides or teachers manuals will reveal such examples as:

1.   to give students examples of Cubist tendencies
2.   to picture life in Japan
3.   to present distinguishing features of phylum arthropoda

Apply the test; substitute "the learners" for "to" in each statement above. While one might argue that "the learners" could be the subject of one or the other of these three statements, it is quite obvious that the writer intended these to be statements of things which the *teacher* will do.   Note carefully that these statements make the most sense when you substitute "teachers" for "to" in each statement.   These are not the kinds of statement of instructional objectives that will prove useful.   Why?   Because the purpose of teaching is to facilitate learning.   Consequently, objectives must describe what the learner, the one who does the learning, will do when he has attained the objective.   What teachers do is also very important, but what they do is not the objective; it is a means for implementing the attainment of the objective.

The following are examples of useful statements of objectives:

1.   to locate a dictionary entry, using guide words
2.   to describe four restrictions of the Bill of Rights
3.   to locate the oceans on a globe
4.   to compose a four-line poem
5.   to hold open the door for the girls in the class

Try the test on these objectives; substitute "the learners" for "to."   Notice that in every instance the statement makes sense; it describes some behavior that the learner will manifest or a product that he will have produced when he has learned what is desired.

The first criterion of a useful instructional objective is this:

> An instructional objective describes something which
> the learner does or a product which he produces.

Can you identify objectives that meet the first criterion?   From the list below, select those statements that could be considered useful instructional objectives.   Then compare your answers with the answers given.

10   To list in writing the four chief agricultural products of the Central States.

·   ·   ·   ·   ·   ·

10   *This is a useful instructional objective according to the first criterion. When you ask the question, "Who is to list?" the obvious answer is "the learners."*

11   To present a rich treatment of the life of the desert nomads.

·   ·   ·   ·   ·   ·

11   *This objective does not meet the first criterion. When you ask the question, "Who is to present?" you would probably answer, "the teacher" or "the unit," or something other than "the learners."*

12   To describe orally the difference between a "go" signal and a "stop" signal.

·   ·   ·   ·   ·   ·

12   *This is a good one. The answer to the question "Who?" is "the learners."*

13   To use a variety of charts, slides, and motion pictures to give the students a full understanding of the process of mitosis.

·   ·   ·   ·   ·   ·

13   *No good! Who is doing the using? It would make no sense to say that the learners are doing the using. The context of this objective indicates very clearly that the teacher should "use a variety of charts, slides, and motion pictures to give the students a full understanding."*

14   To provide rich learning experiences through the study of the poetry of the Romantic Period.

·   ·   ·   ·   ·   ·

14   *This one is also inadequate. The answer to the question "Who?" is something other than "the learner."*

An observable behavior or product   Describing an outcome in such a manner that the *learner* is the subject of the verb is a necessary condition. However, it is not of itself sufficient to ensure that every statement which meets this criterion will be a useful objective. The statement must also describe a behavior or product that is *observable*.

It is unfortunate that many curriculum guides and teachers' manuals use terms that are extremely ambiguous in their statements of objectives. For example, a fourth grade social studies manual states that one of the objectives of a unit is "to appreciate the contributions of the Indians to our life today." There is little doubt that the writer of this objective wants the learners to do the appreciating; the objective, therefore, does meet the first criterion for a useful objective. But the verb "appreciate" is open to a multitude of interpretations. What does the learner who "appreciates" do? Does he voluntarily go to the library to read books about Indians? Does he construct models of Indian villages? Does he say things about Indians which demonstrate some kind of connection between life in an early Indian society and contemporary life in our society? Does he urge his parents to take him to see the pueblos in Mesa Verde National Park during the next vacation? Does he manifest an increased pulse rate when he hears the word Indian? Does he smile when he is told that it is time for another Indian story?

There is no way for one to ascertain what the writer meant when he wrote "to appreciate." *Appreciate* is an ambiguous term because it is not observable. If a number of teachers were to observe a pupil who is supposedly "appreciating," it would be necessary to define this term very precisely before one could expect any kind of agreement among these teachers as to whether the student is doing what the objective requires.

Another word which is used many times in statements of objectives is "know." The physics teacher, for example, says that the objective of his lesson is that the learners should *know* the principles of magnetism. The first criterion is satisfied; the subject of the verb "know" is "the learners." But the second criterion is not met. *Know* does not describe an observable performance. How can a teacher distinguish a learner who *knows* the principles of magnetism from one who does not? The answer is simple—it is impossible to distinguish a learner who knows the principles from one who does not as long as *know* is not defined in terms of an observable pupil performance. Under what conditions will the writer of this objective be willing to say of a learner, "He knows"? Would he be satisfied with a learner who writes several rules about magnetism? Some teachers would. Or would he want the learner to recite three or more descriptive statements? Perhaps he wants the learner to identify examples of magnetism when presented with the physical phenomenon in a form different from that used in the class demonstration. He may have in mind the ability of a student to solve a problem involving the application of a principle of magnetism. He may mean that only those learners who can construct an electromagnet "know the principles of magnetism." He could define "know" as the ability to contrast a bar magnet with an electromagnet in an oral statement of 60 seconds duration or less. Or the writer of this statement could have meant any of hundreds of other things. The objective as it is given is not useful because it does not state the desired behavior in observable terms. You cannot tell what behavior the writer wanted to develop in the learner. Neither can you tell when the learner will have acquired this behavior.

In contrast, the following objectives are stated in observable terms:

1. to construct an angle equal to a given angle
2. to write the dates for these three events
3. to score at least 70 on the Physical Aptitude Test
4. to list the parts of carburetor #P-41

These objectives differ from the "to know" and "to appreciate" examples above. They are not ambiguous. They are not subject to many different interpretations. If five different teachers were to decide whether a given learner has attained any one of these objectives, the probability that all five would agree is very high. Why? Because these objectives are written in observable terms.

Now check your ability to distinguish between objectives written in observable and nonobservable terms. Tell which type each of the following objectives is, and then compare your answers with the ones given.

15 To understand the three chief differences between the Tories and the Whigs.

· · · · · ·

15 Understand *is nonobservable. A learner who "understands" could conceivably give evidence of this understanding in many different ways. He could* write *something,* recite *a number* of *statements,* solve *a problem, list a number of characteristics,* construct *a chart, or do many other things. Any of these could be accepted as evidence of understanding.*

16 To recite the Pledge of Allegiance.

· · · · · ·

16 Recite *is an observable performance term, but this objective does not specify the conditions under which the reciting takes place, nor the standard of quality which the reciter must achieve. These other factors are important, too, but discussion of them will follow later.*

17 To grasp the significance of the 1968 Paris Peace Talks.

· · · · · ·

17 Grasp the significance *is not an observable term. It falls in the same category as "understand."*

18 To understand fully the principles of magnetism.

· · · · · ·

18 *To understand fully is not an observable term. Adding the word "fully" does absolutely nothing to clarify the meaning of "understand."*

19 To solve equations of Type A using the graphic method.

· · · · · ·

19 Solve *is an observable term. When the learner writes the correct solution or speaks the answer, he has* solved *the equation. The product (i.e., the solution) is observable. Any competent observer would be able to distinguish between students who have found the correct solution and those who have not.*

20 To enjoy the music of the Baroque Era.

· · · · · ·

20 Enjoy *is not an observable term. Sometimes we say that we can tell that an individual is enjoying something because he smiles or laughs or because his eyes sparkle. However, it is conceivable that one could enjoy something without manifesting his enjoyment in any overt, observable manner. It is equally conceivable that someone who is smiling or laughing during a performance is enjoying something other than the music of the Baroque Era.*

21   To have faith in one's ability to succeed when an honest effort is exerted.

      •   •   •   •   •   •

21   *To have faith is not an observable term.*[2]

Sometimes a term has a very obvious meaning in a noneducational context, but it should not be used in a statement of objective. If one stated that one of the objectives for a physical education course is "to know how to swim," most people would agree that when the learner swims, the objective has been achieved. However, "to know how to swim" could be defined in terms of a learner's describing or telling how to swim. Certainly such behavior is one type of knowing. It should be apparent that even when a term has a generally accepted popular usage, it does not necessarily follow that it can be used as a performance term describing an observable behavior.

Some verbs may describe an observable behavior in one context and a nonobservable phenomenon in another context. Consider the word "practice." Obviously, "to practice patriotism" must be considered a single term when applying the criterion, which demands that objectives must be stated in terms of observable behavior. To "practice" may or may not be observable; only the context can tell us. To practice *patriotism* is not observable. Specific behaviors, which may be considered patriotic behaviors if the term patriotism is adequately defined, are observable. If an objective is to be written to deal with the practicing of patriotism, it must be written in terms of the specific observable act or acts which constitute patriotism. For example, "to practice patriotism" could be defined to include any or all of these objectives:

1.   to stand at attention when the flag is raised
2.   to recite the Pledge of Allegiance
3.   to donate blood to the Red Cross
4.   to volunteer to work in the voter registration booth at the fair

On the other hand, the piano teacher might ask the learner to practice scales 15 minutes each day. "Practice" in this context stands for behavior which is a good deal more observable than was the case in the example of "practicing patriotism."

Frequently we are interested in an observable *product* rather than an observable *behavior*. When the English department administers standardized tests, it is the score on the test that interests the teacher. If one were to observe behavior during the time the students are taking the test, he might observe them using vertical strokes or horizontal strokes or a scribbling type movement to blacken the rectangles on the answer sheet. Certainly these markings (behavior) are necessary, but they are of no interest to the teacher. The score on the test is the matter of interest.

[2]In examples 20 and 21 we have behaviors that cannot be observed or readily determined. That does not mean that they should be eliminated from the curriculum. They might be expressed in a statement of goals, which are usually long range in nature and not as amenable to evaluation as objectives. More of this will be discussed in Chapter 9.

We refer to a test score as an observable product rather than an observable behavior. The means of obtaining or providing evidence of having obtained the score is rarely, if ever, described in an objective.

If an objective were "to achieve a score of 43 or higher on the freshman consolidated English test," one would be describing a student's product rather than a student's behavior. The behavior (blackening rectangles) is so implicit in the statement of the objective that it is unnecessary to describe it. But there are many other instances in school situations where we are concerned with a product rather than a behavior. These are a few examples:

> In the shop class the students are given an exercise in which parts of a machine assembly are presented pictorially in the left column and randomly arranged names of these parts are printed in the right column. The student is to draw a line from the part to its name. This behavior is known as identifying. However, the operation (that is, the movement of the hand as the lines are drawn) is of no interest to the shop teacher. He is interested only in whether the product is one in which all the lines form proper connections between the pictured parts and the correct names.

> The sixth grade language arts class is learning to make outlines. The students will use handwriting to construct these outlines. The handwriting behavior, however, is not of immediate concern to the teacher. The complete outline, which provides evidence that the student has learned to construct outlines, is the observable element in this example. Here again the teacher focuses his attention on the product, not on the behavior.

> The student orders the four stages in a complete metamorphosis of a butterfly by placing a 1 before the name or description of the first stage, a 2 before the second, and so forth. Or, he may be told to rewrite the four stages in their chronological order. The observable behavior of the student is the writing of the digits or the copying; these are observable behaviors. However, the product, as represented by the correct listing of the numbers or the correct order of the copy made by the student, is of much greater concern to the teacher at this moment than is the writing or copying behavior.

We have discussed two criteria for properly stated objectives. First, when the question "Who?" is asked, the answer must be "the learner." Second, the statement of the objective must describe a behavior or a product which is observable. To help you check your mastery of these two concepts, a number of objectives are listed below. Read each and then tell whether the statement meets the two criteria discussed so far. If the statement is inadequate in terms of these criteria, tell why.

22   To ensure the retention of the facts learned about the Bill of Rights.

•   •   •   •   •   •

22   *Who is to do the* ensuring? *Ordinarily most of us would assume that the teacher is the subject of the verb* ensure. *Consequently, this objective is inadequate with*

respect to the first criterion, since it does not describe something which the learner must do. Certainly there is no observable behavior or product specified here. This statement also fails as far as the second criterion is concerned.

23 To evaluate the significance of the Bill of Rights.

. . . .

23 *It seems obvious that the learner should do the evaluating. This statement meets the requirements of the first criterion. However,* evaluate *is a verb which is open to many and varied interpretations. It is hardly adequate in terms of the second criterion.*

24 To order, according to size, the cities studied in class, beginning with the largest.

. . . .

24 *This objective deals with a function which the learner performs. It meets the first criterion. It also describes an observable behavior—to order and therefore meets the second criterion.*

25 To play the Grieg Piano Concerto in A Minor in order to develop in the students a really genuine appreciation for the Norwegian influence on contemporary music.

. . . .

25 *Who is to play the Concerto? Apparently the teacher is the answer to this question. Someone might contend that the learner is the proper answer. This means that, at best, the objective is ambiguous with respect to the first criterion. The student behavior or product (i.e., appreciation) is not observable. The objective does not meet the second criterion.*

26 To play the Grieg Piano Concerto in A Minor with fewer than six of the technical errors listed on the evaluation card.

. . . .

26 *This statement is adequate in terms of both the criteria discussed. Although the verb is the same in both 25 and 26, the context of 25 leads one to infer that someone other than the student is playing. In 26 the inference that it is the student who is playing seems to be extremely strong.*

A behavior occurring under stated conditions Frequently the conditions under which the observable behavior takes place make all the difference in the world. We have heard of instances of a basketball player making 10 consecutive free throws in practice but missing exactly the same shot in the same gymnasium at the same basket during the final seconds of a championship game. A student might speak her lines in the school play flawlessly during dress rehearsal but "go all to pieces" on opening night. If we want learners to do such things as shoot free throws or speak the lines of a play from memory without error, we must add another element to our statements of objectives: a statement describing the conditions of performance.

Robert Miller[3] has used an example from a military training program to emphasize this point. The military training program included the objective "to run a mile in 10 minutes carrying 30 pounds." This objective certainly meets our first two criteria: it tells what the *learner* is to do, and the performance or product is *observable*. One might even be misled into believing that the objective contains an adequate statement of conditions —carrying 30 pounds. In other words, the learner is to run a mile under specified conditions: he is to run the mile carrying 30 pounds. We can go even further. The learner is given 10 minutes to accomplish this running, and consequently we could say that two conditions are stated in this objective.

Even so, this objective leaves a great deal to be desired. Consider some of the factors which it fails to include:

On what kind of ground: a paved road? through a woods? level? hilly?

On what kind of day: 50° Farenheit? 110° Farenheit? against a strong wind? in the darkness of night?

Wearing what kind of clothing: track suit and shoes? overcoat? GI boots?

With what kind of load: strapped to the back? carried in the arms? in a pail? how bulky? If in a pail, is it 30 pounds of hydrochloric acid? 30 pounds of water? 30 pounds of stones?

Does the objective seem somewhat less adequate than it did at first inspection? It certainly ought to. Any objective which leaves as many questions unanswered as this one does is not very helpful to an instructor. The remedy is to be very specific and very explicit in describing the conditions under which the desired behavior is to take place.

A fifth grade social studies teacher aims to have his students "name the fifty states of the USA." Sally recites the names of the states from memory in alphabetical order. Did she attain the objective? Most of us would say that she did. Dave writes the name of every state on a sheet of paper when he is given an outline map of the United States. But he can write only about two-thirds of the names when he tries to write them without an outline map. Has he obtained the objective? Or to pursue the question even further, has Sally attained the objective but not Dave? Obviously, there is no way to answer this question unless the objective is amended to include a statement of the conditions under which the performance is to take place.

The verb *to name* as used in the illustration above describes an observable learner performance, yet the examples cited are convincing evidence that we need more than a verb which describes an observable learner

---

[3] Robert B. Miller, "Task Description and Analysis," in Robert Gagné's *Psychological Principles in System Development* (New York: Holt, Rinehart and Winston, Inc., 1962), p. 197.

behavior or product if we are to come up with an objective which is not open to varied interpretations. True, we cannot get along without verbs which describe an observable performance or product; however, *the statement of conditions* governing the verb which we use *is the third essential characteristic* of a well-stated objective.

Consider another example:

> "To identify the leaves of the 20 trees growing on the campus" is an objective of a biology course. It is one thing to identify these leaves, given each leaf in a laboratory specimen box. It is another matter to identify these leaves, given a line drawing of each. And it is still another matter to identify them in their natural state, on the trees. The *conditions of performance* are determined by the person writing the objective. He must be very clear concerning the ultimate performance or product that he expects of the learner. This kind of clarity demands a specification of the conditions of performance.

Now check your ability to distinguish between objectives which state a condition of performance and those which do not. If an objective does not state the condition of performance, tell whether it should and give the reason for your answer. Then compare your answer with the one given. If the given objective does not state the condition, try adding words which will remedy the deficiency.

27   To run the 100 yard dash.

· · · · · · ·

27   *On a track? Or through a woods? The conditions of performance are not specified. Sometimes the context will do this. If this objective appeared in a manual on track and field events, certainly it could be assumed that the 100 yard dash is to take place on a track. Then we could agree that there is an implicit statement of conditions. Suggestion: "to run the 100 yard dash on a track approved by the Interscholastic Athletic Association under meet conditions."*

28   To name the three primary colors, given red, yellow, and blue marbles.

· · · · · · ·

28   *This one is adequate. The condition is "given red . . . marbles." (One might ask about the amount of time to be given each learner, but other than that the conditions are clearly specified.)*

29   To distinguish between statements of observation and statements of inference.

· · · · · · ·

29   *Whether the statements are oral or written could make a difference. Another factor which would make a difference is the referent of each statement: are the statements about social phenomena, scientific phenomena, mathematics, or what? Are the statements about pictorial or real phenomena? Obviously, the conditions under which the learner is to do the distinguishing are not spelled out. Sugges-*

tion: to distinguish between written statements of observation and written statements of inference, given pictorial representations of scientific phenomena and statements of observation or inference about the phenomena.

30 To share with a classmate.

.   .   .   .   .   .

30 *This one is very inadequate. Share what? Share when? There are so many ways of interpreting this vague statement that we are offering no suggested reconstruction of the objective.*

31 To print the names of the 50 states without reference to any aid, given an outline map of the U.S.

.   .   .   .   .   .

31 *This objective states the condition of performance, with the exception of the amount of time given the student. The problem of stating time as a condition is our next topic.*

The time that the learner is given to complete the behavior or to produce the product in which we are interested is frequently very important. Consider a typing class. Five students type an assignment without error; one of them completes the assignment in less than one minute, while all the others take more than a minute. Obviously, time in this context is a *standard* of performance. If all other things are equal, we say that the student who typed the fastest did the best job. Physical education teachers and coaches face a similar situation when they deal with track events in which the student who performed a given task in the least amount of time is judged to be the best performer, given a situation in which all other characteristics of his performance are equal to that of his classmates or teammates. Obviously, time can be considered a standard of performance.

However, time can just as easily be considered a *condition* of performance. In the Latin teacher's objective, "to translate any three consecutive sentences from Cicero's First Oration, given a dictionary and five minutes," time is obviously a condition. It is one of the things which is *given* the student. Time is one of the *conditions* of the environment. The student is given three things: a copy of Cicero's First Oration, a dictionary, and five minutes.

Two English teachers, Mr. Shaler and Mr. Witt, had selected for their unit lesson plans the objective "to name the three most important literary figures of Colonial America as agreed upon by at least two textbooks or other references." Note carefully how important time is in stating an objective as you read what happened in the two English classes.

Remember, both teachers were using the identical objective! In Mr. Shaler's class, the students were told to read selections from six important authors of the Colonial period in America. They were given the titles of four specific references and told to find in any one of them the three most important literary figures. Later, during a class discussion, agreement was reached concerning the three figures considered most important. In a timed exercise the following day, the students were asked to recall and to name the three authors. Three weeks later, at the end of the unit, Mr. Shaler included this item in the unit test: "Name the three most important literary figures of Colonial America." They were given no more than one minute to answer this question. Mr. Shaler assumed, justifiably, that all students who responded correctly within one minute to this test item had attained the stated objective.

Mr. Witt, who was implementing the very same stated objective, utilized a different teaching strategy. During the course of his unit, he presented many problems to his students which required that they consult a variety of sources in order to arrive at a solution. Permeating all of the class activities and discussions was an atmosphere of permissiveness; it was not necessary that two students come up with exactly the same answer, since on many occasions two students with widely varying answers would be assured that both were correct. During the course of the unit, Mr. Witt never specifically identified three authors as the most important literary figures of Colonial America. In the unit test, given on the same day that Mr. Shaler gave his test, Mr. Witt asked, "In 30 minutes or less, consult at least four of the references listed below (a list was included) and write the names of the three most important literary figures in Colonial America as agreed upon by any two of the four references consulted." Because of the nature of the references which Mr. Witt supplied, it was possible for students to come up with different answers to this question. Mr. Witt considered anyone who answered this question correctly to have attained the objective, despite the fact that various answers to the question were considered correct.

Recall once again that both Mr. Shaler and Mr. Witt were using the same stated objective. Despite this fact, it is apparent from the anecdote that each was interested in developing a behavior in his students that differed drastically from the other. We could say that Mr. Witt was interested in the development of a study skill in the context of a specific subject matter or discipline. Mr. Shaler, on the other hand, was interested primarily in the recall of specific information. We are faced, then, with this dilemma: we have an objective, apparently well-stated, one which apparently meets the criteria which we have established thus far, but which permits widely differing results. Isn't it possible to state the objective more clearly? Couldn't this objective be written in such a way that these two vastly different results could not occur?

32   Rewrite the objective given above in such a way that you are describing the results that Mr. Shaler desired and rewrite it again to describe what Mr. Witt wanted his students to attain. If you think carefully about time as an important consideration in the listing of the conditions of an objective, you ought to be able to come up with a very satisfactory solution to this problem.

•   •   •   •   •   •

32   *Mr. Shaler: to list from memory the three most important literary figures of Colonial America, as agreed upon by at least two references within one minute.*

Mr. Witt: to list, within 30 minutes, the three most important literary figures of Colonial America, as agreed upon by at least two references, given access to the following four references during the 30 minutes. (References are supplied.)

The example just cited was selected because it demonstrates the necessity of specifying time as a condition in this kind of objective. But is this a typical example? Aren't *most* learning tasks so obvious that time need not be explicitly stated? Consider, for example, the arithmetic teacher whose objective is "to identify addition problems and multiplication problems, given examples of each in both the vertical and the horizontal form." Most teachers who have chosen this objective would probably expect the behavior to occur with 100 percent accuracy *almost immediately* after the question has been asked or after the example has been presented to the pupil. But "almost immediately" is ambiguous! Consider what might happen in a typical classroom, and then decide whether time should be included as one of the conditions in the statement of objectives. Is there any difference in the following four statements of objectives?

1. To identify addition and multiplication problems, given examples which are either horizontal or vertical in format, and given orally the names of the examples. (In a typical class situation, the attainment of this objective would be manifested by a student who answered correctly when the teacher asked a question such as "Is this an addition or a multiplication problem?" and presented the example to the student by means of a flashcard.)
2. To identify addition and multiplication problems with 100 percent accuracy.
3. To identify addition and multiplication problems, within three seconds after the presentation of (a) the example and (b) the orally spoken words "addition or multiplication."
4. To identify addition and multiplication problems, with 100 percent accuracy, within three seconds after the presentation of both the problem and the orally spoken terms "addition and multiplication."

Certainly, the fourth statement is the most precise. Given the fourth statement, a competent observer should have less difficulty recognizing students who have attained the objective and those who have not attained the objective than he would have, given any of the other three. But isn't it extremely cumbersome to put this kind of detail into every objective? For example, is it really necessary to state "within three seconds"?

Ultimately, each teacher is going to have to answer this question for himself. But consider, for a moment, situations such as these. Just how long should a teacher wait for the learner to respond? If a child "really knows" how to identify these two types of arithmetic problems, won't his response occur immediately, or at least almost immediately?

Let's walk into a typical classroom. We observe the students answering just the type of question that we have been discussing. There are five or six children in the class who answer so quickly that it requires less than one second for them to respond after the teacher shows the example. A much larger number of children takes one or two seconds to answer. A smaller number seems to take three, four, or even five seconds to come up with an answer. One or two very slow pupils require more than five seconds to answer. The situation we have just described is graphed for you in the accompanying figure.

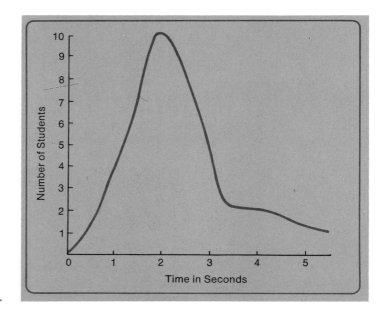

Time required for student response.

Now imagine a situation in which we asked 30 different teachers to indicate which students have attained the objective as it was stated in the first example on page 61, above. Surely we would find only a small number of teachers who would say that only those students who can answer in one second or less have attained this objective. A larger number of teachers would probably say that anybody who can answer the question in two seconds or less has met our requirements. A slightly smaller number might accept as satisfactory the performance of any student who could answer in three seconds or less. Carrying this example to its extreme, it is possible that we might even find a teacher or two who would accept the performance of any student who managed to come up with the correct answer within ten seconds.

What has this to do with the problem of stating objectives adequately? It serves to point out that if we desire precision in our statements of objectives, we will have to deal with all of the conditions which could conceivably make a difference. Most teachers would agree that time does make a difference in the "addition-multiplication example" which we have just considered. Consequently, we shall have to adopt some kind of rule or convention. If *time* is a matter of concern to the teacher, then time must be stated as an explicit condition in the objective. If time is a matter of concern, and the time is not explicitly stated in the objective, the result would be an objective which is subject to varying interpretations and which is, therefore, ambiguous.

Finally, we ought to consider a class of objectives in which conditions, though not stated, are implied. We call conditions of this type *implicitly-stated conditions.* Consider a sixth grade science teacher who is dealing with the water cycle. He wants his students to be able to name the phases in the water cycle in their proper order. He wants the students to be able to state that water evaporates from the surface of the earth, that it is cooled in the upper atmosphere, that it condenses, and finally that it falls to earth in the form of precipitation. The teacher's objective is "to name in the proper order the phases in the water cycle." As this objective is stated, the student will do this ordering in the absence of any visual stimulus. However, if the student were to do this ordering in the presence of a schematic diagram, a diagram in which there are no words, it would be necessary for the teacher to state this condition in his objective. For example, the objective might then be "to name in order the phases involved in the water cycle, given an enlargement in chart form, without words, of the schematic diagram found in the science textbook." One should always be able to assume that there are no supporting factors in the student's environment unless these supports are explicitly stated as conditions in the objective. If no supporting prompts or cues or charts or other stimuli are described, it is implicit that there will be nothing in the student's surroundings or environment other than something such as the question or statement which tells the learner that it is his turn to answer the question or to perform the behavior called for by the objective, for example, "Tell us how a raindrop passes through the water cycle, including all the steps until it becomes a raindrop again."

Check your ability to distinguish objectives which include a description of the conditions of performance from those which do not. If an objective does not state the condition of performance, tell whether or not it should; if it should, try to construct an adequate statement of condition to include in the objective. Then compare your answer with the one given.

33   To name the three primary colors, given red, yellow, and blue marbles.

•   •   •   •   •   •

33   *One might add a phrase such as "given three seconds."*

34   To distinguish between written statements of observation and written statements of inference, given pictorial representations of scientific phenomena and statements about the phenomena.

•   •   •   •   •   •

34   *Add the words "within 15 seconds per example."*

35   To run the 100 yard dash on an approved track.

·   ·   ·   ·   ·   ·

35   Add "given 11 seconds."

36   To print the names of the 50 states without reference to any aid, given an outline map of the U.S.

·   ·   ·   ·   ·   ·

36   Add "within 20 minutes."

A standard of performance   The final characteristic for which one looks in a well-stated objective is a description of the quality or quantity (or both) of the learner's performance or product. If we want him to describe something, we must state how well he must describe. If we want him to spell words, we ought to state how high a score he must obtain. If we want him to identify examples, we ought to state how many of the items he must identify. Statements describing these types of things are called standards. Every good statement of an objective includes a standard for the learner's performance or product. This standard is used to evaluate or, in some instances, to measure whether the learner has reached the desired point.

Sometimes the standard of performance is expressed in terms of a score. "To spell correctly at least 95 percent of the words on pages 3 and 4" is an example of this kind of performance specification. Frequently the only acceptable standard is a 100 percent performance. "To name the capitals of all 50 states" means that the learner must name all 50 capital cities correctly. The objective is not attained if less than 50 are named correctly. "To name at least five of the causes of the War of the Roses" states a criterion. So does the objective, "to make a steel pin with a tolerance of .005″ or less."

Obviously, the examples above demonstrate clearly that if no standard is explicitly stated, the reader has a right to assume that a 100 percent performance is intended. If anything less than a 100 percent performance is acceptable, it is incumbent on the writer of the objective to state this explicitly.

"To swim the length of the pool and back without stopping, in one minute or less, using each of the following four strokes . . ." is an example. Four different strokes are required. "To write four poems of at least six lines each, employing the following four types of meter . . ." specifies a quantity: *four* types of meter. In summary, objectives generally must specify a standard of performance, such as an acceptable score, a quality of performance, a quantity of modes or procedures, or any other criterion which the teacher expects the student to attain.

37 At this time, you should be able to recognize acceptable statements of objectives. First of all, see whether you can name the four criteria for good objectives. What are they?

    •   •   •   •   •   •

37 *The four criteria for good objectives are the following. The objective must*

    a. be stated in terms of learner *behavior;*
    b. describe an observable *performance or product;*
    c. state the condition *of performance;*
    d. state the standard *of performance.*

Tell whether each of the statements below is an acceptable objective. If you feel that it fails to meet any or all of the four criteria for objectives, tell why it is inadequate, then rewrite the objective in acceptable form.

38 To help students gain an understanding of the democratic process.

    •   •   •   •   •   •

38 *There's nothing like starting out with a jack-pot! This objective fails on all four counts. About the only thing it could be used for is to begin a discussion on the subject of stating objectives.*

39 To capitalize the first word of a sentence.

    •   •   •   •   •   •

39 *Learner behavior? Yes! Observable behavior? Yes! Conditions of performance? No—but perhaps this would be unnecessary, since the inference that we are dealing with any English sentence, anywhere, under any conditions, might be defended. However, there might be a difference between capitalizing in a proof-reading exercise and capitalizing one's own writing. Perhaps it would do no harm to add the words ". . . in original writing." Standard? Yes! The meaning is clearly "the first word of every sentence."*

40 To be able to recognize valid statements of inference, given a variety of types of statements and questions.

    •   •   •   •   •   •

40 *Learner behavior? Yes! Observable? Yes—although the words "to be able" do nothing for the statement. Try reading it without these three words. It's just as clear, and you've saved three words. Conditions? Yes—the learner is "given a variety. . ." You might add something regarding time, such as "given enough time to read each statement twice." Standard? Nothing is said about a standard so you must infer that 100 percent performance is expected.*

41 To alphabetize, given lists of words.

    •   •   •   •   •   •

41 *Learner behavior? Yes! Observable? Yes! Conditions? Vague. For example, do lists include words with the same initial two letters, or three letters, or lists in which no two words begin with the same letter? If the writer wanted*

the learner to alphabetize any possible list of words, the objective is probably adequately stated with respect to conditions of performance. Nothing is said about the amount of time given the learner! Standard? It must be assumed that 100 percent accuracy is expected.

42 To understand the procedure for adding pairs of like fractions, given examples in which the answer is a simple fraction requiring no reducing.

· · · · · · ·

42 *Learner behavior? Yes! Observable? No—"to understand the procedure" is quite meaningless. Why not say "to add pairs of like fractions . . ."? Conditions? Technically, you can't specify conditions of performance for a non-observable term, but if you changed the verb, as suggested above, you'd have a very adequate statement of conditions. No doubt the time factor ought to be stated. How much time should the student be given to do this? Standard? By inference, 100 percent must be the acceptable standard. If anything else is to be accepted, it must be explicitly stated.*

Choosing a Means for Attaining the Desired Objective

What tools should a man use to construct a dwelling? Hammer? Saw? Square? Screw-driver? If he were building a wooden house, these tools would probably be indispensable. The term *dwelling*, however, could include stone houses, brick houses, concrete houses, and perhaps houses built of several other materials. *Dwelling* certainly includes apartments, hotels, tents, campers, igloos—to mention only a few. If one were to specify the tools to be used to construct a dwelling, he would have to accept one of two alternatives: either he would list all the tools which would be needed to construct any and every possible type of dwelling, or he would define dwelling very precisely and select only those tools necessary to construct dwellings that are covered by the restricted definition.

The analogy to teaching is obvious. The more specific an objective is, the more precise the teacher can be in selecting a means for its implementation. When an objective is ambiguous, or open to many interpretations, a teacher cannot be specific in selecting a means for implementing the objective. Instead, he will need to compile a huge list of possible means in order to cover all possible eventualities. Just as the list of all the tools needed to construct a "dwelling" is too cumbersome to be useful, so a list of means for implementing ambiguous objectives will contain too many items to have any practical value.

In American education today objectives are determined in various ways and by various individuals. In some schools or classrooms, the teacher is the only one who determines the objectives. In other schools or classrooms, the students may play the dominant role in determining objectives. In still other situations, objectives may be determined cooperatively by teachers and students. Sometimes an institution or an agency outside the school determines the objectives of instruction. This book is not concerned with the question of who determines the objectives. Whether objectives are determined by teachers, by students, by students and teachers, or by some other individual or combination of individuals, it is still critical that the objectives be written in terms that are not ambiguous and not open to varied interpretations. For the remainder of this book we shall refer to teacher-constructed objectives, with full awareness that objectives may be determined by others alone or in conjunction with teachers. The important thing to remember at this time is that even though we refer to objectives as being determined by the teacher, the principles with which we are dealing are applicable to other types of objectives too.

Once a teacher has specified the behavior he wants the student to acquire, he must arrange the environment so that the student will learn in the most effective and efficient way possible. He may lecture, ask questions and react to answers, put up bulletin boards, take pupils on field trips, provide educational telecasts for pupils to watch, show filmstrips, play phonograph records, or do any of the countless things which good teachers do to help children learn.

How can a teacher make a good prediction concerning the means best suited for the implementation of a given objective? Certainly the teacher must consider the characteristics of the learner. For example, some students learn most effectively from pictures while others benefit most if the instructional materials are primarily verbal. If the teacher can identify the characteristics of his students, he will usually be able to select a more effective means of instruction.

In addition to using learner characteristics to determine the instructional strategy, the teacher must consider task characteristics. In other words, the objective will play a large role in determining the means which a teacher employs to cause students to learn. If a teacher wants the students to learn to distinguish a "go" light from a "stop" light, it is quite obvious that, given the choice of a black-and-white or a color film, he would choose the latter. Few decisions concerning instructional strategy are this simple. On the other hand, if a teacher goes about the task systematically, using the best means available to help him make his decision, the task of selecting a medium of instruction will seldom be extremely difficult. Since the primary purpose of this book is to demonstrate a system and method for selecting a means for attaining a specified objective, the development and elaboration of the system will be reserved for subsequent chapters.

Suppose that we have selected a well-written objective which is consistent with our instructional goals. We have taken an inventory of the learners in our class to determine what their learning potential and characteristics may be and what their capability is with respect to the specific learning task at hand. We have chosen the media of instruction and adopted a strategy of teaching within which these media will be employed. This is not the end of our responsibility. We must still go through a final step in our instructional system: evaluation.

Consider the following example from a fifth grade classroom. The teacher wants to interest his students in the new books on space science which the library has purchased. His objective is to lead the students "to

check out and read books on space science during the next month."
There are no doubt many different means which he might use to lead
students to the desired behaviors. Actually, most good teachers would
use several different means. A bulletin board which contains a number
of unusual pictures of astronauts in action might catch the attention of
some students and interest them in reading about space. A film, properly
presented, might cause some students to go to the library in search of
additional information. Or a tape recording of man's first words from the
moon might lead still others to the library in search of good books about
rockets and man-made satellites. These, of course, represent only a
sampling of the many possible means of implementing the objective which
a teacher could use.

Suppose that in this situation the teacher had decided to use only the
film. What would he do next? The showing of the film is not an end;
it is a *means* to an end. The use of the film cannot be justified unless it
can be demonstrated that the desired learning took place. In other words,
if the students checked out and read the specified books after the film
was shown, the objective was successfully implemented. The teacher
would be justified in hypothesizing that the film was an effective means
of instruction. If the students did nothing about the books, the teacher
would be justified in hypothesizing that the film was not an effective means
of instruction.

Whenever the teacher selects a means for implementing an objective,
he must evaluate the results. When this is done, the teacher has a sound
basis for continuing his instructional pattern or for changing it, as the case
may be.

The Relationship Between Means and Outcome

It is insufficient merely to describe (and possibly record for future use)
what one sees. While description is *always* necessary, it should always
be followed by explanation. What does this mean in terms of an instructional strategy?

Several years ago, the September issue of a women's fashion trade
journal reported that the hemline on women's dresses would be higher
than it had been the previous year. For several months following this
announcement, the New York Stock Exchange prices, as measured by a
popular index, increased. The same phenomenon was repeated two years
later, and again two years after that. This is a description. It tells what
someone observed. These are facts. But these facts need an explanation.
Did the change in style produce a change in the stock market? Or was it
the publication of specific information in a women's fashion trade journal
that caused the rise in the stock market? Even with very little knowledge
of either women's fashions or the stock market, one would be inclined to
doubt both explanations. It doesn't seem logical or rational to explain
these phenomena in this manner. Of course, if one had the power to
decree the styles for the coming year, or if one could publish whatever
he wished in this trade journal, the hypothesis could be tested over a
number of years. If a higher hemline was always followed by a rise in

stock prices, and if, through careful manipulation, it were possible to eliminate all other plausible factors as causes of the rise in the market, the explanation could be considered valid. This process is referred to as *establishing a functional relationship.*

There are many functional relationships around us every day. We turn the water faucet on; water flows. We turn the faucet off; the flow ceases. There is a functional relationship between Event *A* and Event *B*.

EVENT *A*	EVENT *B*
Turn faucet on	Water flows
Turn faucet off	Water stops flowing
Turn light switch on	Light shines
Turn light switch off	Light stops shining

Whenever a change in Event *A* produces a predictable change in Event *B*, a functional relationship is said to exist.

Functional relationships are unidirectional. Suppose the light bulb is shining. It can be made to stop shining by screwing the bulb out. Does this affect the switch? Not at all! It remains in the *on* position. In other words, manipulations under Event *A* are followed by a change under Event *B*, but manipulations under *B* are not followed by a change in *A*. When this condition obtains, namely that *A* is always the cause and *B* the effect, and when the direction cannot be reversed, we are dealing with a functional relationship.

While this explanation of a functional relationship is oversimplified, it is adequate for our present purposes. The additional refinements which can be found in a good textbook on educational research are generally too complex for a teacher to apply in the types of classroom situations described below.

Recall the example of the teacher who showed a film to his class in order to implement the objective "to check out and read books . . ." He prepared his students for viewing the film by posing problems and questions for which partial answers could be found in the film. He was careful to suggest only the kind of problem which would require the reading of the type of book mentioned above after the students had seen the film. Following the film, he led the students to ask additional questions, answers to which could be found in the new library books. Then, at the appropriate moment, he told the class of the new books and invited them to go to the library during their library period and inspect the books. During the next three weeks, the teacher periodically set the stage for a discussion of the merits of the new books, and he provided an opportunity for students who had been reading these books to share their findings with their classmates. At the end of the month the teacher checked the library records and discovered that 90 percent of his students had withdrawn one or more of these books. A questionnaire which he used in class revealed that 83 percent of the students said that they had read parts of one or more of these books. Apparently the teacher could say that at least five out of six students in his classroom had attained the specified objective.

The question is this: Did the motion picture have anything to do with the attainment of the objective? The simplest answer is *yes*; the film was shown and following the showing of the film the outcome specified in the objective was manifested. But this is not a way of discovering a functional relationship. Consider the events again.

EVENT A	EVENT B
Students see a film.	Five out of every six students check out and read specified books.

What is missing? Obviously, no one knows for certain whether Event B would have taken place if Event A had not.

Suppose that the teacher had not shown a film, and the results had been the same. What explanation could be offered?

EVENT A	EVENT B
Teacher uses question-and-answer dialogue to bring students to state problems about space.	Five out of every six students check out and read specified books

Here we could hypothesize that the skillful questioning by the teacher caused Event B, and thus we could assume that a functional relationship exists. But we cannot be certain. Indeed, we can be no more certain that the question-and-answer dialogue produced this outcome than we can that the showing of the film produced the outcome. The critical point to remember is that one cannot justify the means of instruction (Event A) solely because the outcome (Event B) occurred after Event A. It is also necessary to determine whether Event B occurred in spite of Event A, or whether it might occur in the absence of Event A.

Evaluation must be more than a description of events. Unless the events are explained, the description is useless. Admittedly, this is a task which even the sophisticated educational researcher finds difficult and, at times, even frustrating. However, unless the classroom teacher attempts to discover functional relationships where they exist, and unless he builds on the functional relationships which others have discovered, he will be in the untenable position of advocating means (or at least using means) which have no demonstrable relation to the ends or goals of his instruction.

One of the most important methods of evaluating the choice of a means of instructing is to try to discover whether a functional relationship exists between Event *A* and Event *B*. Check your ability to apply this concept by responding to the questions below and then comparing your responses with those given.

43   Event *A*, as used in this chapter, always refers to the instructional _____.

·   ·   ·   ·   ·   ·

43   *Event* A, *always refers to the instructional* means.

44   Event *B* always refers to the instructional _____.

·   ·   ·   ·   ·   ·

44   *Event* B *refers to the instructional* objectives.

45   When can one say that a functional relationship exists between Event *A* and Event *B*?

·   ·   ·   ·   ·   ·

45   *A functional relationship is said to exist between Event* A *and Event* B *when a change in* A *produces a predictable change in* B.

46   Students use tape recordings and a programmed textbook in a language laboratory (Event *A*). At the end of the semester they have learned to speak French at a specified level of performance (Event *B*). Is there a functional relationship between Event *A* and Event *B*?

·   ·   ·   ·   ·   ·

46   *If the tape recordings and the programmed text were the only instruction the students received, it would be safe to assume that there is a functional relationship. This is all the information given you, so no other answer is plausible. If, however, the question had specified that a teacher used tapes and programmed texts to* help *him teach these students to speak French, you could not assume a functional relationship. You simply would not know to what factor to attribute the students' learning; it could have been the tapes and text, but it could just as possibly have been any of the other things the teacher did.*

47   A teacher uses many media to teach a unit on Hawaii. Among other instructional means, he uses the bulletin board, maps, charts, the chalkboard, a film, large still pictures, and a phonograph record. The children seem

to enjoy Hawaii at the end of the unit. Is there a functional relationship in evidence? Why, or why not?

    •   •   •   •   •   •

47   *There is no functional relationship possible because Event B is improperly stated. To say that the children "seemed to enjoy Hawaii" is a nonobservable kind of performance, at best. If there is no specific Event B, it is impossible to establish a functional relationship.*

48   The English teacher used a filmstrip in one class section to help him teach students to identify the eight parts of speech. In another section he used a workbook exercise (which consumed about the same amount of time) instead of the filmstrip. After instruction had been completed, he gave a test on identifying parts of speech to each group. The filmstrip group achieved a mean of 96 percent correct, while the workbook group achieved a mean of 87 percent. Do you see a functional relationship here? If so, describe Event *A* and Event *B*. If not, tell why there is no functional relationship.

    •   •   •   •   •   •

48   *This is a difficult one, and if you answered it correctly, you probably can distinguish between functional and nonfunctional relationships.*
    This is not an example of a functional relationship. Event A is quite clear: filmstrip vs. workbook. Event B seems to be just as clear—96 percent vs. 87 percent. But one thing is missing. Did the students learn *to identify parts of speech in this class? There's no way of telling unless we can acquire some information on the* change *in behavior. Remember: learning is a change in behavior.*
    If each group had achieved a mean score of 25 percent correct on a pretest, our relationships could be diagrammed as shown here.

EVENT *A*	EVENT *B*
Filmstrip	Gain from 25 percent to 96 percent
Workbook exercise	Gain from 25 percent to 87 percent

We could assume that there are several functional relations in evidence here. Both the filmstrip and the workbook produce a gain in terms of the test performance. The filmstrip produces a greater gain. It would be safe to assume that for attaining this objective the filmstrip is better than the workbook exercise for the students in these two sections.

Whenever a means of instructing learners has been selected, it is essential to plan some method of evaluating its effect. The best way to do this is to look for a functional relationship between the means and the degree to which the specified objective has been attained.

The Media Selection Rule

The concept of selecting a medium of instruction to implement a specified objective is a very simple one. For example, if the learner is "to describe the process of cell division, given a pictorial representation of the process," it seems only logical that the instructor would use a motion picture at some time during the instructional process, since motion is involved in the process. Furthermore, the motion picture at some time or another ought to be either a silent one or a sound film used without the sound track if the student is to learn to do the describing. The motion picture is used for one reason only: It enables the learner to attain, or to move toward the attainment of, the stated objective by providing an environment in which the *describing* is to take place. Indeed, the concept is so simple that it can be stated as a rule.

> **A MEDIUM OF INSTRUCTION MUST BE SELECTED ON THE BASIS OF ITS POTENTIAL FOR IMPLEMENTING A STATED OBJECTIVE.**

The corollaries are obvious. The objectives should never be determined after a medium has been chosen. Neither should a medium be chosen which does not contribute to the attainment of the stated objective or objectives. It is wasteful and inefficient to use a generalized filmstrip on cells if the only objective that is to be attained at the moment is "to describe the process of cell division." It is possible that the teacher might find selected frames in the filmstrip which would be useful, but it is highly doubtful, given only this brief description of its content, that it would be good teaching strategy to show the class the complete generalized filmstrip on cells. Without a doubt, there would be too many irrelevancies in the film which, at best, would contribute nothing to the stated objective and which, at worst, would interfere with an efficient instructional process.

Although this point will be emphasized later, it should be mentioned that frequently several media may be needed to implement a single objective. It was indicated above that a silent motion picture film might be the most logical medium to employ in the situation involving learning to describe cell division. Perhaps a good filmstrip, several appropriate 35mm slides, and a series of overhead transparencies might be used to present a wide variety of types of cell division, all of which should be included when the learner begins "to describe the process." This concept of a multimedia implementation of an objective is elaborated in the final section of each of Chapters 4 to 10. At this point it is sufficient to note that the rule for media selection applies equally to instances in which a single medium is chosen and to instances in which two or more media are selected to implement a stated objective.

Which of the following examples illustrate a correct application of the rule for media selection?

49 Six teachers of eighth grade science are meeting to choose the films for the next school year. Each teacher is permitted to choose two films. Because of budgetary limitations, each film must be rented for one day only and, consequently, all eighth grade science classes must view each film on the same day. The films are carefully chosen to represent each chapter title listed in the table of contents of the basic text.
Do you agree with this procedure? Why or why not?

•   •   •   •   •   •   •

49 *Obviously, these films are not being selected to implement stated objectives. First, it is highly improbable that all six teachers have identical objectives; if they did, it would not be necessary to permit each one to select two films. Next, teaching is not so predictable that a teacher can tell, long in advance, with what objective he will be concerned on a specific day; it is extremely unlikely that all six teachers would be dealing with the same objectives on a given day, especially when the day is specified many months in advance of the actual use of the film. Finally, the question implies that selection of a medium is possible on the basis of chapter titles; medium selection must be based on objectives, not chapter titles.*

50 The third grade teachers have received notice that a new TV program dealing with the beginning of the transition from manuscript to cursive writing will be telecast during the next two weeks. It will be scheduled daily from 10:30 to 11:00 a.m. One of the third grade teachers indicates a lack of interest in the use of this program on the grounds that her students have already begun the transition, and she needs more advanced instructional materials. The other teachers remind her that there wouldn't be any educational television if everyone adopted her attitude. Who is right? Why?

•   •   •   •   •   •   •

50 *The lone dissenter deserves our support. If her objectives are not concerned with having her students "make the transition from manuscript to cursive," the TV program should not be inflicted on her students. One of the great fallacies persisting in audiovisual education is that "children will always pick up something" from a good film or radio program or telecast. They may, indeed, "pick up something," but if the teacher really wants them to do this "picking up," the instructional experience should be carefully planned and only the best media for the stated objective should be used. Costly media should never be justified on the basis of fringe users. If the TV program used in the illustration can't be justified on the basis of those who really need it, it shouldn't be used.*

51 The biology department is drawing up a list of "most urgently needed" instructional materials for the coming year. A newcomer to the faculty insists that first the department ought to look at the students' scores on the Science Aptitude Test to determine what the areas of weakness are. The others outvote him on the grounds that each teacher has slightly different

goals, and the purchase of materials ought to reflect this diversity. How would you have voted? Why?

. . . . . .

51   *Again, the dissenter's intentions are laudable, but his methods are not clear. The majority is right in this instance. The list of teaching materials ought to reflect the specific objectives of each teacher. Only to the extent that teachers share common objectives can a common list be constructed. An aptitude test is hardly an adequate source of this kind of information. An achievement test might be a good source, providing that the course objectives are consistent with the text content.*

SUMMARY

When objectives are properly stated, they provide a point of departure for selecting the media of instruction. Objectives are well-stated if they answer four questions:

1. Who? The learner.
2. What? An observable performance or product.
3. When? Given stated conditions.
4. How well? At the level of a stated criterion or standard.

A medium of instruction has been correctly selected when one can show that there is a functional relationship between the use of the medium and the desired outcome as expressed in the behavioral objective.

The next chapter describes a five-category system for classifying behavioral objectives, and it answers some of the criticisms which have been offered concerning the use of such objectives.

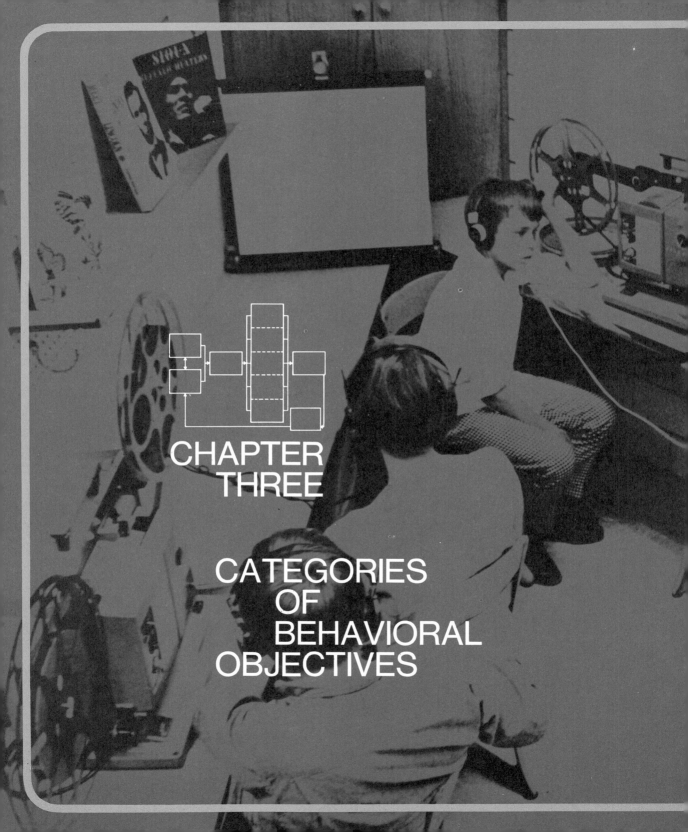

CHAPTER
THREE

CATEGORIES
OF
BEHAVIORAL
OBJECTIVES

WHEN YOU HAVE MASTERED THE CONTENT OF THIS CHAPTER, YOU SHOULD BE ABLE TO:

1.   NAME the five categories of objectives defined in this chapter.

2.   CLASSIFY objectives in one of the five categories, given statements of objectives which meet the criteria discussed in Chapter 2.

3.   CONSTRUCT answers which meet the criticisms of behavioral objectives raised in this chapter.

It is a relatively simple matter to identify well-written objectives as defined in Chapter 2. It is another matter to be able to write objectives that meet the four criteria discussed. The criteria are that the objective must:

1. be stated in terms of learner behavior,
2. describe an observable performance or product,
3. state the condition of performance, and
4. state the standard of performance.

The football fan who sits in front of his television set on a Sunday afternoon easily develops the ability to identify good and bad offensive strategies. But one does not equate this kind of behavior with that of a successful quarterback or coach. It is one thing to identify a good call; it is quite another to make a good call on the playing field in the heat of battle before thousands of roaring fans.

Now that you can discriminate between well-written and not so well-written objectives, you are ready for the next step: to construct well-written objectives which meet the four criteria discussed in Chapter 2.

THE CLASSIFICATION OF OBJECTIVES

This chapter presents a preliminary look at a simple strategy which will help you write objectives. Using this strategy, you should be able to write objectives for nearly all elementary and secondary school learning. First, however, you will learn to classify objectives.

1 What is the objective you should attain before you begin writing objectives?

· · · · · · ·

1 *To classify statements of objectives which contain the four characteristics described in Chapter 2.*

The Five Categories of Objectives

The Science Education Commission of the American Association for the Advancement of Science developed a list of ten words to help science teachers describe objectives in their field.[1] Researchers in the Classroom Learning Laboratory at Arizona State University[2] and in the Southwest Regional Laboratory for Educational Research and Development[3] then reduced this list of terms from ten to five. They revised the definitions to avoid ambiguity and expanded them to make the words apply to content areas other than science. The five words are

1. identify
2. name
3. describe
4. order
5. construct

In the next section each of these five terms is defined and an example given. Following the definitions and examples, detailed instructions concerning the use of these words in classifying well-written objectives are provided.

Identify   When a student *identifies* something, he indicates membership or nonmembership of specified characteristics, objects, or events in a class when the name of that class is given. The objective of the arithmetic student is "to identify examples of cones, given actual cones, cylinders, and pyramids, within three seconds per example." The learner will identify the examples by touching them, removing them from the table, by placing a chalkmark on them or by any other means the teacher might suggest. If the exercise deals with pictures of cones instead of actual cones, the learner will underline, or mark his choice in some other way; he might point, touch, or speak to show which one he is identifying as a cone. Synonyms for identify include select, distinguish between, discriminate between, mark, match, point out, locate, recognize, and classify.

Name   When a learner *names* something, he supplies a label, either orally or in writing, for a specified characteristic, object, or event. Let us use the example of the cone again. The objective is "given examples of actual cones, the learner will name the geometric object within three seconds." Instead of using the word name, teachers might at times prefer synonyms such as label or list.

Describe   In order to *describe* something, the student must report the necessary categories of object properties, events, event properties, and/

[1] American Association for the Advancement of Science, *Commission on Science Education Newsletter.* Vol. 1: 1:3, 1965, 2–4.

[2] Vernon S. Gerlach, Howard J. Sullivan, Robert L. Baker, and Richard E. Schutz. "Programming the Instructional Film."*Audiovisual Communication Review*, 14:3. Fall 1966, 383–406.

[3] Vernon S. Gerlach and Howard J. Sullivan, *Constructing Statements of Outcomes* (Inglewood, California: Southwest Regional Laboratory for Educational Research and Development, 1967).

or relationships relevant to a given characteristic, object, or event. If we assume that the objective is "to describe a cone," and the learner supplies all of the characteristics which have been agreed upon as necessary in a comprehensive description, he has attained the objective. Again, the teacher may prefer to use synonyms for describe; these include define, tell why, tell what happens when, explain, demonstrate, or give examples of.

Order   When a learner arranges two or more things in a specified sequence, we say that he is ordering. As we shall see later, there are two levels of ordering. Sometimes the learner orders things which he is given: "Order chronologically (a) the Mexican War, (b) the Spanish-American War, (c) the War for Southern Independence." At other times the learner is required to provide the things to be ordered: "Tell in order the steps by which a bill becomes a law." Another example would be "to order the steps which must be followed in constructing a cone from a sheet of 6″ x 6″ paper, within one minute, in writing." Synonyms for order include alphabetize, rank, arrange in sequence, and list in sequence.

Construct   The learner is *constructing* when he produces a drawing, an article of clothing or furniture, a map, an essay, or examples of a particular concept. The product must meet specifications which have been given previously. The objective for the arithmetic student might be "to construct a cone, given the geometric parts in scrambled order, within one minute." There are many synonyms for construct; some of them are prepare, draw, make, build, create, or compose.

2   Name the five categories.

     •   •   •   •   •   •

2   *Identify, name, describe, order and construct.*

3   Place each of the following words and phrases under the best of the category headings given below:

a. arrange from left to right	h. give the equivalent of
b. build	i. label
c. classify	j. match
d. compose	k. name from youngest to oldest
e. define	l. prepare
f. describe in order the steps for	m. recognize
g. explain	

Identify	Name	Describe	Order	Construct

     •   •   •   •   •   •

3	*Identify*	*Name*	*Describe*	*Order*	*Construct*
	c, j, m	*h, i*	*e, g*	*a, f, k*	*b, d, l*

Terms Used in Stating Objectives

Unless one has had experience in the classification of instructional objectives, it may seem impossible to classify more than a few tasks in these categories. However, as one works with this classification scheme, it becomes increasingly clear that it is highly inclusive. Furthermore, the kinds of behavior which cannot be classified by use of one of the terms in the list are often behaviors for which a suitable substitute can be found that is not ambiguous. The French teacher wants his students to translate French sentences into English. It would be silly for him to substitute a verb from the list of categories for the verb *translate*. He would gain nothing if he wrote his objective in this manner: "to name the English sentence which is the equivalent of a given French sentence" or "to construct an English equivalent of a French sentence." The use of the verb translate in this instance is better; it is operational, unambiguous, and open to few if any misinterpretations. When one adds to the word translate a statement of conditions and a statement of acceptable performance standard, the word translate becomes adequate in every respect. We find a number of words similar to translate; spell, punctuate, capitalize, multiply are all behavioral terms and they should be used when we write statements of objectives whenever it would be awkward to use one of the words in the classification scheme described above.

These verbs are primarily useful in constructing statements of objectives that deal with knowledge, concepts, and principles. Sometimes we call these areas the *cognitive domain* or *cognitive behaviors*. There are many things with which elementary and secondary teachers are concerned that lie outside the area of knowledge, principles, or concepts. First grade teachers want their children to write (in the sense of manuscript or cursive writing). They want their students to color, to paste, to cut. The home economics teacher wants her girls to sew. The football coach wants his fullback to punt. The industrial arts teacher wants his boys to plane. These are excellent terms and can, when they are accompanied by a proper statement of conditions and a performance standard, be used to write good behavioral objectives. They meet the requirements discussed in Chapter 2 in every respect.

The five verbs may also be used to describe attitudes, interests, and emotions. This subject is discussed in detail in Chapter 9.

Problems in Stating Objectives

Before proceeding with the techniques for writing objectives in each category, let us examine some of the problems related to stating objectives behaviorally. Some problems stem from misunderstandings and are easily resolved; others are thorny ones, and it is quite conceivable that before they are solved we may have to revise some of our ideas about the role and form of well-written objectives.

The intangible outcomes of education   Some scholarly and highly respected educators assert that there are important educational outcomes which cannot be expressed in terms of observable behaviors or products.

They cite examples such as creative thinking or democratic citizenship or the process of inquiry. Indeed, it is extremely difficult to define these concepts. Because they cannot be defined, they are intangible. To the extent that they are intangible, no one knows precisely how to teach in order to insure pupils' attainment of these goals. Robert Ebel points out that

> We may feel intuitively that critical thinking and good citizenship are immensely important. But if we don't know very clearly what we mean by those terms, it is hard to show that the concepts they might stand for are in fact important.[4]

Thus, the discipline imposed on teachers by the need for objectives to meet the four criteria of Chapter 2 will not mitigate against the attainment of "creative thinking" or "democratic citizenship" or "the inquiry process." On the contrary, it will force teachers into a critical analysis and definition process which ought to result in more clearly defined goals. Only as goals become clearly defined can instructional media be effectively selected (or produced) and utilized.

W. James Popham has pointed out that sometimes teachers who say that they are seeking such lofty objectives as the development of democratic citizenship are actually concerned with extremely trivial kinds of student behavior changes, if one is to judge by what occurs in the classrooms of such teachers.

> How often, for example, do we find "good citizenship" measured by a trifling true-false test. Now if we'd asked for the teacher's objectives in operational (behavioral) terms and had discovered that, indeed, all the teacher was really doing was promoting the learner's achievement on a true-false test, we might have rejected the aim as unimportant.[5]

But as long as the teacher states his intent with such imprecise and ambiguous phrases as "developing democratic citizenship" it is virtually impossible to evaluate the objective, the media, or the teaching strategies selected to implement the objective. Perhaps it is difficult to define such terms as "democratic citizenship," but if teaching is to improve in these content areas, it seems clear that an effort will have to be made.

The trivial, measurable outcomes of education Some educators contend that teachers who use behavioral objectives tend to concentrate exclusively on outcomes which can be measured and that such outcomes are trivial.

Schools are concerned to some extent with important outcomes which

---

[4] Robert L. Ebel, *Measuring Educational Achievement* (Englewood Cliffs, N.J.: Prentice-Hall, Inc., 1965), p. 27. Quoted by permission of Prentice-Hall, Inc.

[5] W. James Popham, "The Threat-Potential of Precision," a symposium presentation at the 19th Annual Conference on Educational Research, California Advisory Council on Educational Research, San Diego, California, November 16, 1967. Quoted by permission of W. James Popham.

no one seems to know how to measure. Even the most dedicated specialists in tests and measurement would agree. However, it does not logically follow that because no one today knows how to measure an important outcome that the outcome is not measurable. Someone will immediately ask, "What about honesty? Or patriotism? Or *esprit de corps*?" We will grant that there may be a dearth of paper-and-pencil tests to measure honesty. But if it is possible to identify an individual who has "more honesty" than another, then honesty is measurable, even if the measurement is only a crude one. If the football coach can select a player who has more team spirit than another, then *esprit de corps* is measurable. If a student in a junior American history class, given appropriate data, can reach the decision that Nathan Hale was more patriotic than Benedict Arnold, then patriotism is being measured. And if a teacher, applying agreed-upon criteria, decides that Sue is more patriotic than Mike, patriotism is being measured. Thorndike once wrote that whatever exists at all exists in some amount.[6]

Certainly anything described in a behavioral objective is measurable. The question that we must face is "Does this mean that behavioral objectives must deal only with the trivial?" Obviously, the answer depends in part on our definition of trivial, but if one will grant that such things as honesty, patriotism, and *esprit de corps* are not trivial, then one must also concede that there are measurable characteristics of events which are not trivial. Behavioral objectives cannot, then, be categorically condemned or relegated to the domain of "trivia" merely because they are limited to performances or products which can be measured (i.e., observed).

The difficulty of measuring behavior in the humanities and arts   Hardly anyone who has worked with behavioral objectives will contend that it is as easy to write good behavioral objectives for a literary appreciation course as it is for a course in freshman algebra. It does not follow, however, that the effort should be abandoned any more than it is logical to drop the teaching of spelling (with its hundreds of "exceptions") in favor of arithmetic (which is extremely lawful and has few, if any, exceptions). The problem in arts and humanities stems more from disagreement among the experts in these disciplines as to what is to be taught than it does from any limitation inherent in the concept of writing objectives in a behavioral form.

4   Can the intangible outcomes of education be described by means of well-written objectives which possess the four criteria discussed in Chapter 2? Why, or why not?

·   ·   ·   ·   ·   ·

4   *Even though it may be difficult, it can be done. Actually, one cannot communicate with anyone (not even with oneself) about intangible outcomes unless he does so in language which is not highly subject to misinterpretation. Only to the extent that intangible goals are stated in terms of unambiguous objectives are they useful in teaching.*

[6]E. L. Thorndike, *The Seventeenth Yearbook of the National Society for the Study of Education, Part II* (Bloomington, Ill.: Public School Publishing Company, 1918), p. 16.

5 Do well-written objectives deal mainly with trivial outcomes? Why, or why not?

•   •   •   •   •   •   •

5 *Not necessarily. People whose thinking is confined to trivia will certainly be able to describe their thoughts in acceptable statements of behavioral objectives. But teachers who are concerned with the broad aspects of education (such as values and human dignity) can also develop the ability to describe their objectives in well-written, unambiguous statements if they care to do so.*

6 Are well-written objectives useful for teachers of subjects which are difficult to measure? Why, or why not?

•   •   •   •   •   •   •

6 *Yes. The problem lies not in the characteristics of well-written objectives, but rather in the disagreement of experts concerning what the outcomes of such courses as literature or music appreciation should be. Once this agreement is achieved, well-written statements of objectives can be formulated. It may not be as easy as writing objectives for a science course, but it can be and is being done. You can find examples from the "difficult" areas in the chapters ahead.*

Writing behavioral objectives is not necessarily more difficult in one subject area than another. The source of difficulty lies primarily in the people who do the writing. The more steeped an individual is in writing objectives in a traditional way, the more difficult it is for him to change his behavior. When properly trained, any educator will find that the behavioral objective is easier to write.

SUMMARY

The behaviors or products with which elementary and secondary schools are concerned can be classified, to a large extent, in one of five categories: identify, name, describe, order, or construct. Although some critics maintain that a classification system of this type may lead to undue emphasis on trivial outcomes, or to a neglect of the "important intangible" outcomes, close examination reveals that such criticisms are not based on logic or in fact.

The next seven chapters show how one may use the five categories as a basis for constructing objectives and for selecting instructional media.

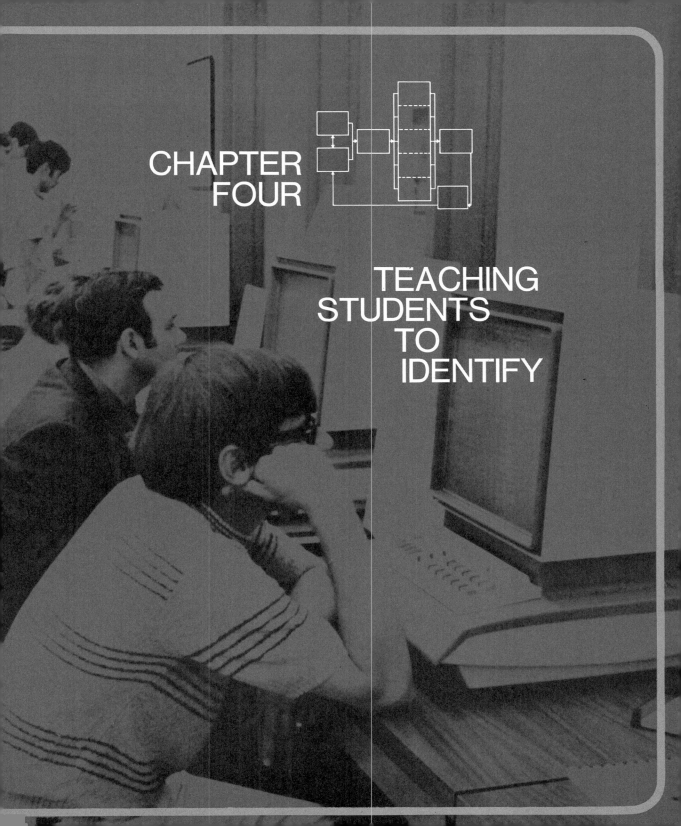

CHAPTER
FOUR

TEACHING
STUDENTS
TO
IDENTIFY

WHEN YOU HAVE MASTERED THE CONTENT OF THIS CHAPTER,
YOU SHOULD BE ABLE TO:

1. DEFINE the term "identify."

2. DESCRIBE school learning situations in which the desired behavior is to identify.

3. IDENTIFY objectives in this category.

4. CONSTRUCT objectives in this category.

5. DESCRIBE the conditions required to teach pupils to identify.

6. CONSTRUCT a rationale for choosing the medium or media best suited for establishing the conditions specified in objectives in the *identify* category.

Whether students are entering kindergarten or completing the final semester of high school, they are confronted with some identifying task almost daily. The five-year-old may find that his teacher wants him to identify the primary colors, and the eighth grader is learning to identify a number of examples of iambic pentameter.

THE NATURE OF IDENTIFYING

What does a learner do when he identifies? He tells whether each of the ten most recent Presidents was a Democrat or a Republican, given the names of the Presidents and the names of the two parties. He underlines each pictorial representation of a vegetable and he circles the pictures of fruit, given the pictures and the names of the two categories. In other words, he indicates whether or not something belongs to a class. He indicates membership or nonmembership of specified objects, events, or characteristics in a class when the name of the class is given. The learner must always be given (1) an object, event, or characteristic, and (2) the name of the object, event, or characteristic, or the name of the class to which it belongs. Unless both these conditions are met, we are not dealing with identifying.

A class is learning about land forms. One of the objectives is "to identify a peninsula on a map, given outline maps containing both peninsulas and other land forms." The diagram below summarizes the nature of the task. The teacher may point to one land form after another, asking

GIVEN₁: The name "peninsula"

GIVEN₂: Peninsulas and nonpeninsulas

STUDENT BEHAVIOR: Correct response to the question: "Is this a peninsula?"

in each instance, "Is this a peninsula?"   If the learner can answer "yes" to each example of a peninsula and "no" to all other land forms, he is identifying.

There are always two discreet elements present in the learner's environment when he identifies something—two things that must be paired. These things may be objects, events, or characteristics, or they may be words or symbols which represent the objects, events, or characteristics.   In the example above we used a word and a symbol.   The word was "peninsula." The symbol was the representation of a land form on an outline map.   The learner could have demonstrated his ability to identify in a number of different ways, all of which would have indicated that he paired or associated the symbol for peninsula with the word peninsula.   He could have demonstrated this ability by circling each peninsula on an outline map and leaving uncircled all other land forms on the map, in response to the teacher's spoken or written direction, "Circle the peninsulas on this map." The word could be a written word or a spoken word.   For example, the learner would also be engaged in an identifying task if the name were presented in the directions, printed at the top of the outline map: "Circle every peninsula on this map."

When the teacher points to Arizona on a map of the southwestern United States and asks, "Is this Arizona?" and the learner responds in the affirmative the learner is "identifying Arizona, given a map of Arizona and the six adjoining states and the audible word Arizona." The student would also be "identifying Arizona" if he responded correctly under the following conditions:

1. The teacher asks the student to go to the wall map and point out Arizona.
2. The teacher tells the students to write AZ on Arizona on an outline map on his desk.
3. The teacher asks the students, "What color is Arizona on this map?" (The assumptions are (a) that the student is able to name the colors used on the map and (b) that on that map no other state is the same color as Arizona.)
4. As the teacher points to Arizona, he asks, "Is this state Arizona, New Mexico, or Utah?"

Pairing as Identifying

Identifying always involves a situation in which the learner is to pair two things.   When he indicates that he has made the correct pairing, he is identifying.   The examples used above are summarized in the table on the facing page.

We walk into a geometry class where the students are practicing identifying three types of triangles.   The teacher holds up a flashcard showing an equilateral triangle and asks, "Is this triangle equilateral?"   The learner is given two things: a triangle with three equal sides and the name of the characteristic of a specified type of triangle ("equilateral").   When the

EXAMPLES OF IDENTIFYING

	Conditions	*Student Behavior*
Given₁	*Given₂*	
Audible "peninsula"	Map containing both peninsulas and other land forms.	Answering "Yes" when teacher points to peninsula and asks, "Is this a peninsula?"; and "No" when teacher points to nonpeninsula and asks, "Is this a a peninsula?"
Written "peninsula"	Map containing both peninsulas and nonpeninsulas.	Circling peninsulas; leaving nonpeninsulas uncircled.
Audible "Arizona"	Map showing Arizona and surrounding states.	Pointing to Arizona in response to teacher's request.
Audible "Arizona"	Map showing Arizona and surrounding states.	Writing AZ on Arizona.
Audible "Arizona"	Map showing Arizona and surrounding states.	Naming the color of Arizona.
Audible "Arizona, New Mexico, and Utah"	Map showing Arizona and surrounding states.	Saying "Arizona."

learner answers "Yes" to the teacher's question, he has identified a characteristic of this triangle.

1. He also identifies the characteristic "equilateral" in many other types of situations. The geometry teacher holds up cards containing an equilateral triangle, a scalene triangle, and an isosceles triangle. He says, "Which is equilateral?" One of the students points to or touches or in any other manner designates the card displaying the characteristic "equilateral." The pupil is identifying.

2. Again, the teacher shows the pupils the equilateral triangle and asks, "Is this an equilateral, an isosceles, or a scalene triangle?" The student responds, "Equilateral." He is identifying an equilateral triangle.

3. The teacher might pass out a dittoed sheet on which drawings of equilateral, isosceles, and scalene triangles appear, as well as the names equilateral, isosceles, and scalene, in random order. He tells the students

to match the words and the diagrams by connecting the appropriate word with the triangle which displays that characteristic. The student who responds correctly is *identifying.*

In the exercise below, we have completed a partial analysis of the situations described in the numbered paragraphs above. Show that you can define some of the components of the term "identify" by completing the blanks in the tables. When you have, check your response with the answer given.

1 Read the example in paragraph 1 above. Then fill in the center cell.

GIVEN$_1$:	Diagrams of equilateral, isoceles, and scalene triangles.
GIVEN$_2$:	
STUDENT BEHAVIOR:	Touching, pointing, naming, etc. the correct diagram.

. . . .

1 *The second given is the audible "equilateral." (The teacher asked, "Which is equilateral?")*

2 Read paragraph 2 above, and fill in the blank cells.

GIVEN$_1$:	
GIVEN$_2$:	Audible "Equilateral, isoceles, or scalene"
STUDENT BEHAVIOR:	

. . . .

2 *The first given is the flash card showing an equilateral triangle. The student behavior is the audible response "equilateral." When the student makes this response, he has demonstrated that he can "identify."*

3 Identify the components of paragraph 3 above, by completing this analysis:

GIVEN$_1$:	
GIVEN$_2$:	
STUDENT BEHAVIOR:	

. . . .

3 *The first given consists of diagrams of equilateral, isosceles, and scalene triangles. The second given is the written "equilateral, isosceles, scalene." The behavior is connecting the appropriate words and diagrams.*

Simple Identifying

In the illustrations above, two types of identifying were illustrated. The less complex type of identifying is called *simple* identifying. In this type of task the learner is presented with *one name* and *one characteristic.* When the teacher holds up an equilateral triangle and asks, "Is this an equilateral triangle?" the student is engaged in simple identifying if he answers correctly. There are always two "givens" in identifying. In simple identifying, each given is restricted to a single object, characteristic, or event (or a single name or symbol representing the object, characteristic, or, event). When a learner is confronted with *one* triangle and *one* name at a time, and he is asked to indicate whether the two belong together, the task is one of *simple* identifying.

Multiple Identifying

Objectives dealing with simple identifying are rarely encountered in school situations except as sub-objectives or as activities leading to a more comprehensive objective. When a learner is presented with (1) several names and a single characteristic, or (2) a single name and several characteristics, or (3) several names and several characteristics, and asked to pair them correctly, he is involved in *multiple identifying*. The word *distinguish* is very frequently used in writing objectives of the multiple identifying type.

In the illustrations used above, we have several examples of distinguishing (or multiple identifying). When the learner is asked to distinguish the three types of triangles, given *three* names and an illustration of *one* of the types of triangles, he is involved with multiple identifying. In a situation such as this, the teacher might point to an equilateral triangle and ask, "Is this equilateral, isosceles, or scalene?"

Or the student might be asked to distinguish the three types of triangles, given an illustration of each of the *three* triangles and *one* of the names. The student would demonstrate his mastery of this objective by pointing to the correct example, an isosceles triangle, when asked to point out the isosceles.

Finally, we have an example of multiple identifying in this objective: "to distinguish the three types of triangles, given an illustration of each of the *three* triangles and the *three* names." The student is asked to give evidence that he can handle this task by drawing a line from each triangle to the corresponding name.

These illustrations have included all the possible combinations with which one can be confronted in writing objectives dealing with multiple identifying. The three possibilities are summarized in the accompanying figure.

Distinguishing is not a separate category in the classification system. The teacher can plan his instruction just as effectively and write his objec-

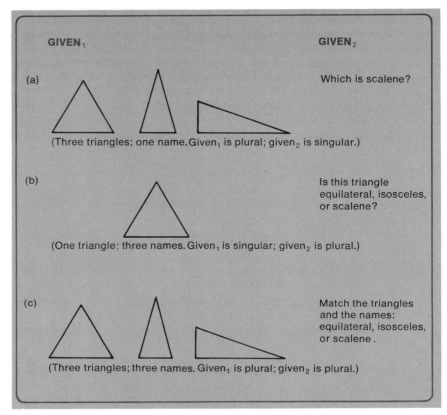

GIVEN₁   GIVEN₂

(a)   Which is scalene?

(Three triangles; one name. Given₁ is plural; given₂ is singular.)

(b)   Is this triangle
                                               equilateral, isosceles,
                                               or scalene?

(One triangle; three names. Given₁ is singular; given₂ is plural.)

(c)   Match the triangles
                                               and the names:
                                               equilateral, isosceles,
                                               or scalene.

(Three triangles; three names. Given₁ is plural; given₂ is plural.)

Multiple identifying.

tives just as correctly if he will think of distinguishing as a form of identifying in which one or more of the givens is plural.

Matching and Classifying

Teachers frequently encounter the words "matching" and "classifying." These, too, are types of identifying. When the fifth-grade geography teacher uses yellow cards on which the names of the states are written and white cards on which the names of the capitals are written and tells the students to pair them, the students are engaged in a matching exercise. In terms of our classification system, such matching is a type of multiple identifying. Whenever the learner is given the elements of a pair, either individually or in combination with other pairs, and is required to indicate whether two elements belong together, or which two elements belong together, he is being asked to identify something.

Classifying as a form of identifying is illustrated in this example: During instruction the class sees a motion picture film depicting the three states of matter. Following the film, each learner is given columns headed Solid, Liquid, and Gas. He is given a list of elements which he is to arrange under the appropriate column headings. This is a task in which the learner is asked to *identify* specified elements according to one of their properties. When he puts iron in the solid column, mercury in the liquid column, and hydrogen in the gas column, he is identifying. All such classifying activities belong in the identifying category.

Tell whether each of the following is an example of identifying. Give the reason for your answer.

4   Mrs. Star is teaching about traffic lights. She points to a classroom model of a semaphore on which the green light is illuminated and asks, "Is this the light that tells you to stop?"

     •   •   •   •   •   •

4   *This is identifying. She provides the name (stop) and the referent (green light).*

5   Mrs. Star asks a student to come up and touch the light which tells us to stop. (There are two lights, red and green, on the semaphore.)

     •   •   •   •   •   •

5   *This is identifying. Mrs. Star supplies the student with two things: a name (stop) and two possible referents (green light and red light).*

6   Mrs. Star says, "Tell me what this light tells you to do," as she points to the green light.

     •   •   •   •   •   •

6   *This is not identifying. The pupil is given only the referent (green light). The pupil must generate (or supply) the name. In the* identifying *category, the learner must be given both the referent and the name. (In case you are curious, this is an example of the next category in the system—"naming." This is discussed in the next chapter.)*

7   Mrs. Star points to the semaphore as she says, "What color is the light that tells us to go?"

     •   •   •   •   •   •

7   *Assuming that Mrs. Star is working with children who had to be taught to name the characteristics "green" and "red," given objects manifesting these characteristics, you would have to say that in this example, she is asking them "to name a color, given. . . ." This goes beyond identifying.*

Someone may argue that the third example (on page 90), in which the learner is asked to identify Arizona by naming its color on a given map, was referred to as an example of identifying. Why have we suddenly changed the rules? Actually, we haven't. In the Arizona example we stipulated that the student has already learned to name the colors on the map. In the semaphore example, we did not stipulate that the learner can name the colors. Consequently, Mrs. Star could be implementing the attainment of the objective, "to name the colors of the lights. . . ."

Admittedly, Example 7 may be a borderline case. We have included it deliberately because it does emphasize the fact that Mrs. Star, as most teachers, often deals with several objectives in a single lesson. She wants her students "to identify the traffic signals" as well as "to name the colors," but eventually she wants them "to name the appropriate response to each signal." Indeed, she will even want them to perform the appropriate action (i.e., stopping or going) in the presence of a simulated traffic situation.

8   Mrs. Star has a representation of a two-light semaphore on a flannel board before her class. She has two felt-backed pictures which the pupils can attach to the flannel board. One of the pictures shows two children waiting on a curb, the other shows them in the act of crossing the street. Mrs. Star asks someone to come up and match the pictures and the lights.

·   ·   ·   ·   ·   ·

8   *This is identifying. It belongs to that sub-category of identifying which was called* distinguishing *on page 93. If you missed this one, study the explanation in the box, but if you answered it correctly, skip ahead to the next section.*

You can see that this is a case of identifying if you diagram the situation:

GIVEN$_1$:	*Picture of children waiting*
	Picture of children crossing
GIVEN$_2$:	*Red light*
	Green light
STUDENT BEHAVIOR:	*Proper classification by placing the pictures next to the appropriate lights.*

Identifying Events

The examples used thus far illustrate identifying membership or nonmembership in a class of *objects* (the peninsula example) or a class of *characteristics* (the triangle and traffic light examples). Identifying may also involve indication of membership in a class of *events*.

When we use the word *event*, we include such things as processes and and procedures. A battle is an event. So is evaporation. Artificial resuscitation is an event. A fifth grade science teacher is teaching a unit on weather, and the topic of immediate concern is the water cycle, which is an event. Before the teacher can deal with the concept of the water cycle he must be certain that the children can describe the phenomena of evaporation and condensation. If the children know nothing about evaporation and condensation, the teacher could organize his instruction to teach them "to identify the processes of evaporation and condensation, given either a demonstration or description of each." This means that, as a result of the instructional procedures which the teacher uses, the students will be able to identify the concepts as in the following example:

GIVEN₁: A demonstration in which water disappeared from a glass which was left in the sun; a demonstration in which drops formed on a sheet of cold metal when it was held in a cloud of steam rising from a beaker containing boiling water.

GIVEN₂: The words evaporation and condensation.

BEHAVIOR: The learner will pair each demonstration with the appropriate word.

It makes no difference whether the teacher would substitute a model for the demonstrations, a motion picture, a filmstrip, a series of transparencies for the overhead projector, a diagram on a bulletin board, or a verbal description of each process. It is essential to remember that in identifying the learner is given the process (event) in any of the several forms listed and that he is given the word which stands for the process.

Write an objective for each of the following:

9   The teacher shows the student a red ball, a yellow boat, and a blue car; the teacher says, "Which is red?" The child picks up (or points to, or touches, or names) the object displaying the characteristic red. (Assume that the learner can name balls, boats, and cars before he begins this task.)

· · · · · · ·

9   *To identify a red object, given objects displaying the primary colors, and given the audible name* red. . . *(In order to meet all the criteria for a well-stated objective, your objective should include a performance standard as well as a time limit. Since decisions with respect to these matters are quite arbitrary, they are not included in the answers to the exercises, but you should keep in mind that the objective is incomplete without these two elements.)*

10   The teacher shows the student a red ball and asks, "Is this red, yellow, or blue?" The child responds, "Red."

· · · · · · ·

10   *To identify the characteristic red, given a red object and given the names of the primary colors. . . (This is an example of multiple identifying, or distinguishing. Notice that the learner is given* one *characteristic and* three *names of characteristics.)*

11   The teacher shows the student a red ball, a yellow boat, and a blue car; he gives the child a card on which the word *red* is printed, one on which *yellow* is printed, and one on which *blue* is printed. He tells the student to match the words and the objects by putting the appropriate card on the object which displays that color characteristic.

       •   •   •   •   •   •

11   To identify the primary colors, given objects of these colors, and given the printed names of these colors...

12   The learners are given three line drawings, one representing condensation, one representing evaporation, and one representing precipitation. The words evaporation, condensation, and precipitation are listed at the top of the page. They are told to write the correct word under each picture.

       •   •   •   •   •   •

12   To identify the processes of condensation, evaporation, and precipitation, given a schematic diagram of each event and given the written words...

13   The students pick up the appropriate object from a collection of objects on a table set for dinner when the German teacher speaks the German word for the object.

       •   •   •   •   •   •

13   To identify the object in a dinner setting, given the spoken German word for each and the actual object...

14   What is the observable behavior in Example 13?

       •   •   •   •   •   •

14   The student picks up or touches the object to indicate that he is identifying it.

Specifying Conditions for Identifying Behavior

When we expect students to identify things, we must present objects, events, or characteristics to them. Sometimes we present words or symbols which stand for the objects, events, or characteristics; sometimes we present both. The things we present may be things which we as teachers arrange. We may hold up cards to show students red balls, equilateral triangles, or the process of condensation. We may use slides or motion pictures to present these things. We are also "presenting" things when we make use of objects, events, or characteristics which we did not bring into the learner's environment. When we use the clouds in the sky which are visible from the classroom window to teach students to discriminate between cumulus and cirrus formations, we are "presenting" two types of clouds. When we analyze the soil in the excavation at the corner of the school property in an effort to teach students to identify the several layers, we are "presenting" types of soil. When we take the kindergarten to the intersection to observe the traffic light, we are "presenting" green, yellow, and red lights. When we teach students to identify, we may provide the "givens" by bringing them to the student, or we may use the objects, events, or characteristics which occur naturally in the student's environment by "bringing the student to them." No matter which, we must develop skill in specifying the conditions which must obtain while the student manifests the desired *identifying* behavior.

IDENTIFYING BEHAVIOR

Comprehending and Evaluating

Identifying is not always an extremely simple, uncomplicated behavior. Frequently, identifying is the evidence which leads us to believe that complex activities, such as *comprehending* or *evaluating*, have occurred. The biology teacher who wants his students "to comprehend the meaning of protoplasm" presents four definitions, none of which has ever been used in the instruction, and directs his students to select the correct one. His evidence of their "comprehension" is based on their identification of the correct definition. In the course of instruction he may have presented motion pictures, slides, drawings, or diagrams of:

1. a complex colloidal system made up of water, proteins, and fats;
2. [cells growing in] a regular progressive series of changes into a more complex unit;
3. a complex mixture of proteins, fats, and carbohydrates, . . . responding to changes in its environment;
4. a complex colloidal system of proteins, fats, carbohydrates, inorganic salts, and enzymes which manifests life.[1]

After repeated practice on a variety of motion pictures, slides, drawings, and diagrams showing each of the above phenomena in a variety of forms the students unfailingly identify as examples of protoplasm only those illustrations depicting cells growing in a regular progressive series of changes into a more complex unit. The learner can identify protoplasm, given pictorial representations of protoplasm or given pictorial representations of nonprotoplasm which might be confused with protoplasm, and given the audible word "protoplasm."

The teacher, however, stated (in his objective) that he wanted his students to "comprehend the meaning of protoplasm," wanted his students to answer correctly in a situation in which the conditions were restricted to verbal definitions of protoplasm (both correct and incorrect). Furthermore, he insisted that the definitions from which the learners were to choose be definitions never used in the instruction.

What is this teacher's objective? His objective is "To identify the definition of protoplasm, given four definitions of the term, three of which are

---

[1] Benjamin S. Bloom, ed., *Taxonomy of Educational Objectives—Handbook I: Cognitive Domain* (New York: Longmans, Green and Co., Inc., 1956), p. 100. Quoted by permission of David McKay Co., Inc.

somewhat plausible but incorrect and one of which is correct; none of the definitions may have been used previously in the instruction; identification must be completed within 30 seconds." How does he present the conditions essential to the development of the behavior specified? He used pictorial materials, moving and still, which illustrate protoplasm and non-protoplasm. His students practiced identifying protoplasm. When they could perform this task without error, he may have had them describe the pictorial phenomena. (Describing as a category is covered in Chapter 6.) When they were able to describe the phenomena in the protoplasm pictures to his satisfaction, he inferred that his pupils could "comprehend the meaning of protoplasm." His inference became certain when he presented the four (verbal) definitions and found that all could select the correct one.

There are two important aspects to consider in this example. The first is that a complex behavior, such as comprehending, may be defined by using a term as simple as *identifying*, provided that the conditions under which the identifying is to occur are clearly specified. The second is that the conditions of instruction may vary substantially from the conditions under which the observation of the desired behavior is to be made. Studying pictures (both motion and still) of cells, tissues, complex colloidal systems, and the like is quite different from reading a list of printed definitions. Yet, the pictures in this illustration bear a critical relationship to the ultimate outcome.

Why do we contend that the pictures are important? Why didn't we confine our presentation of conditions to words (both oral and printed?) First of all, we agreed that comprehension must be defined in terms of new material. The learner must not have been exposed to the definition during instruction. If he had been, his accomplishment would have been pure rote learning which involves no comprehension whatever. An alternative would have been to use a constantly changing set of definitions, all synonomous with, but slightly different from, the set given above. There is no doubt that this strategy would have been adequate, but it would have been far more difficult to accomplish than would the alternative selected in the example (assuming, of course, that the proper motion pictures, slides, photographs, and diagrams were accessible to the teacher). Furthermore, although not specified in the objective, it is highly probable that any biology teacher would be implementing, at the same time, an objective such as "to identify protoplasm, given pictorial representations of examples and nonexamples."[2]

Conditions for Behavior

This example illustrated a "higher level" cognitive task which could be defined in terms of an objective in the *identifying* category. The difficulty

[2]Could one do without pictures entirely if his *only* objective were "to identify the definition of protoplasm . . ."? Since such a situation is unlikely to occur in a good classroom, the question is a moot one.

in constructing objectives for such kinds of learning lies not so much in selecting the correct verb from our list of five (identify, name, describe, order, and construct), as it does in specifying the conditions under which the behavior is to occur. This is true of any kind of objective, no matter whether it is dealing with behavior in the cognitive, affective, or psycho-motor domain.

Consider the following example from the affective domain. Krathwohl, Bloom, and Masia,[3] in discussing "willingness to receive" as a category of educational objectives, point out several factors which are critical to the specification of conditions under which behavior is to occur. They cite "interest in voluntary reading" as an example of *willing* in the broader objective "willingness to receive." They then use a classification task to illustrate the kind of behavior which leads to the inference that a given learner is "interested in voluntary reading:"

> Y means that your answer to the question is *Yes.*
> U means that your answer to the question is *Uncertain.*
> N means that your answer to the question is *No.*
>
> 1. Do you wish that you had more time to devote to reading? (Y).
> 28. Do you have in mind one or two books which you would like to read sometime soon? (Y).
> 41. Is it usually impossible for you to read as long as an hour without becoming bored? (N).[4]

Actually, we can describe the desired behavior very easily: "To identify the questions to which the answer is Yes; No; Uncertain; given the question. . . ." The fact that there is a key for the items cited above clearly indicates that a standard of performance is desired; the learner is expected to answer Questions 1 and 28 "Yes" and Question 41 "No." To the extent that he does not, he has failed to achieve the objective "interest in voluntary reading." Theoretically, we might suggest that the student who answers all questions (i.e., all the questions in the complete inventory) incorrectly has no "interest in voluntary reading" and the one who answers all questions correctly has achieved completely the highest standard attainable with respect to "interest in voluntary reading."

One method to achieve this behavior would be to drill the learner on the test itself until he could identify with complete accuracy the *Yes*, the *No*, and the *Uncertain* items. It would be virtually impossible to find a teacher who would accept this behavior, under such instructional conditions, as evidence of "interest in voluntary reading." But under what conditions would a teacher accept a completely accurate identifying behavior as evidence of the desired outcome? As in the "comprehending proto-

---

[3]David R. Krathwohl, Benjamin S. Bloom, and Bertram B. Masia, *Taxonomy of Educational Objectives—Handbook II: Affective Domain* (N.Y.: David McKay Co., Inc., 1964), pp. 107, 110–11.

[4]Krathwohl, Bloom, and Masia, *Taxonomy of Educational Objectives*, p. 111. Quoted by permission of David McKay Co., Inc.

plasm" example above, previous practice on or exposure to the questions in the inventory should be specifically excluded in the statement of conditions. In addition to this exclusion, the statement of conditions should include exposure to the kind of reading material of interest:

> . . . we are prone to reject and avoid some of the newer art forms. Dissonant music and modernistic art, to name two, would be examples toward which an art teacher might seek a willingness to attend. At this level of the continuum the teacher is not concerned that the student seek it out, nor even, perhaps, that in an environment crowded with many other stimuli the learner will necessarily attend to the stimulus. Rather, at worst, given the opportunity to attend in the field with relatively few competing stimuli, the learner is not actively seeking to avoid it. At best, he is willing to take notice of the phenomenon and give it his attention.[5]

In the voluntary reading example, the instruction might well have included only literary examples of "the good, the better, and the best." There would be little point in introducing into the instruction such competing or potentially inhibiting distractors as comic books, joke books, or lewd magazines. In addition, the instruction might include films showing great men or women (who are admired by students in the class) deriving satisfaction or profiting in some other way from reading. The instruction might also include listening to recordings of good literature being read by excellent speakers or readers.

The conditions described in this illustration are conditions of learning. They are not the performance described in the behavioral objective; instead they are conditions in the learner's history. Review this rather complex concept by studying the outline of the steps involved:

1. The objective: "To achieve a score of X on the *Questionnaire on Voluntary Reading: Test 3.32* when the test is administered according to directions." (As we pointed out above, the nature of the test is such that the student is identifying when he completes the items in it.) "A score of X on the test will be accepted as sufficient evidence that the student has 'an interest in voluntary reading.' "
2. The standard: "a score of X."
3. The conditions: The conditions under which the product (a score on the test) is elicited are specified: ". . . when the test is administered according to directions." Furthermore, one might add that this must be the initial presentation of the test, i.e., the students must not have practiced taking the test; the test should not have been used in instruction.

This is sufficient. The behavior, the standard, and the conditions are adequately specified. But since we are not merely testing, it is essential to remember that we want to arrange conditions prior to the taking of the

[5]Krathwohl, Bloom, and Masia, *Taxonomy of Educational Objectives*, p. 107. Quoted by permission of David McKay Co., Inc.

test in such a manner that the student will achieve a score of X. So, in addition to the conditions listed, we add instructional conditions which we believe are antecedent to the achievement of the behavioral objective. We select conditions which we expect will increase the probability of the learner's achieving a score of X.

1. We create an environment in which there are few competing literary stimuli. We surround the learner with the kinds of things we want him to read voluntarily.
2. We attempt to increase the probability of his voluntary reading by showing him filmed examples of people whom he admires or respects doing voluntary reading.
3. We attempt to establish a favorable disposition toward the literary material by presenting recordings of good literature in the expectation that they will be intrinsically rewarding.

We have purposely chosen two complex examples involving identifying behavior. We have done so because we wanted to forestall the objection that behavioral objectives deal with either relatively simple tasks or with relatively unimportant outcomes. Having demonstrated that behavioral objectives in a class as seemingly simple and mechanical as identifying may be both complex and sophisticated, let us return to a few rather simple exercises. As we move from chapter to chapter, these exercises will involve increasingly more complex decisions. We want to emphasize, however, that this does not warrant the generalization that the earlier categories (such as identifying) deal with less complex instructional problems than the later categories (such as ordering).

Your task in the following exercise is to write a good objective and to specify the stimuli, or conditions, which you would arrange to ensure the learner's attaining the objective. The answers given are merely representative; there are many acceptable alternatives.

15 To identify the process of evaporation. . . .

• • • • • •

15 *Imagine a classroom in which the teacher has demonstrated the process of evaporation. No one would want the learner to identify the process of evaporation only when a demonstration is performed in a science classroom. The skilled teacher will replace the demonstration with several examples of evaporation as presented in a motion picture film. He may ask the learner to identify examples of evaporation given still more abstract referents, such as a diagram in a filmstrip or on a chart. Eventually the teacher will want the learner to identify examples of evaporation when he is given only a verbal description of various natural phenomena. Thus, we see that the teacher may find that even so simple a task as teaching a student to identify evaporation may involve a series of instructional conditions such as (a) identifying, given motion picture representations; (b) identifying, given diagrammatic representations; and (c) identifying, given verbal descriptions.*

16   The industrial arts teacher wants the student to learn to use the gouge to cut away the rough parts of a piece of wood on the lathe, and to use a skew to smooth a round piece of wood.

        •   •   •   •

16   *Again, remember that a considerable variety of answers is possible. The suggested answers are representative.*

> *To identify skews and gouges, given actual examples of each . . .*

> *To identify skews and gouges, given pictorial representations of each . . .*

> *To identify the results of the use of a skew, given a piece of wood to which the skew has been applied . . .*

(There is no explicit statement of a criterion *performance in these objectives. In examples such as this, where there are only two items, it is logical to assume that identification of* both *items is called for. If any other criterion were expected, it would be necessary to state it explicitly.)*

17   The kindergarten teacher asks the children to color (appropriately) the following foods on the poster: carrots, lettuce, beets. (Assume that the children have learned to use crayons in such a manner that their finished coloring stays within the lines.)

        •   •   •   •

17   *Note that the question is not an activity representative of identifying! Do you see why? The color is not given the pupil; only the foods are given. In order to be classified as identifying, both colors and foods must be given. Each of the following meets this requirement.*

> *To identify orange, green, and red, given crayons of each color, and the words. . .*

> *To identify orange, green, and red, given an actual carrot, head of lettuce, and beet, and the audible words. . .*

> *To identify orange, green, and red, given pictures of food items which are predominantly characterized by each of these colors and the audible words. . .*

> *To identify the color which each of the following foods should be colored, given orange, green, and red crayons and an uncolored outline picture of each food: carrot, lettuce, beet. . .*

(Time is an arbitrary condition which should be added to each example.)

18   The geography teacher instructs the class to use upper case letters for printing the names of the states on the map and lower case for the names of the capitals.

        •   •   •   •

18   *To identify each of the 50 states, given the name of the state printed in the appropriate place on an outline map of the U.S.A., and a list of the names of the capitals . . .*

Obviously, this is a rather complex identifying task. Typically, a fifth grader might learn to do this in stages—he learns to identify the states and capitals of the six New England states, then the Middle Atlantic states, and so on, until, after several months of learning and review, he can successfully perform the task with all *the states and capitals.*

19   The junior high school music teacher wants students to recognize some of the best-known music of Beethoven.

·   ·   ·   ·   ·   ·

19   To identify in writing Beethoven's Fifth and Ninth symphonies and the Piano Sonata No. 24 in E Flat, given recordings of each, the names written on the chalkboard, and one minute for responding.

20   The same teacher wants students to distinguish the music of Beethoven from that of Bach and Brahms.

·   ·   ·   ·   ·   ·

20   To identify in writing a composition by Beethoven given recordings of music by Bach, Brahms, and Beethoven and the names of each selection written on the chalkboard, in less than one minute.

21   A tenth grade social studies teacher wants students to be critics of the mass media, particularly in assessing the accuracy of reported news.

·   ·   ·   ·   ·   ·

21   Each student should be able to identify the most accurate account of a presidential news conference, given a transcript or videotape of the complete conference and three newspaper reports of the event.

This objective is one of several which make up a unit on critical judgment. The objective can be reached through specific resources which provide a reconstitution of the event (the transcript or videotape) and the perception of the event (the newspaper accounts). The pupil must analyze each account in reference to the actual event.

Media to Implement Behavior

This chapter has dealt with the objective *to identify*. Throughout the exposition and exercises, a wide variety of media has been used to establish the conditions under which the student does the identifying. It should be clear that there is a wide variety of media available to help students reach each objective. The instructional medium is always selected *after* the objective has been defined. The creative teacher will check all the resources and select those that are available, economically feasible, appropriate for the level of the students, and technically satisfactory. (For a more comprehensive discussion of selection criteria, see Chapter 13, pages 291–97.)

The important principle is that *a medium of instruction must be selected on the basis of its potential for implementing the attainment of a stated objective.* For every objective dealing with "identifying," there are usually several media which might be used to establish the conditions for the attainment of the objective. The choice of media is often obvious, as in Examples 19 and 20 where the conditions call for music. Since it is doubtful that a live symphony orchestra would be available on call, audio tape or records would be the obvious choice. In unusual circumstances a radio or television program or a film or videotape recording might be available.

Name the media alternatives for the following objectives:

22   To identify a correct oral response to the Spanish question, "¿Cómo ésta Usted?" given three oral responses in Spanish, only one of which is appropriate.

· · · · · ·

22   *An audible stimulus is required. The teacher could provide the three alternative responses by means of a live situation; or the alternatives could be recorded on tape for use by individuals in a language laboratory or with an independent tape recorder. The correctness of the response could be confirmed immediately in the face-to-face situation or it could be recorded on tape and compared with a correctly recorded response. Theoretically, one could include the use of motion pictures or television but these media are less accessible and permit fewer choices by the teacher; from a practical viewpoint it is unlikely that they would be acceptable.*

23   To identify ten household objects of the homespun period (1800–1850) given (a) a list of ten household objects and (b) actual household objects (or pictures of objects) from the homespun period and later periods.

· · · · · ·

23   *The actual objects would probably be most appropriate but they may not be available or they might be too small for an entire class to see. Pictures from books and magazines could be displayed on the bulletin board or shown to the whole class with an opaque projector. There may be a filmstrip (or part of a filmstrip) or a set of slides which would help to accomplish this objective.*

Chapter 13 outlines the spectrum of instructional resources available in most contemporary schools. The Media Facts in Part Five outline characteristics, advantages, limitations, and sources of each medium. If you have had difficulty generating ideas for media selection above, it would be helpful to scan Chapter 13 now.

SUMMARY

You have read a description of objectives in the identifying category, and you have practiced constructing such objectives. You have also begun to make decisions concerning the selection of media related to implementing the attainment of these objectives. Look again at the objectives for this chapter. If you feel confident that you have mastered them, continue with the next chapter.

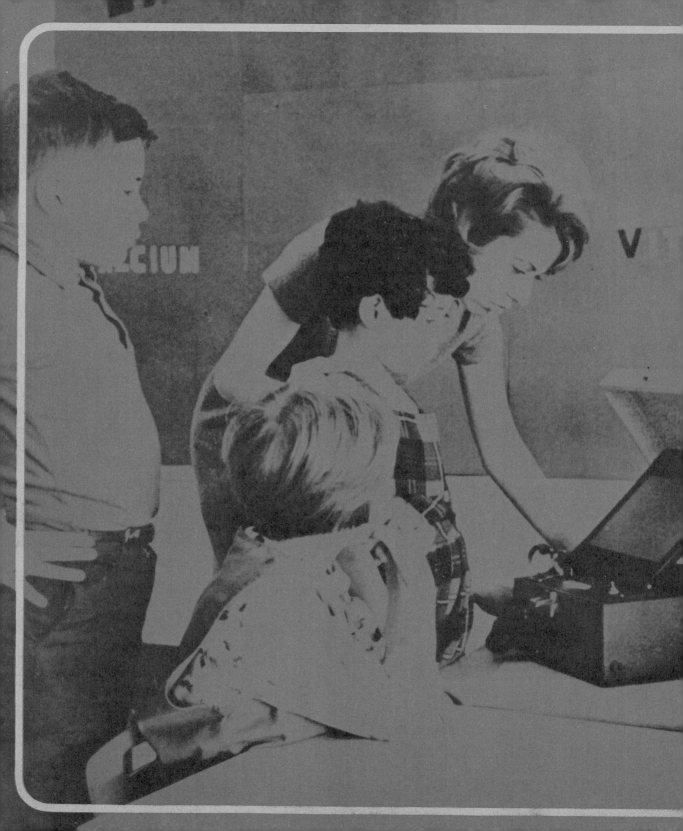

CHAPTER
FIVE

TEACHING
STUDENTS
TO
NAME

WHEN YOU HAVE MASTERED THE CONTENT OF THIS CHAPTER, YOU SHOULD BE ABLE TO:

1. DEFINE the term "name."

2. DESCRIBE school learning situations in which the desired terminal behavior is to name.

3. IDENTIFY objectives in this category.

4. CONSTRUCT objectives in this category.

5. DESCRIBE the conditions required to teach students to name.

6. CONSTRUCT the rationale for choosing the medium (or media) best suited for establishing the conditions specified in objectives in the *name* category.

THE NATURE OF NAMING

Frequently a student will be taught to name an object, a characteristic, or an event after he has learned to identify it. The kindergarten children who have learned to point to the correct object in response to the teacher's "Which car is red?" will soon hear the teacher's question change to "What color is this car?" When this change takes place, the expected learner behavior is changing from identifying to naming. The fifth grader is asked "What state is this?" as the teacher points to Texas on an outline map. When the student responds "Texas," he is naming an object or a symbol. When the high school senior watches the teacher decant a liquid, and then answers "Decanting" in response to the query "What am I doing to this liquid?" he is naming an event (or process).

The definition of *naming* is to supply the correct verbal label (in speech or writing) for an object, a characteristic, or an event when the name of the object, characteristic, or event is not given.

When the learner is asked to identify, he is always required to pair two discrete elements. Since he is required to pair two elements, it is absolutely essential that the conditions for identifying include two givens. Naming, however, reduces the givens to one: the learner is given either an object, event, or characteristic, or he is given some representation of an object, event, or characteristic. His task is to supply the name for the referent given him. Note carefully that the learner is given only the referent in naming; in contrast, he is given both the name and the referent in identifying.

Consider once again the examples that we used in Chapter 4. When the student learns to *identify* peninsulas, the teacher points to land forms on the map and asks in each instance, "Is this a peninsula?" When the

GIVEN: Peninsulas (i.e., nonverbal symbols for peninsulas).

BEHAVIOR: Saying or writing the name "peninsula."

student learns to *name* a peninsula, the teacher points to a peninsula and asks, "What is this?" The diagram of the behavior has one less component than it did for identifying.

Types of Naming

Sometimes the learner's task is to name an *object*. An actual object, or a representation of it, is provided and the teacher asks a question such as, "What is this?" for which the correct answer is the desired name. Likewise, *characteristics* may be named; the teacher may refer to an object or representation of the object and ask questions such as "What color is this?" "What shape is this?" "What is the name of this texture?" and so on. Or the teacher may present *events*, or representations of events, and require the learner to name the event. For example, the teacher may present an actual demonstration of the process (event) of distillation in the science room; he may ask the students to name the event they have witnessed. Or he may provide them with a schematic representation of the process of distillation and ask them questions for which the correct answer is the name of the event. In the examples above, the referents may have been real objects, events, or characteristics, or the referents may have been representations. In any case, the learner's task was to name what he saw or heard or otherwise sensed.

There is still another type of naming which is common in classrooms. Sometimes the learner may be given a verbal referent which describes an object, event, or characteristic. By this we mean that the teacher might give the student a *definition* or *description* of an object instead of the object or a representation of the object. For example, the teacher might hold up a cube and ask the students to name the type of geometric figure; he might hold up a picture of a cube and ask them the same question; or the teacher might give the learners a verbal (either oral or written) definition of a cube and ask them to name the geometric figure defined. When the teacher gives the student a definition of an object, rather than the object or a representation of the object, and asks, "What is this?" he is still asking the students to name. When the teacher describes a historical event and asks the learner for the name of that event, he is asking the student to name. It makes no difference whether the object, event, or characteristic is presented in its real form, in a representational form, or in a verbal form (that is, by means of an oral or written description); if the learner's response is one in which he supplies a correct name for something which is given him, his behavior is called naming.

In Chapter 4 we defined two subclasses of identifying: matching and classifying. We have a similar situation in naming. If the student is given an object, event, or characteristic belonging to one class and is expected to respond with a name belonging to another class, he is naming. To illustrate, if a teacher gives the names of the states, but not the names of the capitals, and tells his students to name the capitals, he is asking them to name. Or if the teacher gives the students an outline map of the United States showing the boundaries of the fifty states and tells them to write the name of the capital anywhere within the boundaries of each state, he is asking his students to name.

Another type of naming is related to classifying. A teacher gives his students a chart with three columns headed Rivers, Mountains, and Plains; when he tells his students to write the names of the physical features of the countries which they have studied in the proper column, he is asking them to name. (The student is required to supply the names to be placed in the columns.) The teacher is also asking his students to name when he points to a body of water, a mountain chain, a lowland, and so on, and has the learners fill in the chart as he points to these physical features on the outline map on the wall. The important thing to remember about this category is that the student is naming as long as he has to supply a name. If, on the other hand, the name is given, he is not naming; most likely such an example is one involving identifying.

OBJECTIVES IN THE NAMING CATEGORY

Classifying Objectives

Below are examples of objectives. Tell whether each objective belongs in the identifying category, the naming category, or neither.

1   To tell whether a given substance is animal, mineral, or vegetable when the instructor (pointing to one object) asks, "What kind of object is this —animal, mineral, or vegetable?" within two seconds.

· · · · · · · ·

1   *This objective deals with identifying. Notice that the learner is given two things: the name and the referent. His task is to make the proper connection or association.*

2   To match a given name of a process with a schematic representation of the process.

· · · · · · · ·

2   *This is another example of identifying. Again, both the name and the referent (a schematic representation) are supplied.*

3   To tell what a process is called after seeing the teacher demonstrate the process.

· · · · · · · ·

3   *This one is naming. The referent is supplied the learner, but he has to supply the correct name for this referent.*

4   With what kind of objective are exercises 1–3 in this chapter dealing?

· · · · · · · ·

4   *Exercises 1–3 deal with an objective in the identifying category. Naming would be the wrong answer because in the directions you are given the names from which to select your answers to these exercises. This is a classifying (or matching) exercise in which you are given two distinct components: (a) names of categories and (b) examples of the categories. Consequently, your answer to this question must be identifying.*

5 To tell in writing all the important characteristics of a pyramid, given a typical pyramid.

. . . .

5 *This is neither identifying nor naming. Actually, this is describing, a category we will discuss in Chapter 6. If someone wishes to point out that the answer to this item could be "naming the characteristics," we'll accept the answer. However, in the next chapter we'll make a clear distinction between* naming *and* describing.

6 To label each of the five marked parts on a drawing of a motion picture projector. (The learner has a copy of a drawing.)

. . . .

6 *This one must be naming. There is no way that you can infer from this statement that the names of the parts are given to the learner. By definition, whenever a learner supplies the names, he is engaged in* naming.

7 To recognize the three most important aspirations of citizens of the emerging nations.

. . . .

7 *This one can't be identifying; neither can it be called naming. The verb* to recognize *is too ambiguous to enable us to classify this objective.*

8 To tell which are the strings, the brasses, and the woodwinds, given in writing only the names of three instruments in each category.

. . . .

8 *This one is obviously naming. The referent is explicitly stated: the names of three instruments in each category. However, there is nothing in the objective upon which you can base an inference that the names strings, brasses, and woodwinds are given the learner. Consequently, the only legitimate assumption is that the learner must supply these three names. Since he is required to, the objective must be classified as a naming objective.*

Constructing Objectives

If you responded correctly to the eight items in the exercise above, you are able to distinguish between objectives in the identifying and naming categories, given objectives representative of each category. Now you should be ready to try something just a bit more difficult. In the exercise below, you are provided with examples of classroom transactions, imperfectly worded objectives, or other statements or descriptions. Your task is to construct an objective which is appropriate to the descriptive material given you in each item. Since you've studied only objectives in the identifying and naming categories, the exercise below is limited to these two categories; if you find a description which demands a verb from some other category, your answer will simply be "other."

9 The auto mechanics teacher is teaching his students the parts of a carburetor. There are four parts which he considers critical. He expects his

students to be able to do two things when they are finished:

a. tell what each part is, and

b. describe the role that each part plays in the functioning of the carburetor.

Write an objective that deals with the auto mechanics teacher's objective as implied in (a) above.

· · · · · · · ·

9   *To name the four parts of the carburetor, given. . . .*

10   The chemistry teacher wants his students to understand fully how important it is to use distilled water in all the experiments in the next unit.

· · · · · · · ·

10   *Actually, there is no way of telling exactly what the chemistry teacher wants. One might assume that he wants two things: (a) students should use distilled water in their experiments, and (b) they should be able to state the reason why it is necessary to use distilled water. If one made this assumption, it would be impossible to write an objective in either the naming or the identifying category. The answer to this item ought to be "other."*

11   To know which three elements are present in sulfuric acid.

· · · · · · · ·

11   *To identify the three elements present in sulfuric acid, given a list of elements which includes hydrogen, sulfur, oxygen, and the name of at least four other elements found in commonly used acids, within 15 seconds. Or, to name in writing the three elements present in sulfuric acid within 15 seconds. These two examples are selected from many possible correct answers. The important points to consider are these:*

a. *your statement must contain a* learner *behavior or product;*

b. *an observable performance or product;*

c. *a statement of the conditions, implied or expressed; and*

d. *a standard, implied or expressed.*

In the second objective stated above, both the statement of the conditions and the standard are implied. It is implied that the learner will name these three elements in an environment which contains absolutely nothing other than the written or spoken words "What elements are there in sulfuric acid?" It is also implied that the standard of performance must be such that the student names all three correctly.

12   To understand the significance of the Declaration of Independence.

· · · · · · · ·

12   *This one probably should be labeled "other." No one can state with any degree of certainty what the writer of this objective meant, but it is fairly certain that no identifying or naming objective would be appropriate for this vague description. Of course, no one can be absolutely certain of this, because the statement is so highly ambiguous.*

13   To learn the multiplication table of 3's.

•   •   •   •   •   •   •

13   To name orally the products for all the problems in the multiplication table of 3's, given the problems in random order, within two seconds per problem. Again, other objectives could be written which would be equally appropriate. For example, one might write an objective for this statement which is in the identifying category. In this case, one would expect the learner to be given both the problems and the products, and he would be asked to match the problems and the products.

14   To know the country in which each of the following historical figures was born: Pulaski, Lafayette, Samuel Adams, William Pitt.

•   •   •   •   •   •   •

14   To identify the country of birth for Pulaski, Lafayette, Samuel Adams, William Pitt, given a map of the world on which the names of all countries in existence in 1770 are printed, within one and one-half minutes. To name orally the nation in which each of the following was born, within 20 seconds: Pulaski, Lafayette, Samuel Adams, William Pitt.

Instructional Problems Involving Naming

As you see, constructing objectives in the naming category is not difficult. However, before proceeding to a detailed consideration of how to specify conditions in objectives in the naming category, we need to consider an instructional problem which was not present in identifying. To illustrate this problem, we shall return to our "peninsula" example.

When the student learns to *identify* peninsulas, the teacher points to land forms on the map and asks in each instance, "Is this a peninsula?" When the students learn to *name* peninsulas, the teacher points to a peninsula and asks, "What is this?" The diagram of the behavior is simpler than it was for identifying:

GIVEN: (referent) Peninsulas on a map.

BEHAVIOR: Supplying (usually orally or in writing) the name "peninsula" in response to "What is this?"

In this example there is one element missing which was present in identifying. No nonpeninsulas are included in the landforms supplied to the student. When the learner is identifying, any landform which is not a peninsula, regardless of its name, can be used as an example of a nonpeninsula. It is as easy for the learner to respond "No" when the teacher points to something which has a simple name, such as an island, as it is for him to say "No" when the teacher points to something which has an apparently difficult name, such as an archipelago. The teacher may use any and every landform imaginable, provided that it is possible for the learner to answer only yes or no in response to the question "Is this a peninsula?"

Obviously, if the teacher is teaching his students to *name* peninsulas, there is a possibility that they cannot name capes and isthmuses. The teacher, therefore, is limited in the number of landforms which he can use. He can point to any peninsula and ask, "What is this?" but he cannot point to an isthmus or a cape and ask, "What is this?" The difficulty which confronts the teacher is that if he is teaching his students to name only one thing, the students may learn to give the correct name not because they are discriminating between the referent of interest and all other referents in their environment, but because they quickly learn that there is only one name which is a correct response. The teacher cannot change this situation unless he can include one or more additional referents from time to time.

Consider the following example: The teacher wants his students "to name peninsulas, given the representation of a peninsula on a map."

Teacher:

(pointing to a peninsula) What is this?

Learner 1:

(apparently examining the referent carefully) A peninsula?

Teacher:

Right! *(pointing to another peninsula)* What's this?

Learner 2:

(apparently examining the referent carefully) A peninsula.

Teacher:

Good! *(pointing to a third peninsula)* And this?

Learner 3:

(almost before the teacher has pointed) A peninsula!

Teacher:

Very good! *(pointing to a fourth peninsula)* What do we call this landform?

Learner 4:

(without even looking at the referent) A peninsula.

Learner 4 was not responding to the presentation of a visual symbol. In other words, he was not "naming a peninsula, given the representation of a peninsula on a map," since he did not see the peninsula to which the teacher was pointing. Why was he able to make the response "peninsula"? Obviously, because the teacher had established an environment in which "peninsula" was a reasonable answer. This answer was reasonable only because the teacher did not intersperse questions which required other names as an answer.

This is an important factor to remember when teaching students to name. The referent must be the factor in the environment which controls the learner's answer, not questions that require the same answer over and over again. The teacher in the example above might have varied the presentation, after noting that Learner 4 was answering without looking at the referent. Assume that the learner can name islands, oceans, rivers, continents, given a map representation:

Teacher:

> *(moving his hand around South America)* What is this?

Learner 4:

> *(again, not looking)* A peninsula.

Teacher:

> Wrong! Look carefully. *(repeating the movement with the hand around South America)* This is not a peninsula! What is it?

Learner 4:

> I remember. We had that word yesterday. It's a continent.

Teacher:

> OK! *(pointing to another peninsula)* What is this?

Learner 5:

> A peninsula.

Teacher:

> *(pointing to the Mississippi River)* And this?

Learner 4:

> *(now watching)* Well, I know it's not a peninsula this time! It's a river.

Teacher:

> *(moving his hand around India)* What is this?

Learner 6:

> A peninsula.

Teacher:

> Right again. *(moving his hand around the Indian Ocean)* This?

Learner 7:

> An ocean.

Teacher:

> *(pointing to the fourth peninsula again)* What is this?

Learner 4:

> It's a peninsula.

The teacher now infers that the members of the class can "name peninsulas, given the representation of a peninsula on a map." The inference is probably a valid one, since the learners' answers now seem to be controlled by the map symbols rather than by an uninterrupted succession of responses, "Peninsula . . . peninsula . . . peninsula. . . ."

Attaining Objectives

Here are examples of a poor method and two better methods of instruction for the attainment of a naming objective.

Mr. Webster is teaching a literature lesson on meter as it is used in poetry. The class has learned to distinguish between a foot in a line of poetry and a number of consecutive syllables in prose. They can count the number of feet in a line of poetry. They were told on the previous day to read a selection in the textbook in which the various kinds of feet are defined. Mr. Webster plays a tape recording of a voice speaking lines of poetry: "Oh, thus be it ever when free men shall stand . . ."

Mr. Webster:

What is the name of the metrical foot used in this poem?

Learner 1:

I can't remember. It goes like this: lah' lu lu, lah' lu lu, lah' lu lu.

Mr. Webster:

Yes, it does! But what is the name of that foot?

Class:

(no one answers)

Mr. Webster:

You just listened to a line of poetry employing dactyl. It is a dactylic foot. *(now playing another portion of the recorded tape: "The King of France went up the hill/With twenty thousand men . . .")* What is the name of that metrical foot?

Learner 2:

I don't know the name. It goes lu lah', lu lah', lu lah'.

Mr. Webster:

Anyone?

Class:

(silence)

Mr. Webster:

That was iambic.

He proceeds in the same manner, supplying the name of each new foot as he gets to it. No one in the class ever names a foot. Mr. Webster does all the naming.

A deductive method   Mr. Webster was attempting to teach his students "to name the following metrical feet, given spoken examples of lines of poetry incorporating each: dactylic, iambic, etc." Apparently the students cannot even identify dactylic, iambic, etc., given a spoken line of each. Mr. Webster might better begin with a procedure such as this:

Mr. Webster:

A dactylic foot is one in which a stressed syllable is followed by two unstressed syllables. The word *tenderly* is an example. Is *eminent* a dactylic foot?

Learner 1:

Yes.

Mr. Webster:

Right. A stressed syllable is followed by two unstressed. How about *quietly*? Is it a dactylic foot?

Class:

Yes.

Mr. Webster:

Right again! How about *decision*?

Learner 3:

No.

Mr. Webster:

Correct. It does not have a stressed syllable followed by two un-stressed. Now let's listen to some lines of poetry which I have on tape. I'll play a line, and you tell me whether it's a sample of dactylic or not.

Mr. Webster plays samples of dactylic and nondactylic until each student can make the discrimination without error. The learners can now "identify a dactylic metrical foot, given a spoken example . . ." Note that the class is not yet supplying the name dactylic; they are merely *identifying*, not *naming*.

Mr. Webster then repeats essentially the same procedure to enable the students to identify iambic feet. When they can do this, he plays selections, in random order, of dactylic and iambic. Near the end of the lesson he gives them three choices (dactylic, iambic, or neither) as he plays recorded excerpts from a wide variety of prose and poetry selections.

Then, *after* the learners can *identify*, he begins to pursue another method of instruction.

Mr. Webster:

(after playing a line of iambic pentameter) What metrical foot was employed in this selection?

Class:

Iambic.

Mr. Webster:

(playing a recorded line of dactylic hexameter) And this?

Class:

Dactylic.

Mr. Webster continues playing randomly arranged selections, until everyone can name correctly the metrical foot employed in the recorded excerpt.

In this example, Mr. Webster used a *deductive method*. He told the class the characteristics of dactyl: "a stressed syllable followed by two unstressed." Applying this rule to each example, the students reached a decision; either the example is a dactylic foot because it possesses the characteristics stated in the rule or it is not a dactylic foot because it does not meet the requirements specified in the rule. This is an example of a deductive method. Usually the deductive method requires that a student learns first to identify, then to name.

An inductive method   Mr. Webster could have used an inductive method:

Mr. Webster:

Class, say "eminent."

Class:

Eminent.

Mr. Webster:

How many accented syllables?

Learner 1:

One.

Mr. Webster:

How many unaccented?

Learner 2:

Two.

Mr. Webster:

Use lah' and lu to stand for the accented and unaccented syllables in eminent.

Learner 3:

Lah' lu lu.

Mr. Webster:

(writing on the transparency on an overhead projector "Evermore = lah' lu lu") How many accented and unaccented syllables?

Class:

One accented and two unaccented.

Mr. Webster:

(after turning off the overhead projector) Give me the pattern.

Learner 4:

Lah' lu lu.

Mr. Webster now repeats essentially the same procedure, using the words *quietly* and *tenderly*:

Mr. Webster:

What pattern is there in all three of these words?

Learner 5:

Lah' lu lu.

Mr. Webster:

How many unaccented and how many accented syllables?

Learner 6:

Two and one.

Mr. Webster:

In that order?

Learner 6:

No—one accented and then two unaccented syllables.

Mr. Webster:

(writing the words on the transparency as he speaks "An accented followed by two unaccented syllables") The name for this metrical foot

is dactyl. Any foot which is composed of an accented syllable followed by two unaccented syllables is a dactylic foot.

Mr. Webster then provides five examples of dactylic feet. He writes the words, one by one, on the transparency and asks whether each exhibits the pattern under discussion. Then he begins to intersperse other metrical feet with dactyl, still asking whether each manifests the pattern. Gradually his question changes from "Does this word have our pattern?" to "Is this an example of dactylic foot?" When the students answer this question correctly, they are identifying dactyl, given the word dactyl and examples of dactylic and nondactylic feet. Soon Mr. Webster begins to substitute lines of poetry on the overhead projector. He continues to ask, "Is this dactyl?" Gradually, under the same conditions, the question changes.

Mr. Webster:

(pointing to a line of dactylic hexameter on the overhead projector) What kind of foot do we find in this line?

Learner 7:

Dactyl.

In the latter part of this anecdote, Mr. Webster first had the students *describe* the characteristics of dactyl. (More about describing in Chapter 6.) Then, using the description which they have generated, the students *identify* dactylic foot and, finally, they *name* it. In this example, an *inductive method* is used; the behavioral pattern began with describing, then changed to identifying, and concluded with naming.

Types of Naming

The variety of conditions one may provide when teaching students to name is infinite. As in identifying, students learn to name objects, events, and characteristics. As mentioned earlier, they learn to name these referents at three levels: actual, surrogate (representational), and abstract (verbal).

Students learn to name such referents as geometric solids, colors of objects, or the process of condensation. All of these referents can actually be brought into a classroom. Sometimes it is either impossible or inconvenient to bring real objects or events into a classroom or to bring the learners to them. Surrogate objects, events, or characteristics may be employed in such instances. The class in Greek history may find the teacher using a model of the Parthenon. The class learns to name the Parthenon, given a three-dimensional model of it. Or the teacher may use a picture of the Parthenon, a 35mm colored slide, a frame from a film-strip, a clip from a motion picture film, a large black-and-white photograph, or a line drawing on acetate which is projected on the screen by means of an overhead projector. All of these are representations of the actual Parthenon; they are surrogate conditions. Again, the teacher may want the learners to name a referent which he describes. For example, he may tell a number of things about the Parthenon without naming it. He wants his students to learn to name the Parthenon, given these verbal abstractions.

When one writes a naming objective, it is clearly essential that the type of condition be explicitly stated.

Naming is a tool which permits the learner to accomplish more complex behaviors. If a learner can name the Parthenon when presented with a picture of it, he can use the naming behavior when he discusses the characteristics of Greek architecture, some of which are found in the Parthenon. For example, he may say that the symmetry of building design such as that found in the Parthenon was a characteristic of the architecture during the Classic period. By naming the Parthenon, he is demonstrating that he has the ability to illustrate a generalization by naming a specific object. Another person, who might hear or read what the student has said or written, would confirm the naming if he had the same referent in his visual repertoire.

MEDIA SELECTION

The task of the teacher, in helping the learner to acquire the ability to name, is to select the appropriate medium or media to reach the objective. A general rule, which has been widely accepted, is that *the more concrete the referent, the more likely a learner will be able to name an object, event, or characteristic when presented with the same stimulus or similar stimuli.* In fact, several conceptual models have been constructed which represent this principle.[1,2]

There are five criteria which can be applied to the selection of an instructional medium once the content has been determined, the objective defined, and the entering behaviors measured. These criteria apply regardless of the objectives of our instruction.

1. **Cognitive appropriateness** (Is the medium appropriate for implementing the attainment of the defined objective?)
2. **Level of sophistication** (Is the medium aimed at the level of understanding of the students?)
3. **Cost** (Is the expense consistent with the potential results in terms of student learning?)
4. **Availability** (Are the material and equipment available when needed?)
5. **Technical quality** (Is the quality of material readable? visible? audible?)

These criteria should be checked when selecting any instructional medium, whether it is real, surrogate, or abstract. In the last chapter an important principle regarding the selection of an instructional medium was stated.

15   What is the media selection principle (rule)?

     •   •   •   •   •   •

15   *A medium of instruction must be selected on the basis of its potential for implementing the achievement of a stated objective.*

[1]Edgar Dale, *Audio-Visual Methods in Teaching*, Third Edition (New York: Holt, Rinehart and Winston, 1969), pp. 107–35.
[2]Jack V. Edling, "Media Technology and Learning Process," in John Loughary, ed., *Man-Machine Systems in Education* (New York: Harper & Row, 1967), pp. 31–44.

When we consider objectives in the naming category it is apparent that a great variety of stimulus materials can be used to help students reach their objectives.

16 Name at least two examples of each of the types of instructional media—actual, surrogate (representational), abstract (verbal)—mentioned in this chapter.

• • • • • • •

16 Actual: *distillation, cube, animal, mineral, vegetable*
Surrogate: *pictures, demonstrations, maps, charts, models, diagrams, drawings*
Abstract: *tape recordings, writing on the overhead projector transparency, speaking*

This analysis of teachers' uses of media is probably quite typical. In teaching and learning within the formal school setting there is very little use of actual objects, events, and characteristics. Most teachers rely upon representational and verbal means to attain objectives. Since actual objects, events, and characteristics are often difficult to provide and even more difficult to use efficiently, teachers will continue to seek those representational and verbal resources which will come as close as possible to replicating the actual object, event, or characteristic. The current interest in and rapid development of simulation activities and educational games are evidence of an attempt to provide students with reality while permitting them to step back and look at what they have done. The increasing use of audiovisual resources is a further attempt to bring representations of reality to the classrooms. While abstract stimuli are extremely important, they are often selected simply because they are readily available and inexpensive. Any decision to use abstract objectives, events, and characteristics (usually in the form of the spoken or written word) ought to be as deliberate as the selection of any other instructional medium, namely, the selection ought to be based on the medium's potential for implementing a stated objective.

Try to apply this principle in the selection of appropriate instructional media to implement the following naming objectives.

17 To name the 14 plants and 5 animals found in a marsh, given examples of each.

• • • • • • •

17 *These actual objects, real plants and animals, are best observed in their natural setting. The student has attained this objective when he responds correctly to the question "What is this?" as the teacher points to a plant or an animal. Spontaneous naming of the specified plants and animals would also fulfill the objective.*

A field trip would be an ideal medium for implementing the attainment of this objective. But suppose the class is in a large urban school and transportation is difficult and expensive to arrange. What media alternatives would help the students to achieve the objective?

Actual objects might still be used if plants or animals could be brought to the classroom. Preserved plants and animals or models of the plants and animals might be used. Other representations might include pictures in slides or filmstrips, in books, or on wall charts. Drawings of the same plants and animals might be made on overhead transparencies or on the chalkboard. There are clearly several alternatives which offer an appropriate approach, geared to the right level, at an economical cost, with reasonable availability and acceptable technical quality.

18   To name in writing the characters in the first act of Shakespeare's *Julius Caesar*, given no supporting clues or stimuli, within three minutes.

•   •   •   •   •   •

18   *One way of establishing the conditions for the students to reach the objective is to make available the drama itself in a "live" format. The students could name each character as he appeared on the stage. Later, after the play is over, they would practice naming the characters, given pictorial representations of each, or given a sound recording of several lines spoken by each, or given a 5-to-10 word description of each. Gradually these supporting stimuli (or prompts) are withdrawn; finally the student can name in writing the characters of the first act when he is given no support or prompt whatsoever. In other words, when he is asked, "Who are the characters in the first act?" he names them with 100 percent accuracy.*

Since live drama is not readily available, a motion picture of the play might be obtained. The same procedure for naming would be followed. There is a filmstrip of the play which would provide still picture representations and might be adequate for reaching the naming objective but it might not be as useful for reaching other objectives. A recording should be considered since there are many available with excellent professional actors playing each role.

Frequently more than one medium is needed to implement the attainment of a stated objective. Seldom is one single medium best for achieving a given objective. The appropriateness of a medium is dependent upon the specific objective being sought at that time; frequently any or several media may be equally acceptable. If you were uncertain about the qualities and variety of media as you completed the exercise in this chapter, it would be useful to review the Media Facts in Part Five at this time.

SUMMARY

This chapter describes objectives in the *naming* category and offers suggestions for teaching students to attain objectives of this type. The writing of objectives in this category requires careful attention to the specification of the conditions under which the naming is to occur. At the beginning of this chapter, six objectives were stated. Check yourself now to determine the extent to which you have attained each objective.

CHAPTER SIX

TEACHING STUDENTS TO DESCRIBE

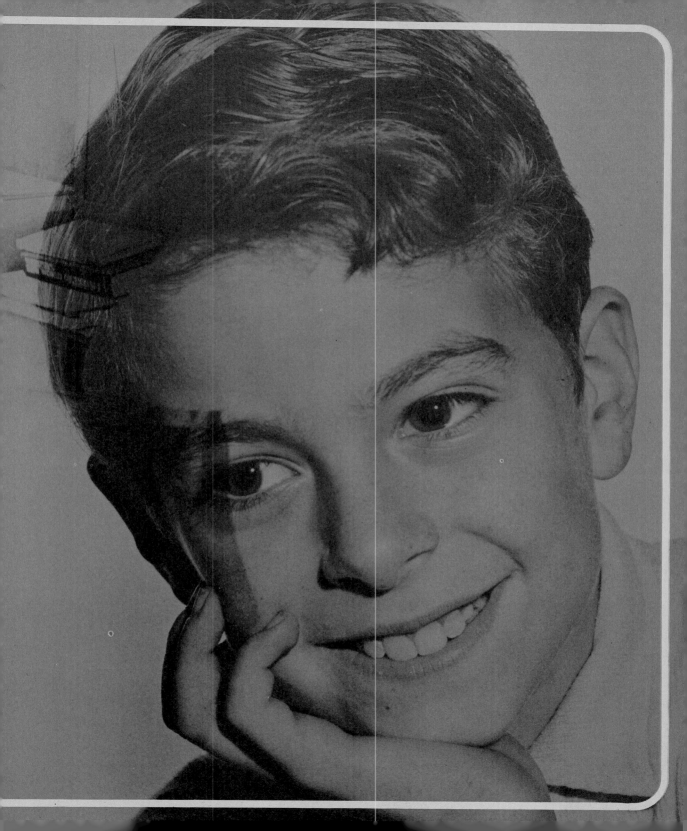

WHEN YOU HAVE MASTERED THE CONTENT OF THIS CHAPTER, YOU SHOULD BE ABLE TO:

1. DEFINE the term "describe."

2. DESCRIBE the school learning situations in which the desired terminal behavior is to describe.

3. IDENTIFY objectives in this category.

4. CONSTRUCT objectives in this category.

5. DESCRIBE the conditions required to teach students to describe.

6. CONSTRUCT the rationale for choosing the medium (or media) best suited for establishing the conditions specified in objectives in the *describe* category.

THE NATURE OF DESCRIBING

Many instructional objectives belong to the category called describing. A student *describes* when he generates and reports the properties or characteristics of objects. He *describes* when he generates and reports events, event properties, and/or relationships relevant to a designated referent. Perhaps *describing* can be clarified by contrasting it with *identifying* and *naming*.

When a student *identifies*, he is always given two stimuli: (1) a name or symbol and (2) the object, event, or characteristic to which the name or symbol refers. When he *names*, the student is given only one stimulus: the object, event, or characteristic to be named. *Describing* is similar to naming in one respect—the learner is given only one stimulus, usually an object, event, or characteristic. But instead of naming it, the student must tell enough about it to meet a specified criterion. Sometimes, on a more complex level, the learner is given only the name or symbol; his task is to produce a description of the object, event, or characteristic for which the name or symbol stands.

Types of Describing

Consider these examples. A mathematics teacher holds up a pyramid. He asks the students to describe the pyramid so well that other students (who can name a pyramid, given a model of one) can tell what the object is even though they cannot see it. The learners who can produce a description which meets this criterion are fulfilling the objective "to describe a pyramid, given a model of a pyramid. . . ."

A science teacher uses a motion picture to show, in slow motion, the germination of a seed. He asks the students to describe the process (or event) with sufficient detail that another student (who can name the process, given a verbal description of it) can name the process being described. The learner who can attain this level of description has attained the objective "to describe the process of germination, given a motion picture (without sound) showing the process. . . ."

The class is studying the 1930's in American history. The teacher uses the word "liberal" to characterize some of the important people in this period, and the word "conservative" to characterize others. One of the class activities is the description (or definition) of the word "liberal" as it is used as a characteristic or property of an individual or group. The student tells enough things about an individual liberal or a group of liberals to enable a competent listener to name the characteristic which he is describing. The student is learning "to describe the characteristic 'liberal' as it is used in American history, given a historical account of individuals who are referred to as liberals. . . ."

Finally, the learner may be required to describe an object, event, or characteristic given only a word or symbol which stands for the object, event, or characteristic. A sixth grade science teacher wanted his students to learn to describe the differences between Monarch and Viceroy butterflies. He used a number of mounted specimens of each species on the first day of instruction. On the second day he used a filmstrip to present pictures of the two kinds of butterflies. The students practiced describing differences in their own words. On the next day this science teacher asked his students "to describe the differences between a Monarch and a Viceroy." In this instance the student is given only the words; he must describe the characteristics of the two objects for which these words stand.

In the first three of the above examples, the description was considered adequate if a competent listener could tell what the student was describing. When students have learned to identify, then to name, and finally to describe, the standard which a learner's describing must meet is simple: *If students who have learned to identify and to name a given referent can name the referent when given only a classmate's description, the description is adequate.* There are many other ways of stating a criterion for describing. The teacher may decide in advance which learner responses will serve as acceptable descriptions. Sometimes the teacher may want the student to be creative in his describing; if so, he might decide (in advance) what kinds of describing will *not* serve as acceptable responses, thus permitting the student to display any desired degree of originality or creativity. Finally, there are many instances in which the teacher will list the attributes which must be included in the description as well as those which should not be included.

Frequently students are required to *define* something. Defining is a type of describing, and, consequently, it is not included as a separate category. If, for example, a student is asked to define a cylinder, he is being asked "to describe the characteristics of a cylinder. . . ." Sometimes define and describe can be used interchangeably. When the conditions of defining or describing have been stated, the choice of one or the other of these two words will usually be a matter of style or personal preference.

Sometimes a description may require a very long response from the learner while at other times a single simple sentence is all that is required. Consider a teacher who is helping his students "to describe the difference between an urban metropolis and a rural village." One description might be, "The urban metropolis is much larger." If this is the only difference with which the teacher is concerned, he would consider the learner who can generate such a statement to have attained the objective. The teacher in the senior course in Problems in a Democracy, however, expects the learner to write a statement which includes a description of at least six differences between the two before he would be satisfied that the student has attained this objective.

Sometimes the length of the description is quite irrelevant. Consider a teacher who wants his students to write descriptions of objects, events, or characteristics which they first encountered in a nonwritten form.

The teacher may show a film on the Revolutionary War to the class. Following the screening, he may ask the students to state in their own words the three phases of the British plan to crush the northern colonies. When the students do this, they are demonstrating their ability "to describe the threefold plan of the British to conquer the northern colonies, given. . . ."

Describing vs. Naming

How does one tell whether to use naming or describing in an example such as "telling the difference between an isosceles triangle and any other triangle"? Suppose that the behavior desired is to produce the following written statements, neither of which was used in the instruction:

1. An isosceles triangle has two sides equal to each other and a third side not equal to the first two.
2. Any triangle with three unequal or three equal sides is not an isosceles triangle.

Wouldn't it be correct to accept either of the following as a correct statement of the desired objective?

1. To name in writing the characteristics of an isosceles triangle . . .
2. To describe in writing an isosceles triangle . . .

We prefer the latter statement, because *describing*, as used in this book, implies that the learner will *generate and report* the categories of object properties. To put it negatively, describing is used when the desired behavior is not simple recall. Naming, however, is generally used for situations where recall is all that is desired. For example, "to name the 50 states of the U.S.A., given an outline map showing the state boundaries . . ." implies simple recall on the part of the learner; he "recalls" the names and then *names* the states by writing the names within the appropriate boundaries. The learner does not generate the names unless the objective specifically demands this.

But what if the learner's task is to recall the list of characteristics of an isosceles triangle? Wouldn't this belong in the describing category? The answer is no—not as describe is defined in this book. The preferred word would be *name*: to name the characteristics of an isosceles triangle.

OBJECTIVES IN THE DESCRIBING CATEGORY

Following are some nonbehavioral objectives taken from teachers' manuals, curriculum guides, courses of study, and similar sources. Read each, then ask, "Did the writer have some kind of 'describing' behavior in mind when he wrote the objective?" If there is a probability that he did, rewrite the objective in good behavioral form. If he did not, select one of the other terms which might indicate what the writer had in mind, but do not write the complete objective.

1 To build the learner's understanding of the concept "area."

     •   •   •   •   •   •

1 To describe orally the procedures for finding the area of a square, given a problem in which the dimensions of a square are stated, within 30 seconds. (Many other "describing" objectives are possible. The answers given in these items are merely illustrative.) Why not use name (or "state" or "write") for this objective? Wouldn't "to name the formula for the area of a square . . ." (or "to state the formula . . ." or "to write the formula . . .") be just as good or better? It would be the correct statement if we wanted the student to recall a formula which we taught him (or which he learned) earlier; it is not the correct term if we want him to discover the procedure.

2 To understand the concept of soil erosion.

     •   •   •   •   •   •

2 Given three one-minute silent motion picture film clips showing eroded areas, to describe in writing the forces and processes of erosion which caused the phenomena, within one-half hour. The description must include at least . . . This objective implies that we want the student to acquire the ability to abstract information from silent films and to state this information in writing. The student's written statements must meet an arbitrarily specified criterion.

3 To appreciate the hardships which the early settlers on the prairie frontier endured.

     •   •   •   •   •   •

3 To compare (or describe) in a written essay a day in the life of a South Dakota farmer of 1890 with a day in the life of a contemporary South Dakota farmer. The learner is given three motion picture films (titles are specified) and three class periods. The essay must contain at least five of the ten contrasts presented in the films, and it must meet the quality standards listed on the chart on the bulletin board.

4 To encourage effective use of the glossary and dictionary.

     •   •   •   •   •   •

4 Possibly the writer wants the student "to find words in a glossary or dictionary." If so, the objective might be stated "to find a given printed word in the glossary within 15 seconds. The learner will give evidence of his having found the word by writing the page number on which the entry is found next to the word."

However, this may not be even remotely close to the goal which the writer had in mind. He may want the students to be able to tell what benefits can be derived from effective use of a dictionary. He shows the class a filmstrip which describes seven uses of a dictionary. He has the students construct a bulletin board picturing and naming these functions. Finally, the teacher describes a problem which a student may encounter in his reading, and then the teacher demonstrates one of the uses of the dictionary which enables him to solve his problem; the students name the function which they see the teacher demonstrate. This teacher is concerned with developing the ability of learners "to name the seven uses of the dictionary, given a demonstration of each use, within five seconds."

Similarly, one could use an illustration in which the name of each function is given and the student describes what he does in each instance. The objective is "to describe orally the seven functions of the dictionary, given the name of each function, within 20 seconds." The assumption is that the learner is generating, not recalling, the functions.

5 **To know the difference between the past and present tense of Latin verbs of the second conjugation.**

· · · · · ·

5 *To identify past and present forms of second conjugation verbs, given examples of each, within three seconds per example.*

To name the tense of second conjugation verbs, given past and present forms, within two seconds per example.

To construct past and present forms of second conjugation verbs, in any given person and number, given the infinitive form of the verb, within 15 seconds per pair.

Obviously, one could also include objectives such as "to describe the characteristics of the past and present tense . . ." or "to describe how to construct the past tense of a verb . . ." or a number of other possible describing objectives.

6 **To help students understand how to make a line graph.**

· · · · · ·

6 *Note that if an objective is stated in nonbehavioral terms, it is possible to allow almost any interpretation of the writer's intent. As a result, nearly any non-behavioral objective can be translated into one which is concerned with describing on the part of the learner. In this example we could legitimately contend that the meaning is that the student should learn "to describe how to make a line graph. . . ." More than likely, however, the writer intended that the learner should construct line graphs.*

Note, too, that as in most examples there is a progression. The best way to teach students "to construct line graphs" is to make certain that they have attained each of the following objectives before proceeding to the next:

a. *to identify line graphs*
b. *to name line graphs*
c. *to describe line graphs*
d. *to describe how to construct line graphs*

Attaining Objectives

As you increase your skill in writing objectives, try to place each objective into a context. Ask, "What behavior will the student need in order to attain this objective?" "What will I have to teach him in order to ensure his attaining this objective?" Invariably, your answers to these questions will lead you to formulate a series of progressively more complex or difficult learner tasks, as illustrated in the example on graphs, above. Consider the following examples of this principle.

Identify–name–describe strategy We have seen how a student sometimes learns to identify, then name, and finally describe; sometimes he learns to describe, then identify, and finally name. Both orders, "identify–name–describe" and "describe–identify–name," represent instructional strategies which are useful in a wide variety of situations.

Mr. Dressel wants the pupils in his fifth grade social studies class to describe the role played by various means of transportation used by Americans in the Westward movement of the 19th century. He analyzes this task and concludes that, among other things, he will have to teach his fifth graders to identify such objects as keelboats, barges, flatboats, Conestoga wagons, and prairie schooners. He finds motion pictures which illustrate each of these, and he uses clips (or short segments of the films) to help the students learn to identify these means of transportation. He uses filmstrips and pictures mounted on the bulletin board to achieve the same purpose. Unobtrusively, using these same media, Mr. Dressel begins to have the students *name* these objects, given pictorial representations. At the same time, he asks questions which elicit from the learners a discussion of the contributions of each mode of transportation to the Westward movement. Still later in the unit, Mr. Dressel has his students discuss the role that each of the above mentioned means of transportation played in the Westward movement. His students are learning "to describe. . . ."

The critical point on which to focus at this time is the developmental nature of Mr. Dressel's teaching. He could not have his students engage in the describing activity unless they first learned to name the modes of transportation listed above. By the same token, it would probably be somewhat inefficient to try to teach these children to *name* the modes unless they first learned to *identify* them. Mr. Dressel used the "identify–name–describe" order as a basis for developing an instructional strategy. His students were to learn to describe, so he asked himself "What are they to describe?" The answer to this question is a list of modes of transportation as they related to the Westward movement; consequently, he reasons, his students should first learn to name the modes of transportation which played a role in this period of our nation's history.

Ask yourself, as you plan an instructional sequence, "Can the students name the objects, events, or characteristics of interest?" If not, provision must be made for them to learn to do so before (or while) they learn to describe. In addition, you should ask yourself, "Can they identify the things which they are supposed to learn to name?" If not, your teaching strategy ought to provide an opportunity for them to learn to identify the objects, events, or characteristics of interest.

Not every lesson involving the "identify–name–describe" sequence can be developed quite this simply. Nevertheless, the pattern occurs so frequently and is so effective that it must be mastered. The literature teacher wants his students to describe the three literary movements of the Romantic period. Since the movements have names, the teacher will teach his students to name the movements before they begin describing them. Furthermore, he will teach the class to identify the movements before he attempts to teach the naming of the movements. The mathematics teacher who wants his students "to describe the characteristics of a pyramid, given . . ." will certainly not begin his instruction unless he has first ascertained whether the class can name pyramids, given examples. If they cannot, he will teach them to do so. Again, before he teaches them "to name pyramids," he will ascertain whether they have learned "to identify pyramids."

Describe—identify—name strategy There are many opportunities to use the "describe–identify–name" strategy. Mrs. Donald wants the students in her English class to use an apostrophe correctly in the possessive form. She decides that her first task is to teach the students to *describe* possessives—"if a word shows ownership. . . ." Next she wants her students "to name possessives given unpunctuated English sentences containing possessive forms. . . ." Finally, she wants her students "to punctuate (i.e., insert or refrain from inserting apostrophes) in unpunctuated English sentences . . ."

Her objectives, in abbreviated form, are:

1.   to describe a possessive form
2.   to identify a possessive form
3.   to name a possessive form
4.   to punctuate a possessive form

Mrs. Donald uses the catalog of her school district's Learning Resources Center in an effort to find instructional material to assist her students in achieving these objectives. A description of a programmed textbook dealing with punctuation catches her attention and she requests a copy. After examining it carefully, she decides to use it for her first two objectives. As you study the programmed text, below, note how it enables the student to attain the first two objectives; later Mrs. Donald will use another means to help them learn the third element in the "describe–identify–name" sequence.

UNIT 5—*Possessives and Apostrophes*[1]

1.   Jimmys jacket
   Which word names the owner?

       (a) Jimmys   (b) jacket   **a**

---

2.   To find out if a word shows ownership, ask yourself two questions:

   First, are you told *what is owned?*
   Second, are you told *who owns it?*

   If the answer to both questions is "Yes," the word shows ownership.

   <u>Steves</u> coat
   Does the underlined word show ownership?
       (a) Yes   (b) No   **a**

---

3.   <u>boys</u> in the lake

Are you told what is owned?	(a) Yes	(b) No	**b**
Are you told who owns it?	(a) Yes	(b) No	**b**
Does the underlined word show ownership?	(a) Yes	(b) No	**b**

---

4.   <u>drivers</u> keys

Are you told what is owned?	(a) Yes	(b) No	**a**
Are you told who owns it?	(a) Yes	(b) No	**a**
Does the underlined word show ownership?	(a) Yes	(b) No	**a**

---

5.   <u>books</u> and records

Are you told what is owned?	(a) Yes	(b) No	**b**
Are you told who owns it?	(a) Yes	(b) No	**b**
Does the underlined word show ownership?	(a) Yes	(b) No	**b**

---

6.   Sometimes the thing that is owned is not really the property of the owner. It still shows ownership.

   <u>teachers</u> class
   Does the underlined word show ownership?
       (a) Yes   (b) No   **a**

---

[1]This unit is adapted from a program developed as a part of a U.S. Office of Education research project. Characteristics and utilization of the program are described in Richard E. Schutz, Robert L. Baker, and Vernon S. Gerlach, *Measurement Procedures in Programmed Instruction* (Tempe, Arizona: Classroom Learning Laboratory, Arizona State University, 1964).

7.	<u>Bills</u> friends			
	Does the underlined word show ownership?	(a) Yes	(b) No	a

8.	Which shows ownership?		
	(a) Bill went home.		
	(b) Bills house		b

9.	Which shows ownership?		
	(a) the boys bike		
	(b) the boys ran		a

10.	<u>uncles</u> boat			
	Are you told what is owned?	(a) Yes	(b) No	a
	Are you told who owns it?	(a) Yes	(b) No	a
	Does the underlined word show ownership?	(a) Yes	(b) No	a

11.	away from the <u>screams</u>			
	Are you told what is owned?	(a) Yes	(b) No	b
	Are you told who owns it?	(a) Yes	(b) No	b
	Does the underlined word show ownership?	(a) Yes	(b) No	b

12.	the <u>shoes</u> below			
	Are you told what is owned?	(a) Yes	(b) No	b
	Are you told who owns it?	(a) Yes	(b) No	b
	Does the underlined word show ownership?	(a) Yes	(b) No	b

13.	then <u>Thomas</u> left it			
	Are you told what is owned?	(a) Yes	(b) No	b
	Are you told who owns it?	(a) Yes	(b) No	b
	Does the underlined word show ownership?	(a) Yes	(b) No	b

14.	from <u>Beckys</u> book			
	Are you told what is owned?	(a) Yes	(b) No	a
	Are you told who owns it?	(a) Yes	(b) No	a
	Does the underlined word show ownership?	(a) Yes	(b) No	a

15. many <u>sisters</u> and brothers

Are you told what is owned?	(a) Yes	(b) No	b
Are you told who owns it?	(a) Yes	(b) No	b
Does the underlined word show ownership?	(a) Yes	(b) No	b

16. the <u>policemans</u> whistle

Are you told what is owned?	(a) Yes	(b) No	a
Are you told who owns it?	(a) Yes	(b) No	a
Does the underlined word show ownership?	(a) Yes	(b) No	a

17. Mr. <u>Lakes</u> voice

Are you told what is owned?	(a) Yes	(b) No	a
Are you told who owns it?	(a) Yes	(b) No	a
What does the underlined word show?			ownership

18. his <u>sisters</u> car

What two things are you told?

(a) _____   (a) What is owned.

(b) _____   (b) Who owns it.

What does the underlined word show?   ownership

19. <u>ducks</u> lake

How can you tell whether the underlined word shows ownership?

(a) _____   (a) It tells what is owned.

(b) _____   (b) It tells who owns it.

20. <u>giants</u> were bold

How can you tell that the underlined word does not show ownership?

(a) _____   (a) It doesn't tell what is owned.

(b) _____   (b) It doesn't tell who owns it.

21. How do you tell whether a word shows ownership?

(a) You must be told_____ . (a) What is owned.

(b) You must be told_____ . (b) Who owns it.

22. You can use the rule you have learned to tell whether a word shows ownership.

Write the rule: When words tell what is owned and who owns it, then the word that tells who owns it shows ownership.

23. Tell whether the underlined word in each line below shows ownership:

students and visitors	(a) Yes	(b) No	b
teachers class	(a) Yes	(b) No	a
paths that are wide	(a) Yes	(b) No	b
the childs smile	(a) Yes	(b) No	a
meetings in the morning	(a) Yes	(b) No	b
trips to many nations	(a) Yes	(b) No	b
etc.[2]			

In this programmed textbook the student learned "to describe the possessive form . . ." (see frame 22). Then, drawing upon this newly acquired ability, he learns "to identify the possessive form . . ." (see frame 23). Later Mrs. Donald will teach him to apply the word "possessive" to appropriate examples. Thus, the "describe–identify–name" cycle will be complete. Teachers who plan their instructional activities thoughtfully will find countless instances where this sequence is effective.

As was mentioned earlier, the teacher, in choosing his strategy, must ask the question, "Do I want to use an inductive or a deductive method?"

[2]The program continues with singular and plural possessives, etc. Then it leads the student to the use of the apostrophe in possessives.

7   Did the programmed textbook which Mrs. Donald used begin with an inductive or a deductive method?   Give a reason for your answer.   (See especially frames 2, 3, and 4 if you can't remember.)

•   •   •   •   •   •   •

7   *Deductive. The learners are given the elements of the rule; they then apply the rule.   Actually, the learners are doing three things in the early frames: (a) identifying expressions that tell what is owned; (b) identifying expressions that tell who owns something; and (c) identifying words that show ownership.*

8   In which frame does the programmed textbook have the student begin to describe one of the characteristics of the possessive form?

•   •   •   •   •   •   •

8   *17.*

9   What do frames 17 through 22 lead the students to do?

•   •   •   •   •   •   •

9   *Describe one of the characteristics of the possessive form.*

10   After the student has learned to describe the possessive form, what does the programmed text book have him do?   (frame 23)

•   •   •   •   •   •   •

10   *Identify the possessive form.*

11   The student identifies the possessive form in frames 2 through 16 and in frame 23.   How do the earlier frames differ from frame 23?

•   •   •   •   •   •   •

11   *In the earlier frames, the learner is given the description of the possessive form and the word(s) which he must identify.   In frame 23, the learner is given only the words; he must supply the description himself.*

Below are three objectives related to *describing*.   Are there any *identifying* or *naming* skills which are antecedent to the stated objectives?   If so, write the appropriate behavioral objectives.   If not, tell why *identifying* and *naming* are not prerequisites for the *describing* behavior.

12   To describe in writing a successful method for indirectly measuring a distance, given a previously unencountered situation in which the distance between two points can be determined by more than one method, within 30 minutes.   The method described must possess all the characteristics enumerated in the list on the wall chart.

•   •   •   •   •   •   •

12   *Such objectives as the following would be appropriate prerequisites:*

   a.   To identify direct and indirect measurement procedures, given graphic illustrations of problems involving each.

    b. To name the method of measurement used, given a textual description of a problem and the method used to determine the distance.

    c. To name the method of measurement used, given a graphic illustration of a problem and the method used to compute the distance.

13   To describe orally a rectangular solid, a pyramid, a cone, and a sphere in terms of their geometric qualities, given the name of the object, within 30 seconds, with such accuracy that the students in the class who have not heard the name can name the object after hearing the description. (The students have acquired the ability to name the objects listed, given an oral or textual description.) The descriptions must not include any non-geometric characteristics.

    •   •   •   •   •   •

13   *To identify rectangular solids, pyramids, cones, and spheres, given . . .*

14   To describe in writing at least three major effects, not previously mentioned in class, of specified changes in climate or topography on economic conditions in given countries.

    •   •   •   •   •   •

14   *To identify functional relationships between changes in climate and economic conditions, given examples of . . .*

    To identify functional relationships between changes in topography and economic conditions, given examples of . . .

    Unless the kinds of effects being studied had specific names, it is possible that no naming *objectives would need to be antecedent to the* describing *objective stated above.*

MEDIA SELECTION

The media selection rule applies to objectives in the *describing* category, just as it does to those in the *identifying* and *naming* categories.

15   What is the media selection rule?

    •   •   •   •   •   •

15   *A medium of instruction must be selected on the basis of its potential for implementing the attainment of a stated objective.*

If a student has been asked to describe the events leading to a landing on the moon by a lunar module, there is an array of media possibilities. Students might have seen the events on television; the teacher could show films obtained from the National Aeronautics and Space Administration (NASA); charts which graphically illustrate the process are available in periodicals and could be converted to slides or transparencies so that all could see. A brief review of other selection criteria should be made at this point.

16   What are some other factors affecting the selection of media?

· · · · · · ·

16   *a.* *Availability of media*
     b. *Cost*
     c. *Appropriateness for level of students*
     d. *Technical quality*

If the selection criteria are used, there is no shortcut to the process. Materials must be reviewed or previewed before final selections are made. Once the objective has been defined and the media alternatives have been considered, the selection can be made. One might infer from the selection criteria that there is one best medium for any one objective, but this is not the case. There may be one medium that is the best of those available at the time of use; there may be one medium that is the best for the amount of money available to rent or purchase; or there may be one medium that is best technically. These are relative criteria and are not absolute. One medium may be best for one use by one teacher and absolutely inappropriate for use by another teacher who is concerned with the same objective.

Another inference might be that only one medium should be used to help achieve an objective. When one medium is selected from a wide number available, the teacher feels that it is best "on the average" to accomplish the stated objective. However, there may be many other objectives en route to the major objective and each of these objectives may require a different medium. There is much to recommend a multi-media approach to teaching and learning.

Mrs. Dahl has prepared the following objective: "The students will describe, in an oral report, the activities of a large dairy farm." After scanning the county film library catalog for a film which might serve as an orientation to help students identify and name various animals, pieces of machinery, and buildings normally found on a farm, she selected the film MILK for her primary class. Other titles about the farm dealt with seasonal aspects of farm life or presented other types of farms. Several titles were for older groups. When the film arrived in the school, she previewed it and used it during the introduction to the unit.

The next day, Mrs. Dahl used slides of farm animals and machinery to determine how well each student was able to name them. This procedure also served as an organizer for a field trip to a farm which was taken the next day. Each student recorded his oral report on a tape recorder to provide feedback to the teacher as she evaluated the extent to which the original objective had been reached.

After selection comes use. Excellent objectives may be formulated. The best media may be ready to help implement the attainment of the objectives, but the manner in which the media are used will finally determine the success of the instructional design. Gagné outlines the events of instruction which provide a context for a discussion of media utilization. These events are applicable primarily to the learning of principles, facts, rules, and generalizations:

1. Gaining and maintaining attention. Obviously, in order for learning to occur, attention must be attracted in the first place, and then maintained. Many of the stimulation conditions that attract attention have been known for a long time, including such things as change, novelty, appeal to dominant interests. Concerning the maintenance of attention, we know somewhat less. Some clarification has surely been gained by Travers' demonstration that we only attend to one thing at a time, regardless of how many media channels may be bombarding us. Presumably, maintaining attention is a matter of achieving a set, related to one or more individual goals, which makes the learner return again and again to the task at hand. Manipulating external stimuli is probably ineffective over the long pull, and one must instead seek ways of reinforcing the motivational state of the learner.

2. Insuring recall of previously acquired knowledge is another important function of instruction. We have seen that recall of prior knowledge is considered an essential condition of learning. . . . When the learner undertakes to learn something new, he must first be reminded of what he already knows which is relevant to that learning.

3. Guiding the learning is done in instruction by verbal or pictorial material that provides "cues" or "hints" to new principles, usually without stating them fully in verbal form. . . .

4. Providing feedback to the learner on his accomplishments is another function of instruction. One of the surest ways, it seems to me, is by defining the objectives of instruction clearly to the learner, so that he will become aware immediately when he has attained each specific goal. Again, the skilled learner may do this himself. Textbooks and other media often seem to neglect badly this essential instructional function.

5. Establishing conditions for remembering and transfer of learning would surely be counted as one of the essential functions of instruction. For purposes of transfer, there needs to be a carefully designed series of problems to which application of the newly learned principle is made. . . . For remembering, there needs to be provision for spaced review, which has often been shown to be an effective technique.

6. Finally, there should be mentioned still another instructional function, often neglected. This is assessment of outcomes. The outcomes of learning and remembering need to be assessed frequently. The administration of a final test or examination for purposes of determining a grade seems often to be a way of consolidating an onerous task which because of its unmanageable scope ends up avoiding the very assessment that should be done. Learning of the *specifics* needs to be assessed, perhaps more so than learning of the generalities. The five-minute daily or weekly quiz has much to recommend it. For the skilled learner, this

function can often be performed with some success by himself. But to test oneself is indeed a highly sophisticated thing to do, and instructional materials should provide as much help as possible in this function.

There are, then, these six major functions that take place in instruction. It may be noted that learning theory does not, in and of itself, say exactly how these are to be put together in the great variety of specific instances to which they are applicable. What learning theory tells us is that when certain ones are not present, learning is improbable. Beyond such theory there must of course be both technology and artistry, whether this be exhibited by the textbook writer, the film-maker, or the master teacher.[3]

Most media available today can perform many of the instructional functions outlined above. Any one medium, or several media in combination, can perform instructional functions. Sometimes media alone can enable learners to attain objectives and sometimes the teacher must consider the media as complementary stimuli. No one medium possesses all the properties which will perform all the instructional functions. Rather, some media perform some functions well some of the time and others not so well.

17   Gagné defines six functions of instruction. What is the first? What is one implication for the selection and use of media?

· · · · · · ·

17   *Gaining and maintaining attention. Media involve several senses thus compelling attention. Media might be used to attract attention, but there is no guarantee that they will hold attention.*

18   What other instructional functions does Gagné list?

· · · · · · ·

18   *To insure recall, the learner must be reminded first what he already knows which is relevant to that learning.*
Guiding the learning by verbal or pictorial cues provides organizers for the new learning.
Feedback to the learner is necessary as soon as possible.
For remembering and transfer, a carefully designed series of problems must be developed for application of the newly learned principle.
The outcomes of learning need to be assessed frequently.

[3]Robert M. Gagné, "Learning Theory, Educational Media, and Individualized Instruction," a paper presented at the Faculty Seminar on Educational Media at Bucknell University, November 16, 1967. Quoted by permission of Dr. Robert M. Gagné.

SUMMARY

At this point you should be able to write objectives using the verbs "to identify," "to name," and "to describe." You should be able to state the media selection rule and to name media alternatives for reaching instructional objectives. Can you?

If so, move on to the next chapter.

If not, return to Chapter 4 for identifying objectives, Chapter 5 for naming objectives and the beginning of this chapter for describing objectives.

CHAPTER
SEVEN

TEACHING
STUDENTS
TO
ORDER

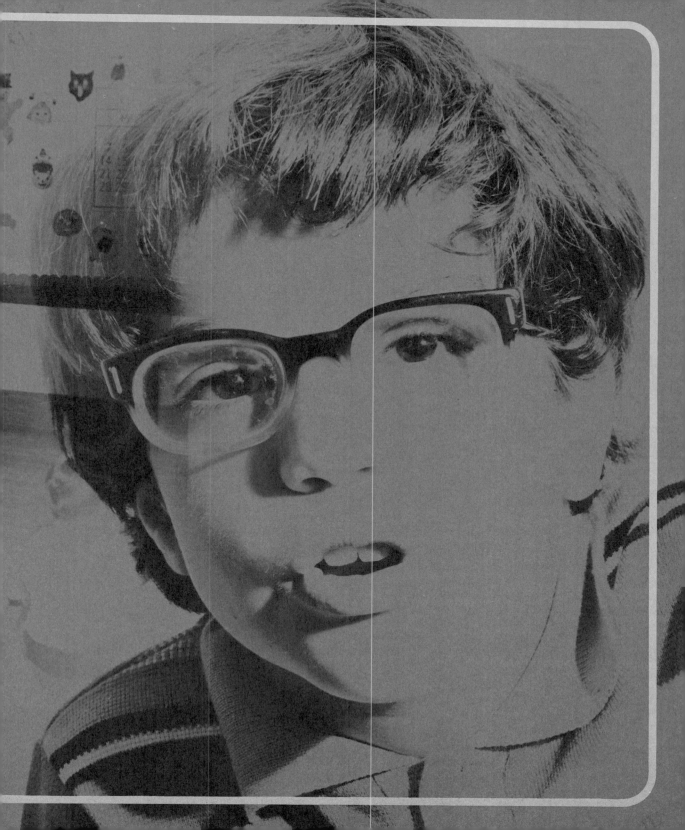

When you have mastered the content of this chapter, you should be able to:

1. DEFINE the term "order."

2. DESCRIBE the school learning situations in which the desired terminal behavior is to order.

3. IDENTIFY objectives in this category.

4. CONSTRUCT objectives in this category.

5. DESCRIBE the conditions required to teach students to order.

6. CONSTRUCT the rationale for choosing the medium (or media) best suited for establishing the conditions specified in objectives in the *order* category.

THE NATURE OF ORDERING

When a learner is required to list or tell or perform in a specified sequence, he is engaged in ordering. He may order objects, events, or characteristics; or he may order words, symbols, or other representations of objects, events, or characteristics. Sometimes he is given that which he is to order. At other times he must both name that which he is to order and do the ordering at the same time. Ordering occurs when the learner correctly arranges two or more referents in the sequence specified in instructions. He may be required to name the referents himself (i.e., to name and order) or he may be provided with a list of referents to order.

Students in schools must learn to do many kinds of ordering. When they alphabetize, they are *ordering* alphabetically. When they list terms, such as inch, foot, yard, rod, furlong, and mile, they are *ordering* according to size or distance. When they tell which event happened first, second, third, and so on, they are *ordering* chronologically.

However not all instances involving arranging belong to the ordering category. If a student is to arrange given garden products in one of two categories—fruit or vegetable—he is not ordering; there is no order, or ordinal characteristic, in an arrangement when it is completed correctly. This is simply and only a nominal classification (an identifying behavior) since it makes no difference whether the student classifies the fruits or the vegetables first. Fruits and vegetables, in this context, have no order. Therefore this is an *identifying* behavior.

Ordering involves varying degrees of complexity. Some ordering tasks are relatively difficult in that the learner must do several things simultaneously. For example, the science teacher wants his students to be able to state the order of the organs and parts of the body through which the blood flows. His objective is "to order the parts and organs of the circulatory system in the order of the flow of blood, beginning with the main aorta, within 30 seconds." This is one kind of ordering objective. The learner is not given the names of the parts which he must order; he must supply both the names and the order.

The same teacher may have used a simpler objective several days earlier: "to order the following names in the order of the blood flow, beginning with the left ventricle, within 30 seconds, given the names: left ventricle, right ventricle, left auricle, right auricle, artery, vein, capillary." This objective is somewhat simpler, since it does not require the student to supply the names of the objects to be ordered.

Somewhere between these two in difficulty would be this kind of objective: "to order the names of the parts and organs of the circulatory system in the order of the blood flow, given a chart of the circulatory system (without names), within one minute." In this case the learner would be required to supply the names in a specific order; he would have the help of a chart symbolizing the parts and organs which he must name, and he would have the freedom of beginning at a point of his choice in the circulatory system.

Ordering does not necessarily involve words. Consider this objective: "to order on the flannelboard the parts and organs of the circulatory system in the order of the blood flow, given flannel cut-outs representing the artery, etc. . . ." In this situation, the learner manipulates flannel symbols of parts rather than words; the performance, or product, is nonetheless ordering. Kindergarten and primary teachers have many objectives in which the learner is involved in arranging objects or nonverbal symbols in a precise order.

Ordering sometimes involves procedures (or processes) for organizing material. Students may be required to order when they learn correct procedures for studying, judging, or criticizing. The student in the geometry class is required to order elements of proof when he is solving a problem. The debate student masters an optimum order for presenting his arguments. The fourth-grade science student must use a precise order in reporting a demonstration or experiment. The girls in the home economics class learn to follow a definite order in baking or sewing.

OBJECTIVES IN THE ORDERING CATEGORY

In each of the following, tell whether the objective is one which involves *ordering, describing, naming,* or *identifying* on the part of the learner.

1 To arrange each of the given colored objects in one of two categories, primary color or secondary color, within two seconds per item.

• • • • • • •

1 *The learner is given an object displaying a certain characteristic (color) and a label. This is identifying.*

2 To arrange each of the eight given color samples according to its wave length, beginning with the color which has the shortest wave length, within one minute.

• • • • • • •

2 *The arrangement must be done in a specified sequence, i.e., according to wave length. This task is* ordering.

3 Given three crystal formations which can be distinguished from each other only by their colors, to state in writing the differences among the crystal formations within one minute. The statement must be sufficiently accurate to enable the teacher to name each formation on the basis of the student's statement.

• • • • • • •

3 *This could be "to name the characteristics . . ." or it could be "to describe the differences. . . ." Sometimes the difference between the choice of the verb*

"name" or "describe" is quite arbitrary. If one can describe an object simply by listing its characteristics and if each of the characteristics has a name, then naming is an appropriate term. If, however, the student must list characteristics of several objects and if he must tell which object possesses which characteristics, it is better to use the term describing. Ultimately it is not as important to quibble about the grey areas where naming and describing may occasionally overlap as it is to recognize that there are times when either term could be used without any danger of misinterpretation. Remember, however, that naming is preferred when we are concerned with simple recall.

4   To describe the sequence of arithmetic operations required to solve three-step problems of the type on pages 67–68 of the textbook, given problems not previously encountered, and given one minute per problem.

• • • • • • •

4   *The teacher wants the learners to state the operations in their proper order: multiply, add, divide; add, multiply, add, etc. The objective is "to order the steps. . . ." There is no plausible way "to describe the sequence . . ." other than to order the components of the sequence in the order in which the student must use them to solve a problem. The answer must be* ordering.

5   To list in writing, from memory and in their correct order, the four steps used in solving story problems, within one minute.

• • • • • • •

5   *To order the four steps . . .*

6   To distinguish between declarative and interrogative sentences, given examples of each, within three seconds per example.

• • • • • • •

6   *The conditions are not clear. If the learner is given the names of the two categories, the task is identifying. If the learner is to supply the names, the task is naming. The use of either of these two verbs would have removed the ambiguity.*

7   Given four formulas for area (rectangle, triangle, trapezoid, and non-rectangular parallelogram), and given a problem in which finding the area of one of the four figures described is required, to select the correct formula within 15 seconds.

• • • • • • •

7   *Think of the givens and the instructions: given the formula; given a problem for which a formula is appropriate; match the two. This is* identifying.

Following are several activities, test items, and descriptions of student performances or products. For each item, ask "Is this related to an ordering objective?" If so, write an appropriate ordering objective. If not, select one performance term to describe the example, and write an appropriate objective.

8 Test item: Which of the following happened first, second, etc.?

Albany Plan of Union
Articles of Confederation
Bill of Rights
Constitution

•   •   •   •   •   •

8 *To order these events chronologically, beginning with the first, given two minutes: Albany Plan of Union, Articles of Confederation, Bill of Rights, Constitution.*

9 Which movement of a sonata is often:

a. rapid and gay?
b. long and complex?
c. sweet and charming?

•   •   •   •   •   •

9 *To name the movements of a typical sonata, given a verbal description of the characteristics, within 30 seconds.*

10 Test item: Name the four stages of the life history of the housefly, beginning with the egg.

•   •   •   •   •   •

10 *To order in writing the stages in the life history of the housefly within one minute.*

11 Activity in a science class: Arrange the following in the two columns shown on the bulletin board:

a. evaporation of alcohol
b. freezing of water
c. burning of a wood splinter
d. melting of paraffin
e. mixing yellow and blue tempera colors

(The bulletin board display includes two columns: physical change and chemical change.)

•   •   •   •   •   •

11 *To identify physical and chemical changes, given verbal examples such as the following:*

a. *evaporation of alcohol*
b. *freezing of water*
c. *burning of a wood splinter*
d. *melting of paraffin*
e. *mixing yellow and blue tempera colors*

The student is given five seconds per item.

12   Activity: The science class has identified a problem. The teacher wants the students to develop sound procedures for studying the problem. He has the students list things which they would do. After the list has been recorded on the chalkboard, he tells them to put a "1" before the step which they would do first, a "2" before the second step, and so on.

        •   •   •   •   •   •

12   *To order the steps which one follows in solving a problem in science within two minutes. (The problem must be one which can be solved if the learner follows the four steps listed in Chapter 1 of his science textbook.) The objective given in Example 12 implies that the student must name and order the steps. You will recall that there are two types of ordering:*

a. either the student arranges in order things which are given, or
b. he arranges in order things which are not given.

The objective as stated above is one of the latter type.

Attaining Objectives

In an actual classroom situation, the teacher would certainly need several objectives to cover the situation described. For example, the students must learn "to name the steps . . ." before they attempt "to order the steps. . . ." Quite possibly they would learn to identify the steps before they begin to name them.

Examine this example more closely. Thus far we assume that the steps have names. The steps must have names, or at the very least one must be able to designate them by means of a phrase or a short sentence. Thus each step is a referent (an event) which can be named. Probably the teacher at some time in the instructional sequence will want the learners to describe each step. Thus, an order or a strategy for teaching can again be constructed by using the terms which have been discussed. In Example 12, above, the teacher might well plan his instruction on the basis of these objectives:

> To identify the steps . . .
> To name the steps . . .
> To describe the steps . . .
> To order the steps . . .

However, the teacher could just as well have decided to use an inductive approach. He would have provided the students with problems and solutions. First, he would have led them to describe the steps in the solution. Next, he would have led them to identify examples of solutions in which the steps were followed properly and solutions in which they were not. Finally, he would have students name and order the steps.

Both approaches are good methods of teaching and both can be used within the framework of our system for describing learner performances and products.

Mr. Borko, the driver-training teacher, uses a mock-up of an automobile to teach specified skills to his future drivers. A mock-up is an "edited model." Mr. Borko's mock-up is a full scale model of those parts of the automobile which the driver must use while in the act of driving.   There is a driver's seat, of course, as well as a steering wheel, instrument panel, the usual foot pedals, and so on.   Mr. Borko uses the mock-up to teach his students to start a car and to shift from a standing position into either low or reverse.   These are psychomotor skills; the learners *do* the actual starting and shifting.

When Mr. Borko teaches his students "to start an automobile . . ." or "to shift into reverse, given a standing automobile, in neutral . . ." he does so only after he has taught many antecedent, or en route, behaviors.   He begins by teaching his students to identify the components in the mock-up which are related to starting and shifting: the ignition switch, the starter switch, the brake, the clutch, and all the other pertinent parts.   He teaches them to name these parts.   He teaches them to *order* the several events which are involved in starting the car.   He uses a set of drawings during the time he is teaching them to identify and name the critical parts.

To teach the students to order the steps in starting an automobile, Mr. Borko uses a sound motion picture.   He shows it many times.   The first showing serves as a general orientation to the task; the entire film is shown, without interruption.   The second time Mr. Borko uses the film, he does so without sound.   The learners describe the sequence of events as they see them happen on the screen.   Later he shows it again without the sound.   This time a learner sits in the mock-up and performs the acts which he sees on the screen.   Mr. Borko stops the projector at any time the learner makes an error, or falls behind, and asks the class to verbalize the correct procedure.   When the student in the mock-up is performing correctly again, the motion picture continues.

On another occasion, Mr. Borko uses the sound of the film, without the picture, to direct the actions of the student in the mock-up.   Finally, he provides a chart containing only a key word to describe each step in the sequence.   Eventually the chart is withdrawn and the student is on his own.   He performs the required operations within the specified time limit without the aid of any of the instructional media which were used while he was learning the en route behaviors.   He has acquired the ability to identify, to name, and to order any objects and events (or steps).   All of these en route behaviors culminate in the terminal behavior: to start the automobile, given a mock-up . . . and to shift from neutral into low or reverse. . . .

Consider the problems which Mr. Borko encountered in his teaching.   To begin with, he wants his learners to behave in an environment which offers as many of the physical characteristics of the real situation as possible.   He wants a steering wheel which is full-size; he wants pedals and levers which are realistic in terms of their spatial relationships to each other.   How can he provide these factors in the learner's environment?   He might use a real car, but he rejects the idea for budgetary reasons.   He might use a small model of a car, but this would not provide the full-scale spatial relationships which he considers essential.   Pictures, even three-dimensional ones, would not provide the opportunity for manipulation which is such an important aspect of the instruction which Mr. Borko wants to provide.   The solution is rather simple: the only instructional medium which has the capacity for providing the desired environment is a mock-up.

Some of the other aspects of the task are not as clear-cut. What about identifying the steps involved in starting the automobile? Each step has a name. The name can be presented orally or in writing. This is no great problem. But what about the referent? How shall the referent for "insert key in ignition switch" be presented? And "check to see that car is in neutral"? Should he actually perform the actions every time he wants to present these referents? Or will a simple line drawing suffice? Or will it be necessary to present these referents by means of a motion picture?

Consider the "live practice." What conditions should govern the student's practice while he is in the mock-up? Words? If so, should they be spoken or printed? Pictures? If so, should they be simple, cartoon-like drawings, detailed drawings, or actual photographs? Or should the student practice under conditions which present both words and pictures? If so, would a set of slides with an accompanying tape recording do the job best? Or would a sound motion picture be required?

MEDIA SELECTION

As indicated in earlier chapters, it is impossible to make a wise choice of instructional media without first deciding what conditions of learning are needed. What kind of environment is required?

In the following, either select, name, or describe the medium or media which could be used in order to facilitate the kind of learning indicated by the objective.

13 To identify the events in the cycle of a two-cycle internal combustion engine, given . . . Select the best answer:

a. still representations
b. moving representations
c. verbal descriptions
d. reality (i.e., the actual engine)

· · · · · ·

13 (b) Since motion is an inherent characteristic of the phenomenon, (a) would be a poor choice, (c) would be far too abstract, and (d), if made of metal, would not permit the learner to see the events of the cycle (even if made of transparent material, the engine would no doubt operate at a speed which would preclude the possibility of identifying the events in the cycle).

14 To order the distances between New York and Tokyo via the great circle route and via a "straight-line" route on any flat projection, given . . .

· · · · · ·

14 Since great circle routes are routes on the globe, a globe showing the two cities is needed. In addition, whatever flat maps are indicated in the "given" would have to include New York and Tokyo. Verbal descriptions of the maps would be virtually useless. Pictures of globes would be of little or no help.

15   To order the planets of the solar system according to size, given . . .

· · · · · ·

15   *A static representation in two dimensions would be adequate. A moving representation of the solar system would impose some difficulty, since comparison of planets which are of similar size would be difficult.*

16   Why not use a list of the names of the planets, in proper order, which the student must memorize?

· · · · · ·

16   *Only if the objective were an isolated one, unrelated to any or all other objectives in a unit on the solar system, would this merit consideration. Even then, there is a question as to whether the learner would be aided by a list which included both the names and some kind of figural or pictorial representation of the planets.*

Once the learning conditions for teaching students to order are defined, selection of a medium is relatively simple. Consider Example 13, above, in which the learner is to identify the events of a cycle. A moving representation is indicated. This could be a motion picture. There are motion pictures which use animation to present this phenomenon. However, several types of mock-ups could be used. These have the advantage of permitting a much wider variation of use by both teacher and students. A cut-away mock-up might be made of papier-mâché, in three dimensions; the parts would be movable, offering the teacher or students the opportunity to run the engine through its cycle. At the other extreme, a very simple two-dimensional mock-up could be made of construction paper or cardboard. The piston and valves could be constructed to move in appropriate synchronization by using brass fasteners to connect the several moving parts. It would be possible to do essentially the same with acetate and thus prepare an overhead transparency which possesses the potential of moving the pertinent parts.

What media would you use to bring about the conditions for learning listed in each of the following examples?

17   To order, from smallest to largest, the fractional parts of a circle, given parts of the circle with the appropriate fractions written on each part. . . . Only proper fractions having a denominator of 10 or less will be included.

· · · · · ·

17   *Flannelboard or magnetic board. The students can easily manipulate and arrange the parts. Changes in order are easily effected. The teacher has immediate access to any combination or permutation. Slides, filmstrips, pictures, and charts would be very poor choices, since they do not offer the flexibility of the boards mentioned above. The chalkboard is a poor choice, since it would be very difficult to maintain the relative sizes if one wished to move parts from one place to another for comparison.*

18   To order the movements of a symphony, given excerpts . . .

• • • • • • •

18   *Obviously, at least two possibilities exist. One might present audible excerpts which students are to arrange. Practice in attaining this objective would require the use of tape recordings and a phonograph. Conceivably the learner could be given excerpts from the symphony score. In that case, the teacher might well use overhead transparencies during the time the students are learning. A large number of transparencies, properly indexed, would provide the flexibility which such an instructional situation demands.*

Although testing as a part of the instructional system will be treated in Chapter 14, it is worthwhile noting now that in this example tapes, records, or transparencies could be used to form the basis of test items for the objective.

These examples lead us to an important generalization:

One of the most important considerations in selecting an instructional medium is the nature of the conditions specified in the objective.

The objective of the instruction will usually limit the media options open to the teacher. If the student is expected to respond to real objects, such as the automobile in the driver-training example, then he must be confronted with the real object (the automobile) or a nearly real object (a mock-up or working model) en route to the use of the real object.

If the student is expected to respond to auditory stimuli, as in ordering the movements of a symphony, then auditory materials must be used at some point in the instructional process.

However, this criterion needs further explanation. Simply selecting the instructional medium which most nearly presents those conditions specified in the objective is not always sufficient. For many objectives one medium is as appropriate as another. In the example concerning the ordering of the events in the cycle of a two-cycle internal combustion engine, a motion picture was selected as the best medium to reach the objective. It was pointed out that a three dimensional cut-away model, a moving paper model, or a "moving" transparency for the overhead projector would accomplish the same purpose. The common element is the movement. At this point other factors such as cost, availability, and technical quality might help to determine the selection. In ordering events chronologically the items can be described in a printed text, displayed as representations on the bulletin board, or projected from slides. In each case there is nothing in the objective which provides a clue as to which medium will be best.

SUMMARY

Check yourself to see whether you can do the things listed in the six statements of objectives at the beginning of the chapter. If you cannot, review the chapter again. If you can, move ahead to the next chapter, which deals with the *constructing* category.

CHAPTER EIGHT

TEACHING STUDENTS TO CONSTRUCT

WHEN YOU HAVE MASTERED THE CONTENT OF THIS CHAPTER,
YOU SHOULD BE ABLE TO:

1. DEFINE the term "construct."

2. DESCRIBE school learning situations in which the desired terminal behavior is to construct.

3. IDENTIFY objectives in this category.

4. CONSTRUCT objectives in this category.

5. DESCRIBE the conditions required to teach students to construct.

6. CONSTRUCT the rationale for choosing the medium (or media) best suited for establishing the conditions specified in objectives in the *construct* category.

THE NATURE OF CONSTRUCTING

When students make drawings, sew clothes, build furniture, draw maps, and create sets for plays they are *constructing*. When students write essays or produce examples of a given concept, they are constructing. The four previous chapters described categories in which we were concerned with either the learner's behavior or a product of his behavior. In this chapter, however, we are concerned solely with the latter; constructing is limited to products of learner behavior. As in the other categories, the product must meet pre-specified standards or criteria.

For example, the learner is constructing when he attains this objective: to write at least two statements of observation and two statements of inference, given pictures of two events. A student in a geometry class is constructing when he masters this objective: to draw an isosceles triangle, given ruler and compass; the equal sides must differ from each other by no more than ⅟₁₆ of an inch. Some of the terms used to designate "construct" are prepare, draw, make, build, and write.

At first glance it seems that most of these examples do not belong to the cognitive area. They seem to deal with motor skills rather than with knowledge. Isn't drawing a map or sewing a dress a psychomotor behavior? The drawing and the sewing are, indeed, motor activities. But so is writing. Yet no one places the objective "to describe in writing the process of currency devaluation . . ." in the psychomotor category, even though writing is obviously a motor activity. Why? Because the emphasis is on the product, not on the overt physical performance which results in the product. It is assumed that the learner already possesses the ability to write.

Likewise, objectives such as the following are used when the instructor is primarily interested in the product:

to make a drawing of the school . . .
to write an essay on education . . .
to sew a dress . . .
to build a footstool . . .

In each of the above, the standards of learner performance will relate to the quality of the drawing, the essay, the dress, or the footstool. The objective will not describe the manner in which the student draws, writes, sews, or builds. The difference between these two types of objectives is illustrated in the following statements:

1. To construct a map of the U.S., in which all states are colored some color other than blue, in which no two adjoining states are colored the same, in which all bodies of water are colored blue . . .
2. To construct with crayons a colored map of the 50 states given an outline map of the U.S., using unidirectional strokes of uniform weight, and holding the crayon in such a manner that the end of the crayon is pointing toward the shoulder as the student colors . . .

The first statement is an example of an objective in the constructing category, while the second is not. In the first example, the emphasis is clearly on the product. In an extreme sense, one could say that this objective permits the teacher to accept any product which meets the description, regardless of the coloring techniques or method employed by the student. The second example is quite different. It clearly implies that the teacher is primarily interested in the student's coloring technique, while the construction of the map merely provides a vehicle for applying the technique. The first objective is a correctly stated one, while the second is not. The teacher who wrote the second objective is interested in a psychomotor activity—coloring with crayons—and he should have written "to color with crayons, using strokes. . . ." Chapter 10, which is devoted to psychomotor objectives, covers this classification in detail.

At this point it is essential to know that you can distinguish between a constructing objective and a psychomotor objective by looking for the point of emphasis. If the objective places primary stress on the product and says little or nothing about the motor skill involved in producing the product, the objective belongs to the constructing category. If the emphasis is on the psychomotor skill, and if the product to be constructed is merely a vehicle, then the objective is not a constructing objective.

OBJECTIVES IN THE CONSTRUCTING CATEGORY

Tell whether each of the following is a constructing objective.

1   To construct a bibliography consistent with the format specified in the manual . . .

      •   •   •   •   •   •

1   *This one is a constructing objective. The emphasis is on the product, a bibliography.*

2   To construct a bibliography consistent with the format specified in the manual . . . using the method of note taking and data gathering discussed in class.

      •   •   •   •   •   •

2   *This one is also constructing. The emphasis is on the product, a bibliography.*
      Don't the words "using the method of note taking and data gathering" refer

to a motor activity? And doesn't this change the objective from a constructing objective to another type?

Actually, no. Certainly the teacher is not concerned with a special handwriting method or a special typing technique which is primarily suited to note taking. On the contrary, the teacher is concerned with the learner's constructing *notes which are suitable to the later construction of a bibliography. Likewise, the method of data gathering is nothing more nor less than the selection and organization of data by means of methods discussed in class. The focus of our attention is a product: a bibliography and a set of notes which meet a specified standard. The entire emphasis of this objective is on the* constructing *of a product, not on the motor activity involved in this constructing.*

The organizing and the note taking are not ends in themselves, but they are activities which lead to the ultimate end (or product), namely, a bibliography. The constructing called for in this objective—the production of a bibliography—is accomplished when, and only when, two other activities are used as means for attaining the terminal goal. The objective is clearly in the constructing *category.*

3   To prepare a table showing the relationship between x and y when $xy = 6$ . . .

    .   .   .   .

3   *This is* constructing. *One might just as well say "construct a table . . ."*

4   To hold the gouge in a manner consistent with shop safety standards while gouging a piece of wood on the lathe, given . . .

    .   .   .   .

4   *This is not constructing. The focus of instruction is on the method of holding the tool, not on the product.*

5   To use the 45° triangle in constructing diagonal lines on a drawing. The method of using the triangle must conform to the three rules on the chart posted in the classroom . . .

    .   .   .   .

5   *This, again, is not constructing. The emphasis is on the motor skills involved in applying the use of the triangle to a problem, not on the product itself. If this objective were to be a constructing objective, it would have to begin, "To construct diagonal lines, given a 45° triangle and . . . (The lines must meet the standards . . .)"*

6   To graph the population of Syracuse at five-year intervals from 1920 to 1965, given (a) references which contain the population figures for these years, (b) graph paper, and (c) pencil and ruler, within ten minutes. The graph must be either a line graph or a bar graph. It must meet the standards described in the film and filmstrip on graph construction shown previously.

    .   .   .   .

6   *This is* constructing. *The emphasis is clearly on the product.*

In summary, we can say that whenever the focus of attention is on the learner's product, the correct word to use is *construct*. When the primary interest is in the learner's behavior or performance while he is constructing the product, the term construct is not appropriate.

The conditions, or "givens," in objectives dealing with constructing behavior have a range even greater than that which was discussed in the chapter on *describing*. In constructing, the student may be given a word or term: construct an equilateral triangle. He may be given a description: construct a paragraph in which the topic sentence is at the end of the paragraph. He may be given a figural representation: construct a joint of the type shown in the sixth frame of the filmstrip. He may be given an actual event: construct a laboratory set-up which can be used to demonstrate the process which the class will observe on the second floor of the electroplating plant during tomorrow's field trip.

The standards which the student's product must meet are expressed in exactly the same manner as the standards for objectives in the *describing* category. The specifications must be stated in observable and identifiable terms. Often a variation from these specifications is acceptable; however, the amount or degree of variation must be specified with precision. The italicized words in the objectives below illustrate several ways of specifying the standards for objectives in the constructing category.

1. To construct an isosceles triangle, given pencil, straightedge, compass, unruled paper, and the instructions that the height of the triangle should be $>3''$ and $<5''$. All the *construction marks* used in the example on page 73 of the geometry text *must be shown*. The two *equal sides must be within* $\frac{1}{16}''$ *of being equal* to each other in length. The *length of the sides must be* within the specified limits, $\pm\frac{1}{8}''$. The student is given three minutes to complete the task.

2. To construct an essay on one of the following topics (a list of topics is included), given 50 minutes and unlimited access to the references discussed in class thus far. The essay *must meet all the standards listed in the summary* at the end of Chapter X in the English textbook. Note that in this objective one accepts, as implicitly stated, that there can be no deviation from the stated standards.

3. To construct an illustration, either graphic or verbal, of the concept "point of diminishing returns," given paper and pencil, within 15 minutes. *The illustration must be sufficiently clear that 80 percent of the members of the class who can name the concept, given the definition, will be able to name the concept given only the illustration and not the name.*

Below are several test items, descriptions of activities, and inadequately stated goals or aims. Write an objective for each which uses one of the five terms in the taxonomy. Your objective must possess the four characteristics of a behavioral objective described in Chapter 2.

7 A fourth grade reading class: The children are drawing pictures of what they read in the story "Up and Down." Each child is permitted to use the opaque projector to help him with his drawing, if he wishes.

· · · · · ·

7 *Apparently the purpose of the activity is to develop the learner's ability to produce a picture which illustrates some aspect of a story. The drawing skill is secondary; the product—a picture that corresponds in some way to the content of the story—is of prime concern. Consequently, the objective ought to be in the constructing category. The objective could be "To construct a drawing depicting some aspect of a given story from the basic reader, given paper and crayons and an opaque projector to be used if desired, and given ten minutes per drawing. The drawing must be of a standard such that 75 percent of the children who have read the story will be able to name the portion or incident of the story which the drawing purports to illustrate."*

8 A ninth grade general science class: the topic is the transmission of electricity. The teacher has prepared a lesson on transformers. His class has raised a number of questions concerning the problems involved in transforming current. The teacher has suggested that they view the motion picture film "Transformers," which contains a number of animated sequences in which both step-up and step-down transformers are described. The teacher wants his students to be able to diagram these two kinds of transformers at the end of the unit.

· · · · · ·

8 *To construct diagrams of step-up and step-down transformers, given paper and pencil, and given ten minutes. The diagrams must include at least the four essentials stressed when the film was shown. Each diagram must be sufficiently clear that 90 percent of the students who can name the transformer, given a written definition of it, will name the transformer given a student-constructed diagram.*

9 The students are given sections from motion pictures related to the period of history being studied. The sections range from three to seven minutes in length. The students are to write summaries which emphasize any cause-and-effect relationships which may be described in the given sections of the films.

· · · · · ·

9 *This one needs to be analyzed very carefully. Notice that they are given motion picture segments which presumably depict (a) cause-and-effect relationships and (b) other events, characteristics, and phenomena. They are to tell which parts of the film deal with the former and, by exclusion, which deal with everything else. In other words, they are to identify the cause-and-effect relationships in the film clips, given (a) filmed representations and (b) two categories, "cause-and-effect relationships" and "non-cause-and-effect relationships." They are to indicate which is which by summarizing the cause-and-effect relationships and by doing nothing with all other material in the films. This is one way of expressing the objective: to identify cause-and-effect relationships, given film clips of three to seven minutes length, by summarizing in writing the cause-and-effect relation-*

ships shown. Each summary must state the cause in one sentence and the effect in one sentence; both cause and effect must be clearly labeled. The student will be given five minutes for each summary, in addition to film-viewing time.

While it is unlikely that anyone would select describe *as the appropriate term to use in writing the objective for this item, there may be someone who selected* construct. *Why isn't "to construct a summary . . ." the appropriate choice? If constructing summaries is the primary goal, then it is the appropriate choice. If, however, the primary goal relates to the content of the history unit and the ability to recognize cause-and-effect relationships in the context of a given historical period, then the objective clearly is one of* identifying. *In this example, writing summary statements is something the learner must be able to do before he begins working on the attainment of this objective. This is no different from expecting a first grader to be able to draw a line before he begins working on the attainment of this objective: "to identify the primary colors, given pictures of objects colored red, yellow, or blue, and given the names . . . The learner indicates his ability to identify the colors by drawing a line from the object to the name of the correct color." In the former example the entering behavior, or the prerequisite, for the attainment of the objective is "to write summaries," while in the latter it is "to draw lines."*

This example should illustrate once again that identifying *is not necessarily an extremely simple type of behavior. It is simple or difficult only in a given context.* Identifying *is called for in kindergarten instruction; it is also an important aspect of instruction in courses in high school or even in graduate school.*

10   Test item: The students watch a motion picture entitled "Joe Is a Pilot Now." Write three sentences. In the first, tell us what Joe did as soon as he saw the plane. In the second, ask someone what Joe did as soon as he saw the plane. In the third sentence, make believe that you were there; tell Joe what to do as soon as he sees the plane.

$$\bullet \qquad \bullet \qquad \bullet \qquad \bullet \qquad \bullet \qquad \bullet$$

10   *It is not likely that the teacher is primarily interested in the student's ability to reconstruct elements of the story which the film told. Rather, it is quite apparent that this test item is designed to ascertain whether the student can write declarative, interrogative, and imperative sentences, given an "idea" for the sentences. Therefore, the proper statement of the objective is "To construct a declarative, an interrogative, and an imperative sentence, given a filmed sequence to provide the 'thought' of the sentence, within two minutes. Each sentence must be a complete sentence with correct terminal punctuation."*

Attaining Objectives

Mrs. Baker teaches English. Each October her students learn to construct outlines. As one of her activities, Mrs. Baker gives the class a five-paragraph prose selection as well as five main headings and ten sub-headings. She leads them to arrange the fifteen components in a suitable order and to include proper indentation and alignment.

What kinds of conditions should Mrs. Baker provide in the learner's environment? We would suggest that samples of outlines, showing physical characteristics such as alignment, are necessary. We would also find it highly desirable to have components which are easily arranged and rearranged until a finished acceptable outline is produced.

Mr. Sullivan teaches chemistry. In a unit on laboratory methods and procedures, he wants his students to learn to distill liquids. He is concerned with their acquiring the ability to set up the proper equipment for distilling, and to use the equipment in conformity with laboratory safety standards. The first objective for his students is "to construct a distillation apparatus within three minutes, given the equipment at a student station. The set-up must include all the elements given on page 12 of the manual. The student may not refer to the manual."

How can he teach his students to acquire this constructing skill? Obviously, a flat picture in a lab manual might provide some help for a learner. If some of the parts are difficult to picture in two dimensions, it might be well to provide a three-dimensional representation of the setup. If a certain order ought to be observed, it might be most effective to choose some means showing how the setup is developed step by step. It is obvious, then, that two characteristics are essential: The instructional material must be three-dimensional or it must be capable of representing three dimensions easily, and the material must have the capability of showing an order in the setting up of the apparatus.

Describe the characteristics of the instructional materials which would be needed to teach effectively for the attainment of the following objectives. You need not select a medium at this time. Merely telling what conditions you want will be sufficient.

11 To construct an angle equal to a given angle, given compass and straightedge, within one minute. Construction marks must be visible. Deviations of 3° or less, as measured with a protractor, will be accepted.

•   •   •   •   •   •

11 *Since there is an optimum order of procedure, a series of illustrations would be required. Examples of several types of angles, such as acute, right, and obtuse, should be presented.*

12 To construct three complete sentences orally, given a situation which the student must describe, within 20 seconds. The sentences must meet the three standards listed on the classroom chart.

•   •   •   •   •   •

12 *A number of alternatives are possible, due in part to the fact that there is a slight degree of ambiguity in the objective. Students could be given a "real" situation: something they can see from the classroom window, or something the teacher or a student has brought to the classroom. Students could be given a "contrived" situation: a classmate or classmates act or dramatize something. They could be given the representation of a situation: a drawing or a photograph or a moving picture. They could even be given words orally; their task could be to complete the story in three sentences. Actually, in a classroom situation a good teacher would probably want to use all of these conditions at one time or another as this objective is being implemented.*

MEDIA SELECTION

These exercises are designed to give you practice in identifying a medium of instruction, given characteristics of instructional conditions. You know the names of the various media. Choose the appropriate medium or media for each example.

13   Mrs. Baker (see p. 166) teaches her students to construct an outline. It has been suggested that she will need samples of outlines, showing such physical characteristics as indentation and alignment. She will also need components which can be arranged and rearranged easily either by herself or by her students. What medium should she employ? Why?

•   •   •   •   •   •

13   *The outline could be printed on a chart. Components of the outline might be prepared in advance and arranged to form a bulletin board. Slides or overhead transparencies could be prepared. A filmstrip could be as easy to use as a set of overhead transparencies. Two aspects of the instruction should be considered. First, the model outline or outlines, prepared in advance on a transparency, would be better than a chart, a set of slides, or a filmstrip. Second, the 15 components, if prepared on acetate strips, can be manipulated easily by teacher or students or both. Thus, faulty arrangements can be discussed whenever they occur, and they can be rearranged quickly and easily. Only the flannelboard offers as much flexibility for this second characteristic. Even the versatile chalkboard is inferior for this instructional task, since a change in arrangement necessitates erasing and rewriting—a needless waste of time when an overhead projector or flannelboard is available.*

14   Mr. Sullivan, the chemistry teacher (p. 167), needs instructional materials which will enable him to present the three-dimensional characteristics of certain pieces of equipment and the order involved in assembling the pieces.

•   •   •   •   •   •

14   *To begin with, three-dimensional characteristics can be portrayed quite readily by a medium other than a mock-up or a model. If Mr. Sullivan wants to show his students a specific angularity which characterizes a piece of glass tubing, he can use a motion picture in which the tubing is turned in various directions as it is photographed. Thus, the students can learn to identify certain three-dimensional characteristics from a two-dimensional medium. The motion picture is also excellent for presenting a predetermined sequence of steps—something which a model, a mock-up, or a real set-up could do much less effectively. If a short motion-picture clip were available, or could be produced, it would be an excellent instructional medium for the purpose described. Local production on silent 8mm film or videotape would be highly feasible, since no sound is necessary.*

       It should be emphasized that other media could be used very well. Frequently a teacher does an excellent job with a second or third choice, simply because the first choice is not accessible.

15   If the 8mm film, or any kind of film, were not available for the problem posed in Example 14, above, what would you choose as an instructional medium?

•   •   •   •   •   •

15   First, remember that there is no one right answer for this question. To teach students to identify the characteristics of the components of the setup, a teacher could use any one of a variety of media: drawings, still photographs, real objects, and the like. These might be presented on a bulletin board (pictures or drawings), on an overhead projector (drawings and certain kinds of real objects), or on an opaque projector (pictures, drawings, or certain kinds of real objects). One might have a series of charts showing the progression, in the required order, of steps involved in setting up the apparatus.

SUMMARY

Now evaluate your own progress. Can you do the things listed in the objectives at the beginning of this chapter? If you cannot, review the chapter. If you can, you are ready for the next chapter, which deals with objectives which are quite different from those discussed in this and the four preceding chapters. We now leave the cognitive area and move into the affective domain.

CHAPTER NINE

TEACHING STUDENTS ATTITUDES: THE AFFECTIVE DOMAIN

W<small>HEN YOU HAVE MASTERED THE CONTENT OF THIS CHAPTER,</small>
<small>YOU SHOULD BE ABLE TO:</small>

1. DEFINE "affective domain."

2. DESCRIBE school learning situations in which the desired terminal behavior belongs to the affective domain.

3. IDENTIFY behaviorally and nonbehaviorally stated objectives in the affective domain.

4. CONSTRUCT objectives in this category, using either of the methods described in this chapter.

5. DESCRIBE the conditions required to teach students an attitude.

6. CONSTRUCT the rationale for choosing the medium (or media) best suited for establishing the conditions specified in objectives related to the affective domain.

Less is known about the subject of developing a learner's attitudes than about any other area discussed in this book. The problem stems from two sources: there is wide disagreement among teachers concerning the nature of attitudes, and there is even more disagreement concerning methods of teaching for the development of attitudes. Despite these areas of disagreement, most teachers believe that attitudes are as important as, or even more important than, cognitive abilities or psychomotor skills. Even though a teacher may ignore attitudes while teaching mathematics or music or history, attitudes will be developing constantly during the instruction. In other words, attitudes may be formed even though a teacher may be consciously ignoring them while carrying on his instructional activities.

Frequently one encounters the term *affective* domain. In Chapter 2 you read that objectives of elementary and secondary school instruction can be classified in one of three domains: cognitive, psychomotor, or affective. The affective domain deals with attitudes. It also deals with students' interests, with how well they like specified things (even with how well they like what they are learning), with valuing, and with motivation. In this chapter the term *attitude*, in its broadest sense. is used to cover all of these facets; the affective domain is concerned with *attitudes* in this broad sense of the word.

WHAT IS AN ATTITUDE?

The words used to describe outcomes in the titles for Chapters 4 to 8 are behavioral terms: teaching students to identify, to name, etc. The title for this chapter, which deals with the affective domain, is worded differently: teaching students attitudes. This is not a behavioral expression; the word *attitude* is subject to many interpretations. This chapter discusses two methods of defining attitudes behaviorally. While these two systems are not the only ones available to a teacher, they are powerful enough to enable anyone to produce behavioral objectives in the affective domain.

The Taxonomy Project System

Developed by David Krathwohl and others,[1] this system is based upon a classification structure for the affective domain which the authors assert

[1]David R. Krathwohl, Benjamin S. Bloom, and Bertram B. Masia, *Taxonomy of Educational Objectives—Handbook II: Affective Domain* (New York: David McKay, 1964).

can be used to classify both objectives and test items. The table of contents of *Handbook II* provides a comprehensive overview of both the structure and the scope of this attempt to develop a taxonomy, or classification scheme, for the affective domain.

1.0 Receiving (Attending)
    1.1 Awareness
    1.2 Willingness to Receive
    1.3 Controlled or Selected Attention

2.0 Responding
    2.1 Acquiescence in Responding
    2.2 Willingness to Respond
    2.3 Satisfaction in Response

3.0 Valuing
    3.1 Acceptance of a Value
    3.2 Preference for a Value
    3.3 Commitment

4.0 Organization
    4.1 Conceptualization of a Value
    4.2 Organization of a Value System

5.0 Characterization by a Value or Value Complex
    5.1 Generalized Set
    5.2 Characterization[2]

Handbook II includes, for each subheading, a number of illustrative educational objectives, a discussion of problems involved in measuring the behavior described by this class of objectives, and selected examples from actual tests. The Taxonomy Project System has achieved a considerable degree of acceptance among educators. There is no doubt that it is helpful to teachers who are concerned about the problem of stating objectives related to attitudes and measuring the degree to which students have attained them. However, the teacher who can construct objectives of the type described in Chapters 4–8 will find that most examples in *Handbook II* can be restated in terms of one of these five categories: identify, name, describe, order, construct.

The Approach-Avoidance System[3]

Hamlet said, "To be or not to be, that is the question." Father tells John, "You can't have your cake and eat it too." The coach advises the basketball player who arrives late for practice, "Shape up or ship out." The college sophomore debates the merits of a 7:00 a.m. section taught by a professor who assigns very little outside reading or a 9:00 a.m. section taught by one who assigns a great deal.

[2]Krathwohl, Bloom, and Masia, *Taxonomy—Handbook II*, pp. xii–xiv.
[3]For an interesting discussion of the Approach-Avoidance System from a psychologist's perspective, view the film *Conflict* (18 min., b & w, sound, McGraw-Hill Textfilms).

Analyze each of these situations. Hamlet is confronted with a conflict concerning life: Is it better to commit suicide or to continue living? To put it differently, he must choose between *approaching* suicide or *avoiding* it.

Examine each of the following. Label each part as an approach tendency or avoidance tendency.

1 You can't have your cake and eat it too. "Having your cake" is something which John wants to———(approach, avoid). "Eating it" is something he wants to———(approach, avoid).

•   •   •   •   •   •

1 *"Having his cake" is something which John wants. One would say that this belongs in the* approach *category. "Eating it" is also something which John wants to do. Obviously, the answer is again* approach. *Note well, however, that the only way one can answer these two questions is by observing what John does. If he keeps his cake for 12 hours, he manifests an approach tendency toward "keeping cake." Note also that there is an obverse, or negative, interpretation possible for each event. If he keeps his cake for 12 hours, John is manifesting an avoidance tendency toward "eating his cake," while if he eats his cake, he is manifesting an avoidance tendency toward "having it." Remember: It is not what John* wants *to do that is a matter of concern; rather, it is what he* does.

2 Analyze the "Shape up or ship out" demand of the coach in terms of approach and avoidance. (Assume that the behavioral definition of "shape up" is equivalent to remaining on the basketball squad, while to "ship out" means that the player drops basketball.)

•   •   •   •   •   •

2 *If the player comes to practice on time, he is manifesting an approach tendency toward "shaping up" or toward remaining on the basketball squad. If he comes to practice on time for 20 consecutive practices, he has attained the following objective: to manifest an approach tendency toward basketball by coming to practice on time for at least 20 consecutive practices. One could also say that the player is manifesting an avoidance tendency toward "shipping out"; he avoids behaving in such a manner that he would be dropped from the squad.*

If he reports late for practice the next day, one could say that he is manifesting an approach tendency toward quitting the basketball squad or that he is manifesting an avoidance tendency toward any of the following:

a. "shaping up"
b. coming to practice on time
c. remaining on the squad
d. basketball practice

What if he was late for practice because he stopped to help a child who had suffered an injury caused by a fall on a slippery patch of ice on the sidewalk? Could one accurately say that the player manifested an avoidance tendency toward "shaping up" if his tardiness took place under such circumstances? The complete answer to this question will be discussed below (pp. 177–82). It is sufficient at this point to say that one might state the objective: to manifest an approach tendency toward basketball practice by reporting on time every day (or for five consecutive practices or for the remainder of the season), unless excused by the coach. Remember, the affective domain is a difficult area; it is impossible to cover every dimension of affective objectives at the very beginning of a discussion.

3 Classify the example of the conflict of the 7:00 a.m. light assignment class vs. the 9:00 a.m. heavy assignment class by using the terms under discussion. Assume that the sophomore is one who has to be called three or four times before he finally gets out of bed mornings and that, given a choice of reading for a class assignment or socializing with fellow students in the dormitory, he does the latter more frequently.

•   •   •   •   •   •

3 *These are all the possibilities. If he registers for the 7:00 a.m. section he is manifesting an approach tendency toward:*

a. *a 7:00 a.m. class*
b. *a professor who gives light assignments*
c. *both*

He is also manifesting an avoidance tendency toward:

a. *a 9:00 a.m. class*
b. *a professor who gives heavy assignments*
c. *both*

If he registers for the 9:00 a.m. section he is manifesting an approach tendency toward:

a. *a 9:00 a.m. class*
b. *a professor who gives heavy assignments*
c. *both*

Or one could say that our sophomore is manifesting an avoidance tendency toward:

a. *a 7:00 a.m. class*
b. *a professor who gives light assignments*
c. *both*

Given the assumptions above, only these alternatives are acceptable:

avoidance tendency — 7:00 a.m. class
heavy assignments
approach tendency — 9:00 a.m. class
light assignments

Obviously, in Example 3 (as well as in the preceding ones) there is a conflict situation. "To be" is in conflict with "not to be." Having one's cake is incompatible with eating it. The basketball player must choose between tardiness and basketball; he can't have both. For the sophomore, it's either "get up early" and escape a considerable amount of study or stay in bed mornings and study late. In school situations objectives in the affective domain are often related to resolution of conflict, but this is not a necessary requirement.

A teacher may try to develop a positive attitude in his students toward lyric poetry without forcing a choice, say, between lyric and narrative forms. An objective for such a situation is "to manifest an approach tendency toward lyric poetry by voluntarily reading at least ten lyric poems from the books on the interest table within the next week." Suppose, however, that the students have a tendency to choose literature of an extremely poor quality for their free reading activities, and the teacher wants to up-grade the quality of their choice of reading material. He could state his goal in either of the following ways, but it would be more likely that he would adopt both statements:

> to manifest an approach tendency toward good literature by voluntarily reading for class only literature listed on the bulletin board and by reading at least five of these selections during the next two weeks . . .

> to manifest an avoidance tendency toward poor literature by reading only selections from the approved list, given a choice of these selections and those of poor quality as defined by the characteristics of poor literature posted on the bulletin board . . .

OBJECTIVES RELATED TO ATTITUDES

How are objectives related to attitudes stated? A cursory glance at typical teacher's manuals, courses of study, or curriculum guides reveals that there is no generally accepted pattern other than that of using ambiguous or easily misunderstood words. Phrases such as "willingness to participate," "acceptance of a viewpoint," "enjoyment of self-expression," "growth in assumption of responsibility," or "readiness to revise judgments" are characteristic of ambiguous or easily misinterpreted statements. Some kind of system is needed to help the teacher translate such statements into behavioral objectives.

Taxonomy Project System Objectives

Two methods of accomplishing this "translation" are explained in this chapter. The first, and more complex, is accomplished by expressing affective objectives in terms of the five cognitive categories: identify, name, describe, order, or construct. Examples taken from the five categories of the Taxonomy Project System are provided below, together with practice exercises designed to enable the reader to do this kind of translation. As a result, it should be possible to take an objective worded in the terminology of the Taxonomy Project System and reformulate it in a statement which meets the four requirements for a well-stated objective.

Why, one has a right to ask, are the statements of the Taxonomy Project the only ones to be considered? Aren't there many other statements of affective objectives? The answer is that there are, indeed! However, it is a fairly simple matter to classify any statement describing a desired affective outcome in one of the Taxonomy System categories. This done, one simply reformulates the statement according to the method explained below. The Taxonomy Project System, then, is used in one of two ways:

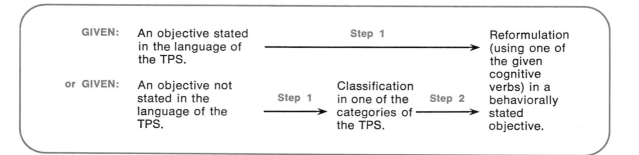

GIVEN: An objective stated in the language of the TPS. → Step 1 → Reformulation (using one of the given cognitive verbs) in a behaviorally stated objective.

or GIVEN: An objective not stated in the language of the TPS. → Step 1 → Classification in one of the categories of the TPS. → Step 2 →

The second, and simpler, procedure for constructing behavioral objectives related to attitudes (or affective behavior) is to express the desired outcome in terms of approach or avoidance tendencies. If it were possible to express all objectives in elementary or secondary schools in this manner, the first strategy would be wasteful and unnecessary. Unfortunately, there are some types of objectives which are too complicated, or not clearly enough understood, to permit this.

4 State this objective in behavioral form: Awareness of the multiplication process as a means of solving problems. (This objective is taken from a modern mathematics course of study for third graders. The learner has been exposed to two processes, addition and multiplication; now he is to "become aware of the greater efficiency of the multiplication process.")

· · · · · ·

4 *The simplest statement of this objective is "to identify the simpler process for solving problems, given the written names* addition *and* multiplication *as alternative processes, and given word problems which can be solved more efficiently by multiplication; the learner must respond correctly to eight of ten examples within five minutes." However, there are other possible answers to this question because no one knows exactly what is meant by the "awareness" objective.*

5 This objective is from the *responding* category of the Taxonomy Project System. Formulate it in behavioral terms: "interests himself in social problems broader than those of the local community."[4]

· · · · · ·

5 *Given a choice of assignments dealing with social problems of the local community as opposed to social problems of the state or nation, to choose the latter.*

[4]Krathwohl, Bloom, and Masia. *Taxonomy—Handbook II*, p. 126.

(Perhaps you have noticed that this is a form of identifying; however, one would hardly use the word identify in this context, since choose is unambiguous and since the expression would be clumsier if identify were used.)

6 Again, many alternative expressions would be just as acceptable as an answer in Example 5. Why?

• • • • • •

6 *No one knows exactly what the learner who has "interested himself" does to show his newly acquired interest. The learner must do something which will permit the teacher to say, "Now Johnny has interested himself in broader social problems."*

7 Another category is *valuing*. One subcategory of valuing is *commitment*. Krathwohl says about this subcategory: "Commitment is never a momentary or occasional enthusiasm or passion which is here today and gone tomorrow or next week. . . . The holding of the value over an extended period of time is not in itself sufficient evidence of a commitment to it. There must also be a considerable investment of energy. . . . There should be actions in behalf of the value, belief, or sentiment—actions which by their very nature imply a commitment."[5] As an illustration of an objective in this category, he cites "Faith in the methods of experiment. . . ."[6] Reformulate the objective in behavioral terms; as you do so, try to include the thoughts expressed in the quotation concerning the meaning of commitment.

• • • • • •

7 *Given problems amenable to solution by experiment and given other types of problems, to select problems of the former type; the two types of problems must be of such nature that a somewhat greater investment of time or energy is required for solving the former type. The learner must persist in this behavior from the time that the subject has been covered in both class and laboratory at least until the end of the semester.*

Once again, many alternative answers are acceptable. The critical points are that (a) the behavior endures over a period of time—"until the end of the semester"; (b) there must be a considerable investment of energy involved in the decision and in the consequences of the decision to use an experimental method.

8 The fourth category in *Handbook II* is *organization*; a subcategory is organization of a *value system*. An illustrative objective is "Rejects stereotypes of people of various races. . . ."[7] Reformulate this objective. (Assume that the meaning of this objective includes exposing the learner to conditions under which he has the alternative, among others, of rejecting stereotypes presented to him.)

• • • • • •

8 *Given motion picture clips showing members of the Negro, the Chinese, and the American Indian races in stereotyped and nonstereotyped roles, the learner will*

---

[5]Krathwohl, Bloom, and Masia, *Taxonomy—Handbook II*, p. 150.
[6]Krathwohl, Bloom, and Masia, *Taxonomy—Handbook II*, p. 150.
[7]Krathwohl, Bloom, and Masia, *Taxonomy —Handbook II*, p. 161.

identify as giving him pleasure those which present people in nonstereotyped roles; he will identify as the objectionable elements in the film clips those segments which portray the subjects in a stereotyped role.

Obviously, the teacher will look for consistency and perserverance in rejecting the objectionable portrayals; when he finds this consistency and perseverance, he will infer that the learner "rejects stereotypes of people of various races." The degree of consistency and perseverance can be stated in precise terms, e.g., in 100 percent of the situations presented.

The fifth category, characterization by a value or a value complex, is so difficult to work with that no exercise is provided in this book. Krathwohl says of this category, "Rarely, if ever are the sights of educational objectives set to this level. . . . Realistically, formal education generally cannot reach this level, at least in our society. . . . The maturity required at this level [is] not attained until at least some years after the individual has completed his formal education."[8]

In Examples 4–8 all the suggested answers employed the term *identify*, or an equivalent. This does not imply that the categories of the affective domain can be equated with identifying; indeed, objectives in each of these categories can be expressed, generally, in terms of all of the five cognitive verbs. In the exercises below, reformulate the objectives using verbs other than identify or its equivalents.

9   Mrs. Steel teaches "Problems of Family Living" in a senior high school. She tries to show how important nonvocational activities are in the life of adults in modern society. She employs a large number of film clips to show nonvocational activities and to contrast the life of an adult who devotes some time to nonvocational activities with the life of one who does not. When asked to state her objective, she replied, "I want my students to realize how important nonvocational activities are in adult life."

Restate her objective. If it is helpful to you, think first of one of the affective categories listed on p. 174. Then express the outcome in terms of one of the five verbs discussed in Chapters 4–8, or, if you prefer, use any other unambiguous verb.

· · · · · · · ·

9   *The objective is an example of one belonging to Category 1.0, Receiving (Attending); Subcategory 1.1, Awareness.*

Given film clips showing adults whose lives are balanced and other clips showing adults whose lives are not balanced, the student will name the nonvocational activities manifest in the former, and he will refrain from attempting to name nonvocational activities when presented with the latter. The student will perform this task perfectly, given 15 seconds to respond orally to each clip. (Many other answers are acceptable.)

10 Mr. Gardner wants his students to show that they have begun to form their own dominant values. He uses a method of role-playing to simulate

[8]Krathwohl, Bloom, and Masia. *Taxonomy—Handbook II*, p. 165.

conditions under which the examples should manifest themselves. Yesterday Mr. Gardner used a slide projector to show his class the frescoes which Michelangelo painted on the ceiling of the Sistine Chapel. Then he asked for reactions to the paintings. Each student is permitted to record his own reactions on tape. Later the class discusses these recordings in terms of six types of values: (a) theoretical, (b) economic, (c) aesthetic, (d) social. (e) political, and (f) religious. Each student attempts to determine which value system is dominant in his own life. Mr. Gardner attempts to help each learner accept (or change) his own value system and to develop behavior patterns consistent with the individual's chosen dominant value system. What is Mr. Gardner's objective? (Again, go through the affective categories en route to your statement if it helps you to do so.)

• • • • • • •

10 *Category 4.0, Organization; Subcategory 4.2, Organization of a Value System. Suggested objective: to construct a system of dominant values; given situations to which a reaction occurs, the reactions will be classified as belonging to a single one of the following six categories at least 75 percent of the time. . . Reactions should occur within 30 seconds after completion of the presentation of the situation. (This is only one of many possible answers.)*

11 Mrs. Roberts wants her fifth graders to extend their interests in the field of literature. She believes that children should enjoy reading on a variety of themes, and she uses bulletin boards as one means of helping to create wider interests. When the unit of instruction, which requires three weeks, is completed, she compares the students' responses on a post-unit inventory with those which were gathered on a pre-unit inventory. Students were directed, on each occasion, to list in order of their personal preference the themes about which they enjoy reading. Mrs. Roberts rated the responses in two ways: (a) she assigned a score value based on the number of themes listed and (b) she assigned another score value based on the degree to which the order of the students' preference corresponded to a value scheme discussed in class. What was Mrs. Roberts trying to accomplish, in terms of behavioral objectives?

• • • • • • •

11 *Category 2.0, Responding; Subcategory 2.3, Satisfaction in Response. Her objective: to enjoy reading books on a variety of themes; this enjoyment manifested by:*

a. naming an increasing number of themes from which enjoyment is derived and
b. ordering these "enjoyed themes" in a manner consistent with the value scheme discussed in class, in which themes that glorify or glamorize crime are rated lowest and themes that praise unselfishness (as manifested by man's service to his fellow man) are rated highest.

The question may be asked, "Is naming (or ordering) on an interest inventory the same as enjoying?" There is no right or wrong answer to this question. If

Mrs. Roberts is satisfied with this kind of definition of enjoying, *then she should use it. If someone else feels that enjoying involves more or less than the naming and ordering described above, then it is up to him to state what it is that students do when they are* enjoying.

Are responses to questions on an attitude inventory equivalent to the attitude? In the illustration above, does the student who names *and* orders *in a manner which meets Mrs. Roberts' criteria really enjoy reading on a variety of themes? Again, this is a question which Mrs. Roberts must decide. In order to decide intelligently, she ought to know something about test validity and other matters related to educational measurement. Additional considerations involved in the use of media for testing or measurement are discussed in Chapter 14.*

12   Mr. Tyler wants his students to develop the desire to attain optimum health. He uses films, still pictures, tape-recorded anecdotes, and several other media to show good health habits and their consequent benefits as well as poor health habits and their undesirable consequences. During the course of instruction, he leads the students to verbalize both orally and in writing, principles which they ought to follow if they wish to attain optimum health. At the end of the unit he asks a student to state a health principle.

•   •   •   •   •   •

12   *Category 3.0, Valuing; Subcategory 3.1, Acceptance of a Value. The objective: to describe practices which help one attain optimum health, given examples of good and poor health habits and the results of each.*

The preceding four examples provided an opportunity for translating nonbehavioral objectives into behavioral ones using the Taxonomy Project System as an intermediate aid. If this two-step procedure, from nonbehavioral statement to (1) Taxonomy Project System category to (2) behavioral objective, seems to work well for you, it is absolutely essential that you acquire *Handbook II* and master its content to the extent that you can easily and consistently categorize nonbehavioral objectives dealing with affect. Some teachers may prefer the one step method: to go directly from the nonbehavioral statement to a behavioral objective. The prime advantage of the two-step procedure is that the Taxonomy Project System provides a checklist; it helps one guard against the inadvertent omission of desired outcomes in the affective domain.

Approach-Avoidance Objectives

The approach-avoidance method of describing outcomes in the affective domain may appear, at first glance, to be much simpler than the Taxonomy Project System. It may be. However, the problem of specifying conditions under which the desired approach or avoidance behavior is to occur is somewhat formidable. When all is said and done, the choice of the system must ultimately be decided on the basis of the answer to the question, "Which works better for me?"

In the following exercises, decide what it is that the teacher is trying to accomplish. Then write an objective to describe the desired outcome using the approach-avoidance procedure.

13   Mr. Reid wants his students to display an interest in voluntary reading.

.   •   •   •   •   •   •   •

13   To manifest an approach tendency toward reading (excluding any reading required to complete c, below) for at least 20 minutes on at least four days each week, given 30 minutes free time each afternoon in which he may (a) read, (b) draw or paint, or (c) work on any of tomorrow's assignments.

14   Mr. Watson wants his students to enjoy a musical experience. In order to achieve this end, he decides to build positive, interesting, meaningful images in preparation for the musical experience itself. He feels that if he sets a tone of pleasing excitement and anticipation, the new experience will have pleasant associations. Try to express, in terms of approach or avoidance behavior, what Mr. Watson wants to accomplish.

•   •   •   •   •   •

14   Given a choice of listening to music or engaging in another activity for which the learner has previously manifested an approach tendency, the learner will manifest an approach tendency toward the music listening at least 50 percent of the time.

This is an example of learning an "attitude." Sometimes students can learn attitudes by association. Mr. Watson uses certain motion picture films which the children enjoy; he knows that they enjoy them because, when given a choice, the children ask to see these films in preference to others. The background music is the type which Mr. Watson wants his children to enjoy. He expects the favorable attitude toward the films to become gradually associated with the music. Ultimately, if the instructional strategy is effective, the students will manifest an approach tendency toward the music, even in the absence of the films.

There is also potential danger in teaching attitudes by association. The propagandist capitalizes on the fact that the learner may not think about whether the new object really merits the same response as the old one. If a teacher uses this technique to present as equivalents things which are not, he is doing the learner a disservice. An attitude which ought to accompany the kind of instructional strategy just described is one of analysis.

15   Mr. Watson wants his students to keep checking their attitudes because he wants every individual to be certain that his attitudes are appropriate and relevant to the new situation. For example, he wants each student to be certain in his own mind that enjoying music is an appropriate attitude for him. Try writing this objective in behavioral terms.

•   •   •   •   •   •

15   As was pointed out earlier, there are many instances where it is virtually impossible to decide whether an objective belongs in the cognitive or in the affective domain. This is a good example. However, because this section deals with the approach-avoidance system, most readers will have attempted to write an approach or an avoidance objective:

> *Given a set of criteria for determining whether an attitude is relevant or appropriate, to choose music listening in preference to watching films without music only when the music meets the standards of the given criteria and to avoid (i.e., not choose) music listening when the music does not meet these standards.*

It is obvious that there is a great deal of cognitive behavior implicit in this objective:

> *to identify attitudes which meet acceptable criteria and which do not meet these criteria, given examples of each . . .*
>
> *to order one's attitudes according to the degree to which they meet specified criteria . . .*
>
> *to construct a system for deciding whether one's attitudes are relevant and appropriate to a particular situation . . .*

This points out once again the importance of teaching for the attainment of many objectives simultaneously. It is impossible to think of any objective in the affective domain that is not related to one or several cognitive or psychomotor objectives; neither are there cognitive objectives which can be attained in an affective vacuum. Robert Mager develops this concept in an interesting little book, *Developing Attitude Toward Learning.*[9] Read it. It will provide you with a thoroughgoing analysis of the approach (but not the avoidance) system for writing behavioral objectives related to the affective domain.

16   Mrs. Wall teaches first grade. In her health and safety curriculum one of the goals is to teach the children to respect the deadliness of certain types of poison. One of the symbols which she uses is the skull and crossbones. Write an objective related to this situation.

   •   •   •   •   •   •

16   *To avoid poisonous materials by refraining from opening, handling, or touching containers marked with a skull and crossbones, given an opportunity to do so, 100 percent of the time.*

Mrs. Wall is limited to instruction at school, during school hours. Since there are no poisons in the child's school environment, Mrs. Wall must teach in such a manner that the avoidance behavior will be maintained outside the school. This is not a simple task. However, Mrs. Wall will do much to help her children achieve the objective if she shows films or filmstrips depicting the unpleasant, or even deadly, consequences which may occur when the skull and crossbones is not avoided. She may also use mock-ups of poison containers in a simulated home environment in order to provide an opportunity for practicing the avoidance behavior.

[9]Robert F. Mager, *Developing Attitude Toward Learning*, (Palo Alto: Fearon, 1968).

17 Why would Mrs. Wall choose mock-ups instead of real objects in this lesson?

* * * * * *

17 If real objects (actual containers of poison) were used, there is a danger that a child might be inadvertently harmed. The mock-up[10] guards against the possibility of such an undesirable accident.

18 In Mr. Darsie's class of seventh graders, all but two boys seem to dislike poetry. He wants them to develop a genuine liking for poetry. Write an appropriate objective. Tell what medium of instruction you would use and why.

* * * * * *

18 To approach poetry by choosing to read poetry on at least 50 percent of the occasions, given a choice of reading poetry or reading dramas.

Mr. Darsie decides to capitalize on the general need of seventh grade boys for masculine approval. He finds examples of famous persons, respected by seventh grade boys, who in some way or other manifest an approach tendency toward poetry. He then produces a series of 35mm slides and accompanying tape recording to present this information.

Ronald Lippit once said, "It is easier to smash an atom than to break a prejudice."[11] One should not believe that a single instructional act, such as the one just described, will succeed in overcoming a group of seventh grade boys' hostility to poetry. However, the example might be one in a long chain of acts which leads to the attainment of the objective.

19 Mr. Reese decided to acquaint his students with local ecology and the problems of pollution in their school and community. With what category from the affective taxonomy was he probably concerned?

* * * * * *

19 Awareness.

20 Write an objective related to the awareness category; state the conditions in such a manner that your selection of the media of instruction is apparent.

* * * * * *

20 Given a series of previously unencountered still pictures, color slides, and 8mm film clips depicting individuals or institutions in the act of polluting the environment, the students will demonstrate an awareness of the various forms of pollution by correctly identifying all examples of pollution.

Mr. Reese listed still pictures, color slides, and 8mm film clips in his statement of conditions. You may wonder why a field trip was not mentioned. Actually, Mr. Reese took his students on a field trip *during the*

[10]Remember: A mock-up is an edited version of something real. In this case, the mock-up might be a thoroughly clean bottle which once contained poison and which still has its label with the skull and crossbones.
[11]Ronald Lippitt, "Preface," *The Journal of Social Issues*, V. 1, No. 3 (August, 1945), pp. 1–2.

time of instruction. In order to reconstruct the acts of pollution, Mr. Reese took pictures both before and after the field trip, and he encouraged his students to take pictures during the field trip. These pictures served as a record of the field trip; some of them were used subsequently as instructional, or learning, materials and some of them were used for testing at the end of the unit. The field trip frequently needs to be recorded if it is to be of maximum utility in teaching.

21   As a kindergarten teacher Mrs. Garner is aware of the fact that all but three of her students prefer Saturday morning television cartoons to the educational television programs which are designed specifically for kindergarten children and which are broadcast at that time. Mrs. Garner wants the children in her class to develop an interest in the instructional television programs, since she feels that these programs will help the children in their academic activities and that they will help the children develop better attitudes toward television in general. Write an objective.

•   •   •   •   •   •   •

21   *To manifest an approach tendency toward educational television programs, given a choice of viewing either these or the cartoon programs on Saturday mornings, by selecting the educational program.*

During the week, Mrs. Garner uses slides and tapes provided by the educational television station to introduce some of the characters and events that will be appearing on the Saturday programs. She creates further interest by having students, the following Monday, discuss the events and their reactions to the instructional programs. In other words, Mrs. Garner uses two media (slides and tapes) to motivate her students to accept a third medium (television).

22   As a fifth-grade teacher concerned with the good dental health of her students, Mrs. Davis finds that nearly all who eat lunch in the cafeteria select cookies or cake rather than fruit for dessert each day. Mrs. Davis feels that all of her students would benefit from rejecting cookies and cake as preferred desserts for school lunches. What is her objective?

•   •   •   •   •   •   •

22   *To approach foods that will develop or preserve good teeth, and to avoid foods which are most likely to cause tooth decay, given a choice of each type of food as a dessert for the school lunch.*

23   How might Mrs. Davis use media to help her students attain this objective?

•   •   •   •   •   •   •

23   *Mrs. Davis presents a series of photographs from the American Dental Association that demonstrate the chemical reaction that takes place in tooth decay. She then poses the problem of how to get children to select the proper foods. She suggests to the students that they might like to develop their own tape-filmstrip presentation that could be shared with other children in the primary grades at their school.*

24   Mr. Ryan teaches mathematics in a junior high school. A manufacturer of computers has installed three teletype terminals which provide access to a time-sharing computer system. Teachers are free to explore possible uses of this medium with their students. Mr. Ryan wants students to become familiar with the computer as an aid in solving problems in mathematics and he wants them to appreciate the medium. State an objective with which Mr. Ryan might be concerned.

      •   •   •   •   •   •

24   *To manifest an acceptance of the value of the computer for solving problems by selecting the computer, given the opportunity to solve problems "by hand" or "by computer." ("Selecting" is, of course, a euphemism for "identifying.") Or, to manifest an approach tendency toward computers by selecting the computer when provided the choice of solving problems in mathematics "by hand" or "by computer."*

25   What medium or media would be helpful in implementing the attainment of objectives such as these?

      •   •   •   •   •   •

25   *Mr. Ryan could use films showing people using the computer for the types of problem-solving activity in which he wants his students to engage. If these films demonstrate a great increase in accuracy of results and/or a great saving in time, as a result of computer utilization, students may tend to manifest a stronger approach tendency toward the computer.*
      Perhaps the most important of all possible media is the computer itself. Given the actual experience of increasing his problem-solving accuracy or saving time as a result of having "tried out" the computer, the student will no doubt find the result sufficiently rewarding to warrant an increased use; in other words, the computer is an effective medium of instruction in this instance because it is intrinsically motivating.

In this example, any medium is likely to be a good choice if it enables the student to display a new competence; essentially, this is what educators and psychologists are concerned with when they speak of "experiencing a feeling of efficacy." Before there were educators and psychologists, good teachers tried to implement the maxim "Nothing succeeds like success." Perhaps it is a truism to tell teachers to choose a medium which will help students succeed. Nevertheless, it is good advice; any medium which enables a learner to display a new competence in the shortest possible time is an effective medium. If this is true with respect to cognitive objectives, it is doubly true of the affective domain. Remember: If you want a student to develop an approach tendency toward something new, use that "something new" as a medium of instruction, if at all possible, and make very certain that his experiences with it are successful.

SUMMARY

Can you do the things stated in the objectives at the beginning of this chapter? If not, take time for a review. If you can, you are ready for the chapter on motor skills, Chapter 10.

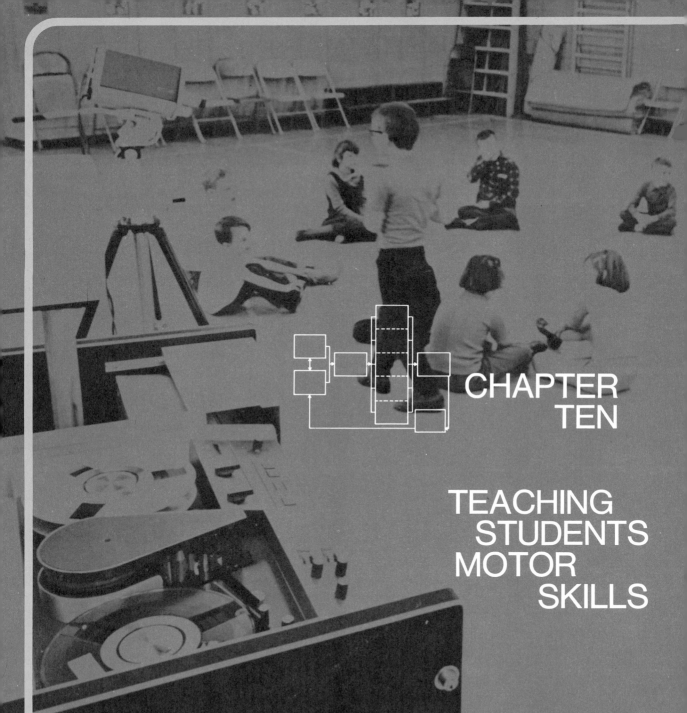

CHAPTER TEN

TEACHING STUDENTS MOTOR SKILLS

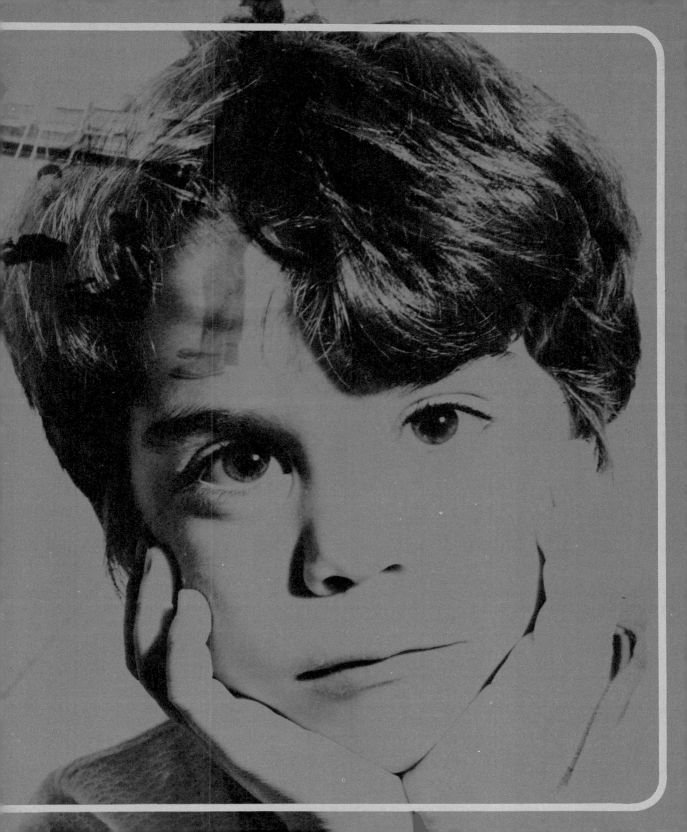

WHEN YOU HAVE MASTERED THE CONTENT OF THIS CHAPTER,
YOU SHOULD BE ABLE TO:

1. DEFINE "motor skills."

2. DESCRIBE school learning situations in which the desired terminal behavior is a motor skill.

3. IDENTIFY properly stated objectives related to motor skills.

4. CONSTRUCT behavioral objectives in this category.

5. DESCRIBE the conditions required to teach students a motor skill.

6. CONSTRUCT the rationale for choosing the medium (or media) best suited for establishing the conditions specified in objectives related to motor skills.

THE NATURE OF MOTOR SKILLS

Motor skills are those activities in which the learner moves a muscle or his body. If the learner must engage in this muscular movement or body motion in order to complete a desired act successfully, then we refer to the behavior as a motor skill. Some textbooks make distinctions between perceptual motor skills and psychomotor skills. These distinctions, while useful or even necessary in some contexts, are not analyzed in this book. The distinction between fine motor skills and gross motor skills is also useful in certain contexts, but it is not one which is essential to the understanding of this chapter.

Students are engaged in behavior in the motor skill category when they play basketball, draw designs, do their handwriting assignment, use the bench saw to cut a board, use pinking shears to cut a piece of cloth, or color an outline picture with wax crayons. Many motor skills are merely mediating behaviors; they are behaviors which must be learned by the child as he moves toward the attainment of a terminal behavior, but they are not terminal behaviors themselves. When a child is asked to identify the primary colors by drawing a line from a colored object to the name of the color, his behavior is termed identifying. Yet it is obvious that only the child who has learned a motor skill—to draw lines—can perform this identifying behavior. The motor skill (line drawing) is one of the means which the child uses to manifest his cognitive ability (identifying colors). Similarly, the student who writes an essay (constructs an essay) employs a motor skill (either handwriting or typewriting) as a means to an end. The motor skill is a mediating behavior.

OBJECTIVES RELATED TO MOTOR SKILLS

Unlike Chapters 4 to 9, this chapter does not define and explain a behavioral category, nor does it present a procedure for translating objectives from one system to another. Remember, the reason for using the procedures described in Chapters 4 to 9 is to reduce uncertainty or ambiguity. Statements of objectives ought not to be subject to multiple interpretations. In earlier chapters it was repeatedly stressed that verbs which are unambiguous should be used whenever possible. There is no point in saying that the desired terminal behavior is "to order the letters of a word according to accepted orthographic standards . . ." when one means "to spell," nor is it advisable to say "to construct (or name) the product of a multiplication problem involving a two-digit multiplier and a two-digit multiplicand" when one wants the learner "to multiply two two-digit numbers. . . ." Verbs such as *spell* and *multiply* are not ambiguous; nothing is gained by expressing statements of objectives dealing with these behaviors in the kind of jargon used above. Words such as *spell* and *multiply*, when used with adequate statements of conditions and criteria, should be used in constructing behavioral objectives.

The behaviors in the motor skill domain are generally described by using verbs which, like *spell* and *multiply*, are relatively unambiguous. Basketball coaches teach learners "to dribble the ball . . ."; art teachers "to draw outline pictures using . . ."; first grade teachers "to write a row of a's, in manuscript writing . . ."; industrial art teachers "to cut a board, using the bench saw . . ."; home economics teachers "to cut a piece of fabric, using a pinking shears . . ."; and the kindergarten teacher "to color an outline picture, using wax crayons. . . ." A great deal of variety and latitude can be built into each of these statements, but not because the verbs are ambiguous. Whatever variety or latitude there is in these statements exists because the statements of conditions and standards have been omitted.

A few negative examples are included to serve as warnings of pitfalls to avoid. Aside from these few examples, everything can be summarized in one short rule: when writing objectives related to the motor skill domain, always use verbs which describe an identifiable or observable behavior. Avoid such expressions as

> to acquire increased dexterity . . .
> to develop eye-hand coordination . . .
> to build strength and endurance . . .
> to develop a sense of balance . . .
> to increase one's peripheral vision . . .
> to heighten one's kinesthetic sense[1] . . .

Write a behavioral objective in the motor skill domain for each of the following situations.

---

[1]The authors do not accept the notion of a general kinesthetic sense and do not use the concept in this chapter. They do accept the view that proprioception (or kinesthesis) is *specific* to a given task, or *specific* to the part of the body or the test involved in a given skill. However, those who do accept the notion of a general kinesthetic sense will have no difficulty adapting the procedures of this chapter to objectives related to kinesthesis, provided only that the objectives are written behaviorally.

1   Miss Norman teaches girls' physical education. Her curriculum guide includes, as one objective for the year, to develop increased manual dexterity. Miss Norman uses the age-old game of "jacks"[2] as one of the exercises to help implement the attainment of this objective.

•   •   •   •   •   •

1   To complete five consecutive pick-ups in a game of jacks; a successful pick-up is one in which the child drops the ball from a height of 15" or less and picks up one jack and catches the ball in the same hand before the ball strikes the walk the second time.

2   Mr. Lund wants the players on the football team which he coaches to increase their strength. In order to accomplish this, he has outlined a weight-lifting program. Because many of the boys have not seen the type of weight-lifting which Mr. Lund has specified, he provides an 8mm silent cartridge film showing the exercise.

•   •   •   •   •   •

2   To lift 25 pounds more at the end of the second week of practice than he was able to lift on the first day of practice, using a press as shown in the film; position of the hands, knees, and hips must be consistent with that shown in the film before, during, and after the lift.

3   Mr. Travers wants the players on his hockey team to increase their peripheral vision. (Before attempting this one, make certain that you remember the concept of an operational definition as discussed on pp. 51–52.)

•   •   •   •   •   •

3   Mr. Travers is not dealing with a motor skill as it is defined in this book.

4   If you missed Example 3, try again. This time think of it as a cognitive skill; formulate an objective.

•   •   •   •   •   •

4   The simplest answer would involve identifying. Mr. Travers wants his players "to identify objects at a greater angle after two weeks of practice than they were able to the first day...." To illustrate, the learner skates down the center of the rink while two teammates skate along the boards. These two each carry 12 inch plastic discs, one side of which is green and the other red. From time to time one or the other or both rotate the discs. The task of the skater in the center is to call out whether the discs are the same color or different at any given instant.

[2]Jacks: The child, while kneeling, bounces a small rubber ball on a hard surface such as a sidewalk; he then picks up a small metal object and catches the ball in the same hand before the ball strikes the sidewalk the second time.

During the first day of practice, most players could do this with 100 percent accuracy only if the angle were something like this:

Mr. Travers' objective is to get the center skater to increase the angle at which he can make a correct identification consistently, thus:

Attaining Objectives

Before working on the problems of media selection for motor skill objectives, a few general principles should be considered.

Attention to specific environmental stimuli during practice facilitates the learning of a motor skill. A student may practice for hour upon hour, but if he practices a mistake he will not attain the desired objective. The student in a typing class ought to be able to tell himself whether his typing is rhythmic. If he falls into an unrhythmic typing pattern, there ought to be a relevant cue which could guide him to an improved performance. In many instances these relevant cues are stimuli which occur naturally as the learner acts upon his environment. The student who learns to drive an automobile with a standard transmission learns to operate the clutch smoothly because of the annoying jerking of the car when he does not and because of the satisfactory response of the car when he does. The typist is rewarded with acceptable copy when she operates her typewriter properly; the acceptable copy is a relevant cue which tends to improve her performance, or, at the very least, to maintain an already satisfactory performance.

Teachers use films or video tapes to direct the learner's attention to cues of this type. Handwriting teachers show students proper posture and correct hand position by means of film. These films may lead the learner to develop his own set of relevant cues which assist him in improving his performance. The track coach shows his dash men the proper starting position by means of videotape recordings. The runners develop relevant cues which may lead to improved performance.

There is considerable evidence to indicate that a learner who wants to improve will do so faster than one who is unconcerned. The teacher will do well to establish conditions which motivate students to improve their motor performance. If it is essential for the student to improve his flute playing, the teacher should attempt to develop an approach behavior in the student with respect to practicing the flute.

MEDIA SELECTION

Many teachers seem to believe that a complex motor skill is best acquired if the learner practices very slowly in order to concentrate on accuracy. The burden of proof lies almost entirely on the teacher who follows this type of strategy. Generally, practice should approximate the desired terminal behavior as nearly as possible. A music teacher teaches his drummers by having them follow a model drummer recorded on videotape. The novice drummers imitate the model at the proper speed from the very beginning. Gradually the volume is raised so that both the picture and sound serve as relevant cues. Next, the picture is gradually faded and a notation is superimposed on the picture. Ultimately the sound is faded, too, until the learner's drum playing is controlled completely by the notes on the TV screen. While this technique incorporates a number of principles regarding motor skill learning, the emphasis at the present time is on the nature of the practice and the extent to which it approximates the desired terminal behavior. Remember, there is very little evidence to indicate that artificial practice (for example, practice at half-speed or quarter-speed) facilitates acquisition of desired terminal behavior.

Most experts in motor learning agree that short practice periods interspersed with short rest periods over a given period of time are more effective than long practice periods followed by long rest periods over an equal length of time. Distributed practice is more effective than massed practice. Visual materials, such as a motion picture film, may increase the learner's ability to attend to relevant cues if such aids are used during the rest period.

More effective retention usually occurs when students are required to overlearn a motor skill. As was stressed in Chapter 2, acquisition (the first occurrence of a desired behavior) is the goal of almost every conceivable instructional activity. Overlearning is essential to the development of maintenance.

Most teachers of motor skills seem to be unaware of the importance of mental practice or image practice. While it is certainly true that no one learns a motor skill unless he practices (or performs) that skill, it is also true that many teachers find themselves in situations which permit only one or only a few members of a large class to engage in actual practice. What do the other students do while waiting? If the teacher wants to use this waiting time to maximum advantage, he will have his students rehearse the motor skill in their minds. The auto mechanics teacher who is teaching his class to assemble a carburetor will find that the efficiency of his instruction can be markedly increased if he will use a programmed text or a set of programmed slides to lead the waiting students through the steps of the assembly procedure.

Many motor tasks involve serial learning. The student who learns to operate a motion picture projector is involved in serial learning. In most types of serial learning, that which is learned first is retained longest, that which is learned in the middle is retained for the shortest time, while the material learned last is retained longer than that learned in the middle, but not as long as that learned first. Films or tapes might be constructed in modules so that the learner may begin his practice at various positions in the task. For example, the student may learn to operate the motion picture projector by following these steps:

1. unpack
2. plug in power cord
3. extend arms
4. attach feed-and-take-up reels
5. etc.

For his second practice run, he might be directed to a station where the first four steps have been completed, and he begins the threading portion of the task. Another practice session may consist of running and rewinding the film and repacking the projector, followed by a practice session consisting of the first four steps (i.e., the set-up module). For each of these modules, consisting of several steps, 8mm silent cartridge films or audiotape cassettes are available to help the student learn.

The nature of cues may vary from one type of learning task to another. When a student is beginning a task, visual cues seem to be much more useful than they are at more advanced levels. For most types of motor skills, visual cues should be as close to the learner as possible. In addition, the cues should be as specific and precise as possible. An audiovisual coordinator who is teaching the members of the high school AV projectionists group to operate the four types of tape recorders in the school would be ill-advised to try to teach his students to operate all four from a single generalized schematic or drawing. Likewise, a large wall chart posted at the front of the room is much less effective than a diagram or flip-chart which the learner can place next to the machine which he is learning to operate.

When all is said and done, however, it is very difficult, if not impossible, to formulate a set of general statements regarding the nature of visual stimuli and methods of using them for teaching motor skills. Media which have been found very useful or even indispensable in one experiment or situation are found to be useless or even detrimental for another instructional task. Ultimately, each teacher must determine whether a functional relationship exists between the medium which he is using and the outcomes which he has observed. Until a more solid knowledge base is available, teachers will continue to use motion pictures, videotapes, slides, and other visual or auditory media to add variety to their teaching routine, to increase the probability of desired approach or avoidance behaviors, and to assist learners in acquiring verbal behavior which is related to the acquisition of a specific motor skill.

SUMMARY

Check your progress! Can you do everything which is required in the statements of objectives for Chapter 10? If you can, you are ready for the Part Two summary exercises below.

SUMMARY EXERCISES FOR PART TWO

At this point, you should be able to *construct objectives* according to the criteria described in Part Two.

1   What are the characteristics of a good objective?

   •   •   •   •   •   •

1   *A good objective:*
   a.   *Describes something which the* learner *does or produces.*
   b.   *States a* behavior or a product *of the learner's behavior.*
   c.   *States the* conditions *under which the behavior is to occur.*
   d.   *States the* standard *which defines whether the objective has been attained.*

You also should be able to *describe the process of assessing the entering behavior* of each student.

2   What factors should be considered in assessing entering behaviors of the learner?

   •   •   •   •   •   •

2   *Knowledge of entering behaviors will depend upon the objectives being sought. Most commonly, teachers will want to measure the degree to which any of the students have already attained the objectives, e.g., which terms, concepts, and generalizations (if any) have been mastered. Many teachers also want to assess the aptitudes of the students—their potential for learning. In some cases it may be helpful to obtain a description of attitudes held by individual students toward the subject matter.*

You should be able to *name and to order the components of the instructional system* described in Chapter 1.

3   Write the components of the instructional system in the appropriate box in the chart on the next page.

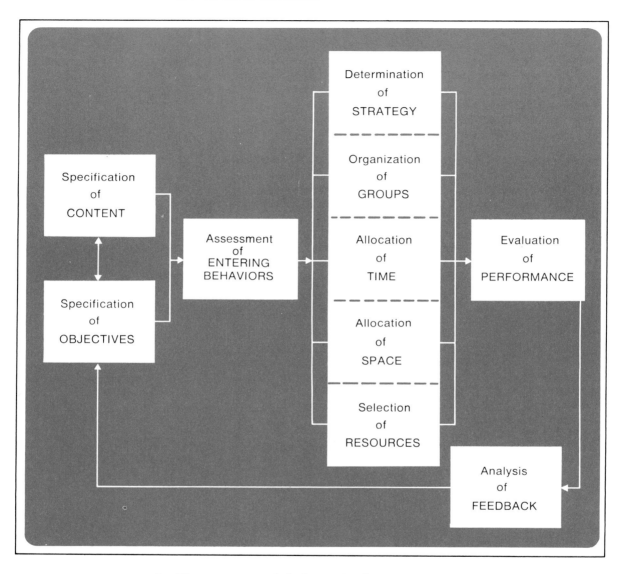

3   The components of the instructional system.

If you have demonstrated your ability to perform these behaviors, you may proceed to Part Three. However, if you cannot, you should return to the earlier chapters and re-read the information.

SELECTED READINGS FOR PART TWO

Bloom, B. S., M. D. Englehart, E. H. Furst, W. H. Hill, and D. R. Krathwohl (eds.), *Taxonomy of Educational Objectives, Handbook I: Cognitive Domain*. New York: David McKay, 1956.

Describes a hierarchy of instructional goals applicable to the cognitive domain. Definitions and exemplary test items are provided for each level of the hierarchy.

Deterline, William A., "The Secrets We Keep from Students," *Educational Technology*, Vol. VIII, No. 3, February 15, 1969.

Present practices of not telling students precisely what should be learned are examined. Recommendations for improving present practices are made, and the effects of the recommendations are discussed.

Gagné, Robert M., "Educational Objectives and Human Performance." In *Learning and the Educational Process*, ed. J. D. Krumboltz. Chicago: Rand McNally & Co., 1965. Pp. 1–24.

Discusses the difference between educational and instructional objectives.

———, "The Analysis of Instructional Objectives for the Design of Instruction." In *Teaching Machines and Programed Learning, II: Data and Directions*, ed. R. Glaser. Washington, D.C.: Department of Audiovisual Instruction, National Education Association, 1965. Pp. 21–65.

Discusses the relationship between objectives and a task analysis.

Gerlach, Vernon S., *Describing Educational Outcomes*. Inglewood, Calif.: Southwest Regional Laboratory for Educational Research and Development, 1967. 34 pp.

———, "Selecting an Instructional Medium." In *Media Competencies for Teachers*, ed. W. C. Meierhenry. Educational Resources Information Clearinghouse, 1966. Pp. 70–100.

Describes a strategy for media selection, beginning with behavioral objectives. Shows how to match media characteristics with conditions specified in objectives.

———, and Howard J. Sullivan, *Constructing Statements of Outcomes*. Inglewood, Calif.: Southwest Regional Laboratory for Educational Research and Development, 1967. 38 pp.

Two self-instructional programs that teach the construction of behavioral objectives and the definitions of several behavioral terms.

————, Howard J. Sullivan, Robert J. Berger, Robert L. Baker, and Richard E. Schutz, *Developing the Instructional Specification*. Inglewood, Calif.: Southwest Regional Laboratory for Educational Research and Development, 1968. 52 pp.

A self-instructional program that teaches a method of prescribing variables relevant to implementing behavioral objectives.

Gronlund, Norman E., *Stating Behavioral Objectives for Classroom Instruction*. New York: Macmillan, 1970. 60 pp.

Describes the methods used in identifying and defining instructional objectives as learning outcomes. Discusses the use of *The Taxonomy of Educational Objectives* related to the process of selecting instructional objectives.

Instructional Objectives Exchange Catalog. Los Angeles: Instructional Objective Exchange, 1969.

A continually updated catalog of behavioral objectives contributed from various sources for an array of subjects. Request for behavioral objectives for specific subject matters should be addressed to:

> Instructional Objectives Exchange
> Center for the Study of Education of the
> University of California at Los Angeles
> 145 Moore Hall
> 405 Hilgard Avenue
> Los Angeles, California 90024

Kapfer, Phillip G., "Behavioral Objectives in the Cognitive and Affective Domains," *Educational Technology*, Vol. VIII, No. 11, June 15, 1968.

Discusses methods of relating behavioral objectives in the cognitive and affective domains to more broadly stated goals.

Kibler, Robert J., Larry L. Becker, and David O. Miles, *Behavioral Objectives and Instruction*. Boston: Allyn & Bacon, 1970.

Identifies functions which behavioral objectives can serve in improving instruction. Describes the nature of objectives, assists teachers in writing them, and provides examples of well-written behavioral objectives.

Krathwohl, D. R., "The Taxonomy of Educational Objectives—Its Use in Curriculum Building." In *Defining Educational Objectives*, ed. C. M. Lindvall. Pittsburgh: University of Pittsburgh Press, 1964.

Describes the role of objectives in deciding what pupils are to learn.

————, B. S. Bloom, and B. B. Masia, *Taxonomy of Educational Objectives, Handbook II: Affective Domain*. New York: David McKay, 1956.

Describes a hierarchy of educational goals applicable to the affective domain. A definition and exemplary test items are provided for each level.

McNeil, J. D., "Antidote to a School Scandal," *The Educational Forum*, 1966, *30*, 69–77.

How the use of behavioral objectives improves teaching.

Mager, Robert J., *Goofing Off with Objectives*.   Mager Associates, 13245 Rhoda Drive, Los Altos Hills, California   94022.

An amusing 14 minute 16mm film which might be used in an in-service program related to instructional objectives.

————, *Developing Attitude Toward Learning*.   Palo Alto, Calif.: Fearon Publishers, 1968.

Discusses the problem of defining attitudes in behavioral terms and procedures for developing such attitudes.

————, *Preparing Instructional Objectives*.   Palo Alto, Calif.: Fearon Publishers, 1962.

A self-instructional text that teaches the identification of behavioral objectives and test items appropriate to behavioral objectives.

————, and Kenneth M. Beech, *Developing Vocational Instruction*.   Palo Alto, Calif.: Fearon Publishers, 1967.

Describes procedures for developing instruction.   The focus is on vocational education, although the procedures are generalizable to other fields.

Miller, Robert B., "Analysis and Specification of Behavior for Training."   In *Training Research and Education,* ed. R. Glaser.   Pittsburgh: University of Pittsburgh Press, 1962.   Pp. 31–62.

————, "Task Description and Analysis."   In *Psychological Principles In System Development*, ed. R. M. Gagné.   New York: Holt, Rinehart & Winston, Inc., 1962. Pp. 187–230.

The two Miller articles are excellent discussions of task analysis.   Anyone who wishes to select effective media should read these.

Payne, David A., *The Specification and Measurement of Learning Outcomes*.   Waltham, Mass.: Blaisdell, 1968.

Describes procedures for measuring learning outcomes.   Chapter 2 discusses the relationship of objectives to test construction.

Plowman, Paul, *Behavioral Objectives and Teacher Success*. (Unit 1).   Chicago: Science Research Associates, 1968.

First of a series of short writings relating to behavioral objectives in education and various subject matters.   Others include:

Behavioral Objectives in English and Literature, (Unit 2), 1969.
Behavioral Objectives in Social Science, (Unit 3), 1969.
Behavioral Objectives in Science, (Unit 4), 1969.
Behavioral Objectives in Biology, (Unit 5), 1969.
Behavioral Objectives in Mathematics, (Unit 6), 1969.
Behavioral Objectives in Art and Music, (Unit 7), 1969.
Behavioral Objectives in Reading, (Unit 8), 1969.

Popham, W. James, *Educational Criterion Measures*.   Inglewood, Calif.: Southwest Region Laboratory, 1968.

A self-instructional program that teaches procedures for constructing tests that measure behavioral objectives.

————, Elliot Eisner, Howard J. Sullivan, and Louise Tyler, *Instructional Objectives*. Skokie, Ill.: Rand McNally, 1969.

A series of papers discussing problems in the utilization of behavioral objectives in education.   Solutions to some of their limitations are proposed.

Sanders, N. M., *Classroom Questions: What Kinds?* New York: Harper & Row, 1966.

Basic types of questions are defined and illustrated.   Assistance is provided for evaluating questions to broader cognitive opportunities they present to the student.

Tyler, R. W., "Some Persistent Questions in Defining Objectives."   In *Defining Educational Objectives*, ed. C. M. Lindvall.   Pittsburgh: University of Pittsburgh Press, 1964.

PART THREE

ARRANGING THE VARIABLES FOR TEACHING AND LEARNING

In Chapter 11 we will consider the development of an instructional *strategy* as part of the system. The *organization of groups*, the *allocation of space and time*, and the *selection of instructional resources* follow in Chapters 12 and 13. The system is now beginning to take shape prior to *assessment of performance*.

When you have mastered the content of Part Three, you should be able to:

1. Describe the procedure for determining an instructional strategy, given the learner's objectives.
2. Describe the procedure for organizing groups.
3. Describe procedures for allocating space and time, given objectives for the learner.
4. Name the types of resources available to teachers.
5. Construct a plan for teaching and learning based on the components of this instructional system.

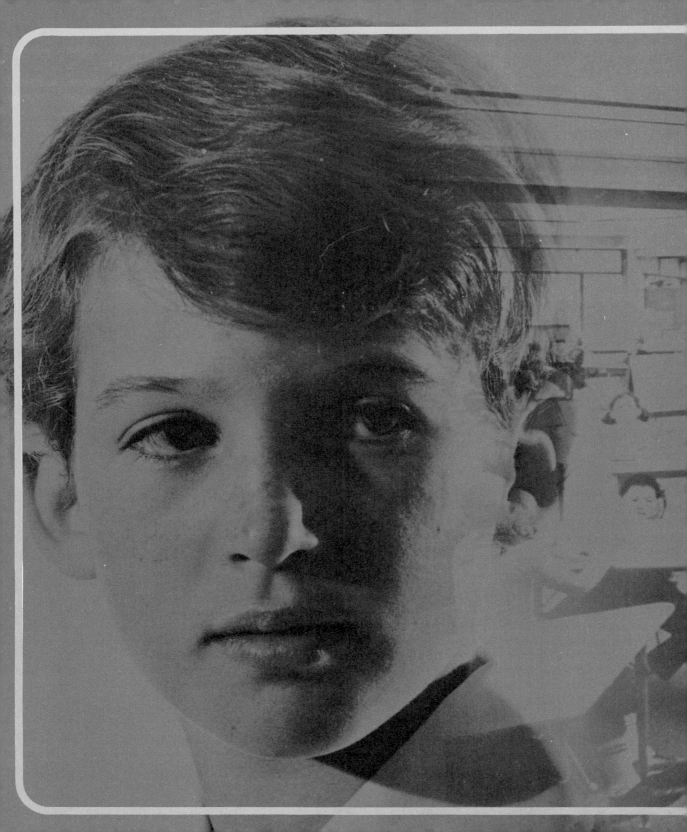

CHAPTER ELEVEN

STRATEGIES FOR TEACHING

WHEN YOU HAVE MASTERED THE CONTENT OF THIS CHAPTER, YOU SHOULD BE ABLE TO:

1. IDENTIFY the strategy being used by a teacher when observing a class in session.

2. NAME the characteristics of expository and inquiry teaching.

3. NAME the techniques which are generally available to teachers.

4. CONSTRUCT a strategy for teaching and learning, given an objective.

> **strategy** . . . **2a:** a careful plan or method or a clever strata-
> gem **b:** the art of employing or devising plans or stratagems
> toward a goal[1]

In the systematic approach to teaching and learning, *strategy* is concerned with the way in which content is presented in the instructional
environment. It includes the nature, scope, and sequence of events which
provide the educational experience. The strategy must take into account
the objectives that have been defined, and the entering behaviors of the
learners.

The word strategy is obviously borrowed from the military. Over the
centuries, armies have developed strategies to accomplish military objectives. The objectives are usually clear and the results observable. Before
the performance begins, the strategy is carefully spelled out. Squads,
platoons, companies, and battalions are deployed; time decisions are
made; space to be occupied is determined; and the supplies are carefully
placed for support of the effort. The objectives of education are far removed from those of military activities, but the process is strikingly similar.

DETERMINING A STRATEGY FOR INSTRUCTION

Since the late 1950's, many new and experimental teaching procedures
have been tried. Almost without exception, these experiments have attempted to link objectives with teaching strategies, seeking to determine
the most efficient and effective classroom procedures for reaching stated
objectives. An instructional strategy is a plan for attaining learning objectives. It is made up of methods and techniques (or procedures) which will
ensure that the learner does in fact reach the objective.

In an assessment of the current status of the new social studies, Edwin
Fenton outlines one way to view teaching strategies.

A TEACHING CONTINUUM

Exposition	Directed Discussion	Discovery
(all cues)	(questions as cues)	(no cues)

[1]*Webster's Third New International Dictionary* (Springfield, Mass.: G & C Merriam Co.,
1966), p. 2256.

At one pole of the continuum lies an expository 'lecture' in which the teacher tells students both the generalizations and the evidence for the generalizations which he expects them to learn. . . . A skilled lecturer can often promote thinking if he knows his students well and challenges them to reflect on topics they care about.

Discovery techniques lie at the other pole of the continuum. In this type of strategy, teachers assume a nondirective role. They provide stimulus material in the form of words, pictures, or sound for students to think about with minimal guidance from the teacher.[2]

Expository and Inquiry Approaches

The continuum suggested by Fenton is a useful way to look at the selection of an instructional approach. The poles of the continuum offer two extremes of methodology with many points between. The teacher must decide which approach will help to reach the instructional objective. While a simple answer of "expository" or "inquiry" may seem sufficient, the fact is that few teachers are "purely" expository or "purely" inquiry oriented. But the dominant approach must be identified since it will affect the size of groups, the learning spaces required, the allocation of time, and the selection of resources.

Identify the dominant approach being used by each teacher in the following examples.

1 The kindergarten teacher is telling the children the rules for crossing the streets, using posters to illustrate each rule: cross at the corners, wait for the green light, etc.

      •   •   •   •   •   •

1 *This is an expository approach. The teacher is communicating generalizations which the children are expected to follow.*

2 The kindergarten teacher is using the 16mm motion picture *Safety on the Way to School* to help learners plan the best route to school from their homes and to state the rules for a safe walk to and from school.

      •   •   •   •   •   •

2 *The film is an expository medium if it is designed to tell viewers what to think or what to do. This film apparently is an expository film—at least while it is being shown and the students are recipients of information. There may be a shift from an expository stance to inquiry (or discovery) if the teacher permits each youngster to plan his or her own route to school. Such an assignment would cause each child to raise a host of questions before he could come up with a tentative solution.*

3 In helping high school students to demonstrate a negative attitude toward drugs, the health teacher plays five brief excerpts of tape recordings made

---

[2]Edwin Fenton, *The New Social Studies* (New York: Holt, Rinehart and Winston, Inc., 1967), pp. 33–34.

by former addicts describing the pain and expense of their experience with drugs. The teacher asks for questions after all the recordings have been played.

    •   •   •   •   •   •

3   *The focal point of the instructional design is on inquiry, but the stimulus materials were presented in an expository fashion. This illustrates the difficulty of planning for "pure" exposition or inquiry.*

4   The language arts and social studies teachers on a middle school teaching team want their students to state and defend positions on a proposed route for a new super highway which would go through a residential section of town. They organize teams for affirmative and negative points of view and relate the objective to the students along with an anticipated date for the debate to take place.

    •   •   •   •   •   •

4   *This is an inquiry approach.*

A Case Study

The middle school mathematics and science teachers have decided that the metric system will be used in all courses next semester. They have developed a series of objectives having to do with competencies in using the metric system. One reads: "The learner will be able to measure common objects in the classroom (such as the desk top, books, window panes) using the metric system, given a meter stick and 30 seconds for each measurement."

The team has decided to use an inquiry approach. However, the class session will begin with an expository segment outlining the current status of the metric system. The fact that this system is used for scientific work around the world and that most nations follow the metric system will be the essence of the expository portion of the introduction. The objective is shared with the students, and they are told that a test will be given at the end of the class period. A test at the beginning of the semester indicated that only four students were able to use the metric system. These four were assigned the task of timing the measurement exercise.

What techniques should be employed?

Lecture?
Discussion?
Demonstration?
Doing?
Field Trip?
Role-Playing, Simulation, and Gaming?
Student Reports?
Audiovisual Materials?
Combinations of the Above?

Consider the alternatives:

It is unlikely that the *lecture* is the best choice for the objective, ". . . to measure."

Certainly some *discussion* will occur in the form of questions and answers, but discussion alone probably could not produce the desired outcome.

A *demonstration* of measurement would be helpful, but could everyone see it? A simple closed circuit television system could magnify the demonstration so that all could see. Is it worth the time and cost of setting up such a unit? Probably not.

Doing is certainly a serious contender. If the objective is "to measure," then the learner actually will have to measure at some point during the instruction. Each person would need a meter stick. The cost is not prohibitive.

A *field trip* would serve as motivation for use of the metric system if the class visited an industry where the metric system was used continually. However, this technique is not directly appropriate at this time.

Role-playing, simulation, and *gaming* might offer a possibility for trying to transfer the principles of metric measurement to an actual situation where such measurement was required. This approach could use a case study as a simulated activity and help individuals to realize the applicability of the system, but this is not the objective under consideration.

Student reports? Not much to report on in this exercise.

Audiovisual materials ought to be considered. Is there a film or filmstrip which could communicate the principles of metric measurement in a brief, yet efficient manner? A current film library catalog[3] lists two choices which might be considered:

> *Metric System* (13 minutes, color, junior and senior high school level, produced in 1966 by McGraw-Hill, rental: $7.00)
>
> How do we measure length? The apparent randomness of multipliers used to convert one unit to another serves as motivation for the introduction of a more convenient system: the Metric System. The meter (unit of length of this system) is defined as one ten-millionth part of a line from the north pole to the equator. It is then compared with the English System by expressing it in terms of inches. Greek prefixes are introduced to show multipliers. After length comes area. Film shows the Metric System to be used throughout the world today to measure such things as ribbons, vegetables, milk, and distances. A guide accompanies film.
>
> *Metric System* (11 minutes, color, junior and senior high school level, produced in 1958 by Coronet Films, rental: $4.25)
>
> The history of the metric system and its uses today are included in this film which clearly illustrates the basic units. English and Metric units are compared, and the advantages of computations in the metric system are demonstrated.

[3]Descriptions from the 1970 edition of the Syracuse University Film Rental Library catalog.

The *Index to 35mm Educational Filmstrips* lists two filmstrips which could be considered, but the lack of grade level indicators and cost information might limit further consideration. (Once filmstrips are identified in the *Index*, it is necessary to go to the catalog of the producer or distributor to get further descriptive information, age level emphases, and price lists.) The two filmstrips are:

> *The Metric System of Measuring* (50 frames, color, produced in 1966 by Encyclopaedia Britannica Educational Corp.)

> Uses investigative problems and simple explanations to explain how uniform, accurate systems of measurement make physical science a precise field of study.

> *The Metric System* (44 frames, color, produced in 1961 by McGraw-Hill Textfilms)

> Introduces and summarizes some important topics in general mathematics (correlated with 'Using Mathematics 9' by Henderson).

Is there programmed instructional material which would be relevant? A check of Hendershot's *Programmed Learning: A Bibliography of Programs and Presentation Devices* revealed no programs currently available.

5   Which approach would most likely implement the objective?

·   ·   ·   ·   ·   ·

5   The observable product, measurement of objects with a metric stick, is a skill which would probably be learned equally well from a teacher using either exposition or inquiry. Inquiry questions such as, "How much liquid is in a liter of gasoline?" or "How far is a 100 meter dash?" are inquiry-type questions which might lead to a desire to learn the metric system which would then be taught using an expository approach. Likewise, a good presentation, together with a demonstration, followed by a session in which students practice measuring would no doubt produce the desired results.

6   Following an expository approach, which technique(s) would be most efficient and effective?

·   ·   ·   ·   ·   ·

6   There is no single best answer since individual differences among teachers make the selection of techniques a difficult choice. Such variables as the personal dynamism of the teacher, the ability to use an audiovisual medium effectively, and the creative approach to question-raising all contribute to a teacher's style. However, we do not have to dodge the question. A first step could be a demonstration with an explanation. Whether this is accomplished by a motion picture or filmstrip or by the teacher using a chalkboard or an overhead projector depends upon availability of the necessary resources and the teacher's ability to use them effectively. A second part of the plan would provide opportunities for each student actually to measure using a meter stick. Evaluation would take place by actual observation or by a written test which would stem from actual measurements. This is one example of the way in which techniques are selected to implement an instructional objective.

Inductive and Deductive Approaches

Another way of looking at the differences between inquiry and exposition is to review the premises of the inductive and deductive approaches to teaching. Inductive teaching and inquiry are close relatives, although purists may try to draw clear distinctions. Likewise, deductive teaching and exposition are in the same generic camp.

To induce is "to lead on" or "to tow." The teacher who is using an inductive approach begins by providing unorganized information in various formats to the learners. The learners study the information relating it to the problem at hand. The teacher works cooperatively with the students to develop guidelines for searching out additional facts. From the observations and research, the students are asked to state hypotheses which can be subjected to various tests. During the process, the teacher using the inductive approach begins with the learner's experiences and helps to narrow down these experiences until a tentative generalization or hypothesis is stated which is later analyzed for acceptance, rejection or modification. The inductive procedure can be generalized as follows:[4]

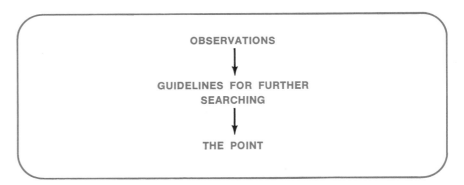

OBSERVATIONS

↓

GUIDELINES FOR FURTHER SEARCHING

↓

THE POINT

To deduce is to "lead or draw out from." The deductive approach to teaching is related to expository approaches to teaching. A teacher who uses the deductive approach states a law, a principle, or a generalization. The teacher begins by making statements regarding discoveries he has made or information that he has found to be useful. Then the learners are asked to apply the statement to problems of their own. Often opportunities to discover these examples are created. For example, the experiments in the chemistry or biology laboratory have historically been structured so that the learner will come out with specific illustrations to support generalizations presented in class.

[4]Adapted from *Straight Talk about Teaching in Today's Church* (p. 39), by Locke E. Bowman, Jr. Copyright © 1967, The Westminster Press. Used by permission.

Contrast the following generalization of the deductive process with the inductive diagram at left:[5]

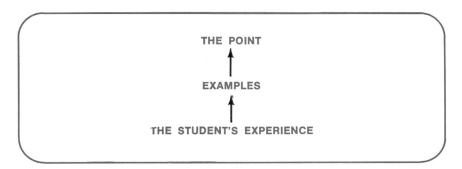

Application of Approaches

Use the next example as a test of your ability to construct an instructional strategy, given an objective.

7   An art teacher wants his students to be able to name the type of black markings on white paper, given a piece of white paper with marks made from pencil, charcoal, India ink, felt tip marking pen, and ball point pen; no errors are allowed. What strategy would you follow in an expository approach and how would you design an inquiry approach?

· · · · · · ·

7   *The exact words you use to describe each strategy will differ, but you should see common elements between your statement and those proposed below.*

In an *expository* presentation the teacher presents his objective. (He might omit this step; many teachers do.) He then describes the qualities of each source of black, talks about the amount of carbon in each substance, and mentions the drying quality of each substance and its proneness to smudge. He demonstrates each substance on a large white pad, while repeating key points about the quality of each. After answering questions which the students raise, he gives a quiz asking each student to name correctly each of the five substances from a group of eight different black markings on white paper. There is little doubt that the students will learn.

With an *inquiry approach*, the teacher states the objective first. Or, in an even less structured situation, the teacher may simply ask a question: "What drawing substances will show the darkest blacks and which will show the lightest blacks?" He then provides an assortment of marking instruments which produce black marks and circulates among groups of learners. He continues to raise relevant questions. Questions from the student to the teacher are usually answered with a "What do you think?" response or a simple "Yes" or "No." At the time when the teacher has observed that the students have the ability to identify the types of markings made by a variety of substances, he asks them to summarize what they have found.

There is a type of teaching between exposition and inquiry which is called *directed discussion*. The art teacher places the objective on the chalkboard or reads it to the class. He has the five marking substances and instruments at each student's work station. He asks them to make several lines with each type of marker on a piece of white paper. A series of questions then follows:

"What differences did you notice as you made a mark using each instrument?"
"Which substances make the blackest black? The lightest black?"
"Which instrument would you prefer to sketch with? Why?"
"Which substance would make a better reproduction? Why?"

To determine whether the objective has been reached, the teacher asks each student to make a mark with each of five different black substances and to identify each one on a separate sheet of paper. Then he directs students to work in pairs and to test each other. If any individual makes an error, his partner is instructed to redraw the five marks in a different order and to test again until all five are named correctly.

From the standpoint of time, the *expository* approach would reach the objective most quickly. The teacher's generalizations are prepared and are easily presented. The *inquiry* approach probably consumes the greatest amount of time since less direction is provided and students have to spend varying amounts of time attempting to raise appropriate questions and finding satisfactory answers. The *directed discussion* takes less time than the inquiry approach but somewhat more time than the expository approach. The structure helps the class to move along, yet answers are not readily provided by the teacher.

The use of resources varies from one approach to the other. For *expository* teaching, the instructor uses a large white pad and the five drawing substances during a demonstration. That is all. For *inquiry* teaching, each one of the students has a set of five drawing instruments and some paper at his work station—a somewhat more expensive procedure. In *directed discussion*, one set of five instruments is provided at each work station.

The decision regarding approach is a first step. We must realize that these are not hard and fast categories. From time to time, a teacher may find it beneficial to jump back and forth from exposition to inquiry as in the case of a history teacher who provides detailed insights into material previously read by the entire class outside of class. After a formal (expository) presentation of details, one or two questions can quickly shift the strategy to inquiry. However, it is important to inform the learners about the change in signals.

CRITERIA FOR DETERMINING STRATEGY

The teacher or teaching team will determine the instructional approach to be followed. There are times when additional instructional consultants, such as an instructional media specialist, a curriculum supervisor, or a librarian, might work with the teacher or team, but since it is the teacher who ultimately has to work within the context of the method selected, it follows that the final decision must be one which is acceptable to him.

The starting point for determining the instructional approach must be the objectives which have been established. If the teacher knows what a learner ought to be able to do at the culmination of the learning activity, the question of method naturally follows. "Which approach will be most effective and most efficient in helping each learner to reach this objective?" This question is both very simple and very difficult.

The question of approach is simple because it seems obvious that a method should be selected to help the learner achieve the defined objective in the easiest and most productive fashion. The first step, as we discussed earlier, is to define the objective in terms of what a learner should be able to do, under what conditions, and at what level of attainment. Once this is done, and the student shares the knowledge of the objectives with the teacher, the approach may be a secondary matter.

But the question of approach is difficult because each student is different and each teacher has different abilities and qualities. It is difficult because there are often affective, or emotional, objectives of feelings and attitudes which are more difficult to describe and measure. When an instructional method is selected for implementing a specific cognitive objective, the decision is usually the best estimate for achieving the goal to the highest degree possible for the greatest number of students. But the teacher should not stop at this point. There are opportunities for reaching the individual student today as never before. Groups of students with varying capabilities can receive individual attention through a number of different media of instruction. Individual filmstrip and slide viewers with tape recorded commentaries are used for one group while the teacher works directly with another group. The learning objectives are the same, but the techniques to reach them, and the organization of groups, may vary. In this case, the method may be expository, or inquiry, or somewhere between. The instructional media and group size *do not* dictate the approach.

Once objectives have been defined, a general model for selection of an instructional approach is:

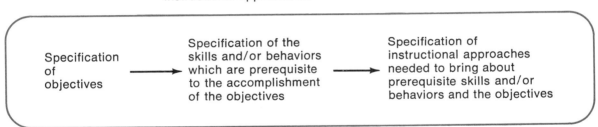

Specification of objectives → Specification of the skills and/or behaviors which are prerequisite to the accomplishment of the objectives → Specification of instructional approaches needed to bring about prerequisite skills and/or behaviors and the objectives

How are instructional approaches selected? By efficiency and effectiveness criteria.

Efficiency Criteria

Given a cognitive objective such as "to identify six types of fish found in the Columbia River, given unlabeled pictures of ten fish" it might be most efficient to give a learner a labeled picture of the six fish to be identified and ask him to study the picture while the teacher points out unique characteristics of each fish. Then ask him to test himself until he is ready to demonstrate his competence on a brief quiz. Another objective: "to name the chemical formula for ethyl alcohol, given the elements of organic compounds." To help a student name the chemical formula for ethyl alcohol, it probably would be most efficient to give him a copy of the formula, perhaps with formulas for other types of alcohol and point out the similarities and differences of each compound. Ask him to write the formula several times and to repeat it to himself. When he feels he is ready to be tested, he can request the test. If he can name the formula on a test, he has exhibited the desired behavior.

Expository teaching is probably the most efficient method to accomplish rote learning. Factual data can be efficiently transmitted via verbal expository methods. Techniques common to this method are the lecture, the demonstration, and the use of expository motion pictures and filmstrips.

To reach the same objectives via an inquiry approach would probably take longer and might produce the same results. There might be additional useful learning, not directly related to the defined objectives, but for the present, the concern is reaching the specified objectives, nothing more.

Using the objectives above, the teacher who chooses the inquiry approach might show slides of fish indicating that some are common to all fresh water bodies in North America but some are found only in waterways with an ocean outlet. The question would be: "Which fish are found in the Columbia River?" Questions from the group might pertain to the location of the Columbia River, the fish in the river, etc. The teacher answers "Yes," "No," or "Maybe" to the students' questions. This drives them to their textbooks and some to the encyclopedia. Some go to the map of the United States hanging on the front wall. Others ask to see the slides of the fish again. After giving the class a reasonable amount of searching time, the teacher calls the group back together. He shows the slides again and asks random individuals in the group to identify each fish and to indicate whether it is found in the Columbia River and why. He asks, at the end of the assessment period, for the characteristics of fish that live in fresh water bodies which flow to an ocean. Evidence is sought to support or reject the hypotheses being tested.

This method leads the learner to the same point as the expository approach did, but the process of getting the "right" answers required considerably more time. The inquiry process, however, leads to some useful principles of data gathering, hypothesis formulation, and testing of an hypothesis.

Effectiveness Criteria

Efficiency must balance with effectiveness. The most efficient method does not always yield the most effective result. Thus efficiency can become wasteful if the terminal behavior is not reached.

Has the learner demonstrated that the defined behavior has been attained, in the proper conditions, and at the stated level? If so, the objective has been implemented, but *how* effectively?

One way to test for effectiveness is to determine the transferability of the principles learned. Given the objective, "to construct a circle with a six inch radius on the chalkboard, given a piece of chalk, a piece of string more than six inches, and a ruler" the teacher could approach the objective from either an expository or an inquiry standpoint.

Efficiency and effectiveness should be considered together. If an objective is accomplished in less time with one method than another, it is more efficient. If the retention or transfer of the information or skill learned is greater for one method than another, then it is more effective for reaching that objective. In any case, when determining the approach to be followed, the best estimate of both efficiency and effectiveness will have to be followed. If the approach is studied carefully, future predictions will be based on empirical data of past experiences and they will probably result in better teaching.

8   How would you reach the objective using an expository approach?

     •   •   •   •   •   •

8   *In an expository approach, the teacher might tie the string around the chalk, measure six inches from the chalk to a point where the string is held firmly between the index finger and the thumb, and inscribe the circle on the chalkboard using the point where the string is held by the finger and thumb as the center of the circle. He then might ask six children to come to the chalkboard to construct similar circles. When they are finished, and judged accurate, six more would come to the board, etc. The whole class could demonstrate in less than five minutes that they have achieved the objective.*

9   How would you reach the objective using an inquiry approach?

     •   •   •   •   •   •

9   *Your response might be very different from this one, but that is the way* inquiry *works! In an inquiry mode, the teacher might state the objective and ask six pupils to come to the chalkboard to perform until they have satisfactorily reached the objective. The remainder of the class would be asked not to look at the board nor at their neighbors when they are at the board. At the end of about fifteen minutes, 31 of the 33 students in the class might have reached the objective.*

10 Is inquiry or exposition more effective? The expository approach appears to be efficient, and on the surface it would appear that the expository approach is more effective. But do we really know?

●   ●   ●   ●   ●   ●   ●

10 *No, we don't know unless an evaluation of learning is made. It might be handled this way: Two weeks later both groups are asked to construct a circle with a three inch radius on the paper using a pencil, a piece of string, and a ruler. Suppose that only half of the first group of 35 could do this in the three minutes allotted for the task but that 30 of the 33 in the inquiry group could accomplish the objective in three minutes or less. If this were the result, the inquiry approach was more effective than the expository approach. If the results were reversed, we would conclude that the expository approach was more effective.*

Other Criteria

Still another important consideration in making the determination of method is the degree of student involvement. The inquiry method usually demands more intensive student involvement. He is required to formulate his own hypotheses and to discover sources of data to validate his hunches. In expository situations, the student tends to be more passive. The teacher is more active in presenting information. If it is important that facts be mastered, then exposition is probably the better way.

It should also be noted that exposition and inquiry are very seldom used exclusively by any teacher. The creative teacher will look at the objectives and the current level of student achievement and attitudes and then select the approach which will achieve the objectives in the most efficient and effective manner. There are points between exposition and inquiry which will probably be the locus of most teacher and student activity. The *directed discussion* is not just a compromise, but a valid device for alternating methods during formal classes or during an entire unit of study.

At the beginning of a class in tenth grade world history the teacher chooses exposition since one of the objectives in the unit on valley civilizations is to identify the rivers and geographical characteristics of the valley civilizations. This teacher uses a current political outline map on the overhead projector to locate the area in today's terms. He shifts to a transparency of a physical map of the area to show terrain and physical features of the land. A third map is used to show the location of the tribes inhabiting the area in the Fifth Century B.C. This is overlaid on the physical map to provide an orientation and to permit each learner to name the rivers and geographical features on a piece of paper at each desk. After each question, the teacher provides the correct answer so that the learner knows immediately about the correctness of his answer. At the end of the test, the teacher determines the individuals who have not reached the objective and meets with them in the corner to review the maps.

Meanwhile, the teacher moves to another objective: "to describe the sources of food, given an understanding of the geographical features of the Tigris and Euphrates Valley." The groups who have demonstrated their competency with the first objective are asked to establish research teams to reach the next objective. The teacher writes the objectives on the chalkboard and indicates that the library is open and that the librarian is expecting groups from this class to come for research. There are two filmstrips and a filmstrip viewer on the reference table and some clippings from *Life* magazines. As the research groups begin their efforts, the teacher joins the group which did not achieve the first objective. When the teacher arrives, they are looking at the maps used on the overhead projector.

The switching that goes on in the previous example is more common and appropriate than complete commitment to one method or another. Too often a total commitment imposes unnecessary restrictions on both the teacher and the learner from which it is difficult to escape when the directions clearly indicate that methods should be changed.

Back to the example. About one-half hour later, the groups have finished their research and the slower group has achieved the initial objective. The teacher brings the whole group together once again and, through directed discussion, draws out the individuals who have done the research on the sources of food while encouraging members of the remedial group to raise questions of classmates who have used the resources. A quick quiz or an informal questioning around the entire group provides sufficient feedback to convince the teacher that both objectives have been reached.

SELECTION OF TECHNIQUES

Techniques are the ways and means adopted by a teacher to direct the learners' activities toward an objective. Techniques are the tools of the teacher. The effective teacher has a multitude of techniques at his disposal and must be prepared to select the ones which will be most efficient in leading the learner to the desired terminal behavior. Techniques are the means for reaching an objective and can be part of expository or inquiry approaches. Certain techniques may be more appropriate for exposition and others more suited to inquiry, but almost any technique can be used for either approach.

11   Techniques (sometimes called methods) can be observed in any formal teaching and learning situation. Name as many techniques as you can recall from your own experience or the examples given in this book.

⋅   ⋅   ⋅   ⋅   ⋅   ⋅

11   *Lecture, discussion, demonstration, direct experience, field trips, role-playing, audiovisual materials. . . .*

Types of Techniques

Each of these techniques will be discussed further with examples. The objective of the authors at this point is to help the reader construct a strategy for teaching, using efficient and effective techniques, when an objective is given.

12   What are the alternative techniques for a high school chemistry laboratory instructor who wants his students to measure dry and liquid chemicals with 100 percent accuracy given an analytic balance, weights, and an unknown quantity of sulphur and a container of hydrogen peroxide?

· · · · · ·

12   a. *The teacher could* tell *the students how to use the balance, verbally supporting his comments with illustrations on the chalkboard.*
      b. *He could* raise questions *about the concept of balance and invite suggestions about handling the chemicals and making preliminary estimates of the weight. He could ask for questions from the class.*
      c. *A* demonstration *would be a good choice, if everyone could see. The use of a simple closed circuit television camera and several receivers could make the demonstration visible to the entire class.*
      d. Direct experience *could be provided simply by stating the objective, giving each student the materials, and asking him to indicate when he is ready to be tested.*
      e. *If the catalog of* audiovisual materials *indicates that there are films, filmstrips, slides, or overhead transparencies, these could be used if they are accessible and available.*
      f. *Combinations of the above techniques could also be considered. It would be stretching the options to include field trips and role-playing techniques here.*

13   What names have been given to each of the techniques (a)–(e) mentioned in Example 12?

· · · · · ·

13   *(a) lecture, (b) discussion, (c) demonstration, (d) direct experience, and (e) audiovisual media.*

Lecture

14   One of the most prevalent techniques is the lecture. Why?

· · · · · ·

14   *Lecturing is probably the most common of all techniques. On the surface it is the easiest, the least expensive, and the most readily available procedure. It can involve extensive preparation or can develop spontaneously. It can be highly organized and logical in its development, or it can be a stream of consciousness with no visible order. Lecture implies a formal presentation while telling and explaining are more descriptive of informal presentations.*

Telling, explaining, and lecturing are the most efficient techniques for communicating facts, generalizations, terms, principles, and theories. Giving directions or providing explanations can be accomplished in an optimum fashion using this technique.

Discussion

15   While the lecture technique is considered to be one way (teacher to student) of interacting, most teachers and students strive for additional

means of interaction. What are the characteristics of the discussion technique and what purposes does it serve?

· · · · · ·

15   *Discussion or conference techniques include all those activities which tend to develop an interchange of ideas between the teacher and the learner and among learners themselves. The basic procedure is to present a topic or an issue. Often the purpose is to give everyone in the class or group an opportunity to speak and voice an opinion on the topic under discussion. If the discussion format is varied to carry on a debate or forum, there is usually an attempt to come to a conclusion and to resolve an issue. The teacher usually acts as a moderator or discussion leader.*

16   Is the discussion technique primarily inquiry or expository in approach?

· · · · · ·

16   *Sometimes discussions are thought of as inquiry with opportunities for an open and free-wheeling exchange of ideas. However, discussions can be expository or inquiry depending upon the strategy selected by the teacher. In an expository discussion, the teacher is a dominant leader and steers the discussion to predetermined conclusions. There are "right" and "wrong" answers. Emphasis is placed on logical development of thought processes, and random questioning is discouraged.*

It is important to note that *recitation* is not discussion. When a teacher asks a question and seeks a particular answer, he is merely using another form of the expository lecture. The student, rather than the teacher, is providing the data. It is a change of pace and a valid procedure, as long as the teacher and the learner accept the technique for what it is—an attempt to assess the learner's knowledge about a particular object or event. When opinions rather than facts are sought in a formal context, the strategy is more inquiry-oriented than expository, but opinions must be honestly elicited and respected. There are no absolutes in opinion formation.

Inquiry-oriented discussion   A guidance counsellor uses the 16mm film, *Phoebe: The Story of a Teenage Pregnancy*, with an eleventh grade class in a group guidance situation. The objective is for each learner to state the consequences of pre-marital sex. The discussion technique is selected to ensure opportunities for participation by as many individuals in the group as would want to speak. A committee of four previews the film independently before it is used to gather information which could be used to prepare the class for viewing the film. They also write down several questions which might stimulate discussion at the end of the showing. A motion picture is selected because it portrays realistically a series of events with which the teenage audience could identify. This particular film was chosen because it is "open-ended." No conclusions are reached. No moral judgments are made. No alternative solutions are presented. All of these missing elements must be provided by the viewers, and it is this type of active involvement which high school students seek. In this case the teacher is available as a counselor and guide but is not the leader. As the film is discussed the teacher does not participate, since the students carry the discussion and present the alternative solutions.

Variation on the discussion technique   The panel discussion permits students to prepare statements concerning an assigned topic. These statements are presented formally to the class or to other groups as an individual's analysis of the topic. This could involve facts and opinions. Members of the panel interact with each other and then permit individuals in the audience to ask questions. This procedure can be either expository or inquiry-oriented, depending upon the topic being discussed, the approach of the students, and the direction given by the teacher.

Discussion can best be summarized as the flow of information and ideas from teacher to learner, from learner to teacher, and from learner to learner.

17   We have discussed two techniques (the lecture and discussion) which involve verbal interaction between the teacher and learners. Which techniques serve as surrogates for real experiences?

·   ·   ·   ·   ·   ·

17   *In one sense the lecture and discussion are surrogates for real experience but are usually on an abstract verbal level. More realistic, or vicarious, are those techniques which involve the real object or event or representation of the object or event. For our purposes we will call these techniques (a) demonstrations, (b) field trips, (c) role-playing, simulation, and gaming, and (d) audiovisual media. We will be expository in presenting the characteristics and case studies concerning each technique. At the end of the chapter, you should be able to* name *each of the techniques and* describe *their possible uses in expository and inquiry strategies.*

Before we look at each technique, we ought to explore briefly the concept of direct experience. If the other techniques are surrogates, we ought to be able to describe the characteristics of the actual object or event.

Direct experience   This is life itself—often under controlled conditions in the school. The phrase "learning by doing" is applicable here. The actual performance is usually preceded by telling and showing. Demonstrations are often provided. The student operates a piece of equipment or completes tasks under controlled conditions. This technique is more familiar in home economics, industrial arts, or vocational education programs than in the academic areas. Kindergarten children make cookies and plant seeds to gain the experience of doing. Seventh grade students play in the school band or sing in the chorus. Learners wire a simple electric circuit in a ninth grade general science course. High school juniors in Spanish III talk with a visitor from Mexico using the Spanish language. These "doing" activities are the most direct means of education. They provide concrete referents for future activities of a more abstract nature.

Activities involving direct experiences are highly inquiry-oriented. The student here is an active participant rather than the passive observer of the lecture or even discussion situation. The teacher defines objectives as for any learning task. Since students are involved in "real life" events, even though they may be in controlled environments, there is more of an opportunity to explore than at times when other media and symbols are used as surrogates for the real event. The student can discover for himself the many facets of his experience and take from it more than was intended. The semester in a foreign country sponsored by many colleges and universities is an illustration of the extra benefits which accrue to an individual beyond the primary goals of learning to speak a language, gaining specific knowledge about the music and art of the country, and earning academic credit toward graduation.

Demonstrations   The demonstration technique is always accompanied by telling or explaining. A demonstration is used to show how something works. Accurate procedures and operations are shown. Models, mock-ups, and actual equipment are used to accomplish the successful demonstration. Demonstrations usually tend to be highly expository since they are dominated by the teacher who is performing a predetermined routine which will lead to a highly predictable result. There are ways to build in inquiry dimensions in a demonstration. A chemistry laboratory demonstration is presented up to a point when the teacher asks which of several alternatives should be followed. The teacher permits a student to make a decision and to act upon that decision. If the action is correct, the demonstration is completed. If not, the resultant action is analyzed and reasons for lack of success are elicited from the class.

Demonstrations are useful because they provide concrete referents for objects or events. Students relate terms and concepts to those events which they have observed.

Field trips   Field trips (or school journeys) are difficult to classify since students are taken to real places to see real people doing real things. The field trip tends to be more of a demonstration than a "doing" event. The students are passive as they observe rather than active in living the event they are observing. However it may be classified, the field trip is a technique which is valuable in the repertoire of any teacher. It provides a dimension of reality which the classroom cannot supply.

Role-playing, simulation, and gaming   There are sound psychological bases for involvement of the student in the process of learning. Robert Travers has pointed out that "Information is not satisfactorily stored when a passive learner is passively exposed to inputs though some learning may occur under such circumstances."[6] Some teachers have attempted to bring into the classroom situations which actively involve students on

[6]Robert W. M. Travers *et al., Research and Theory Related to Audiovisual Information Transmission* (Kalamazoo, Mich.: Western's Campus Bookstore, 1961), p. 259.

the assumption that if a student assumes a role, other than the one he normally holds, he will act in accord with the new role he has assumed or been assigned to perform.

In an effort to learn "to describe the functions of an elected official in city government," members of an eleventh grade social studies class are assigned to various positions in the city government. Jim acts as mayor, George as chairman of the council of supervisors, Mary as chief of police, and Tony as fire marshal. Other members of the class assume the roles of deputies and members of electoral districts serving on the city council. They take over city government for a day. After a briefing by the official, each individual has an opportunity to view first-hand the decisions which have to be made and the pressures which are placed on public officials in serving those who elected them to office. With this experience as a reference point, the group returns to the classroom the next day with important raw data (information) about the city government. They begin to practice "describing the functions . . ." as they share this data with the class. The creative teacher who arranges for this role-playing experience uses the experience as one of the means for achieving the defined objectives.

Role-playing does not have to be an elaborate undertaking. The classroom can become a grocery store to provide a realistic environment for third graders to learn how to identify the value of coins and how to make change. It can become a courtroom for the replication of the trial of Sacco and Vanzetti. In human relations, role-playing situations are created for parent-child relationships. A simple verbal description sets the scene: "It is 12:30 a.m. and Julie has just come home from a date. The rule, to which she agreed, was 'Arrive home before midnight.' This is the second successive week in which Julie has broken the rule." Jean is assigned the role of the mother, George will be the father, and Lynda is Julie. "Begin the action." The teacher, in this case, must maintain a careful observation of the action to be certain that the "play" stays within bounds.

There are other *simulations* which are more sophisticated. Some of the driver training simulators place the student driver in a behind-the-wheel situation where he actually manipulates the steering wheel and uses the pedals on the simulated automobile as he views a motion picture screen resembling the road and real traffic conditions. The student is expected to take appropriate action as events occur on the screen. The objective, in this case, is in the psychomotor domain: "to move steering wheel and pedals when stimulus conditions indicate that certain moves must be made, in less than two seconds." More complex simulators can be found in training schools for pilot instruction. The cockpits are as complete as those in an actual airplane. The landing strips are presented by means of projected pictures, either still or motion.

A more recent development, but one closely related to the role-playing and simulation activities, is *gaming*. Many of us have played board games such as "Monopoly." Now games have been developed especially for use in teaching-learning situations. There is usually a board or some other organizing element. There are objects to be moved, built, traded, or obtained. There are markers to determine the status of each player. Frequently money or items of value are used to carry on business. There is a set of operating rules, and there are players. The players assume the role of an historical figure, or a stock broker, or a geologist whose job it is to predict whether a given tract contains oil. They are given the rules and must operate within the stated constraints. Markers or score cards or status cards are given to each player. If money or other objects of value are used, each player receives his allocated amount. From this point on, the resemblance between the academic game and the ordinary table games diminishes.

A game may be played by one or two people, or by small groups or even entire classes. Games are sometimes played between schools, and there are even national academic Olympic games held each year.

The idea behind gaming in the classroom is that when a student assumes an active role in the process of learning and is responsible for the consequences of his actions, he will gain a knowledge of the decision-making process and the rules which apply to the situation in everyday life.

The objectives in gaming are both product- and process-oriented. In the game of *Empire*, for example, junior high social studies classes should be able to describe the conditions involved in mercantilism and trade during the eighteenth century. Each student should be able to describe the decision points required by merchant-leaders in a nation when confronted with economic problems and trade regulations.

There are several games in the social sciences. *Empire* was developed by Abt Associates for Educational Services, Inc. and is now distributed by Random House. The Center for the Study of the Social Organization of Schools at Johns Hopkins University has developed and tested many games: *Consumer*—a model of the consumer buying process involving players in the problems and economics of installment buying. Consumers compete to maximize utility points for specific purchases while minimizing their credit charges. Credit agents also compete to make the most satisfactory lending transactions. *Democracy*—a game that simulates the legislative process, in which players act as representatives, giving speeches and bargaining with other players. Representatives get re-elected by passing those issues which are most important to their constituents. There are still more complex games that have been developed for use on the computer.

Academic games represent an attempt to provide instructional materials which support the inquiry approach to learning. For most of the games there is no absolute conclusion. There are time limits and the "winners," if there are any, are determined at that time by the performance record during the game. Games involve the students in dynamic learning activity and discourage passivity.

Audiovisual materials   There are several synonyms for the term *audiovisual*. Much of the federal legislation uses the term *educational media* to designate these materials. In some schools the broad term *instructional materials* is used to include all auxiliary items which help the teacher to accomplish the teaching task. Instructional materials would include all the traditional audiovisual materials but would also include items such as chalk, paper, textbooks, workbooks, and globes. In some schools, *learning resources* is the label used to identify all the teaching materials available to teachers and students. In essence, all these terms are interchangeable although there may be shades of difference. We will use all the terms from time to time for the sake of variety and to acquaint the reader with the several usages of the terminology.

There are five broad categories of audiovisual materials:

1. Real materials and people
2. Projected materials
3. Audio materials
4. Printed materials
5. Display materials

Examples of materials in each category are spelled out in Chapter 13, and comprehensive descriptions of each medium are located in Part Five, Media Facts.

Audiovisual materials may be used with expository or inquiry approaches. Many media fall between the expository-inquiry extremes of the continuum. Once again, the stated objectives are the point of reference in selecting audiovisual materials. Some audiovisual materials should follow expository or inquiry objectives while others ought to precede. A basic question must be: "Can this audiovisual material help me to accomplish an objective as well or better than any other means available?" There are some obvious answers when objectives relate to identifying, naming, describing, ordering, and constructing of knowlege or events which are far removed from the school (such as foreign lands); items which are too small or too large to bring to the classroom for everyone to see (such as microscopic images and elephants); processes which are too slow or too fast to observe (such as the opening of a flower or an exercise on the parallel bars); and people who are inaccessible (such as famous people who have died or are unavailable for school appearances).

It is sometimes possible to use a motion picture in either an expository or inquiry fashion. An objective for a fourth grade social studies class is to describe the geographic, living, and economic contrasts in Mexico. The first teacher, who has decided to follow an expository approach, has selected the following film:

Mexico: The Land and the People (20 min., Encyclopaedia Britannica Films, 1961, color, intermediate, junior high)

We see a Mexico of the past existing within a Mexico of the present, people whose customs have changed little since the period of Spanish rule some 400 years ago—in striking contrasts with modern manufacturing centers and luxurious seaside resorts. There is the Mexico of the Indian village and primitive open-air markets within a few minutes drive of a city with beautiful parks, fine theaters, and office buildings.

Because he is using the expository approach, the teacher places key phrases on the chalkboard before the film is shown: "Contrasts in Mexico," "geography," "homes," "buildings," "manufacturing." He asks the students to look for these contrasts during the film showing. The film is shown and followed up by a discussion about the contrasts written on the chalkboard. Three students are selected to summarize the class session with an oral statement about contrasts in Mexico.

The other teacher, who decided to use an inquiry approach, has the same objective. She located the same film in the catalog, ordered it, and previewed it. During the preview she was conscious of the fact that the narrator described everything that was shown in the film and left little to the imagination of the viewer.

When the day arrived to use the film, the teacher restated the objective to the students, wrote the word "contrasts" on the board, and asked one of the students to define it. She then pointed out that there are contrasts *among* countries and contrasts *within* countries. She indicated that they would look at some contrasts in Mexico by means of a film—almost as if they were taking a short field trip to that country. The projector was started, but the sound was deliberately turned off. The class saw a silent version of a sound film. They assumed the posture of observers in a strange land and were required to interpret what they saw as they would on a trip without a guide. When the film ended, the teacher asked for comments on the contrasts which were observed. No attempt was made at this point to separate them into geographical, living, and economic contrasts. Soon the students were talking about people and the ways in which they lived. Someone pointed out that many of the same contrasts exist in our own country. Home craft industries seemed to be the major source of income in rural areas as compared with manufacturing in the urban areas. The session ended when all students had made a contribution to the discussion.

The next day the film was shown again without the sound; students took turns supplying the sound track. Notice that this teacher had the learners practice the terminal behavior described in the objective: "describing . . . contrasts in Mexico." As time progressed, students continued to practice "describing . . . contrasts," given less and less support in the form of a motion picture, words on the chalkboard, or other cues.

18   Are there other techniques which have not been highlighted?

18   *There are several more: laboratory techniques in the sciences and language, the use of student reports, and individual tutorials. There may be others. Combinations of some of the techniques may create new labels for such amalgamations, but the techniques discussed in this chapter are the major procedures followed in the design of instruction.*

19   What techniques have been discussed in this chapter?

19   *(a) lecture, (b) discussion, (c) direct experience, (d) demonstrations, (e) field trips, (f) role-playing, simulation, and gaming, and (g) audiovisual media.*

Problems in Technique Selection

20   As you reviewed some of the case studies and examples for the purpose of selecting the best technique(s), what were some of the problems in making your decision?

       •   •   •   •   •   •

20   *You probably wondered about* availability of resources. *If you selected a certain technique, would the material and equipment be available? Another concern probably centered on* cost. *If you selected the technique that you felt was the best, could the school afford to supply you with the materials and equipment which would be required? These matters are often called the "logistics" of instruction.*

    Logistics refers to planning, handling, and implementation of materials and facilities. This means that if a tape recording is to be used in a classroom, a tape recorder will be available at the time it is needed and someone will be able to operate it. If a recorder is not available, or if no one can operate it, planning to use a tape recorder, even if it is the very best technique to achieve the defined objective, will not matter. *Availability* of materials, equipment, space, or personnel is one aspect of logistics.

    A second consideration has to do with *cost*. A French teacher in Kansas City may feel that the best way to help her advanced students speak French in a stress situation is to take them to a French-speaking city such as Montreal or Quebec. The school board agrees that this would be an ideal experience to achieve the desired behavior, but the budget is already committed and a request for Spanish classes to go to Mexico City might come up next. An alternate solution would have to be found, such as locating one or two French-speaking people in Kansas City to come to the class or to institute a telephone connection with a class in Montreal. *Economic feasibility* is another logistics factor.

    If the materials, equipment, space, and personnel are available and the costs are within reason, the teacher can then proceed to the instructional criteria to help select the best techniques. We must remember that there are times, however, when instructional criteria must come first and that availability and cost problems often can be solved if the argument for instructional productivity is sufficiently strong.

21   Are there other factors which affect your selection of techniques?

       •   •   •   •   •   •

21   *Of course there are—probably too many to include here if we attend to every detail. Let's look at the instructional aspects of selecting the most appropriate technique. Before a technique is selected, the objectives must be clearly defined in behavioral terms and then the content must be determined. The teacher must also know the entering behavior of each individual. These data should help make the selection of techniques an easier task than it might otherwise be.*

The difficulty in making this selection is that there is no formula for matching objectives and techniques. What sometimes "works" for one teacher is a failure for another. The technique that may stimulate eighth graders in Atlanta may bore eighth graders in Memphis. The many variables operating in any classroom make it almost impossible to predict the results of using any technique; consequently we must construct hypotheses based on experiences and research of teachers who have used certain techniques.

SUMMARY

Once objectives, content, and entering behaviors have been determined it is then possible to select appropriate teaching strategies and techniques. Two major approaches, expository and inquiry teaching, offer points of departure for the design of a systematic instructional strategy. The strategy then points to the ways in which a variety of techniques may be used. The techniques described in this chapter include: lecture, discussion, demonstration, doing, field trip, role playing, simulation and gaming, student reports, and audiovisual materials. Techniques are the means for reaching an objective and can be used in both expository and inquiry teaching.

Categories like exposition or inquiry are not always distinct. There are points between. Creative teachers change approaches from time to time as objectives vary. Likewise, techniques should be used at various times according to effectiveness and efficiency criteria. Considerations of cost, availability, and appropriateness also help to determine the best technique to use to achieve an objective.

The guidelines provided in this chapter should permit the teacher to select a strategy for teaching and learning and then to determine the techniques which will help to reach the defined objective.

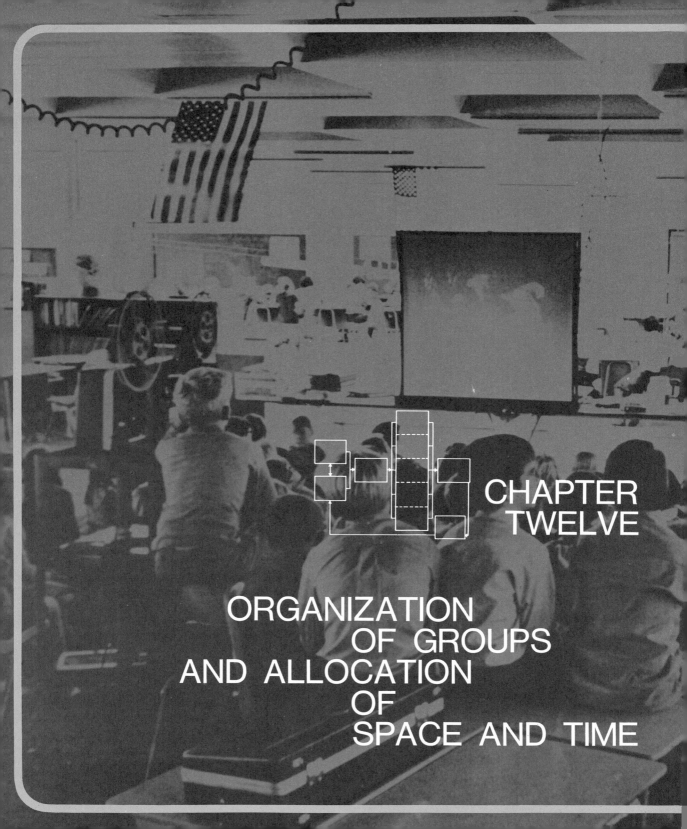

CHAPTER TWELVE

ORGANIZATION
OF GROUPS
AND ALLOCATION
OF
SPACE AND TIME

WHEN YOU HAVE MASTERED THE CONTENT OF THIS CHAPTER, YOU SHOULD BE ABLE TO:

1. ORDER the three components of the teaching-learning system discussed in this chapter according to the original model presented in Chapter 1.

2. STATE three questions which assist in planning the management of the teaching-learning system.

3. DESCRIBE procedures for grouping students and teachers.

4. CONSTRUCT a model student schedule based on large group, medium group, individual study modes using the principles of flexible scheduling.

An invincible nation is a nation of invincible people, united—
for life, liberty and the pursuit of happiness. What people?
All the people? Yes, but each. We unite for the good of the
person. In our nation the most important number is "1"—
the single individual.[1]

No matter which element of the system we are considering, we must
always return to objectives. Precisely what outcomes do we expect the
learner to achieve? Objectives must be the point of reference as we work
with any step of our systematic approach to teaching and learning.

When objectives and content have been specified, the entering behaviors measured, and the strategies selected, then decisions concerning
management functions of the system must be made. We are considering
simultaneously the organization of groups (options for the deployment of
students to various size groups); the allocation of space (options for locating individuals and groups in available classroom and auxiliary spaces);
and allocation of time (options for using time according to the tasks being
performed). These elements are grouped because each affects the other
to a high degree. If we decide to divide a class into five groups, the
space must be available and apportioned accordingly. The amount of
space required for a five minute problem-centered discussion is quite
different from that required for a fifty minute small group discussion.
Obviously, group organization and space and time requirements are highly
interrelated and although we will look at each component as an entity for
the purposes of discussion, we will also consider, later in this chapter,
how to synthesize the three elements.

There is a basic premise underlying our concern for the group-space-
time synthesis in planning for instruction. Historically, schools have been
concerned with providing "the greatest good for the greatest number."
The emphasis is changing to a concern for providing the *best for each*.
It seems incongruous that when our schools have more students than ever
before, and when these students are attempting to cope with more information than ever before with proportionately fewer teachers, we emphasize our concern for the individual.

Today we can do a better job of designing individual learning experiences for students. This can be attributed partly to the fact that technology is available for individual instruction and partly to the fact that

[1]William W. Caudill, *In Education the Most Important Number is One* (Houston, Texas: Caudill, Rowlett and Scott, 1964), p. 4.

objectives are being written in behavioral or operational terms. Once again the important factor is the specification of objectives in terms of an observable action or product, because such objectives enable us to design instruction based on specific guidelines.

MANAGEMENT OF THE LEARNING PROCESS

One way of proceeding toward the management of the learning process is to ask the following questions *after objectives have been specified:*

1. Which objectives can be reached by the learner on his own?
2. Which objectives can be achieved through interaction among the learners themselves?
3. Which objectives can be achieved through formal presentation by the teacher and through interaction between the learner and the teacher?

Answers to these questions will provide useful data for determining how groups should be organized. Some objectives which can be reached independently by the learner should be implemented through the use of the independent study mode. Others require interaction; they demand the use of small groups. Finally, some objectives can best be attained through formal presentation; large group sections will be organized for these.

As we make decisions regarding the organization of groups, we will also consider how to allocate space. Obviously, groups will be assigned to space which is compatible with size of the groups. In some cases this will mean alteration or adaptation of existing space.

The allocation of time will be a function of the nature of the objectives and the learner's efficiency in attaining them. In some cases the administrative organization of the school may dictate time constraints which will have to be adapted to the instructional system.

The Ontario Curriculum Institute has described a very unusual elementary classroom. Notice, in the excerpt below, the dynamics of the teaching-learning process, including the components just discussed. Note, too, the extensive use of instructional media in this school.

> The classroom is completely different. At first the difference may seem to lie in the abundance of materials and equipment, in the grouping of students' desks, or in the existence of two eight foot dividers that swing out into the classroom for the corridor wall. A visit with the class in session reveals the basic differences.
>
> Students in this room are self-directed. They have established purposes and rules of conduct themselves. The teacher's role here is to inspire, advise, and occasionally remind. Learning resources are essential to this kind of program.
>
> The classroom has its own filmstrip projector, aquarium, screen, record player with headphones, books, microscope, encyclopaedia, globe, filmstrip viewer, and self-contained 8mm cartridge-load projector. In an adjacent storeroom there is a 16mm projector and a portable science lab to be shared by four classes.

The school itself is well supplied with learning materials by current standards. In addition to the library, there is a resource center to which individual students may come. The center has reference books, tables and chairs, and a variety of audiovisual equipment located in five carrels along one wall. There is a tape recorder with headset, a record player, two filmstrip viewers, and an 8mm cartridge projector. Mounted on the walls are filmstrips (about four hundred), recordings, and 8mm films. A number of models and devices are also located on shelves in the room.

Each of the eighteen classrooms in the building has its own light control, wall screen, radio reception, and filmstrip-slide projector. The school as a whole is served with two 16mm projectors, three tape recorders, three record players, two 8mm projectors, two television sets, and two overhead projectors, in addition to the equipment in the resource center and the atypical classroom.

To complement the school's resources, the Board of Education provides films and other materials through a daily delivery service, and extra equipment on long term loan. School buses are available so that field trips are taken at no expense to students.

The teacher in what we have chosen to call the "atypical" class has made all materials directly available to her students, without restriction. They move freely about the classroom, view 16mm films in the adjoining storeroom, and work in the resource center if they so desire. Students work in groups, exploring problems and topics co-operatively. When a group has satisfied itself that it is ready, a topic is presented to the whole class. Non-book materials are used by the students in their presentations.

This shift in emphasis from teaching to learning has remarkable consequences. Surrounded with a variety of materials, the students analyze, synthesize, and create their own meaning, rather than paraphrase the encyclopaedia in the customary manner. Their abilities to evaluate and then to articulate are heightened. They use learning resources as sources of information and experience, and as creative media of expression. This full exploitation of contemporary media is all too rare.[2]

1   What conditions permit the learner to reach objectives on his own?

•   •   •   •   •   •

1   *The abundance of resources and the free access to them probably contribute more to independent study by individuals than any other factors. Each pair of headsets for the record player becomes an individual carrel; the adjoining storeroom where students may view 16mm films is another independent learning space. Access to the school's resource center by individuals is a key facilitating factor for independent learning.*

[2]Ontario Curriculum Institute, *Technology in Learning* (Toronto: The Institute, 1965), p. 87. Quoted by permission of The Ontario Institute for Studies in Education.

2   What evidence is there in this case study that objectives are reached through interaction of the learners?

•   •   •   •   •   •

2   *First, there are facilities for small group work: the eight foot dividers that swing out into the classroom create new spaces for small groups; the moveable desks ensure the possibility of easy groupings. One of the strategies is obviously inquiry-oriented when "Students work in groups, exploring problems and topics co-operatively."*

3   Does the teacher make formal presentations and interact with the students?

•   •   •   •   •   •

3   *"The teacher's role here is to inspire, advise, and occasionally remind." Whether this is done in a formal sense is not indicated, but by inference, the teacher probably does present information when necessary. The shift is clearly from teaching to learning. The teacher probably interacts with individuals and small groups as he inspires, advises, and reminds.*

4   What are the three questions which can help the teacher to organize groups, and to allocate time and space?

•   •   •   •   •   •

4   *a.   Which objectives can be reached by the learner on his own?*
     b.   Which objectives can be achieved through interaction among the learners themselves?
     c.   Which objectives can be achieved through formal presentation by the teacher and through interaction between the learner and the teacher?

The three questions, then, are the focal point for making decisions regarding the organization of groups and the allocation of space and time. While each element will be discussed separately, we should remember that all three components of the model discussed in this chapter interact with one another and that the three constitute a simultaneous concern.

ORGANIZATION OF GROUPS

The three basic group structures are individual study, small groups, and large groups. These units may be further divided according to the differences among individuals, groups, and content. Students are grouped and regrouped, when necessary, according to general ability, achievement, interest, need for remedial work, and capacity for self-direction. Students move from one group to another whenever evidence of achievement or need for another type of instruction seems appropriate—not just at the end of a unit, the book, the semester, or the year. The learners complete the work of a grade or a defined level of achievement at various times of the year.

Decisions regarding the amount of time to be spent, sequence of subject matter, and the use of instructional resources may cause new groupings to take place. It may be, for example, that the small group of 15 should be divided into three groups of 5 for exploration of a topic. Sometimes group sizes between those of the small group of 15 and the large group of 100 or 200 are needed. Medium sized groups of 15 to 60 or 75 might be appropriate because of classroom configurations or enrollment in a course or grade. The patterns of organization will vary from school to school. There are really only two certainties:

1. no longer will one teacher be responsible for teaching an entire subject or combination of subjects to groups of 25 to 30 students meeting for five times a week, and
2. the organization will be a direct function of the objectives which have been defined.

There will be frequent need to regroup students in order to cope with the varying rates of learning and with the changing interests which most students display. Flexibility of grouping is a basic characteristic of this system. If the objectives and the learners' needs are the most important factors in determining group structure, we should witness a gradual disappearance of such traditional practices as deciding several weeks before the school year begins to keep students in a specified group for a semester or a year. Nothing in the educational structure should prohibit a student from learning at the time he is ready to do so. To hold a student back in science because he is not doing well in history is a violation of the principle that each learner should be able to move according to his individual ability.

The permanent class organization of 25 to 35 students, so common in today's schools, will give way to the new concept in grouping. The traditional size is too small for the type of activities conducted in large groups. The cost of maintaining this size cannot be justified in terms of the learning. Students learn just as well in a group of 100 as in four groups of 25 when the method is largely expository. The traditional arrangement of 25 to 30 students, especially in the secondary school and college, must be stultifying for most teachers who have to repeat the same information for several classes each day, with the subsequent result that they have little time or energy for productive planning, for creation of teaching materials, and for individual contacts with their students.

A class of 25 to 35 is too large for effective independent study. In an independent study mode, each individual should have the opportunity to move about as he seeks resources and as he creates new materials and formulates new ideas.

A class of 25 to 35 is also too large for effective active discussion. Research on the interaction of groups indicates that a group should be no larger than 12 to 15 if all students are to benefit.

Ungraded Organization

It was in the mid-nineteenth century, when the Quincy Grammar School opened in Boston, that the idea of grading began. The predominance of one-room schoolhouses had perpetuated the practice of an ungraded organization since the first appearance of formal American schools. The latter half of the nineteenth century saw the rapid development of grouping children by age and moving them ahead as a group at the end of the school year. Eventually the "passing" or "promoting" of an entire group to the next grade became an annual ceremonial ritual performed regardless of whether the student had mastered the content of the grade level.

The graded school is still very common. There are many reasons for its continuing in this century-old pattern. Both state curriculum guides and new curricula being developed by committees and commissions from within the disciplines presuppose the organization of schools by grade level. The publication of textbooks and various audiovisual materials for specific grade levels often limits the potential use of these resources. Many of these instructional materials receive "state adoptions" which, in effect, establish sanctioned materials for specific grade levels throughout a state. In some cases the textbooks themselves become the curriculum outlines.

The concept of grade levels began to break down as team teaching, flexible scheduling, and technology of individual instruction began to appear. Students of various levels of achievement were divided into homogeneous discussion groups, and materials were created for self-instructional purposes. The construction and renovation of learning spaces to provide for large group, small group, and independent study broke down the egg crate model which had been used for classrooms within the school. The next logical step was to introduce the opportunity for individual student progress through an ungraded organization of the curriculum. In this sense, we are back to the one-room schoolhouse in modern dress!

A nongraded (or ungraded) school is:

> . . . a place which makes arrangements for the individual student to pursue any course in which he is interested, and has the ability to achieve, without regard either to grade level or to sequence.[3]

The teachers in a nongraded school are organized in a team teaching mode with a cadre of teaching aides and assistants. Students are assigned to certain "levels" which are defined according to ability rather than by chronological age. Within each level the subject matter has been organized according to phases which are designed to group students in relation to their achievement. In a Florida high school, which has pioneered one form of a nongraded concept, each subject is divided into five phases:

Phase 1   Subjects are designated for students who need special assistance in small classes.

Phase 2   Subjects are designed for students who need more emphasis on the basic skills.

Phase 3   Subject matter is designed for students with average ability.

[3]B. Frank Brown, *The Nongraded High School* (Englewood Cliffs, N.J.: Prentice-Hall, Inc. 1963), p. 43.

Phase 4 Subject matter is designed for capable students desiring education in depth.

Phase 5 Challenging courses are available to students with exceptional ability who are willing to assume responsibility for their own learning and go far beyond the normal high school level.[4]

A basic procedure in this approach is to measure the entering behavior of each student in each area of study. Without regard to grade level or sequence within the curriculum, the school allows any individual learner to take any course for which he can demonstrate the appropriate prerequisites. A student might be in Phase 2 of English, Phase 3 of social studies, Phase 3 of biology, and Phase 4 of mathematics. Phase 4 of mathematics, which might emphasize differential equations, could include students who are 14, 15, 16, and 17 years of age. Some might be taking mathematics for the first time, while others might have completed two or three prerequisite courses.

The same fundamental procedures are followed in the elementary school. Students are permitted to proceed through reading and arithmetic as rapidly as they are able. From time to time they are tested for mastery of essential skills and move from one achievement group to another. If the criteria are not met, then the student remains in the group or he is given remedial work in those areas where he needs specific assistance.

The nongraded school encourages independent study to a far greater extent than does the conventional school. It is one of the best illustrations of the shift from "the greatest good for the greatest number," which characterized our schools in the past, to "the best for each."

Psychologist William Clark Trow describes another benefit which can be derived from the new attempts to individualize instruction:

> It is probable that a large block of undesirable school behavior will be eliminated as the students find themselves faced with tasks at their own levels of ability, neither so easy as to be a bore, nor so difficult as to produce excessive frustration with the consequent apathy, anxiety, aggression, or hostility.[5]

Other Approaches to Grouping

Although the groupings mentioned above are the most common, there are other approaches. Some of the other approaches are: multiclass teaching, schools within schools, and educational parks.

Multiclass teaching Sometimes a teacher is able to have several different groups in the same room at the same time. It is possible to provide a number of courses or to handle several grades simultaneously. With

---

[4]Brown, *The Nongraded High School*, p. 50.
[5]William Clark Trow, *Teacher and Technology* (New York: Appleton-Century-Crofts, 1963), p. 134.

the aid of instructional media, multiclass teaching can be very effective. For example, some students may be using programmed instruction, while some are in a group around a television monitor, and some are listening through headsets to a prerecorded tape made by the teacher.

The multiclass approach is used in the one-room school or in ungraded classes. Children are grouped according to their level of achievement, and while the teacher works with an individual or small group, the remainder of the group does assigned work. Today's version of the one-room

The open school of today is an enlarged and up-dated version of the one-room schoolhouse.

schoolhouse is a large, open, carpeted room. Two to six classes of the traditional 25 to 35 students are located there. Common resources are used, such as a room library, science and audiovisual equipment, and display surfaces. From time to time, students are regrouped according to their abilities and interests. If one of these multiclass teaching rooms has two third grade classes and two fourth grade classes in one large room, small groups of children from third and fourth grades may be "mixed" for reading or mathematics, but the entire group of third and fourth graders may gather for a Spanish lesson when the visiting foreign language teacher comes. In some schools the folding wall permits quick changes of room configuration for multiclass teaching, since classes can combine when the walls are opened. Again, common resources are shared and teachers operate as teams.

Schools within schools   To combat the bigness of some schools, attempts are being made to create smaller units within the larger complex. Again, as with multiclass teaching, the building is the agent which makes this arrangement possible. A school with an enrollment of 2000 students is broken down into four "houses" of 500 each. Various terms such as "houses" or "pods" are used to describe the little schools within the big

Large modern schools are sometimes divided into smaller units called "houses" or "pods."

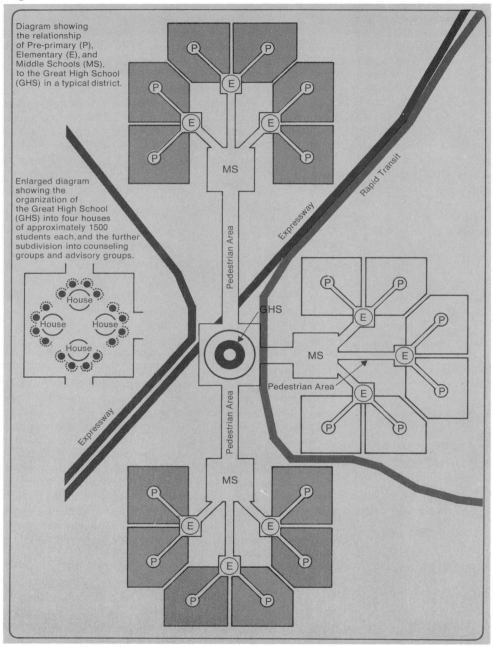

Diagram showing the relationship of Pre-primary (P), Elementary (E), and Middle Schools (MS), to the Great High School (GHS) in a typical district.

Enlarged diagram showing the organization of the Great High School (GHS) into four houses of approximately 1500 students each, and the further subdivision into counseling groups and advisory groups.

complex. There are common eating, physical education, and learning resource facilities within the complex. Large group instruction takes place by television or in a space which will hold a large group, such as a "cafetorium." Small group and independent study situations occur within each unit.

The grouping of students in the school within a school arrangement is made by grade level or by multigrade level. Under the grade level arrangement, all of the first grade classes are together, all of the second grade classes, and so on. Under the multigrade level arrangement, one group of primary and one group of intermediate learners are located in one house with another group of primary and another group of intermediate students in a second house. While the number of schools using this arrangement is not large, most of the schools that do use it feel that the new arrangement permits students to identify more closely with their school and that teacher and student morale has improved. The problems seem to center on the joint use of space and staff.

In some secondary schools, houses have been set aside for certain languages; for example, a single large school might include a Spanish house and a French house, where the language is used in some of the instruction, even in nonlanguage classes. Separate vocational, agricultural, and business houses have been established because of the specialized equipment required.

Educational parks   Once considered an avant-garde plan for solving educational and social problems, the educational park or campus, where many levels of education are combined on the same site, is appearing with increasing frequency. Every educational program from preschool through junior college and adult education is located in a single campus setting. Through centralization of services and resources, some economies can be effected. For example, some educational parks use a distribution network for getting information from a central location to the point where it is needed in minimum time.

· · · · · · · ·

5   Name and describe the approaches to grouping students which have been discussed in this chapter.

5   *a.   Grouping by size—large group, small group, individual study.*

b.   Ungraded grouping—students are placed in groups for which they have qualified regardless of age or grade level; they may be at different levels or phases for each subject.

c.   Multiclass groupings—several groups or classes at approximately the same level are taught simultaneously by one teacher.

d.   Schools within schools—to combat the bigness of some schools, several grades are grouped together in a house or pod, but this procedure is more an administrative operation than a decision based on ability or achievement.

e. Educational parks—*an educational campus which brings together, in one central location, many learners at many levels, often from preschool to college, to gain efficiency in the availability of resources and the cooperative use of expensive facilities.*

Grouping by the Teacher

The grouping of students is a major management decision, often made by the school administration. The use of some of the newer approaches to grouping, such as multiclass teaching, educational parks, and schools within schools, depends largely on the facilities available and is, therefore, outside the domain of the classroom teacher. There are, however, several basic decisions which must be made by the teacher who is using a systematic approach. These decisions involve the procedure for grouping those students for whom the teacher is designing instructional experiences. There are three basic alternatives: students can be grouped by ability, by interest, or by achievement rate. The group to which a specific student belongs may vary from subject to subject and from project to project.

Grouping by ability   Homogeneous grouping refers to grouping by ability. If the implementation of one's objectives indicates that students with similar intellectual abilities should be placed together, this can be accomplished easily. No matter what the ability level, there is reason to believe that students can achieve their maximum potential if they are challenged and surrounded by those who have approximately the same level of intellectual development. However, students may become stereotyped with respect to ability, and such students seldom move from one group to another. Even in primary classes, the group of slow readers is readily identified by the other children, and the stigma of such placement can continue beyond the immediate situation.

Grouping by interest   Grouping by interest tends to be a self-selection process. It is usually project-oriented. Those individuals who want to do research on transportation in the state can work together. Those who want to study the natural resources of the state form another group. The students interested in manpower work together as still another group. This committee structure has worked well over the years and will continue to be a useful method of grouping.

Grouping by achievement rate   Very often the grouping by ability or by interest will, in fact, determine the pacing of any group. Teachers should realize, however, that individuals may have different rates of learning even though their measured abilities are similar. A very able group, for example, may choose to probe a topic in depth and therefore prolong the time spent in a project. On the other hand, students in another group may have the ability to reach an objective, but their learning style, as a group,

Campus plans include more than one building and are often designed for the full spectrum of education.

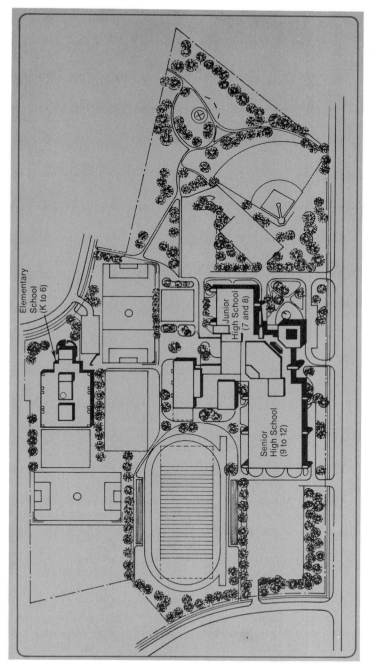

tends to be more deliberate and plodding. The objective is reached in each case, but at different rates.

When the teacher is faced with the organization of groups, it will be necessary to analyze the objective and the individual ability and interest of each student. It will be possible, in any given group, to find many who are "more or less" alike. There will be natural groupings for many situations, but the alert teacher has to be aware of changes, ready to regroup when necessary. We must constantly return to our starting point. What is it we want a student to be able to *do*, and how can his placement in a group help him to reach this objective?

6 What options does the teacher have for grouping students regardless of administrative organization of the school or school system?

• • • • • •

6 a. *Students can be grouped by* ability—*those with similar intelligence potential are placed together.*
   b. *Students can be grouped according to* interest—*most frequently oriented around projects when individuals are selected to work toward common interest goals.*
   c. *Students can be grouped by achievement rate—the actual level of attainment in any given subject determines placement of the individual learner.*

7 What grouping is used for ungraded programs?

• • • • • •

7 *Achievement rate is the primary determinant of placement, whether it be for individual instruction or for groups.*

8 Is there one achievement level for all students regardless of the subject?

• • • • • •

8 *No; students are grouped for each subject and may vary in level from one subject to another.*

Grouping of the Teachers

Sometimes the concern for the individual differences of learners and the attempts to provide appropriate experiences for helping them achieve defined behaviors tend to obscure another critical problem, namely, individual differences among teachers. The tasks teachers perform vary greatly in type and degree of responsibility. In recognition of differences among teachers and the tasks they perform, two new types of organization have emerged: team teaching and differentiated staffing.

Team teaching The concept of the teaching team evolved as an attempt to permit teachers to use their talents most effectively. Today, team teaching is widely used and sometimes misused. Misuse occurs when one teacher is teaching and other team members are doing nothing. It has become part of the fabric of instructional design, especially at the elementary level and to a lesser extent at the secondary level.

What is team teaching? The Shaplin and Olds definition is useful:

> Team teaching is a type of instructional organization, involving teacher personnel and the students assigned to them, in which two or more teachers are given responsibility, working together, for all or a significant part of the instruction of the same group of students.[6]

Team teaching has several advantages. Teachers who work in teams specialize. In the elementary school, the specialization is usually by subject matter—reading, science, mathematics, or social studies. In the secondary school, specialization may be defined by areas of content, within a field; for example, members of the English team may be specialists in literature, speech, writing, and criticism. The advantage for the student is that in some fields he is exposed to several teachers with higher degrees of competence than he would be with one generalist who is not equally competent in all phases of a field. However, generalists are still needed to provide coordination and to help in the integration of knowledge.

There is an element of cross-fertilization that results from individuals working as a group toward a common goal. The teaching team may include both experienced and new teachers. The neophyte teachers can learn from the more experienced. Teacher aides are often part of the team. These assistants handle routine reporting, record keeping, production of simple materials such as duplicated papers and copies of transparencies for the overhead projector, and they are available for the time-consuming sub-professional tasks which are always a part of classroom management. Use of such sub-professionals affords increased opportunity for the teachers on the team to discuss teaching strategies and problems of individual students during planning meetings and to observe the teaching of fellow team members. The discussion which follows such an observation can yield high dividends to new and experienced teachers alike.

The grouping of teachers into teams implies the grouping of students into various size units. The large group–small group–independent study pattern is a logical solution to the deployment of students. If the three third grade classes of 30 students each are taught by a team, there will be 90 students in the large group sections at various times during the week. While one teacher has the primary responsibility for the group, the others may be observing or working on preparations for future sessions. Team planning and team presentation provide consistency of instruction and eliminate needless repetition of materials. There is no known difference in the results of using a film clip three times for three groups of 30 and the results of showing it once for a group of 90. The use of the information gained will take place later during a small group discussion session.

[6]Judson T. Shaplin and Henry F. Olds, Jr., eds., *Team Teaching* (New York: Harper & Row, Publishers, 1964), p. 15.

With some time freed from formal and often repetitive presentations, teachers can spend more time in planning and creating the instructional materials which will be used in the large group, small group, and independent study situations. Planning time for these kinds of activities is seldom available when the teacher is responsible every hour of every school day for a group of students.

A number of questions concerning team teaching have been raised. This arrangement means that one teacher may do more work than another, since the decision regarding the use of time is usually left up to the individual teacher. Some critics say that research has yet to show that team teaching results in more learning. There is little evidence to challenge this criticism. There is also the problem of cost. If teacher aides are employed, additional salary is required. Since team teaching usually requires more teaching materials, the budget would probably have to be increased. The question of efficiency and effectiveness has to be answered in order to meet this criticism.

The criticisms have not seemed to blunt the growth of team teaching. Teachers are now actively involved in this enterprise in nearly every state[7] and are responding enthusiastically to the new perspective they seem to gain about teaching because they are vitally involved with the ideas in which they are most interested.

Differentiated staffing   Differentiated staffing allocates instructional tasks among a teaching staff. It is an attempt to make maximum use of teacher talent. There is a variety of models currently being tried in many school districts, but no one plan prevails. Differentiated staffing began as an antidote to inefficient use of human resources, since all teachers have traditionally been treated as equals in the instructional role. "The basic purpose of differentiated staffing is to provide a more individualized program. . . . Differentiated staffing corrects this [inefficient use of talent] by assigning teachers on the basis of matching their various combinations and degrees of talent to children's needs."[8]

Smith outlines the types of personnel who might be involved in a differentiated staff organization:

> The new staff organization model makes use of teacher aides, educational technicians and teacher clerks who may have little or no formal college training. It also utilizes people with a year or less of college training, as well as junior college graduates and university doctorates. Some categories might be satisfied by a professional in the arts or a competent scientist or journalist.[9]

[7]*Nation's Schools* (April, 1967) reports that so many schools are using team teaching that it is no longer considered to be a major innovation. In a study of 7237 accredited secondary schools, about 41 percent reported the use of team teaching on a regular basis.
[8]Fenwick English, "Questions and Answers on Differentiated Staffing." *Today's Education*, March, 1969, pp. 53–54.
[9]Rodney Smith, "A Teacher is a Teacher is a Teacher?" *Florida Schools*, September-October, 1968, p. 4. Quoted by permission of Florida Department of Education/*Florida Schools* magazine.

One of the pioneer school systems to introduce differentiated staffing organizes functions on a four level teaching hierarchy (see illustration[10]):

1. An Associate Teacher, who is a novice, and has a less demanding schedule than other teachers;
2. A Staff Teacher, who has a full teaching load and is aided by clerks, technicians, and other paraprofessionals;
3. A Senior Teacher, who might be characterized as a "learning engineer"—a specialist in a subject, discipline, or skill area; and
4. A Master Teacher, a scholar-researcher with curriculum development competencies, who translates research and theory to classroom applications.

Besides the obvious efficiency which differentiated staffing offers, there is an equally compelling argument for its use. Within the school organization there is an incentive system which permits teachers to advance as *teachers* rather than to advance by assuming nonteaching positions as supervisors or administrators. When differentiated staffing is in full operation, some advocates feel that it will be possible for some teachers to earn $25,000 per year or more and command authority and status in the educational system equivalent to that of some administrators and beyond that of many others.

[10]Rodney Smith, "A Teacher is a Teacher," p. 5. Adapted by permission of Florida Department of Education/*Florida Schools* magazine.

Model of differentiated staffing.

			Non-tenure
		Non-tenure	Master Teacher Doctorate or Equivalent
	Tenure	Senior Teacher M.S. or Equivalent	
Tenure	Staff Teacher B.A. Degree and Calif. Credential		
Associate Teacher A.B. or Intern			
100% Teaching	100% Teaching Responsibilities	3/5's Staff Teaching Responsibilities	2/5's Staff Teaching Responsibilities
1–10 Months	10 Months	10–11 Months	12 Months
Academic Assistants A.A. Degree or Equivalent			
Educational Technicians			
Clerks			

Differentiated staffing provides a promising solution to separating teacher roles and offering career advancement within teaching. Classroom teaching remains the base and core responsibility for all positions in the hierarchy. Support is provided by clerks, technicians, and paraprofessionals.

9 What arguments would you use to justify team teaching to your chief school administrator?

•   •   •   •   •   •   •

9   *a. Individuals on a teaching team use their best talents; they do those things which they are best qualified to do.*
     b. On a teaching team there is an active exchange of ideas during planning and evaluation.
     c. Assistance from teacher aides and other paraprofessionals releases the teacher from routine and nonprofessional tasks.
     d. More time is gained for planning and preparation of instructional materials.

10 Would you prefer to participate on a teaching team or in a differentiated staffing organization? Why?

•   •   •   •   •   •   •

10   *Your answer depends on your life style and professional preparation. You would probably choose team teaching if you feel that you would prefer to participate in a coordinate role with your colleagues. On most teaching teams, each individual has equal weight in decision-making—and equal salary as well. On a differentiated staff, you would be in a hierarchy with opportunities for upward mobility. The senior teacher and master teacher play an active leadership role and are rewarded accordingly with higher salaries than those of the associate teacher or staff teacher. Be ready to make your choice if you are asked during an interview for your next position.*

ALLOCATION OF SPACE

Independent Study

The answer to the question, "Which objectives can be reached by the learner on his own?" may lead to a design for independent study. An extreme case of independent learning would be the "self-educated man" who has achieved a significant position in the world with a minimum of formal schooling. These people are highly motivated and goal-oriented. Goals are set by the individual himself, and his actions or the products of his actions are certainly observable. Unfortunately we cannot formulate a rule on the basis of the exception, but we can observe the results of strong drive and clear goals.

Consider several ways in which independent study can be carried out. When the teacher assigns Chapter 8 to be read for the next history class, the student might do this studying independently during his "study hall." When the teacher assigns 30 problems for arithmetic "homework," the student will probably study independently at home. When the teacher allots the final 20 minutes of the English period for the reading of "Aes Triplex," the students will be engaged in independent study as they read the essay. There is, however, a world of difference between the assignment to read Chapter 8 on the Industrial Revolution in England for a test the next day and the kind of independent study which we are considering.

Suppose we ask the student to learn to name the inventions which contributed to the Industrial Revolution and to describe the changes in the life of a working man in 18th century England as a result of the Industrial Revolution, given the information provided in Chapter 8 of the textbook. The differences, of course, lie in the fact that the objectives in the latter case are unambiguous; thus reading the chapter becomes a means for the attainment of a clearly and explicitly stated end.

Some carrels are very simple.

As he endeavors to attain his objectives, a student in an independent study situation may use a variety of methods and media. He may read, listen to records and tapes in a resource center, or view slides or filmstrips himself. He may experiment in an independent laboratory carrel or investigate mathematical problems using a computer console. Independent study time can be used to write, create, memorize, or record. Self-criticism can take place after the student listens to a recording of a recitation given earlier in the day. Independent study time may be used for visits to museums, to local businesses, or with resource people—including the teacher. Regardless of how the time is used, independent study is a vital element of the learning process when the student pursues specific goals in a variety of locations on his own.

Carrels   One of the most prominent "symbols" of the new interest in independent study is the carrel. The concept has been revived from the Middle Ages when monks did their study and scribing in places called carrels. Libraries in colleges and universities have traditionally provided a small number of carrels for faculty and graduate students who need space for doing research and writing in the library.

Today carrels are found not only in the library, but in classrooms, resource centers, and even the school hall. The carrels are no longer

Contemporary carrels should have access to electrical service.

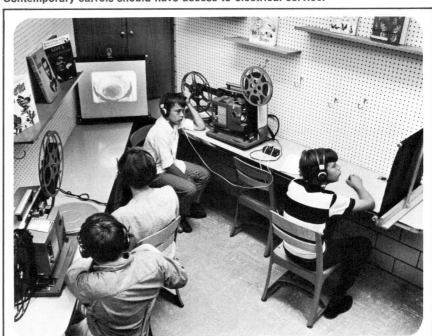

Clusters of carrels provide privacy.

limited to use by faculty and graduate students; elementary and secondary students seek out such areas to pursue individual interests in relative privacy. Modest carrels of this type often contain only a chair and a working surface. For some purposes such carrels are completely adequate. However, just as the patterns of group organization and scheduling practices are changing, so the stark atmosphere of the medieval carrel and the traditional university carrel has given way to attractive enclosures with comfortable chairs, bright working surfaces, and access to electrical service for a wide range of audiovisual equipment.

Carrels are not *required* for individual study, but they do help to ensure privacy when it is wanted. Many libraries and resource centers offer open tables for six or eight individuals as well as clusters of carrels for those who prefer the privacy. When you next go to a school library or resource center which contains both types, observe the number of students at the open tables and in the carrels. It has been the authors' experience to find most students seeking out the privacy. A study involving students from four institutions in the Connecticut Valley concerned with the design

Small, lightweight equipment can be checked out for use in a carrel.

of individual study spaces indicated that college students preferred small spaces, away from noise, with good lighting, control over ventilation, large work surfaces, and chairs that "fit."[11]

Carrels with no equipment other than a desk and semi-isolated surface are known as "dry" carrels and those with electricity as "wet."

In a "wet" carrel, a study lamp, an electric typewriter, or small individual previewers for slides, filmstrips, and 8 mm films can be used. Tape and disc playbacks can be used with headsets. It is a simple matter to check out small, lightweight audiovisual units from a central location for use in any type of wet carrel. Other self-instructional units that require electricity, such as reading pacers and some types of teaching machines,

[11]Stuart M. Stoke et al., Student Reactions to Study Facilities, The Committee for the New College, 1960.

could be used in a wet carrel. It may be easier in centers where there is constant demand for certain types of audiovisual equipment, to set up some carrels with equipment and assign students to the unit where appropriate equipment is located. In this case, it would be necessary to check out the materials only.

In some situations, it may be necessary to provide spaces for more than one person but fewer than five. For example, if three or four students want to listen to a recording of Ogden Nash reading his own poetry, listening posts located on an open table would make the recording available to as many listeners as there were jacks for the headphones. Several students should be able to preview together a silent 8mm film in a cartridge projector.

The specifications for these facilities, unlike specifications for computer terminals or dial access audio retrieval systems, are not too advanced for

Where there is a constant demand for the use of audiovisual equipment, carrels can be permanently set up.

A listening center permits all students with headsets to listen to a tape or disc recording.

even the most modest school. Carrels can be set up in classroom or other spaces within the school building without major alterations. A simple plywood or wallboard divider can be used to convert an ordinary table into a series of carrels. Listening posts and preview corners can be set up almost anywhere in the classroom. Individuals or small groups can use these makeshift but highly functional areas. For individuals who do not require the use of equipment but do need isolation and quiet, areas in the classrooms, the halls, the library, and unassigned space may be converted to independent study space.

Dial-access systems   A recent development in the area of independent study facilities and resources is dial-access or remote-access technology. The basic outline of the system appears in the accompanying illustration. A central control facility makes studio information (usually on tape) and audiovisual information (on videotape or film) available in answer to a request which is dialed-in from a remote location.   The central control houses many banks of tape recorders which have audio programs ready to play.   In centers where audiovisual information is available, several

Carrels can be inexpensively built.

videotape playback units and motion picture projectors stand ready to run materials. At the other end of the line is an individual in a carrel who has a telephone dial, a set of headphones, a television receiver, and a catalog of programs available from the central control. The individual carrel is connected to the central control by a wire. The carrels may be located anywhere. In a public school system in New England, the control center is in one of the high schools, while carrels are located in a high school library, in a viewing room, in most of the high school class-rooms, and in three elementary schools. At a large midwestern university, the control center is located in one building while the carrels are located in the library, the student union, the music building, the listening center, and in several dormitories and fraternity houses.

The number of available recordings or films in most systems varies from 40 to 100, depending on requests by the faculty and demands of the stu-dents. The recordings and films are listed in a catalog. A student may

Listening posts and preview corners can be set up almost anywhere in the classroom.

want to hear the inauguration address of John F. Kennedy. If it is listed
in the catalog, he dials the correct number, thus activating the tape recorder in the control center. If someone else is using the tape, the new
listener joins the other listener "in mid-stream" and continues until the
end when the tape repeats. The system can operate at any hour, and its
capacity can be increased almost infinitely. Most systems offer the audio
component only, although the number offering video is steadily increasing.
In some communities the control system is connected to the regular telephone system to make the collection available to students in their homes.

Small Group Discussion

To determine which objectives can be achieved best (1) through interaction between the learner and the teacher and (2) among the learners
themselves, it is necessary to look at small group organization. There is
no absolute number for "small," but 15, or fewer, students will be considered a small group in this book.

The group might meet in a corner of the classroom or in a conference room. While this is primarily a student activity, a teacher is usually in attendance. Student leaders are also used. But what is the remainder of the class doing? They may be in other groups, with a teacher aide or assistant, or with a tape recording made by the teacher. They may be working independently with programmed instructional materials or on a project designed for individual study.

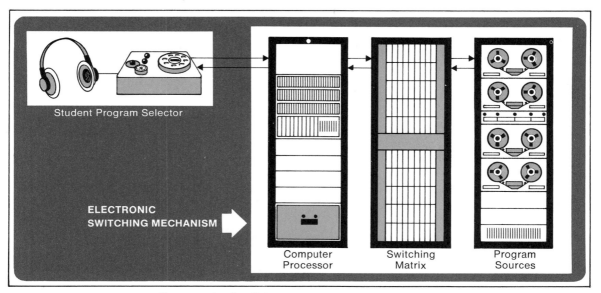

Student Program Selector

**ELECTRONIC
SWITCHING MECHANISM**

Computer
Processor

Switching
Matrix

Program
Sources

Components of a dial-access system.

In small groups, issues are discussed to determine areas of agreement or disagreement. Groups examine terms, concepts, and problems to gain a depth of understanding and to clarify points of uncertainty. One of the fringe benefits of the group situation is the improvement of interpersonal relationships.

The small group provides a setting in which teachers and students can come to know each other better than they could in a large group. Ideas from large group meetings are probed. Opportunities for interaction permit mutual questioning and discussion of the content as well as the development of interpersonal skills. Since leadership in small groups may rotate, more students are given a chance to practice leadership. This unique function of small group units cannot be easily achieved in any other way.

Attainment of small group objectives is often implemented through *discussion* of concepts which were presented either in the textbook or in a large group session. Other methods of attaining objectives in small groups include *answering questions, laboratory work, solving problems*, and *remedial work*. Small groups may be well suited to process objectives such as those related to *leadership, participation* in a group, and *social awareness.*

Sometimes we need to group students according to their abilities. Students requiring remedial work should be together, as should those who have demonstrated mastery of objectives and those who have gone beyond the specified level of competence. The slower student is able to work on areas of specific deficiency and to solidify earlier learnings, while the talented student has an opportunity to dig deeper or to follow individual and group interests.

It is necessary to regroup when ability levels become too extreme, when interests wane, or when smaller units are preferable. A small group may begin with 14 students; after several days two groups of 7 may be

A central bank of tape playback units is the "heart" of a dial-access system.

more desirable in order to permit intensive work in selecting a topic for further study or in group research activity.

The small group permits an active student to be *involved* in learning. He assumes the leader's role from time to time. He feels free to raise questions that he probably would not pursue in a larger group. In the small group he learns to listen and to respect the opinions of other members of the group. The learner gets to know other students in new ways. He knows his teacher as a counsellor and guide as well as a presenter of information. He works with other teachers if a team approach is being followed. This provides more adult contacts. If one contact with one adult does not elicit a desired response, perhaps contact with another will. This flexibility is possible in small groups. The small group is one answer

In a dial-access system, each student station is equipped with a dial, a headset, a program, and sometimes a television set.

to the problem of the impersonal school and the resulting loss of identity which many students feel.

The student uses a dial or Touch-Tone to select a program from the central source.

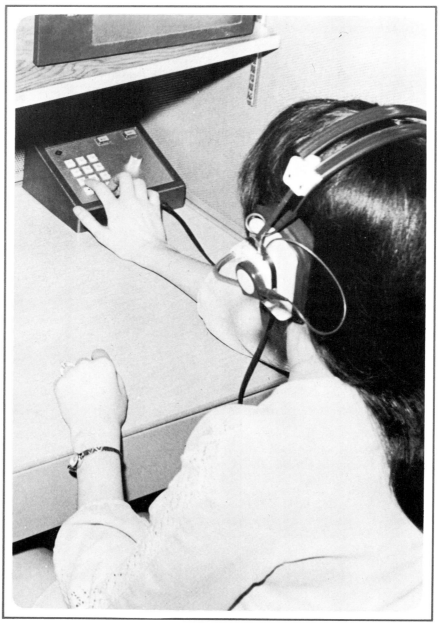

The small group makes the teacher's task more interesting. It provides the opportunity for active interchange of ideas. Many teachers feel that in a small group they truly serve the essential functions of a teacher, for it is in this setting that questions are raised, clarification is given, and ideas are explored. Teachers know their students on a more personal basis than they otherwise might. Previous student activity can be assessed by observation as well as by testing. Responses in small groups enable teachers to predict future responses in other situations. The feedback assists in planning future learning activities and helps in regrouping when needed. From the small group comes data about individuals which can help to identify new individual learning problems. Working with a teaching team means that individual teachers will move from group to group, when appropriate, thus ensuring a better acquaintance with all the students in the area.

Large Group Instruction

"Which objectives can be achieved through presentation by a teacher, a competent resource person, an audiovisual medium, or a combination of a teacher and an audiovisual medium?"

Large group instruction involves a number of activities for which small or medium size grouping is not required. Since the method of large group instruction is largely an expository one, the number of students in the group does not have to be limited for any reasons other than the capacity of the room, its acoustical properties, or the students' ability to see chalkboards, charts, or any other items which might be used by the teacher. The research on group size does not indicate that learning will be impaired because of group size. There is no maximum size for learning when expository teaching is used. Much of the teaching in the intermediate grades and junior and senior high schools which is carried on with groups of 25 to 35 students might as well involve 50, 100, or 200 student classes. Student reaction or questioning is not an apparent element of the instruction.

In new school buildings, large group instruction occurs in facilities which have been especially designed for this purpose. In older buildings, auditoriums and cafeterias serve to handle groups of this size. Some classrooms which were originally built as "study halls" are being converted to large group instruction rooms, and little theaters are often available in the school during the day. When television is introduced into the school system, it is possible to send signals to any location where a television receiver is installed. The use of television increases the opportunity to present instruction to far more students than the 100 or 200 which would be physically present in a classroom or renovated facility.

What activities occur in the large group instruction periods? New topics are introduced. Objectives of the unit are presented together with reasons for the study of the topic. New knowledge is related to previous knowledge. Tests are given to assess the entering behavior of the students. The large group situation provides an opportunity for motivational

In new school buildings, large group instruction occurs in facilities which have been especially designed for this purpose.

activities and prepares students for what is to come. The teacher raises questions for immediate or long range consideration. Problems are identified, future activities are explored, and methods or approaches to the study are presented. Enrichment materials are introduced. Content not readily available to students for small group work or individual study is provided through guest speakers or use of audiovisual materials. A variety of evaluative techniques is used. These activities are more efficiently handled by large group organization than by the small group or individualized approach.

Large group instruction looks very much like traditional classroom instruction in groups of 25 to 35. Since traditional teaching is largely expository in nature, the large group is an extension of the group *size* rather than a change in the method employed. At this point the similarity ceases and new characteristics are evident.

The use of the most highly qualified teacher is typical of the large group approach. Members of the teaching team serve in large group instruction according to their academic strengths. Teachers plan together, but during the actual class time those teachers who are not making a presentation may observe the teaching efforts of a colleague or prepare for work with a future large group or small group session. Trump and Baynham have indicated how a teacher's day will be spent when the large group, small group, independent study plan is followed (see illustration[12] next page).

Teaching large groups of students almost always requires the use of instructional media. Such basic considerations as voice amplification (so that everyone may hear) and visual projection (so that all may see) are minimal requirements. The efficiency of previously prepared transparencies for the overhead projector leads teachers to develop visual materials before the class meets. The help of a graphic artist or media specialist in some schools frees the teacher from the burden of trying to

[12]Adapted, by permission, from J. Lloyd Trump and Dorsey Baynham, *Focus on Change— Guide to Better Schools* (Chicago: Rand McNally & Co., 1961), p. 44.

produce esthetically pleasing materials when he lacks the necessary artistic ability. However, many teachers have discovered the ease of creating their own transparencies with clear acetate (or even reclaimed X-ray film) and felt pens or china marking pencils. The important thing is that valuable class time is saved by preparing materials before the class meets. These visuals are saved and revised from semester to semester. They also serve as references for students who were absent during the class. The chalkboard is simply not adequate for large group instruction.

Frequently slides, duplicated work sheets, and recordings may be created especially for large group instruction. Teachers often preview films which might help students to reach a defined objective. They select those segments of the film which might be useful instead of showing an entire film, parts of which are irrelevant.

When teachers meet large groups, more effort is usually devoted to preparation of the presentation. Usually administrative support is given in the form of time to specify media needs and staff to create materials. This type of support encourages the development and use of instructional media.

The same basic selection rule applies in this situation as in any other

Time allocation of a teacher's day when the large group, small group, independent study plan is followed.

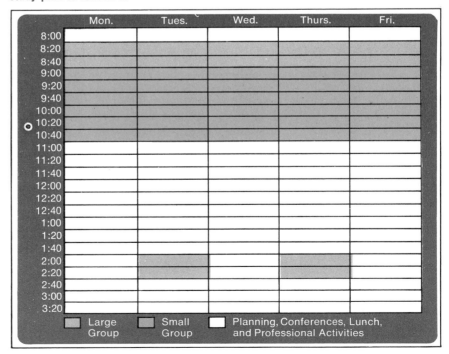

circumstance: *A medium of instruction must be selected on the basis of its potential for implementing a stated objective.*

As an example, a teacher has formulated the objective that "each learner will be able to describe the process of cell division by the end of the class period when asked to write the description, given five minutes." (The absence of any prompts or supporting stimuli is implicit.)

Each student has read a section of the textbook dealing with the concept of cell division. As a review of the reading, the teacher makes an overhead transparency showing the process in a static form. In addition, he feels that the learners will be better able to describe the process if they see it in motion. After consultation with the media specialist, he finds three films which show the process. The media specialist also suggests the use of a television camera through a microscope lens to demonstrate "live" cell division. Still another alternative is the videotaping of cell division in the laboratory; thus the teacher can show the process whenever he wants students to see it.

When teaching large groups, it is almost always necessary to use media so that all can see and hear.

The teacher considered the alternatives and selected one of the films after studying the catalog descriptions. He felt that the eight minute color film, made by a world-renowned photomicrographer, presented the information needed for his purposes. In addition, it could be repeated if necessary. The $3.50 film rental fee would be most economical since the cost of production of a locally made film would far exceed that amount and the quality could never approach that of a professional production.

There are other alternatives, such as filmstrips, programmed instruction, slides, and transparencies for the overhead projector, but the film seemed best able to provide the conditions demanded by the stated objective.

When we are involved in large group instruction, we must remember that the prime concerns are the selection of content for large group instruction and the techniques which will be used. In a study conducted by the National Association of Secondary School Principals, a number of secondary schools used large-group instruction on an experimental basis. One conclusion of the study was that achievement in large classes generally ranked as high as that in traditional classes of comparable ability, and sometimes it ranked higher.[13] When large group instruction is blended with the small group and independent study approaches, a new potential for exciting teaching and effective and efficient learning is released.

11   What are the implications for the use of instructional media as individuals and groups meet in spaces of various sizes?

      •   •   •   •   •   •   •

11   *For independent study—there is a wide variety of resources which students can use as individuals: books, programmed instruction, audiotapes and discs, slides, filmstrips, and 8mm films. In planning for the use of independent study spaces, teachers use many media which are available as well as some which they have made. All such spaces should be equipped with at least two electrical outlets and appropriate equipment. The use of headsets provides audio isolation for listening.*

For small groups—various media which students have found in their independent study research will be shared with the small group; recordings on audiotape and videotape can be made for future reference and for the teacher's review when he is not in attendance. Good acoustics are required for these spaces so that sound will not be easily transmitted to other spaces and so that recordings can be made with minimal noise in the environment.

For large groups—materials which cannot be easily used or those which are too expensive for independent study or for small groups can be used, e.g., videotape recordings, long films, visiting resource people. Chalkboards are not very useful in large group spaces; therefore overhead projectors are necessary. Large screens for two or three images are often required.

[13]Trump and Baynham, *Focus on Change*, p. 75.

ALLOCATION OF TIME

The activities of most schools today are guided by the bell. The secondary school is more bell-oriented than the elementary school, but even in the latter the scheduling of regular and special events, such as music, art, and physical education activities is usually rigidly prescribed. A school totally without organization would be chaotic, but some breakdown of the inflexibility of scheduling time for teaching and learning is necessary and is being accomplished by new instructional resources.

Planning for optimum use of time must be coordinated with the organization of groups and the allocation of space. One of the most promising innovations for organizing and allocating time is found in the plans for flexible scheduling.

Flexible Scheduling

Along with the attempt to establish nongraded organizations in the schools came an obstacle in the form of time blocks throughout the school day. The 50-minute period, particularly in the secondary school, was antithetical to nongrading with its emphasis on individualized instruction. In addition, the development of teaching teams to replace the individual teacher prompted new organizations of time and space. A partial answer has been sought through flexible or modular scheduling. *Flexible scheduling* can be defined as:

> . . . the organization of the school day, pupils and course units into modules of 5 to 20 minutes (or combinations of these modules) according to specified instructional objectives.[14]

Some schools are extending the 50-minute time period while others are dividing it to create shorter modules which can be combined into periods of varying lengths. When a school day contains 24 20-minute modules instead of 9 50-minute periods, the management of time becomes extremely complicated. Fortunately, computers can be used for the scheduling of individual students who are following a nongraded program according to a flexible schedule. The illustration on the next page represents several approaches to modular scheduling compared with conventional scheduling.

The pioneer work in flexible scheduling was accomplished by Robert Bush and Dwight Allen at Stanford University. The assumptions on which their work was based provide a rationale for flexible scheduling:

1. Groups of students pursuing various courses of study possess sufficiently distinct needs to require discrete programs of study.
2. Each subject includes four basic types of instruction: (a) individual, (b) small group, (c) laboratory, and (d) large group.

[14]For a comprehensive overview of flexible scheduling and reasons for its use, see *A New Decision for Education*, 16mm sound, color film produced by the Stanford University Education Project.

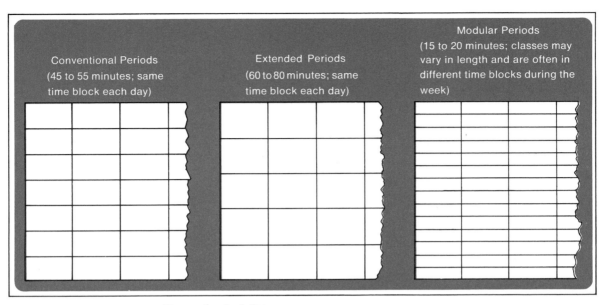

Types of scheduling.

3. Each subject requires teachers who are highly knowledgeable senior teachers and less highly trained assistants.
4. The nature of the subject, the objectives of the unit, the teaching strategies, and the entering behavior of students determine the size of the class, the length of time spent in achieving objectives, and the number and spacing of classes.
5. The computer is a useful tool which makes possible the implementation of a schedule which takes all of the above factors into consideration.[15]

The figure at the right illustrates a flexible course schedule. To read this figure, it is necessary to understand three terms: *course structure, phase*, and *section*. *Course structure* is the total allocation of time and grouping over a one week period. A *phase* is a subdivision of the course structure. A *section* is a subdivision of a phase. The letters A through E represent the five phases of the course structure illustrated. The phases can vary in length of time. If the entire course structure is five hours per week, phases A, B, and C are one-half hour each; phase D is one and one-half hours; and phase E is composed of one hour sessions which meet twice a week. Each section is a subdivision of a phase.

Extending the School Day, Week, and Year

Several pressures are forcing the consideration of extending the school day, week, and year. Increasing amounts of knowledge to be learned in a

[15]Robert N. Bush and Dwight W. Allen, *A New Design for High School Education* (New York: McGraw-Hill Book Co., 1964), p. 27.

A flexible course schedule.

fixed amount of time have caused educators to find time to incorporate the new knowledge into the curriculum. The artificial barriers to continuity of study created by long vacation periods are being questioned. The economic pressures to use facilities more fully are causing educators to consider year-round operation. The need for community centers for continuing education of adults causes leaders to turn to the schools to provide this resource. Even the students are seeking access to the school building, particularly the library and resource center, as they pursue independent study in the late afternoons, evenings, and on weekends. Learning doesn't stop at the end of the school day, they argue. If they are correct, how can one deny them access to learning resources after four o'clock?

Some schools, in response to such demands, have extended library and resource center hours to the late afternoons, evenings, and Saturdays. While the independent study facilities are open for regular students, the adult education program is using the classroom space occupied during the day. Adult classes run the gamut from enrichment and recreational courses to career studies for advancement on the job and to preparation for new careers. The school system is rapidly becoming an around-the-clock operation.

While most of the resistance for use of the school facilities during the summer months has come from parents who would have trouble adjusting vacation times, there is a growing number of schools operating year-round, with the summer term as an optional term. A few high schools are following the college trimester plan which permits students and teachers to select the two terms during the year in which they will be in attendance. Although many schools have developed summer programs for remedial and enrichment purposes, only a handful have tried the extended school year for academic purposes. When the extended year program is established, it is usually some version of a four quarter system.

The New York State Education Department has developed a plan which makes fuller use of school resources during the year.[16] By moving to an extended school year of 210 days or more, they can achieve the goal of student acceleration (see the illustration[17] at right). One year of schooling (K–12) is saved; hence economies in the school budget can be made over a period of years if the school is committed to the plan. The summer vacation period is not omitted, even though it is shortened. All students are expected to attend every day school is in session, but the school day is not lengthened.

12   How can schools make better use of time?

·   ·   ·   ·   ·   ·   ·

12   *If the amount of time is fixed, flexible scheduling of the time available will probably help to make the use of that time more efficient. Additional time could be gained by lengthening the school day, extending the week (by using evening and weekend times), and extending the school year by various manipulations of the calendar.*

13   What are the three elements of the model of the systematic approach described in this chapter?

·   ·   ·   ·   ·   ·   ·

13   *Organization of groups, allocation of space, and allocation of time.*

14   After the teacher has specified objectives and content, assessed entering behaviors, and determined strategies, what three questions can help him organize groups, and allocate time and space?

·   ·   ·   ·   ·   ·   ·

14   a. *Which objectives can be reached by the learner on his own?*
      b. *Which objectives can be achieved through interaction among the learners themselves?*
      c. *Which objectives can be achieved through formal presentation by the teacher and through interaction between the learner and the teacher?*

[16]"The Rescheduled School Year," *NEA Research Bulletin* (October, 1968), pp. 68–69.
[17]Adapted by permission of the National Education Association from "The Rescheduled School year," *NEA Research Bulletin* (October, 1968), pp. 68–69.

Extended Year	Curriculum Adjustment Necessary to Save One Year of Schooling Out of Seven		
1	Kindergarten 180 Days		Grade 1 30 Days
2	Grade 1 150 Days		Grade 2 60 Days
3	Grade 2 120 Days		Grade 3 90 Days
4	Grade 3 90 Days		Grade 4 120 Days
5	Grade 4 60 Days		Grade 5 150 Days
6	Grade 5 30 Days		Grade 6 180 Days

Operation of the continuous school year plan for rescheduling the school year.

15 Given the objective that each student will be able to multiply two digit numbers, how would you group a fourth grade class with some students already able to demonstrate mastery of the objective, some able to multiply single digits, some able to multiply single and two digit numbers but with no consistent performance, and some who have not begun to grasp the multiplication concept?

· · · · · · ·

15 *Students would be grouped according to their achievement. This apparently has been measured and would serve as a guide for grouping. It might be possible to consider using the students who have already mastered the objective as "tutors" for those who have almost reached the objective, i.e., that group which is inconsistent in its accuracy even though there are occasional correct answers. It may have occurred to you that the class could be grouped by ability. Remember, even though measured abilities may be the same, the rate of learning can be quite different. You might have grouped by ability at the beginning of the unit, when all the learners were more or less at the same level of development, but the information you have about current performance requires a grouping by level of achievement.*

16   As a new member of a middle school faculty, you have been requested to join a seventh grade teaching team. What information would you need to know about the current members of the team and what kinds of information would you need to provide to the team leader?

• • • • • •

16   *After determining the major field or fields of emphasis for this particular team, you would probably want to know what specialties are already present in the members of the team and where your interests and abilities would complement those already present. You would want to know how time is allocated and for what kinds of responsibilities. You would want to know what types of teaching strategies are usually prevalent. You would want to know what types of instructional media are most commonly used and how those media are obtained or produced. You would probably want to see the spaces allocated for the team—for planning, large group presentation, small group discussions, independent study, and for counselling with individual students.*

    You would want to make your specialties known. You would indicate what types of activity you feel you can do best. You would indicate where your weaknesses are and where you need help.

17   Describe the difference between team teaching and differentiated staffing.

• • • • • •

17   *These two concepts are close relatives in that they each capitalize on the individual abilities of teachers. Each provides an organization which permits the best use of the talents of a group of teachers. On the teaching team, individuals serve coordinate positions, with one person usually designated as team leader. Each teacher appears to have an equal voice in the decision-making process. Functions are assigned to individual teachers according to their particular talents. Differentiated staffing is much more hierarchical in its organization with very specific delineation of responsibility according to training and ability. A plan for upward mobility of those who perform at high levels is basic to the concept. It permits a teaching base for professional advancement.*

18   Construct a schedule for a ninth grade general science course which includes components for small group, large group, laboratory, and individual study according to the principles of flexible scheduling.

• • • • • •

18   *This is a difficult one since you do not know the objectives or the entering behaviors of the students. However, a generalized schedule should incorporate four phases and sections as subdivisions of several phases. One example is given here. It shows a flexible schedule for a five clock hour course where phase A is*

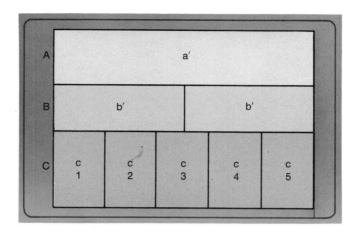

large group instruction for two hours per week, phase B is two small group sections for one hour per week, and phase C is five independent study sections for two hours per week.

SUMMARY

If you are satisfied that your answers to the last seven questions closely approximated the answers given, you have successfully completed this chapter. You can state the three questions which assist in planning for a systematic approach to teaching and learning. You will be able to group teachers and students and, if requested, there is a very strong likelihood that you could construct a student schedule for large group, medium group, and independent study using the principles of flexible scheduling.

CHAPTER
THIRTEEN

THE SELECTION
AND USE
OF
INSTRUCTIONAL MEDIA

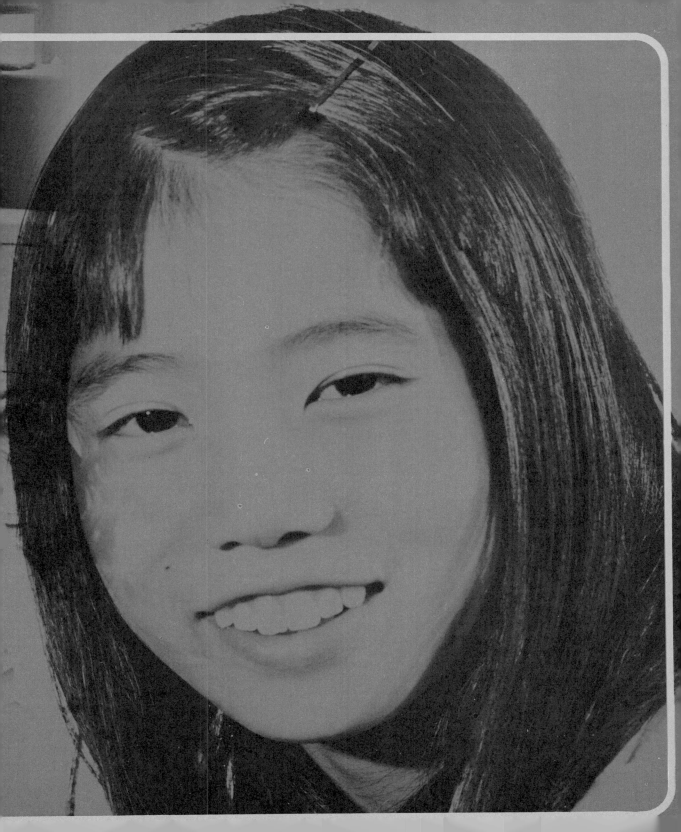

WHEN YOU HAVE MASTERED THE CONTENT OF THIS CHAPTER, YOU SHOULD BE ABLE TO:

1. STATE the basic rule for media selection.

2. APPLY the media selection rule, given an instructional objective which offers the alternative of selecting two or more media.

3. NAME the eight categories of instructional media and examples of each.

4. DESCRIBE the three properties of media discussed in this chapter.

5. GIVE *examples* of the ways media properties are functionally related to objectives.

A fundamental component of the systematic approach to teaching and learning is the *selection of instructional media*. The basic rule for media selection is:

> **A MEDIUM OF INSTRUCTION MUST BE SELECTED ON THE BASIS OF ITS POTENTIAL FOR IMPLEMENTING A STATED OBJECTIVE.**

A question stemming from this rule is: "What medium (or media) will be most likely to help establish the *conditions* for the learner to identify someone or something?" There is no medium, *per se*, which is better than any other to teach one to identify or to describe, so we choose the medium best able to establish the conditions. Name the behavior and the condition in the following examples.

1   To identify lepidoptera, given pictures of both the lepidoptera and the hymenoptera categories. . .

* * * * * *

1   The behavior is "to identify" and the condition is "given pictures..."

2   To describe the organization of the United Nations, given only the chart of organization on p. 67 of the textbook. . .

* * * * * *

2   The behavior is "to describe" and the condition is "given only the chart..."

The placement of the *Selection of Instructional Media* in the present model might seem to indicate that this is the last step in choosing the strategy for instruction. This is not necessarily true. It is concurrent with all the steps which take place *after* the definition of objectives, specification of content, and measurement of entering behavior, but *before* the performance.

THE NATURE OF INSTRUCTIONAL MEDIA

A Definition

Instructional media play a key role in the design and use of systematic instruction. A *medium*, broadly conceived, is any person, material, or event that establishes conditions which enable the learner to acquire knowledge, skills, and attitudes. In this sense, the teacher, the textbook, and the school environment are media. In the context of this book, however, *media* will be defined as "the graphic, photographic, electronic, or mechanical means for arresting, processing, and reconstituting visual or verbal information."[1]

Every medium is a *means* to an end or to a goal. For example, an organization chart of the U.S. Government is a representation, or a means of abstracting reality. The chart is a medium which represents real people and their relationships to one another. It has fixed each position and has reconstituted the organization of government on one sheet of paper.

3   Why is a photograph of a scene from the senior class play a medium?

     •   •   •   •   •   •

3   *Because an event was fixed on photographic emulsion (film) and the event is reconstituted each time someone views the picture.*

4   Why is an audiotape on which are recorded the comments of a visiting foreign student a medium?

     •   •   •   •   •   •

4   *A recording of an electromechanical device which arrests and processes an event.*

The picture of the scene from the senior class play and the audio recording of the foreign student are considered to be *information* in current parlance. Information today may be found in books, on computer tapes, on recordings, on photographic film, or on microfilm. Information is found in many media all of which are forms of storage. The retrieval of this information from its storage is a reconstitution of the event or report of the event. When the picture of Roosevelt, Churchill, and Stalin at Yalta is taken from the file, the event has been reconstituted for the viewer. When a student plays the record of Robert Frost reading his poem "Stopping by Woods on a Snowy Evening," he is reconstituting the reality of the actual event.

5   Mr. Lee wants to provide a wide range of media resources for his eleventh grade students who are attempting to describe the economic, political, and social conditions in the cities of the United States in the 1930's. They are

---

[1] J. V. Edling and C. A. Paulson, "Understanding Instructional Media," in *The Contribution of Behavioral Science to Instructional Technology* (Monmouth, Oregon: Teaching Research Division, Oregon State System of Higher Education), p. IV–6.

using an inquiry approach. What events could be reconstituted through which media?

· · · · · · ·

5 *For an overview of the period, encyclopedia yearbooks and almanacs might be used. Specific events, once identified, could be looked up in old newspapers— probably on microfilm. A search of the catalogs of recordings would yield titles such as* I Can Hear It Now, *with the actual voices of the personalities who were recorded during that period. Some film documents are also available and would provide for the reconstitution of events at that time. There are probably other sources which you have named that illustrate the concept of reconstitution of an event.*

An orderly analysis of the instructional media spectrum includes a description of (1) the characteristics of each medium, e.g., motion, sound, color, etc.; (2) the ways in which each medium can be presented, e.g., a still picture can be displayed on a bulletin board, projected with an opaque projector, or copied photographically in a slide format for use in a slide projector; and (3) the ways in which each medium can be used effectively.

Ways of Looking at Media

The classification of media may appear to be an elaboration of the obvious. After all, media such as slides and tapes are commonplace. However, the process of reviewing an orderly classification of media should help to identify new uses of these resources. Looking at old ideas in a new light often produces new insights.

Specific information about each medium is outlined in Part Five, Media Facts. Included in Media Facts are details about computers, educational games, simulations, filmstrips, slides, motion pictures, overhead transparencies, phonograph records, programmed instruction, still pictures, tape recordings, and television. For each medium there are definitions, illustrations, description of physical characteristics, a summary of advantages and limitations, and a list of sources and references.

When considering instructional media, one must distinguish between the materials and the equipment, since both are usually implied when media are discussed. The material itself can exist in several formats, e.g., a still picture may be printed in a textbook; it may appear in a filmstrip or on a slide; it may be transferred to an overhead transparency or placed on a bulletin board. The still picture is the *material*; the projector with which to show it or the bulletin board on which to display it is the *equipment*. The material and the equipment together constitute the *medium*. Actually, the picture without a projector has limited use, while the projector without the picture is useless.

The terms "hardware" and "software" are being used with increasing frequency. The terms probably originated with the computer manufacturers who referred to the computer and its associated equipment as "hardware" and to the programs written for the computer as "software." The terms have spread to the entire field of instructional media, and now almost any machine is referred to as "hardware" and any material which is used on the machine as "software." These generalizations ought to be clarified.

The materials and equipment which store and/or transmit instructional stimuli or content constitute *hardware*. Examples of hardware are motion pictures and motion picture projectors, overhead transparencies and overhead projectors, videotapes and videotape playback units with television receivers.

The stimuli (content) which are stored and transmitted are software. For example, the information and concepts in a motion picture are the software, not the photographic film itself.

A third dimension of the hardware-software concept is that of *technique*. Techniques are procedures for utilizing hardware to transmit software. Examples of technique include educational games and simulation and computer assisted instruction.[2]

6   Many educators say that there is a sufficient amount of hardware in the schools; software is the greatest need at the present time. What does this mean?

•   •   •   •   •   •

6   *Following the definitions above, it would imply that there is equipment (projectors, recorders, computers) and there may be materials (filmstrips, recordings, and computer programs) but the content of the materials is not sufficient in quality or quantity. In other words, the materials which are currently available are inappropriate, inaccurate, or insufficient in content. There may be plenty of film titles and recordings on the shelf of the instructional materials center, but the person who commented on the need for software was asking for improved content in the media.*

7   To help students become more active in the learning process, Mr. Druger has created an audio-tutorial laboratory for his tenth grade biology classes. He has recorded his formal presentations on tape and has produced slides, 8mm films, and programmed work sheets to accompany the taped lectures. Students come to the laboratory at scheduled times and in their free time to work at individual carrels, each having a tape player and the necessary viewing equipment. Identify the hardware, the software, and the technique.

•   •   •   •   •   •

7   *The* hardware *is the equipment (tape playback units and viewing units) as well as the tapes, slides, 8mm films, and programmed work sheets. The* software *is the content (the facts and ideas recorded on tape and on the slides, films, and worksheets). The* technique *is called audio-tutorial (or multimedia).*

[2]Dale Hamreus, "What's Media?" a presentation given at the Department of Audiovisual Instruction Convention, Portland, Oregon, April 27, 1969.

The Properties of Media

Good teachers have been using instructional media for centuries. Jesus drew pictures in the sand and used objects in the environment as teaching media. Comenius wrote *Orbus Pictus (The World in Pictures)* in 1658; it was the most popular illustrated textbook ever written for children. Pestalozzi held that sense impression is the only true foundation of human knowledge. His influence was felt throughout the nineteenth century. As new inventions brought about new technologies, the educational community derived benefits from the new developments—printing, recording, photography, cinematography, radio, television, and the computer all contributed to the vast array of resources now available to nearly every teacher.

Three properties of media help to indicate why they are used and what they can accomplish that teachers alone cannot accomplish (or can accomplish less efficiently). These properties affect the ways in which each medium is used.

The fixative property   This property permits the capture, preservation, and reconstitution of an object or event. Photographic film, audiotape, and videotape are raw materials for fixing these objects and events. Once a photograph is made or a voice recorded, the information has been "saved" and is then available for reproduction at any time. This property enables the record of an event to be transported through time. Large libraries of photographs, tapes, and films provide instant resources for the reconstitution of historical events. Even the videotape of a student discussion made last week can be preserved for later re-use and analysis.

8   Why is the fixative property important to you as a teacher?

•   •   •   •   •   •

8   *Objects or events which have been "fixed" in some media format are available for use at any time. Events which occur only once in history can be recorded and reconstituted. Complicated laboratory procedures can be fixed for later reproduction as often as may be required. The performance of an individual or group can be analyzed and criticized by the individual or group after the performance and as often as necessary.*

The manipulative property   This permits the transformation of an object or event in many ways. The event can be speeded up as in the opening of a flower bud which is recorded by time-lapse photography with a motion picture camera. Or an event may be slowed down by replaying a motion picture film or videotape at a slower speed than that at which it was recorded. For example, the approach in pole vaulting or the reaction of chemicals can be observed through this manipulative approach. Action can be arrested, as in a still photograph. It can be reversed, as in a motion picture which is run backwards. Media can be edited. Audiotape may be used to present excerpts of a speech by cutting out irrelevant parts.

Events occurring over a period of time may be sequenced and selected to create a film document such as *The Rise and Fall of the Third Reich* which is composed of excerpts taken from thousands of feet of film collected over a 20-year period and edited to form a three hour documentary film. Resequenced films and tapes can be misused, and viewers can be confused and deceived by erroneous sequences which might cause a modification of attitudes and ideas. There is, of course, a danger of misinterpretation when audio and visual data are juxtaposed in such a fashion, because the record of the original event is altered in the process. Historians have argued that any editing of an event is a historical distortion. The protests are even stronger when stock footage (for example, a battle scene from World War II) is used as visual support for narration when there is no relationship between word and picture.

9   What are the advantages of the manipulative property of media?

> •   •   •   •   •   •   •

9   *Manipulation, or editing (a "softer" word) of real objects or events can save time. The process of growing and harvesting wheat, milling the wheat for flour, and using flour for bread can be condensed into one brief film which presents sufficient information to permit students to describe the process. Special motion picture effects such as time-lapse photography and high speed filming can show events that would otherwise be unavailable to the human eye. Complex details may be simplified by highlighting important components of an object. For example, the cut-away model of the internal combustion engine shows the essential parts and motions but omits all the elements which are not essential for understanding the basic concept of internal combustion.*

The distributive property   "While the fixative property of the media allows us to transport an event through time, the *distributive* property permits us to transport an event through space, simultaneously presenting each of potentially millions of viewers with a virtually identical experience of an event."[3]   The distribution of media within the educational setting is usually limited to a single classroom or, in the case of closed circuit television, to several classrooms within a school district or a region. Once an object or event is recorded on film, tape, or the printed page, it can be reproduced in almost any location at any time. Further, with mass distribution systems, such as television and radio, the potential number of viewers and listeners is dramatically increased.

10   What is one of the most significant advantages of the distributive property?

> •   •   •   •   •   •   •

10   *Once information is recorded in any medium it is available for reproduction as*

[3]Edling and Paulson, "Understanding Instructional Media," p. IV–9.

often as necessary and in almost any location. It is available for simultaneous use in many locations or for repeated use in one location. You may feel that an important advantage is the accuracy of reproduction. Once the information is recorded in any medium it can be used and re-used and the reproduction will be exactly the same as the original. The potential for the same content to be transmitted to different audiences is enhanced.

A CATALOG OF INSTRUCTIONAL MEDIA

While the three properties discussed above do not assist directly in the selection and use of instructional media, they do help to demonstrate the utility of media and the reasons for using a wide range of resources. What are the options available to the teacher once the objectives are defined, the content selected, and the entering behaviors measured? This section outlines the physical characteristics of media and shows ways in which the media may be presented. As we go through the range of media, note that a given medium frequently may be presented in a variety of ways.

The term instructional media includes a wide range of materials, equipment, and techniques: chalkboards, bulletin boards, filmstrips, slides, motion pictures, television, programmed instruction, models, demonstrations, charts, maps, books, and combinations of these. Each of these materials and their associated equipment and techniques have a unique set of physical characteristics that can be classified in eight categories. For example, a still picture may be presented as a textbook illustration, as a slide or filmstrip frame, as an overhead projection transparency, or as an illustration on a television program, yet it is a still picture. A motion picture could be in 8mm or 16mm format, it could be presented to an individual in a carrel or to a group in a large class, and it could be presented through a closed circuit television system or played back as a videotape recording.

Types of Media

In presenting the eight types of media, it is important to note that more than one presentation mode usually can be used to distribute the same medium.

Real things   This category includes people, events, objects, and demonstrations. Real things, as contrasted with other media, are not substitutes for the actual object or event. They are, in fact, life itself, often in its natural setting. Second graders are brought into contact with real things by means of a field trip when they visit the local bakery and each child tastes the fresh bread as it comes from the oven.

There are countless real things in the immediate community. When these real materials or people are readily and economically available and when they help in the attainment of an objective, we should use them! The third grade teacher who brings an Edam cheese and passes out pieces to the class when she is describing the products of Holland is providing a real object for the children in her class. The ninth grade mathematics teacher who passes out data processing cards to each student when he is teaching them the binary number system is providing a concrete example of the application of this system to everyday affairs.

Not only do *things* provide first-hand data but so do *people* who are intimately associated with a process or event. The seventh grade social studies teacher who brings the president of the local historical association to class when the history of the community is being discussed is making use of a prime resource person. The doctor who has treated patients addicted to drugs can give an authentic report about the dangers of drugs. The examples are many. The values are extensive. The costs are low. The involvement is high. These people and materials are resources which should be used more frequently to implement the attainment of worthwhile objectives.

Taking the class to the location of an event or process may accelerate the achievement of objectives. If the second grade teacher wants her students to describe the process of milk distribution from the cow to the consumer, she could arrange for a field trip to a nearby farm to observe the milking and storage process. An additional field trip to the dairy could provide the first-hand observation of pasteurization and packaging.

The demonstration can occur in the classroom or, in the case of a field trip, at the actual location of the event or process. Sometimes the demonstration is the actual event, such as the operation of the wood lathe in the industrial arts shop. Sometimes it is a substitute for the event, as in the arrangement of iron filings to reveal the magnetic field around a mag-

Verbal representations   This category includes printed materials, such as textbooks and workbooks. Projected words on slides, filmstrips, transparencies, or motion pictures also belong in the category. (Audio-verbal representations are discussed below.)

Chalkboard notations, titles on bulletin boards, or any written or printed words which are used to convey an idea, skill, or attitude are included. The printed word is the most common verbal representation, but aural verbal representations are also common media.

Verbal representation is frequently used in combination with other media, for example, captions on filmstrips and printed guides which accompany audiotapes for language instruction, or sound tracks on films. The output of computer consoles used for computer assisted instruction is verbal representation whether it is printed or in graphic form displayed on a cathode ray tube associated with the computer console.

Graphic representations   Charts, graphs, maps, diagrams, drawings— any rendering which is produced with an intent to communicate an idea, skill, or attitude is included here. Graphic representations may appear in textbooks, in programs for self-instruction, on wall displays, on a filmstrip frame, or on an overhead transparency.

Still pictures   Photographs of any object or event constitute still pictures. Photographs may appear as textbook illustrations, as bulletin board materials, as slides, filmstrip frames, or overhead transparencies. A still picture is a record or a copy of a real object or event which may be larger or smaller than the object or event it represents. Even though there is no motion, it may be suggested, such as in a still picture of a boy running toward first base. It may be in color or black and white.

Motion pictures (including television)   A motion picture or videotape recording is a moving image in color or black and white produced from live action or from graphic representations. Objects or events may be in normal motion, in slow motion, time-lapse, or stop motion. Objects or events may be edited for abbreviating or highlighting. Film or videotape may be silent or with sound. Sound may be synchronous with the visual portion or may be narrated "over" the action.

Audio recordings   Recordings are made on magnetic tape, on discs, or on motion picture sound tracks. These are reproductions of actual events or of sound effects. Sounds are genuine and are presented in the sequence in which they actually happen unless the recording is edited. Obviously, one of the most important types of audio recording is verbal material.

Audio recordings may be used by individuals or played directly to an audience or over radio or a central sound system.

Programs   Programs are sequences of information (verbal, visual, or audio) which are designed to elicit predetermined responses. The most common examples are programmed textbooks or instructional programs prepared for teaching machines or computers.

The presentation of information is made through any one medium or combination of media, e.g., printed words, slides and tapes, motion picture sequences, and filmstrips. An active response is required of the learner before new information appears. The learner is informed immediately of his success or failure. Some programs (branching type) build in remedial units for responses which are incorrect.

Simulations   Simulation is the replication of real situations which have been designed to be as near the actual event or process as possible. Examples would be the use of a simulated driver's position in an automobile with road conditions presented on the screen. Educational games which simulate economic or geographic conditions demand active decision making on the part of the learner. Many media, including the computer, tape recordings, motion pictures, slides, and objects, can be used for simulation.

The simulation may present the complete environment, as in pilot training, or it may contain elements of the whole, as in several stock market games.

11 A friend has heard that you are taking a course which is concerned with instructional media. He asks you, "What can these media do that a good teacher cannot do?" What would your answer be?

. . . .

11 You might say that instructional media have three unique properties: (a) Instructional media record the events of the present so that they can be used at a later time (fixative). (b) They can be arranged so that events that are otherwise unobservable to the human eye can be seen (manipulative). (c) They can be displayed to a large group or to individuals as often and in as many different locations as they are needed (distributive).

12 You want your students to identify Tanzania, given a map of the world, in less than 10 seconds. What media alternatives are open to you?

. . . .

12 Of course this depends on where you are teaching and how large the group is. It also depends on whether individuals in the class have already discussed the location of Tanzania. Let's say that this is a group of 30 sixth graders in a classroom and that you are reviewing the nations of Africa. If the students' textbook is adequate, there is a good map of Africa in it. This would be the easiest and most economical medium, since each student has a textbook at his desk. You may have a map in the front of the room. Can everyone see it? You may have a permanent overhead projector in your room with a set of transparencies on African nations which you used earlier in the unit on the geography of Africa. But wait! If Tanzania is labeled on all these maps, you may not achieve your objective because the students may respond to the name "Tanzania" printed on the map rather than to the shape or location of Tanzania. Would an outline map be better? Do you have spirit duplicator masters of Africa, or better still of the world, which you can run off on the spirit duplicator? Wouldn't these help you to determine whether each student can identify Tanzania, given a map of the world? These are some alternatives. There are many others.

13 You are teaching a ninth grade class in general mathematics; your objective is for each student to describe how to multiply with the slide rule using the "C" and "D" scales, given a photograph of the slide rule in the textbook, in one minute or less. What are the media alternatives?

. . . .

13 Again, this depends on whether this is something new to your students or a review of information previously discussed. It also depends on the number of students in your class and the location of the learning activity. Let's say that you are meeting in the regular classroom with a group of 12 students who were not able to describe this operation after it was presented by a film in class. You have a large model of a slide rule in front of the classroom and a dozen slide rules. Now, what will you do?

You could use the large model of a slide rule which is hanging in the front of your classroom and demonstrate the process. You could pass out individual slide rules with which the students may practice as you demonstrate. You could reshow the film, stopping at appropriate points for clarification and for practice on the individual rules. You could "talk through" the operation, asking the students to follow your directions with one set of numbers and then to perform the operation without help with different numbers. As you go through the process you are using an actual object.

14   You have just worked with examples involving graphic representations and real things. Now, name the other six categories of instructional media.

⋅   ⋅   ⋅   ⋅   ⋅   ⋅

14   *Verbal representations, still pictures, motion pictures, audio recordings, programs, and simulations. Is it important to memorize these classifications? No, not if you know where to get the information. But if you do memorize them, you have a quick checklist for selecting a medium (or media) for implementing specific objectives.*

15   What is the media selection rule?

⋅   ⋅   ⋅   ⋅   ⋅   ⋅

15   *A medium of instruction must be selected on the basis of its potential for implementing a stated objective.*

MEDIA SELECTION

Just what does the media selection rule mean in operational terms? It means that you have to start at the beginning by stating the objectives in behavioral terms. There is no shortcut. For every medium that is properly selected, the objective is the reference point. For a quick overview of the alternatives, look at the illustration on the next page. It presents many of the variables which should be considered when selecting an instructional medium.

Even though the media selection matrix illustrated is a thoroughly practical device, it may not always provide a solution in an actual school situation. For example, teachers may go through the media selection process according to the rules, but then find some additional factors which must also be applied at the time of selection. These factors are discussed in the next section:

1. *Appropriateness* (Is the medium suitable to accomplish the defined task?)
2. *Level of sophistication* (Is the medium on the correct level of understanding for my students?)
3. *Cost* (Is the cost worth the potential learning from this particular medium?)
4. *Availability* (Are the material and equipment available when I need them?)
5. *Technical quality* (Is the quality of the material acceptable: readable? visible? audible?)

Without answers to these key questions, there is not much point in selecting the best medium to accomplish the defined objective. Because these

| | Real Things | Representations | | Pictures | | Audio Recordings | Programs | Simulations |
		Verbal	Graphic	Still	Motion			
SELECTION FACTORS								
Appropriateness								
Level of Sophistication		These factors must be considered first. If no barriers are present, then move to objectives below. If barriers are present, ask if they can be eliminated so that selection can be based on objectives.						
Cost								
Availability								
Technical Quality								
OBJECTIVES								
To Identify								
To Name								
To Describe								
To Order								
To Construct								
To Display Attitudes								
To Perform Motor Skills								

Media selection matrix.

check points should be reviewed first, they are placed on the media selection matrix ahead of the instructional criteria.

Factors in Media Selection

Appropriateness   If a teacher knows what he wants to teach and what he wants his students to be able to do, it should be possible to select a medium which helps the students acquire the behavior which the teacher wants them to exhibit. For example, if he wants the students to identify faulty speech patterns and to correct these patterns, the students must be able to hear themselves. An audiotape recorder would be a good selection. A videotape recorder would be better if both hearing and seeing are essential to identifying and correcting speech patterns.

If an elementary school teacher wants children to describe the climate and vegetation of areas inhabited by the lion, a motion picture would probably be a logical selection. A trip to the local zoo might provide useful data about the size and appearance of the lion, but very little information about his natural habitat. There is probably no single criterion which is more important than *appropriateness* since the selection of the medium is tied directly to the objective(s) being sought.

16   The teacher wants each student to be able to describe the famous ride of Paul Revere and the events leading up to it. What media would be appropriate to implement this objective?

            •   •   •   •   •   •

16   *If we can assume that the content is accurate and is related to the objective, a motion picture, a filmstrip, a recording, a series of overhead transparencies, or a set of still pictures would all be appropriate. There are, in fact, at least four motion pictures,[4] two filmstrips, a recording, and a series of still pictures which would be appropriate media to use in reaching the objective. But the media alone will rarely be enough to ensure that the learner reaches the objective. The effectiveness of any medium depends on the creativity of the teacher using it. Media are most often teaching and learning tools, even though they often have the potential of assuming many teaching functions.*

Selection of the medium cannot be based on appropriateness alone. Once a medium has been verified as appropriate, it should be subjected to four other criteria: level of sophistication, cost, availability, and technical quality.

Level of sophistication   While the content of an overhead transparency or a filmstrip might be highly appropriate to the implementation of one's objectives, the treatment or level might obscure its usefulness. Many commercially prepared materials are, unfortunately, aimed at a wide range of grade levels so that there is a potentially large market for the product. One should examine the level of sophistication, the vocabulary, the rate at which content is presented, the type of visualization, and the approach to the subject matter in an effort to make certain that the material is suited to the age group with whom it is to be used.

A motion picture portraying family life in India designed for junior high school social studies classes offered an excellent visual document for a college class in comparative religions, but the vocabulary level was far below that of the college sophomore or junior. The professor wisely turned off the sound track and narrated the film himself.

One of the characteristics of programmed instruction is the step-by-step development from one concept to the next. This is a painful process for some students who are capable of jumping in larger steps than the program is designed to permit. Perhaps there is a branching, rather than a linear, program which would accomplish the same objective more effi-

[4]16mm films: *Paul Revere's Ride* (Film Associates, 10 min., color); *Paul Revere's Ride* (McGraw-Hill, 10 min., color); *Midnight Ride of Paul Revere* (Coronet, 11 min., color); and *Midnight Ride of Paul Revere* (Encyclopaedia Britannica Films, 11 min., color).

ciently. If not, it is probably wise to seek out another medium—perhaps a good book—to accomplish the objective.

17 How can you determine the level of sophistication of any medium you may be considering?

•   •   •   •   •   •

17 *The only certain procedure for assessing the level of sophistication is to preview or audition the medium under consideration. There are cues in the catalogs and indexes, but these are overly general and can be used only as a first screen in the process. The most common divisions of level are: primary (p), intermediate grades (i), junior high (jh), senior high (sh), college (c), and adult (a). Previewing or auditioning can help you to determine whether the medium will be acceptable for your students. You may have to adapt the material for your objectives by using only a portion of it, by adding your own commentary, or by deciding to use it more than once.*

Cost   A high school social studies teacher is seeking resources for an introduction to the United Nations. It is possible to locate a wide spectrum of media which could be used to help students describe the organization of the United Nations Security Council, General Assembly, and Secretariat. A school can rent the film, *Workshop for Peace*, for about $7.50. The U.N. also sells a filmstrip, *Structure for Peace*, dealing with the topic for $3.00. There are large charts showing the organization pattern of the U.N. and overhead transparencies which could help any learner achieve the objective. But suppose every student has a textbook with the same charts and an explanation of the organization's operation? The economic question looms large when there are constant demands on school budgets. However, the economic argument should not deter teachers from specifying the optimum medium to accomplish educational objectives. Many an opportunity for learning can be lost simply because the least expensive method is employed.

School systems sometimes turn to technology to solve pressing economic problems. Faced with a shortage of elementary foreign language teachers, art teachers, and music teachers, one school system turned to closed circuit television. The special teachers prepared telecasts for daily use in the various grades. They followed up these telecasts with personal visits to schools on a scheduled basis. The learners acquired the basic vocabulary and speech patterns which had been one of the first objectives. The cost per student was less than the expenditure required to employ teachers in all the schools if they could be found. Cost should be compared with the learning benefits anticipated.

Availability   A high school English teacher, while attending a summer institute at a university, heard John Ciardi deliver a brilliant lecture on current trends in poetic criticism. A videotape of the lecture was made by the university's audiovisual department. The following September the teacher inquired about the availability of the tape. The university said that they would duplicate the tape if the teacher would provide a blank tape. When this teacher checked with the school's audiovisual department, she learned that the school's videotape recorder and the university's unit were not compatible and that it would do her no good to acquire the duplicate tape.

18   If you were this teacher and were determined to obtain this recording for your class, what would you do at this point?

·   ·   ·   ·   ·   ·

18   *A request for an audiotape recording of Ciardi's lecture would have been appropriate. The audio recording very easily could have been made from the videotape. Since the audio element was the prime carrier of the content, and since audiotape recorders are compatible, there is no doubt that a practical solution was available. It simply was not used!*

A first grade teacher decided after school had opened in the fall that the class should see *Autumn on the Farm*, since it had proved useful in the past for teaching children to describe the signs of the season. An inquiry to the county film library yielded a "not available until February" reply.

19   If you were this first grade teacher, would you forget about any objectives concerned with autumn on the farm? Are there other alternatives open to you?

·   ·   ·   ·   ·   ·

19   *No, it is not necessary to forget about these objectives. A field trip to a nearby farm might help her students reach the defined objectives. A check of the school's materials collection might reveal a filmstrip or slide set which could help to achieve the desired objective.*

Some of the most appropriate materials, geared to the right student level, and within the price range of the school, simply are not available when needed. Other alternatives should be considered.

Technical quality   A Spanish teacher wanted to provide authentic language experiences for advanced students. Radio broadcasts from Mexico could be monitored at night and recorded at that time for future use. A friend recorded several news broadcasts, a few singing commercials, and an interview. When the teacher auditioned the tape through headphones in the audiovisual center it was quite adequate, but in the classroom the combination of a small speaker, a large room, and poor acoustics prevented its use.

A seventh grade science teacher discovered a set of slides in a catalog from a science supply company. Fortunately, he was able to preview the slides before requesting purchase. The slides were in black and white, but color would have been more appropriate; many of the slides were out of focus.

20 The teacher found that the content was appropriate and at the right level, the costs were reasonable, and the slides were immediately available. Is poor technical quality a sufficient reason to eliminate the use of these slides?

・　　　・　　　　　・　　　・　　　　　　・　　　・

20 *It certainly is! How can objectives be reached if a teacher is depending on a medium to accomplish certain objectives but images are not visible or legible or sounds are indistinct? Media with poor technical quality should not be used. There are other factors regarding technical quality which ought to be considered as well.*

Artists can be creative or condescending in their attempts to visualize ideas. Overly slick, cute, or crude cartooning detracts from an otherwise good presentation. By the same token, abstract and overlysubtle art work leads students down interpretive paths which may be incompatible with the primary objectives. One of the fallacies found in the world of instructional media is that "if an idea is visualized it is good, and if it can be visualized it should be." Sometimes visualization turns out to be merely the substitution of a poor medium for a good one. For example, an outline of a speech is put on an overhead projector and projected on the screen. Or a poem from an anthology, which every student owns, is placed on the chalkboard. The head and shoulders shot of a teacher lecturing is put on television and distributed to 10 groups of 30 students rather than presented live to 300 in the auditorium.

21 Is there anything "wrong" with the use of the overhead projector, the chalkboard, and closed circuit television in the examples above?

・　　　・　　　　　・　　　・　　　　　　・　　　・

21 *No, there's nothing "wrong," it's just that the media are superfluous; they are apparently not needed to accomplish any instructional objective. There is very little that these media can do that the teacher could not do without them.*

Practice in Media Selection

The seventh grade social studies teacher wants each student to be able to name the three branches of government and the title of the person or body which best represents each branch. The students have studied local and state government. They have never learned that the federal Constitution specifies the three branches of government nor have they learned the names of those branches, although they do know the people (by titles) who serve in each branch. The teacher who wants his students to name the three branches has several media alternatives. Since it is his task to decide which conditions will permit his students to learn most efficiently, he reviews several alternatives for the next day's lesson:

"I could simplify things by just telling them what the three branches of government are. Perhaps I could write them on the chalkboard.

"I could check the catalog in the instructional materials center to see if there is a filmstrip which would cover the topic as well or better than I might in a formal presentation.

"Perhaps the local film library has a motion picture which I might use.

"If there is a chart in the social studies textbook, they could all see it at once while I describe the organization of our government.

"I might consider making a simple overhead transparency which could build up the ideas as I add overlays dealing with each branch of government.

"But wait . . . all of these techniques are expository in nature. I would like to use an inquiry approach, if at all possible.

"I could say, 'There are three branches of government. What are they?' and direct them to a copy of the Constitution in the appendix of their textbook.

"Could I approach this inductively by recording leading discussion questions on tape for three groups? Group discussion could lead to discovery of the three branches."

22 What would you do? Why?

•   •   •   •   •   •

22 *It would be necessary to determine whether to use an expository approach or an inquiry approach, since this will determine the media which are selected. If an expository approach is selected, the media would most likely be formal presentations of information under the control of the teacher, e.g., filmstrips, motion pictures, charts, overhead transparencies. If inquiry is followed, some of the same media might be used, but information would be sought out by the students who would be guided by questions.*

23 Which technique and media would you use?

•   •   •   •   •   •

23 *For establishing the conditions which will help students achieve the naming behavior, the telling and chalkboard notation is probably the most effective and efficient procedure. But later, as we look at other behaviors, we would have to raise the question again. When we ask a student to name and describe the three branches of the U.S. government and their function and relationships to each other, we will have to consider other media which will establish conditions having the potential to achieve the behavior.*

MEDIA USE

Selection of an instructional medium cannot be made without a view to the use which this medium will have. Therefore, selection must be based on a consideration of how the medium will be used in actual instruction. When we speak of utilization, we must always remember that the principles of good utilization depend upon valid selection, i.e., upon the proper application of the media selection rule.

There are no "hard and fast" rules or formulas which dictate that specific media will yield specific results when used to implement the attainment of a specific objective. It would be helpful if we knew that still pictures are the best medium to help learners to identify, but such precision is lacking in the research literature. There are, however, guidelines which assist the teacher in selecting the most appropriate medium once the objective has been defined in behavioral terms.

A high degree of transfer from the learning situation to actual practice will occur if the content and procedures of the medium elicit responses which are very similar to or identical with the desired terminal behavior.

For example, if the objective is to splice two ends of 16mm film so that the film will not break when subjected to a slight "tug," the use of the motion picture *How to Splice Film*[5] would be useful. This film demonstrates the process of film splicing from the observer's point-of-view, breaks the process into steps, and allows for covert viewer participation. A good demonstration, in which the learner can see each step, would be a reasonable alternative.

In some tasks there are the things which a person must see if he is to perform the terminal behavior properly. For example, anyone who can see would be well-advised to use his sense of sight to thread a tape recorder or to operate a sewing machine. There is some evidence to indicate that in learning to perform tasks of this type the use of visual presentations is desirable.[6]

24   A teacher could use a dialog in a textbook to reach the objective, "to make correct responses containing personal biographical information to questions asked in French," but the printed dialog is a substitute for the auditory form. It is not as adequate as another medium which would be closer to the desired terminal behavior. What is it?

·   ·   ·   ·   ·   ·

24   *Auditory language—whether it is "live" or recorded on tape, disc, or a motion picture sound track would be closer to the desired terminal behavior. Practice with this medium in the form of a question and answer dialog will most likely transfer to the actual situation.*

The learning of verbal facts and concepts is likely to occur if those facts and concepts are presented with accompanying visual cues.[7]

[5]*How to Splice Film*, 9 min., black and white, 16mm, Michigan State University, 1964.
[6]George L. Gropper, "Why a Picture is Worth a Thousand Words," *AV Communication Review*, II (July-August, 1963), 78.
[7]A. A. Lumsdaine, "Cue and Response Functions of Pictures and Words," in Mark May and A. A. Lumsdaine, *Learning from Films* (New Haven: Yale University Press, 1958), pp. 123–49.

When the facts and concepts are concrete, specific, and structured, visual examples and cues are more effective in eliciting verbal responses than are words and other symbols. For example, in foreign language instruction the use of a picture of a house, a dog, and a tree would ensure more effective learning of the appropriate noun than would the printed word in English or the foreign tongue. Thus a picture of a house would help the learner acquire the ability to use the proper foreign word for house.

25 A physical map usually uses color coded cues to represent land features: green for the plains, dark brown for high mountains, and so forth. Does this illustrate the previous principle? If so, how?

. . . . . .

25 *Yes, this is a fairly good illustration of visual cues guiding verbal learning. Each color should elicit recall of a verbal repertoire based on information about the land formation represented.*

Media used as examples of the concept to be learned can assist in the process of learning.

When the second grade teacher is attempting to communicate the concept that the whole is the sum of the parts, she may use an apple which has been cut in quarters and a piece of paper that has been cut in half to facilitate the acquisition of the concept.

26 How might media be used to accomplish the objective, "to describe Ohm's law"?

. . . . . .

26 *A laboratory demonstration would probably best show how resistance in an electrical circuit varies with the current and voltage. If the student has sufficient experience with the actual objects of the demonstration, a pictorial representation might be sufficient to help him attain the objective. A student with still more background might simply require the formula R = E/I as a sufficient cue to reach the objective.*

Since most visuals are saturated with information (i.e., they usually present more than one fact or concept), the learner has the opportunity to discover relationships that are not always discernible in written materials.[8]

For example, a teacher who wants students to learn to name community helpers will find that the use of a picture of a milkman delivering milk opens a host of related questions. Why is milk delivered? How is it kept cool? Does it cost more to have milk delivered than to buy it in the store? Does the milkman deliver anything else besides milk? Where does he get

[8]Gropper, "Why a Picture," pp. 80–81.

his milk? If the teacher wants children to raise these kinds of questions while they learn to name community helpers, it would be well to use the picture. If, however, the teacher wants to avoid the possibility of having to deal with such questions, the use of the picture might be avoided.

The "change of pace" in classroom procedure when visuals are used often justifies their use for attracting attention.

This guideline is an example of what we can learn from others in the media business, such as advertisers. If learning is to occur, attention must first be attracted and then maintained. Frequently we need to cause learners to attend to the stimuli being presented, especially during a potentially monotonous learning situation. There are stimulus conditions which attract attention: change, novelty, and appeal to dominant interests. Teachers and other instructional designers should use these principles.

SUMMARY

When the teacher considers the selection and use of instructional media as a component of the teaching-learning system, it should remain clear that the media selection rule is the primary reference point. It should also be clear, after reading this chapter, that there is no single medium which is best suited to accomplish any objective. It seems likely that combinations of media are required to achieve the kind of instruction which is effective and which exploits the unique properties of media to the fullest advantage. The eight categories of instructional media (real things, verbal representations, visual representations, still pictures, motion pictures, audio recordings, programs, and simulations) should provide each teacher with a guideline for media alternatives. Knowing the fixative, manipulative, and distributive properties of media should assist with the selection of the most appropriate medium to implement an instructional objective.

For more specific information regarding each medium, use Part Five, Media Facts.

SELECTED READINGS FOR PART THREE

Strategies for Teaching

Joyce, Bruce A., *The Teacher and His Staff: Man, Media, and Machines*. Washington, D.C.: National Education Association, 1967.

Describes a school of the future in which teams of professionals and paraprofessionals help children learn by employing a variety of materials, machines, and innovative practices.

Organization of Groups and Allocation of Space and Time

Class Size. Washington, D.C.: National Education Association, Research Division, 1968.

Summarizes research findings on the effects of class size.

Classroom Teachers Speak on Differentiated Teaching Assignments. Washington, D.C.: National Education Association of Classroom Teachers, 1969.

Describes the attitudes of teachers toward differentiated staffing and the implications of differentiated staffing for professional organizations.

Davis, Harold J., and Ellsworth Tompkins, *How to Organize an Effective Team Teaching Program*. Englewood Cliffs, N.J.: Prentice-Hall, 1966.

Defines team teaching and describes its rationale and use in elementary and high school. Planning for large group, small group, and independent study, and procedures for evaluating the results of team teaching are also discussed.

Howard, Eugene R., and Roger W. Bardwell, *How to Organize a Non-graded School*. Englewood Cliffs, N.J.: Prentice-Hall, 1966.

Describes present uses of nongradedness, emerging concepts of nongradedness, the types of facilities nongradedness requires, procedures for implementing and operating nongraded programs, and what nongradedness can and cannot do.

The Rescheduled School Year. Washington, D.C.: National Education Association, Research Division, 1968.

Describes various plans for rescheduling the school year and summarizes relevant research.

Swenson, Gardiner, and Donald Keys, *Providing for Flexibility in Scheduling and Instruction*. Englewood Cliffs, N.J.: Prentice-Hall, 1966.

Discusses flexible scheduling at Brookhurst School and the rationale for its adoption. The mechanics of flexible scheduling, its promise as an innovation, procedures for breaking lock step instruction, and providing instruction for groups of various sizes are also described.

Westley-Gibson, Dorothy, and Fred T. Wilhelms, *Grouping Students for Improved Instruction*. Englewood Cliffs, N.J.: Prentice-Hall, 1966.

Describes origins of present grouping practice and research and criteria relevant to making decisions about grouping. Innovations that aid effective grouping and problems that administrators face in grouping are also discussed.

The Selection and Use of Instructional Media

Brief Guide for Evaluation. New York: American Film Library Association, 1965.

A concise summary of effective film evaluation techniques.

Film Evaluation—Why and How? New York: American Film Library Association, 1963.

Discusses film as communication, an art, and a teaching tool. Describes detailed procedures for evaluating films for libraries, schools and specialized use.

Selection and Use of Programmed Materials: A Handbook for Teachers. Washington, D.C.: Department of Audiovisual Instruction, National Education Association, 1964.

Discusses procedures for the selection and use of programmed instruction materials.

Torkelson, Gerald, *What Research Says to the Teacher—Instructional Media*. Washington, D.C.: Department of Audiovisual Instruction, National Education Association, 1969.

Summarizes the research relevant to various media. Describes the characteristics of different types of media and procedures for media selection.

PART FOUR

ASSESSING
AND EVALUATING

No instructional system is complete until the results of the use of the instructional components have been evaluated. No matter how well the objectives may be stated, no matter how logical the media selection and the allocation of space and time may be, the instructional process is incomplete unless it is accompanied by a continuous process of evaluation. Types of evaluation and the relationship of media to the evaluation process are discussed in this section.

CHAPTER
FOURTEEN

THE
EVALUATION
PROCESS

WHEN YOU HAVE MASTERED THE CONTENT OF THIS CHAPTER,
YOU SHOULD BE ABLE TO:

1. DESCRIBE how to use feedback in a teaching context.

2. DESCRIBE how to use media in evaluation.

TYPES OF EVALUATION

Generally speaking, two factors are evaluated in the educative process: students and systems. Most readers are quite familiar with the practices of evaluating students. A test is administered and a judgment is formed on the basis of the student's performance.

Sometimes this judgment involves placement, as when a college freshman is given a French examination in order to determine the section in which he should enroll. Sometimes the evaluation process includes a decision about whether a student should be advanced to the next unit of a course or to the next course. Sometimes the evaluation process involves a decision concerning a grade or credit for a course. These illustrations are sufficient; every college student can recall dozens of instances in which he was evaluated for one reason or another. The end result of this process is that some kind of judgment is made *concerning the qualities or characteristics or abilities of a student.*

Feedback

Another kind of evaluation involves using such student data to form judgments concerning materials and methods of teaching. This is the heart of the systematic approach. It involves the concept of *feedback*. Think of the heating system mentioned earlier (in Chapter 1). You could conceivably turn the furnace on by operating a hand switch. You could adjust the intensity of the flame by manually operating a valve which controls the flow of fuel. When you felt warm enough, you would make an appropriate change in the system, such as reducing the flow of fuel or turning off the switch.

1 The heat produced by the furnace is "fed back" to you. How do you react to the "feedback," i.e., the increase in temperature which you notice?

·   ·   ·   ·   ·   ·

1 *You change something in the condition of the furnace to reduce the output of heat.*

This, of course, is a tedious and inefficient process. Instead of manually operating the controls, you use a furnace on which the controls are changed by electrically operated switches (or relays). Instead of constantly attending to the temperature in your house, and reacting accordingly, you use a thermostat to "sense" the temperature and to send a signal to the switches or relays which operate the controls on your furnace.

2   The furnace emits heat. When this heat raises the temperature of the room to a given point, the thermostat senses it and effects a change in the condition of the controls on the furnace. What name is given to the process of providing information to the thermostat?

•   •   •   •   •   •

2   *This process is known as feedback.*

3   How does the thermostat use this feedback?

•   •   •   •   •   •

3   *It tells the furnace to produce more heat. (Or, it changes the state of the furnace controls so that the furnace will produce more heat.)*

In the instructional cycle we are concerned with the student instead of the furnace (of course!). What the student does is observed by the teacher (or, in some instances, by the pupil himself) with the aid of tests, quizzes, rating scales, checklists, or other instruments of measurement or observation. Information from these sources is assimilated and used to help the student continue his performance or to change his behavior.

However, one should never forget that in many situations the information received from the measuring instruments tells us something about ourselves as teachers. If our measurements or observations tell us that student performance is inadequate, this is usually a signal for us to change our methods, to use better media, to group students differently, or to use the available time or space more effectively. Feedback in education, then, tells either the students or the teachers or both to "change their state," to "produce more (or less) heat."

You remember that one expresses objectives in behavioral terms in order to be able to determine when an aim or goal has been achieved: When a student manifests the behavior or displays the product specified in the objective, the aim or goal has been achieved. You also know that one selects methods and media of instruction on the basis of two factors: the desired behavioral outcome and the conditions under which the behavior is to occur.

4   You have selected media and methods to help you implement the attainment of a group of objectives. You employ these media and methods. You discover a functional relationship: When you use these media and methods, the desired student outcomes occur, and when you do not, the

desired student outcomes do not occur. What will lead you to continue using these media and methods?

. . . .

4 *The results which you achieve lead you to continue using the media and methods.*

5 What is the name of this process, i.e., using evidence of student learning on which to base a decision concerning further use of specified media and methods?

. . . .

5 *This process is called* feedback. *Feedback provides the data on which evaluation is based.*

Sometimes feedback is positive, as in the example just cited. Sometimes feedback is negative: You have carefully stated your objectives and selected your media, but the results in terms of learner behavior or product are unsatisfactory. When you receive negative feedback, you are faced with two alternatives.

6 The high school baseball coach has installed a pitching machine to help his batters increase their skill. He uses video recordings and films to provide instructions. His goal is to have each boy hit into fair territory at least 9 of 10 pitches thrown by the machine. After two weeks none of his players has reached the goal; furthermore, although almost everyone has shown improvement, performance tends to level off at approximately 7 successful hits out of 10. What two alternatives does the coach have on the basis of this kind of feedback?

. . . .

6 *He can do one of two things:*
   a. He might lower the standard in his objective. He should consider the possibility that high school baseball players, given the best instruction possible, might not be able to attain an objective which requires 9 out of 10 successful hits. If he can find evidence to indicate that a more realistic maximum standard is 7 out of 10, he should revise his objective.

   b. He might revise his instruction. Perhaps videotapes and films are not as effective as some other medium. Or perhaps no medium other than the live teacher will be effective. This may be a case where a one-to-one relationship between teacher and student, in an actual situation, is demanded. At any rate, the second alternative is to reevaluate the media and methods.

A word of caution: The downward revision of standards in one's objectives should be done only after careful consideration. Generally speaking, a teacher who does this should have evidence that it is not possible, given the resources and time at his disposal, to attain the standards originally established. Any other course of action is likely to lead to the "normal curve syndrome"; in this type of teaching, standards are determined by the class. Any performance attained by the average member of the class is, by definition, satisfactory, since standards are always established after the instruction and testing have been completed, not before.

7   Name two purposes for evaluating in education.

•   •   •   •   •   •

7   *a.   To rank, classify, or describe students.*
    b.   To identify, on the basis of student performance, adequate instructional media and methods.

8   What is the name of the element in the instructional system which provides information concerning the effects or results of instruction?

•   •   •   •   •   •

8   *The element (or process) is called feedback.*

Thus far we have concentrated on the concept of feedback as a process which involves the teacher in making a decision concerning his practices, i.e., he may decide, on the basis of feedback, to continue with his present media and methods or he may decide to change either his objectives or his media and methods. Before discussing the procedures for obtaining feedback, it is necessary to examine briefly one other aspect of the concept, namely, feedback to the learner.

There is no doubt that in nearly every type of learning, effectiveness and efficiency are increased when the learner is kept informed concerning his progress. The basketball player who misses a free throw will usually attempt to make some change in order to increase his accuracy, while the one who makes the free throw will endeavor not to change his style. The third grader who misspells a word will undoubtedly change his spelling behavior if he is told that his effort is incorrect.

The best example of the learner's use of feedback is found in programmed instruction. (For information regarding programmed instruction, see section 7 in Part Five, Media Facts.)

9   How is the feedback principle employed in a programmed text?

•   •   •   •   •   •

9   *The learner is told whether his answer is correct.*

Unfortunately the concept of feedback has not been widely employed in instructional materials. Only recently have publishers begun to produce films, filmstrips, tapes, and other instructional materials employing this principle.

However, teachers are not limited to commercially prepared materials which provide feedback to the learner. The overhead projector provides an excellent means of presenting feedback. Mrs. Marcus, an elementary school music teacher, uses the overhead projector in conjunction with her "music memory" activities. While an excerpt from a composition is presented to the students by means of a tape recording, the students write the name of the composition and composer on their work sheets. As the students complete each item, Mrs. Marcus reveals the correct answer which she has previously written on a transparency and which is now covered with a sheet of paper. When the students are ready to compare their answers with Mrs. Marcus', she slides the covering sheet down just far enough to reveal the first answer:

1. *Für Elise*—Beethoven

After the students have completed their second response, Mrs. Marcus slides the covering sheet down one more line:

1. *Für Elise*—Beethoven
2. *Träumerei*—Schumann

Obviously, this technique provides a great deal more flexibility than would the writing of the key on the chalk board.

10 Mr. Eric teaches a tenth grade speech class. His students are presenting persuasive talks. The class has developed a list of five criteria for evaluating these talks. How could Mr. Eric make use of overhead transparencies to employ the principle of feedback in this situation?

•   •   •   •   •   •

10 *The criteria could be written or printed on a sheet of acetate. Following each talk, the class could discuss whether the speaker had attained the standards listed.*

Evaluation should not be considered merely a terminal activity. Most instructional situations involve sub-objectives or en route objectives. We have considered examples such as constructing lines of poetry employing iambic pentameter. The student must first learn to identify, name, and describe iambic pentameter; then he engages in the terminal behavior, that is, he constructs lines of poetry. It would be foolhardy for a teacher to provide no opportunity for the learner to evaluate his performance until he reached the terminal behavior stage. On the contrary, the teacher will make provision for continuous feedback to students; when students are learning to identify, the teacher will use questions, exercises, quizzes, and so forth to help them determine whether they can identify iambic pentameter. The teacher will continue to make provisions for feedback when the students are learning to name or describe iambic pentameter.

11 Describe how the English teacher could use media to provide feedback in sub-objectives such as naming and describing iambic pentameter, given audible examples of lines of poetry.

•   •   •   •   •   •

11 Naming—*Lines of poetry of varying meter and length could be presented on a tape recorder, including a five-second pause following each example. After the pause, during which the learner makes his response, the correct answer is presented via the recording, together with a reason for the answer.*

Describing—The pupils could be told to describe iambic pentameter in writing, using accent marks ('), breves (˘), and slashes (/). Correct answers for comparison could be presented on an overhead transparency. Or the learners might be required to do their describing in words: "a metrical foot composed of an unaccented syllable followed by an accented; five feet in a line." The correct answers, with which the learner compares his own, can be presented by means of an overhead projector or a tape recorder.

The most important thing to remember about the above example is that it shows the feedback principle in operation long before the learner manifests the terminal behavior. Evaluation is a continuous process which should be found at every stage in the instructional process.

The machine-scored answer sheet has become commonplace in elementary and secondary schools. Unfortunately machine scoring of tests often limits the degree of feedback or the usefulness of feedback for the learner. It is rather cumbersome to discuss incorrectly answered test items when the responses are on a machine-scored answer sheet. Some teachers have overcome this limitation by making overhead transparencies of the master key. When this is done by a machine process, such as the thermal copying method, the transparency is produced in a matter of seconds. This transparency can be used in two ways. First, it can be projected during the discussion of the test, thus providing a visual referent. Or it can be used in exactly the same manner as a mask; when the transparency is placed over an individual's answer sheet, the right and wrong answers are immediately apparent.[1]

The use of feedback or evaluative techniques to facilitate learning is one of the most important techniques in education. However, there is always a concurrent activity which can be conducted by the alert and informed teacher. We have already indicated that this second concept of feedback is evident when a teacher uses information about student performance to reach a decision concerning the use or revision of instructional media and methods. In a very real sense, the teacher must always be a learner, too. He must learn whether his instructional strategy is the most effective and efficient possible in a given situation.

PROBLEMS IN EVALUATION

Two problems confront the teacher who wishes to adopt the concept of evaluation presented here. The first is the tendency for administrators and supervisors to place an undue emphasis on content at the expense of actual goals or outcomes of instruction. Sullivan has pointed out the dangers inherent in treating content of the program as the most important criterion for evaluation:

[1]Additional information concerning this subject can be found in Vernon S. Gerlach, "Preparing Transparent Keys for Inspecting Answer Sheets," *Journal of Educational Measurement*, Vol. 3, No. 1, 1966, p. 62.

The content of an educational program is simply the materials and methods employed by the teacher. Barring public relations complications and financial considerations, any given content may be installed at will by a teacher or school administrator. Although it should be apparent that the content of a program is an educational means, not a goal in itself, it is not always treated as such. From time to time certain methods and materials, often classified as "innovative," become cherished in educational circles. For example, the present educational climate is such that few self-respecting teachers would admit that they do not employ a problem-solving or discovery-learning approach. The popularity of these cherished programs and program components is often based more upon some sort of intrinsic appeal or other elusive factors than upon empirical evidence of their effectiveness. Nevertheless, teachers and educational programs are often evaluated on the basis of whether or not they employ certain favored methods and types of materials, with little attempt made to determine the effectiveness of this content in improving learner performance. The presence or absence of discovery procedures, individualized instruction, multi-media materials, or a multi-sensory approach clearly is not an appropriate criterion for evaluating instruction.[2]

Another problem in evaluation is caused by the tendency to confuse activities with desired behavioral changes. This is exemplified by a fourth grade teacher who wanted her children to identify Indian dwellings. One of the activities in which the students engaged was mural constructing. Frequently in the course of classroom procedure an activity of this type becomes the basis for evaluation while the desired behavioral change is forgotten. Sullivan describes several examples of this problem when he points out that evaluation sometimes is focused on learner behaviors that occur even though these behaviors do not represent actual changes in the learner.

Student enjoyment, involvement, and self-expression in the classroom are conditions that imply certain pupil behaviors whose frequent occurrence in class is highly desired by teachers. "Fun-type" classroom activities, often containing related instruction, are introduced in the hope that students will enjoy them and participate actively in them. The activities selected are such that the student enjoyment and participation would have occurred in response to the same types of activities at either an earlier or a later date without the particular enjoyable classroom sequence. Rarely is any evidence obtained to indicate that the children will subsequently be happier, more involved, or more self-expressive in either the same or different situations. In short, these conditions in the classroom normally do not constitute student learning. They are responses that the child has already

[2]Howard J. Sullivan, "Improving Learner Achievement through Evaluation by Objectives," in W. J. Popham et al., eds., *Instructional Objectives* (Chicago: Rand McNally & Company, 1969), p. 66. Reprinted with the permission of author and publisher.

learned to make in similar situations, and the classroom activity provides him with an additional opportunity to make these learned responses.[3]

In the following examples, the teacher is making an error involving evaluation. Tell what the error is and how it can be corrected.

12 Mrs. Arthur is teaching the students in her music class several types of rhythmic patterns. She uses tape recordings to present examples of music written in 3/4 and 4/4 time. She has the students practice identifying these rhythmic patterns in a great variety of types of music, including vocal, instrumental, and orchestral compositions. After considerable practice, all the students in her class can identify 90 percent of the examples of 3/4 and 4/4 rhythm, which was the standard given in her objective.

At the end of this unit, Mrs. Arthur gives her students a test which includes an item in which they listen to two musical excerpts, one written in 3/4 time and one written in 4/4 time. The students are then required to describe the difference between the two rhythmic patterns. Most of the pupils fail this item.

What should Mrs. Arthur do?

. . . .

12 *Mrs. Arthur's first alternative would be to have her students, during their instruction, practice describing rhythmic patterns when they are presented with excerpts from musical compositions. If they learn to do this kind of describing during their instruction, there is a strong likelihood that they will perform satisfactorily on the test item which Mrs. Arthur used. One might state this differently: Mrs. Arthur should change her objective from* identifying *to* describing, *because her test item indicates that she is interested in having her students describe rythmic patterns.*

Another alternative is to alter the test item. Obviously, the test item is not measuring the behavior that Mrs. Arthur had her children practice during instruction. If the behavior in which the students engaged during instruction is what Mrs. Arthur really wants, then her test items might better read something like this: "Listen to each of the recorded musical excerpts. Immediately after each excerpt has been concluded, tell whether it was written in 3/4 or 4/4 time by circling the appropriate time signature on your paper. You will be given a 10-second pause after each excerpt is completed in which to record your answer." Notice that this test item would now be consistent with Mrs. Arthur's objective: "to identify. . . ."

13 Mr. Franklin wants his students to construct (write) accurate reports of incidents which they have witnessed. The reports must exhibit all of the

---

[3]Sullivan, "Improving Learner Achievement," pp. 66–67. Reprinted with the permission of author and publisher.

five characteristics of good factual reports discussed during the instructional periods. Mr. Franklin reads excerpts of descriptive material from daily newspapers, such as reports of accidents, stories of sporting events, and descriptions of society functions. He reads each account once and then has his students write a summary of what they have heard; the summary must include all the essential facts and must possess the five characteristics of good reports.

In the examination at the end of the unit, Mr. Franklin uses excerpts from motion pictures. He projects a short two- or three-minute film clip and then asks the students to write a factual narrative description of what they have seen. After reading the test papers, Mr. Franklin notes that a substantial number of the students seem to have forgotten how to write good factual reports; their reports are not as good as those which they wrote during the instructional periods. He concludes that his instructional media or methods were in some way inadequate. He revises his strategy. Instead of reading excerpts from newspapers, he chooses examples from great literature which are obviously much better written than the newspaper excerpts. In addition, he reads each excerpt twice instead of once.

What is wrong with Mr. Franklin's tactics?

· · · · · · ·

13 *Mr. Franklin's commitment to the idea that no instructional strategy is good unless it produces the desired terminal behavior is a laudable one. However, Mr. Franklin is probably doomed to an almost endless series of revisions if he continues his practice. Obviously, the conditions under which the terminal behavior occurred in instruction are quite different from the conditions under which he tried to elicit the terminal behavior in the evaluation or testing situation. In the instructional situation, the students were supposed to report factual events in good narrative form given a pictorial representation of the event.*

   It is absolutely essential to remember that the terminal behavior should be evaluated under the conditions that were present during the instruction. If the conditions are not the same in both situations, then we are not dealing with the same objective.

14 In a college audiovisual education course, one of the objectives was to operate a 16mm motion picture projector according to the standards specified in the laboratory manual. The instructor had the students practice on 16mm projectors in their laboratory until they were able to perform satisfactorily. After one week, all the students were able to operate the projector according to the criteria specified, within the time given.

   In the final examination at the end of the course, the instructor presented four brief film clips showing individuals operating a 16mm projector. In three of these sequences, an error was made, while in one of the sequences the projector was operated correctly according to the standards specified in this course. The instructor was highly gratified with the results of this test, since 98 percent of the students answered the item correctly. He therefore concluded that his instructional media and methods for his objective, "to operate a 16mm projector . . . ," were satisfactory.

Do you agree or disagree with his conclusion? Why or why not?

•   •   •   •   •   •   •

14 *His conclusion concerning the appropriateness of his media and methods was totally unwarranted. There is nothing in the final examination which tells whether the learners can operate a 16mm projector satisfactorily. All that can be determined from this evaluation is that students can identify correct examples of projector operation, given motion picture sequences illustrating correct and incorrect examples of a desired behavior.*

15 Mr. Pophan is a seventh grade English teacher. He wants his students to punctuate their own compositions correctly. He prepared overhead transparencies to present examples of poorly punctuated sentences and paragraphs to his class. As his instructional activity, he has the students correct the errors that they find in these materials.

At the end of the unit, Mr. Pophan has his students write a five-minute essay on an assigned topic. He corrects the papers, marking only the punctuation mistakes, not the mistakes in spelling, usage, or capitalization. He gives 10 percent of the students an A, 25 percent a B, 30 percent a C, 25 percent a D, and 10 percent an F. The following day he privately informs the students who received an F that they have failed to attain the objective and they will have to participate in remedial sessions after school each day for the next week.

Discuss Mr. Pophan's evaluation strategies.

•   •   •   •   •   •   •

15 *The purpose of evaluation may include assigning grades to students. However, the error which the teacher made in this illustration was that of placing the blame for lack of achievement on the students. Even worse, there is no way of telling whether any student in this class attained the desired objective. We know nothing at all of the performance of even the very best students in this class; we know only that the students who were in the top 10 percent of their class received an A. But the students who received A's may have been woefully inadequate in the behavior specified.*

Actually, Mr. Pophan used as his instructional strategy a proof-reading activity which may or may not be closely correlated with the desired terminal behavior. In other words, it would be necessary for him to demonstrate a functional relationship between the type of instruction which he used and the successful attainment of the objectives. Since we do not have any evidence of whether the objective was successfully attained, there is no point in discussing whether the instructional strategy was adequate.

SUMMARY

Performance assessment is indeed a "fine art," to use John DeCecco's description. However, it is an art which begins with a description of desired learner outcomes. We look at the student before we begin instructing him because we want to know whether or not he already possesses the desired behaviors. If he does, there is no need for instruction. If he does not, we make a decision concerning his entry behavior—does he possess the necessary prerequisite behaviors, or readiness, to profit from instruction?

At every point in the teaching process, we use information to evaluate. We decide whether the methods, the media, the grouping procedures, the time allocation, and the space utilization are contributing to the prespecified desired outcomes. If these factors are functioning properly, we have increased our knowledge about teaching, and we push on. If not, we go "back to the drawing board" to reformulate our hypotheses—to try other methods, to select different media, to group students in new patterns, to use space and time in yet another way.

Above all, we must remember that evaluation is the process by which we discover whether *our instruction* is adequate, not whether *our students* are adequate.

SELECTED READINGS FOR PART FOUR

Ebel, A. L., *Measuring Educational Achievement.* Englewood Cliffs, N.J.: Prentice-Hall, 1965.

An especially good reference on judging the quality of a classroom test and on assigning marks.

Gorow, F. F., *Better Classroom Testing.* San Francisco: Chandler, 1966.

Describes procedures for designing and developing classroom achievement tests. Objective tests are emphasized, but essay examinations are also discussed.

Making the Classroom Test: A Guide for Teachers. Princeton, N.J.: Educational Testing Service, 1959.

Describes procedures for constructing instruments to measure learning outcomes. (Free)

Multiple Choice Questions: A Close Look. Princeton, N.J.: Educational Testing Service, 1963.

Describes the applicability of multiple choice test items for measuring a variety of educational objectives. Examples are provided. (Free)

Payne, David A., *The Specification and Measurement of Learning Outcomes.* Waltham, Mass.: Blaisdell, 1968.

Describes the nature of measurement; the relationship of measurement to instructional objectives; the planning, constructing, and evaluating of measuring instruments; the reporting of test results. Standardized tests, their use and misuse, and the assignment of marks are also discussed.

Short Cut Statistics for Teacher-Made Tests. Princeton, N.J.: Educational Testing Service, 1964.

Describes how to compute some simple statistics that can be used in evaluating classroom tests. (Free)

PART FIVE
MEDIA FACTS

Teaching without media in today's schools is a distinct handicap, for teaching with media can extend the opportunities for learning. But there is no inherent magic in media—there must be a context for its use which relates media to objectives. For this reason the earlier parts of this book present the *design* for instruction. This part emphasizes the *things* of instruction.

A good design is necessary for the best teaching and learning to occur but actual changes of behavior are brought about by the materials of instruction. The Media Facts sections highlight the media which are used to implement objectives throughout the book. Here are the specific details about each medium.

CHAPTER
FIFTEEN

MEDIA FACTS

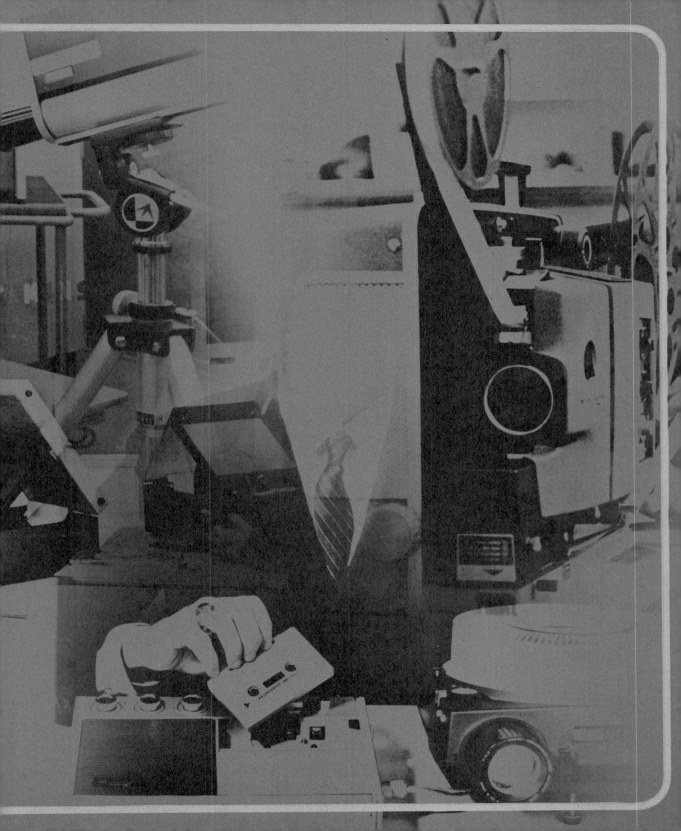

INTRODUCTION

Any book concerned with teaching and media should provide a reasonable amount of information about the media *per se.* The body of this book is not cluttered with miscellaneous data about the materials and equipment which are the tools of the systematic approach to teaching and learning. Instead, the Media Facts sections following provide information about each significant medium. Thus, readers who are already familiar with given materials or equipment are spared interruptions. Those who want a quick refresher on any medium can use the Media Facts for a capsule review. Those who are unfamiliar with a particular medium will find sufficient information to permit them to identify a medium and to describe its use in the classroom.

References to additional books, pamphlets, and articles are given to help the reader who is seeking further depth. Another useful reference is the list of audiovisual materials pertaining to each medium. These films, filmstrips, and recordings provide additional concrete information when specific demonstrations are required. These media have been selected by the authors as the best materials currently available to present an overview of the medium and its uses. Additional titles may be found in a comprehensive reference, *Instructional Materials for Teaching Audiovisual Courses,* available for $2.00 from Film Marketing Division, Syracuse University, 1455 East Colvin St., Syracuse, N.Y. 13210. Over 700 titles are listed with data concerning types of media, length, date of production, and purchase source, as well as a brief annotation. Chapters in this useful reference include administration, communication, class activities, computers, programmed instruction, projected materials, broadcast and recorded materials, nonprojected materials, display materials, photography, and graphic materials. Producer sources are listed.

Each of the ten Media Facts sections follows the same format. This makes them easy to use and should help you to move from medium to medium in order to compare the advantages of the various media. Each Media Facts section includes:

1. *Definition* and *illustration* of the medium and the equipment associated with it
2. *Physical characteristics* of the medium and the associated equipment
3. The unique *advantages* of the medium
4. The *limitations* of the medium

5. *Sources* locating the materials
   a. Comprehensive references
   b. Producers (complete names and addresses are listed on p. 392)
   c. Local sources (where to look)
6. *References* for more information about the medium
   a. Books, pamphlets, and articles
   b. Audiovisual materials

A word about terminology is in order. In common usage, the term *media* has come to mean the *combination* of the materials and equipment used in an instructional setting. A 16mm film without a 16mm projector is worthless. By the same token, the 16mm projector without a film serves no purpose. Some materials do stand alone, such as a programmed textbook, but if the same material is transferred to microfilm, a microfilm reader is required before it can be read. The important point to remember is that media is a generic term which includes the materials and, if required, the associated equipment.

COMPREHENSIVE REFERENCES

There are five comprehensive references to audiovisual equipment which go beyond the scope of this digest. They offer excellent information regarding the principles of equipment operation, basic information on audiovisual optical and electronic systems, equipment specifications, and prices:

The Audio-Visual Equipment Directory, National Audio-Visual Association, 3150 Spring Street, Fairfax, Virginia 22030, $7.00 (published annually).

NAVA surveys all manufacturers and distributors annually to determine current equipment specifications and prices. Nearly every piece of audiovisual equipment currently available is included with a photograph.

Raymond L. Davidson, *Audiovisual Machines*, International Textbook Co., Scranton, Pa. 18515, $4.75 (1969).

This manual is about audiovisual equipment. It is designed to help teachers understand how the equipment works and how to operate all types of machines most efficiently. It can help teachers determine when equipment is operating properly, to make minor adjustments and repairs, and to provide proper care. Especially useful are the chapters on videotape recorders, systems of equipment, machines for individual use, and auxiliary equipment not normally included in other equipment manuals.

Sidney C. Eboch, *Operating Audio-Visual Equipment*, 2nd ed., Chandler Publishing Co., 124 Spear Street, San Francisco 94105, $2.25 (1968).

The principles of equipment operation are presented graphically. The fundamentals of optical systems, electronic components, and basic manipulation of equipment are thoroughly represented.

Fred J. Pula, *Application and Operation of Audiovisual Equipment in Education*, John Wiley & Sons, Inc., 605 Third Avenue, New York 10016, $8.50 (1968).

This is a comprehensive overview of audiovisual equipment: characteristics, how it works, and how to operate it. Detailed descriptions of each type of equipment supported by extensive graphic and photographic illustrations make this a useful reference handbook for people who use audiovisual equipment.

Technology in Education, School Product News, 614 Superior Avenue, West, Cleveland, Ohio 44101, $12.50 (1969).

This reference includes information on a wide variety of audiovisual equipment, classroom furnishings, and other teaching hardware. Case studies of exemplary programs in schools and colleges are also covered.

1
THE COMPUTER

A *computer* is a machine especially designed for the manipulation of coded information, an automatic electronic machine for performing simple and complex operations. There are two types of computers, the digital and the analog.

The *digital computer*, which is the most common, operates with numbers expressed directly as units in a decimal, binary, or other system.

The *analog computer* operates with numbers represented by directly measurable quantities (as voltages, resistances, or rotations).

Computer systems are complex arrays of electronic components. However, all computer systems have four basic elements: the *input*, the *processor*, the *storage*, and the *output*. For instructional purposes, the input is usually a typewriter keyboard console. A cathode ray tube input can be fed directly to the computer and often shares the computer with many other typewriter consoles. On request of the user, the computer calls up the appropriate program from the storage (or memory) of the computer. The request is processed and the response of the computer, or output, is usually typed out on the typewriter keyboard console or displayed on a cathode ray tube, which is similar to a television set.

The equipment of the computer system is referred to as "hardware." The various components are machines which perform at the command of an individual, but the machine can only do what it has been instructed to do.

The instructions for the machines are referred to as *programs*. Programs are often referred to as "software." A computer program for instruction is a sequence of carefully constructed items which leads a student to mastery of a subject with minimum error. There are other types of computer programs which are designed to solve programs, analyze data, and interpret information.

The computer programs are developed by specialists called *programmers* who work with teachers in subject matter fields. From time to time, people in the various disciplines learn computer programming and do not require assistance. There are attempts to create programming "languages" which do not require extensive coding and thus permit a person to program and use a computer with minimal instructions.

The student usually "talks" with a computer through a keyboard console very similar to a typewriter. This console provides a cathode ray tube for display of information.

Computer assisted instruction (CAI) can take many forms. At the most basic level, the interaction is limited to a relatively elementary sequence without evaluation, interpretation, or variation on the part of the computer. The instructional material is presented via a display unit such as a typewriter console or cathode ray tube (CRT); the student scans the presentation and indicates by means of a switch his readiness to go on. The computer then may give further information, or it may present questions whose answers are to be recorded in a notebook or programmed textbook. Again the student notifies the computer when he is ready to proceed, and so on to the end of the lesson.

The computer presents nearly all the instructions, and it records the student's responses. The computer can score the student's work and present the results to him. Ultimately, as CAI approaches its full development, the computer will continuously evaluate the student's responses and lead him through remedial material if he fails to demonstrate understanding of key points in the main presentation.

There has been considerable optimism expressed concerning the future use of the computer in education. There are hundreds of schools using this instrument at the present time. Those specialists who are active in computer-assisted instruction agree on several unique qualities of the computer in the instructional setting.

1. Because CAI is a computer-based system, it never gets tired, distracted, angry, or impatient, and it never forgets.
2. CAI can use the storage facilities of the computer to assess individual progress and to initiate and monitor remedial work as it is needed.
3. Through the use of time-sharing, CAI can accommodate many students, each of whom appears to have exclusive use of the computer.
4. Through the use of tele-processing, one computer can service many terminals and many locations. Terminals can be separated by hundreds of miles.
5. The control of the learning process is always vested in learning sequences created by instructional personnel. CAI permits the teaching staff to take on the coordinator's role in the teaching-learning process. The teacher can use his time more productively, e.g., in individual counseling and in guidance of students who require additional assistance.
6. CAI can perform its functions with less error and more speed than a human instructor.

A typical computer system for instructional purposes.

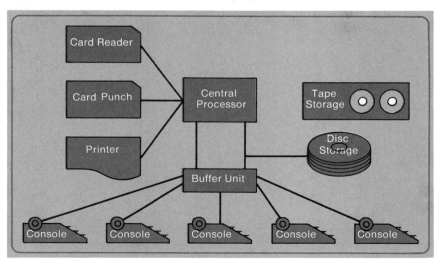

```
SAMPLE      13:42    PX SYSP 11/11/9

IN DRIVE
IN .FIRST
IN SIMP

WHICH STATEMENT BEST DESCRIBES THE CAPABILITIES
OF EXPER?
    A. A LANGUAGE DESIGNED FOR SCIENTIFIC CALCULATIONS.
    B. A LANGUAGE DESIGNED FOR BUSINESS APPLICATIONS.
    C. A LANGUAGE DESIGNED FOR USE BY INSTRUCTORS
        WITH A NEED TO WRITE LESSONS TO BE ADMINISTERED
        BY A COMPUTER.
    D. ALL OF THE ABOVE.
? D
WRONG.EXPER IS A C.A.I.(COMPUTER ASSISTED INSTRUCTION)
AUTHOR LANGUAGE.WITH THIS INFORMATION TRY THE QUESTION
AGAIN.

WHICH STATEMENT BEST DESCRIBES THE CAPABILITIES
OF EXPER?
    A. A LANGUAGE DESIGNED FOR SCIENTIFIC CALCULATIONS.
    B. A LANGUAGE DESIGNED FOR BUSINESS APPLICATIONS.
    C. A LANGUAGE DESIGNED FOR USE BY INSTRUCTORS
        WITH A NEED TO WRITE LESSONS TO BE ADMINISTERED
        BY A COMPUTER.
    D. ALL OF THE ABOVE.
? C
THATS RIGHT.EXPER IS DESIGNED FOR EASY LESSON WRITING
WITH CAPABILITIES FOR MATCHING RESPONSES AND BRANCHING
ON THE VALUE OF SCORE COUNTERS.

WHEN YOU FINISH TYPING, ALWAYS PRESS THE 'RETURN' KEY TO TELL
THE COMPUTER YOU HAVE FINISHED.  OTHERWISE IT WILL CONTINUE TO
WAIT FOR YOU
            AND WAIT
                AND WAIT
                    AND WAIT

TRY IT. TYPE THE LETTER 'A' AFTER YOU SEE THE QUESTION
MARK AND THEN PRESS THE RETURN KEY.

    ?Q

OOPS. YOU MISSED. JUST PRESS THE KEY WITH 'A' ON IT AND
THEN THE RETURN KEY.
    ?W
'THESE QUESTIONS TOO TOUGH, DUMMY?'
                        DON RICKLES
TRY IT ONE MORE TIME.
    ?A

GOOD. ALWAYS REMEMBER TO PRESS THE RETURN KEY WHEN YOU
HAVE FINISHED TYPING.

THERE ARE SOME OTHER THINGS YOU SHOULD KNOW ABOUT THE
TELETYPE AND THE COMPUTER.

FIRST, THERE ARE ONLY UPPER CASE LETTERS ON A TELETYPE.
THESE ARE TYPED AS ON A NORMAL TYPEWRITER KEYBOARD WITHOUT
USING THE SHIFT KEY.

LETS USE THESE LETTERS TO SAY HELLO TO THE COMPUTER.TYPE
THE WORD 'HI'AFTER THE QUESTION.MARK AND THEN PRESS THE
RETURN KEY.
    ?HI

HELLO. THIS IS YOUR FRIENDLY G.E. 255/265 COMPUTER.
ISN'T THIS FUN?
```

The print-out shows how a student interacts with a computer.

LIMITATIONS

The excitement generated by this glamorous new tool often overshadows some of the problems related to its use. Some of the problems which exist now may fade in the future.

1. Computers are very expensive educational instruments. While there have been some fantastic claims regarding very low cost per student hour, the fact remains that the initial investment in the equipment, the programs, the training program for the teachers, and the additional personnel required to handle the equipment adds substantially to the cost of instruction.

2. The individual nature of the instruction provided by the computer confounds the arrangement of the student's daily program. When shall a student use the computer? What will other students be doing while several are at the console?

3. There are problems regarding physical location. Where should the console be located? In the classroom? In the library? In a special carrel or room? The noise of keyboards and the distraction of cathode ray tubes are disrupting elements when other students are around. How can isolation be provided, yet supervision maintained?

4. Most of the programs available today are quantitative in nature. There is a preponderance of programs in the sciences and mathematics with very little in the social sciences and the humanities. If programs are developed and validated in all disciplines, the value of the computer will be enhanced.

5. If a computer exists for instructional purposes, can it be used for administrative and guidance purposes? It can, but who has the priority? How can the equipment be used optimally without limiting the instructional program?

6. There is a danger with any new instrument that it will be considered a panacea for educational ills. With almost every new device that has been invented, a group of zealots has promoted the new invention as the solution to many educational problems. This type of media myopia prevents an honest assessment of possible alternatives to solving the problems. Some researchers have found, for example, that the computer was being used to teach material that could have been taught just as well (and much less expensively) using traditional programmed instruction. In effect, the computer had become an electronic page turner. The reference point for the use of any new medium must still be the objectives which have been defined prior to the determination of a strategy or the selection of instructional resources.

SOURCES

The sources of the software or programs for use in CAI depend upon the type of computer being employed. Each major computer manufacturer provides a catalog (or library listing) of the programs which are available for the computer(s) manufactured and distributed by that company. The programs are not always interchangeable from the computer of one manufacturer to that of another. The points of contact are the manufacturers themselves. Some of the best contacts are:

Control Data Corp., 8100 34th Ave. South, Minneapolis, Minnesota 55440

Digital Equipment Corp., Maynard, Massachusetts 01754

Honeywell, Inc., Wellesley Hills, Massachusetts 02181

IBM, Thomas J. Watson Research Center, P. O. Box 218, Yorktown Heights, New York 10598

Information Systems—Education, General Electric Company, 13430 North Black Canyon Highway, Phoenix, Arizona 85023

Philco-Ford, C and Tioga Streets, Philadelphia, Pennsylvania 19134

RCA, Instructional Systems Division, 530 University Avenue, Palo Alto, California 94301

Remington Rand, 1290 Avenue of the Americas, New York, New York 10019

REFERENCES

Before considering the applications of the computer to instruction, it is necessary to know something about the computer itself. One of the best references regarding computer operation is "How the Computer Gets the Answer," a reprint of an article that originally appeared in *Life* magazine. The 14 page, illustrated article contains photographs of specially-designed models which graphically demonstrate just what goes on inside a computer as it solves a simple problem in addition. The text explains the process in clear, step-by-step progression. The minimum order is five copies at $.40 each from Life Educational Reprint Program, Time-Life Building, Chicago, Illinois 60611.

For a quick overview of computer applications in education, the November, 1967 issue of *American Education* features a 15 page section, "There's a Computer in Your Future," which highlights the computer as a counselor, a planner, a patient, a professor, a tutor, and a paper pusher. Reprints of the feature are available for $.20 from the Superintendent of Documents, U.S. Government Printing Office, Washington, D.C. 20402.

There are several books which provide more information on the application of the computer to education. The reader should be somewhat familiar with computers before consulting these sources.

Don D. Bushnell and Dwight W. Allen, *The Computer in American Education*, John Wiley & Sons, Inc., 605 Third Ave., New York 10016 (1967).

Ralph W. Gerard, ed., *Computers and Education*, McGraw-Hill Book Co., 330 W. 42 St., New York 10036 (1967).

John L. Goodlad, John F. O'Toole, Jr., and Louise L. Tyler, *Computers and Information Services in Education*, Harcourt, Brace & World, Inc., 757 Third Ave., New York 10017 (1966).

John W. Loughary, *Man-Machine Systems in Education*, Harper & Row, Publishers, 49 E. 33 St., New York 10016 (1966).

For keeping up to date with the fast-breaking developments in this area of instructional technology, it is necessary to subscribe to newsletters which report on current items of interest in computer assisted instruction. Two such newsletters are:

Automated Education Letter, Box 2658, Detroit, Michigan 48231 ($18 per year).

ENTELEK News About Computer Assisted Instruction, 42 Pleasant Street, Newburyport, Massachusetts 01950 (free).

Several films have been produced which describe the nature of computers and computer assisted instruction.

The Computer in the Classroom, 16mm, 13 min., sound, b & w. Depicts by candid photography a group of gifted ninth and tenth graders as they respond to a summer course devoted to practice at an LGP-30 computer, to programming, flowcharting, testing, and explanations of computer circuitry and computer chess. (Rand)[1]

Introduction to Feedback, 16mm, 10 min., sound, color. Shows a presentation of the feedback idea, its growing importance in our culture, and some examples of tools developed to facilitate its use. (IBM)

CAI, 16mm, 17 min., sound, color. Describes the 192 station CAI system serving 16 elementary schools in New York City. Includes comments on CAI by a principal and teacher at P.S. 87. (RCA)

Educating a Computer: A Report on Dartmouth Time-Sharing, 16mm, 15 min., sound, color. Reports the use of the time-sharing computer facilities at Dartmouth for educational and research purposes. (GE)

Living Machine, 16mm, 59 min., sound, color. Explores progress in electronic technology and the new frontiers of knowledge and experience man-made machines will open to man himself. The film demonstrates "artificial intelligence." Another segment explores the impact of computer technology on our society. It shows experiments in duplicating, electronically, our sensory perceptions. (Sterling)

[1]The names and addresses of the producers appear on page 392.

2

DEFINITIONS

A *filmstrip*[2] is a length of 35mm film containing a series of still pictures intended for projection in sequence one at a time. Some filmstrips come with a tape or disc recording that contains the narration. When the proper equipment is used, a low frequency signal activates a mechanism to advance the filmstrip one frame. (The filmstrip is sometimes called a *strip film* and a *slide film*.)

A *filmstrip projector* is an instrument designed to accept 35mm filmstrips. It is often equipped with an adapter to accept 2″ × 2″ slides. Models are available with manual advance and remote control.

A *slide* is a film transparency contained in either a 2″ x 2″ or 2¼″ × 2¼″ mount. Lantern slides are 3¼″ × 4″.

A *slide projector* is an instrument designed to project 2″ × 2″ or 2¼″ × 2¼″ or 3¼″ × 4″ mounted transparencies; slides may be shown by individual handling or may be placed in a slide cartridge and operated by manual or remote control. Projectors which accept only 3¼″ × 4″ slides are usually referred to as *lantern slide projectors*.

CHARACTERISTICS

A filmstrip contains a series of still pictures in color or black and white on film which is 35mm wide. The film is perforated along both edges for movement through the projector. Each picture in a filmstrip is called a *frame*. Each frame is one-half the size of a 35mm slide. Commercially prepared filmstrips vary in length; some are as short as three frames, while others may contain from 70 to 80 frames or more. The filmstrip format is less expensive than a set of individually mounted 35mm slides containing an equal number of pictures. It is far less expensive to print a series of pictures on a strip of film than it is to print, cut, and mount the same pictures in a set of slides. The most typical slide, the 2″ × 2″ transparency, is made from a strip of 35mm film with a width twice that of a filmstrip. After processing, the slides are mounted in cardboard or glass mounts for easy use and for protection.

The equipment for using filmstrips and slides varies widely. Inexpensive viewers for less than $15.00 are often used for individual study purposes. Small projectors, intended for small group use, sell for around $20–$40. Classroom models cost $80–$150, while auditorium models are

---

[2]The definitions used in Media Facts have been adapted from Donald P. Ely, ed., *The Changing Role of the Audiovisual Process in Education: A Definition and a Glossary of Related Terms* (Washington, D.C.: Department of Audiovisual Instruction, National Education Association, 1963), 148 pp.

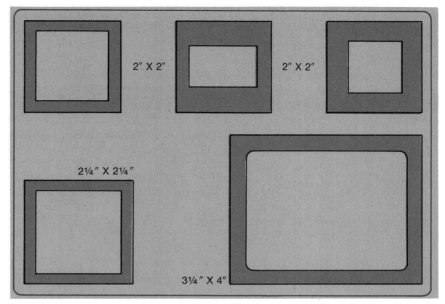

Each of the several slide sizes requires a different projector.

A comparison of the 35mm filmstrip and a 2″ X 2″ slide. One slide equals two filmstrip frames.

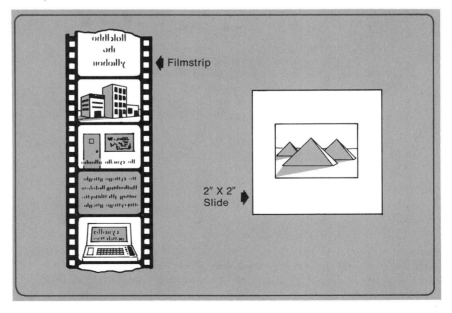

still more expensive. Some projectors will handle only filmstrips or only slides, while many classroom models will handle either filmstrips or slides. A simple and quick change of the film channel converts the projector from one use to another.

ADVANTAGES

The filmstrip is a widely used instructional medium because of its many advantages.

1. The sequence of pictures is always the same. Careful planning has preceded the production of each filmstrip.
2. Individual pictures can be held on the screen for class discussion for as long as desired.
3. Pictorial or graphic materials can be used alone or in combination.
4. The small size of the filmstrip permits easy storage and handling.
5. Filmstrip equipment is relatively inexpensive, lightweight, small, and easy to operate.
6. The room need not be extremely dark for projection.

Inexpensive viewers permit individuals to preview filmstrips.

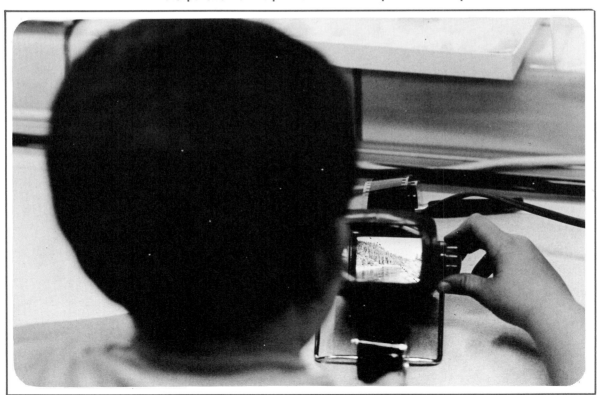

Small groups use small viewers of various types.

Slides offer many opportunities for creative use:

1. The sequence of slides can be altered to meet specific needs.
2. Slides are easily made with an inexpensive 35mm camera. Copying materials with the same camera is a relatively simple task.
3. All of the advantages of the filmstrip also apply to the slide, except the fixed sequence.

LIMITATIONS

1. The fixed sequence does not permit easy flexibility.
2. Filmstrips lack the attention-compelling qualities of the motion-picture and television which are more familiar to students.
3. Filmstrips cannot be made easily in the local school, and therefore selection is confined to materials made by commercial producers.

Classroom filmstrip projectors are used with large groups.

Slides overcome some of the filmstrip limitations. They do permit arrangement according to the wishes of the teacher or learner and they are easily produced.

SOURCES

The major source guide for 35mm filmstrips is the *Index to 35mm Educational Filmstrips* published by R. R. Bowker Co., 1180 Avenue of the Americas, New York, N.Y. 10036. It sells for $34.00 and is scheduled to be updated by means of regular supplements. It has been compiled by the National Information Center for Education Media at the University of Southern California.

Other guides are more specialized and not as comprehensive as the NICEM *Index*. They are:

Educators Guide to Free Filmstrips, Educators Progress Service, Randolph, Wisconsin 53956, $7.00 (issued annually).

Educational Sound Filmstrip Directory, DuKane Corporation, Audio Visual Division, St. Charles, Illinois 60174, free.

Some Sources of 2 × 2 Inch Color Slides. Motion Picture and Education Markets Division, Eastman Kodak Co., Rochester, N.Y. 14650. (Since there is no master list of 2″ × 2″ slides, it is necessary to consult a wide variety of sources which specialize in slides for art, architecture, science, religion, medicine, travel, and space.)

There are many filmstrip producers in the United States, and nearly all of them permit free previews of their materials when the requesting school intends to purchase the filmstrips that meet the approval of the teachers. Catalogs can be requested directly from the producers. Some of the large producers are:

Stanley Bowmar Co., Inc., 4 Broadway, Valhalla, N.Y. 10595.

Encyclopaedia Britannica Educational Corp., 425 N. Michigan Ave., Chicago, Ill. 60611.

Enrichment Teaching Materials, 246 Fifth Ave., New York 10001.

Eye-Gate House, Inc., 146–01 Archer Ave., Jamaica, N.Y. 11435.

Guidance Associates, 23 Washington Ave., Pleasantville, N.Y. 10570.

Scott Education Division, 104 Lower Westfield Road, Holyoke, Mass. 01040.

McGraw-Hill Book Co., 330 West 42nd St., New York 10036.

Popular Science Publishing Co., Audio-Visual Division, 355 Lexington Ave., New York 10017.

Society for Visual Education, 1345 Diversey Pkwy., Chicago, Ill. 60614.

Weston Woods Studio, Inc., Weston, Conn. 06880

Many filmstrip projectors can also accommodate 2″ X 2″ slides.

REFERENCES

There are several audiovisual materials about the use of filmstrips:

Children Learn from Filmstrips, 16mm, 16 min., sound, color, $200. Illustrates effective and imaginative ways to use filmstrips in the classroom. (McGraw-Hill)

The Filmstrip Projector, filmstrip, 41 frames, color, $6.50. Describes the basic construction of a filmstrip projector, preparation system, and movement of film. (NFBC)

Slides can be made easily with a 35mm camera and a simple copy stand.

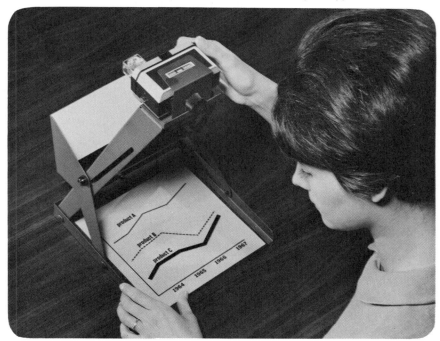

Filmstrips and the Teacher, filmstrip, 45 frames, color, $6.50. Defines and analyzes filmstrips and their uses. (NFBC)

Using Filmstrips in Teaching, filmstrip, 52 frames, color, $6.00. Shows different techniques for using filmstrips in teaching. (Basic)

3

GAMES AND SIMULATIONS

DEFINITION

A *game*, or *simulation*, is a simplified, operational model of a real-life situation that provides students with vicarious participation in a variety of roles and events.

CHARACTERISTICS

When the student plays a game in the classroom he assumes a role and participates in the decision-making process. The objective of the game and the rules under which it operates are clearly stated.

The properties of a game include:

1. A small, fixed set of players striving to reach a goal.
2. Rules which define the legitimate actions of the players.

A game is a model of a real-life situation.

3. A basic sequence and structure within which the actions take place.
4. A time limit.

ADVANTAGES

Games and simulations permit students to experience life-like situations in which there is social interaction and an observable outcome. The ability to observe the consequences of actions permits a student to reflect on the process as well as on the actual result of the game. Games contribute more to the development of social processes than to the acquisition of information or basic learning content. There are other unique advantages:

1. The student seeks to solve problems in which he is intimately involved.
2. The student is satisfied when he senses a new insight as new ideas and concepts are formulated.
3. The student is placed in a more realistic environment than in any other form of learning (except when the actual experience occurs).
4. A full range of audiovisual media can be used to create realistic simulated environments. Audiotape, films, slides, television, and other media offer opportunities to capture and distribute useful stimuli.
5. A high degree of interest is generated through realistic participation.

LIMITATIONS

Some of the objections are:

1. Games often distort the social situation they are attempting to simulate. In an attempt to simplify the social context students may gain false confidence.
2. Since games are fabricated by people, the assumptions of a game's designer often distort reality or project a bias.
3. Games are time-consuming activities in the classroom. Many games run for several hours or for several days. When schedules are organized for changing classes every 40 or 50 minutes, the cumulative effect of a game is lost by stop-and-start activities.
4. Most games require only a few people to play. Should the same game be played by several groups? Should one game rotate throughout the class from time to time? How can entire classes be involved in a simulation?

SOURCES

In a rapidly growing area such as games and simulation, it is difficult to keep up with all the current resources. Most of the efforts in gaming have been focused on secondary school level social studies with little attention to the elementary level. The resources listed below are publishers and distributors of games. There are several organizations involved in the development and testing of games that do not act as marketing sources. The organizations listed below offer specific games for classroom use.

Academic Games Associates, Center for Study of Social Organization of Schools, The Johns Hopkins University, 3505 North Charles St., Baltimore, Md. 21212. (Games of CONSUMER, DEMOCRACY, DISASTER, ECONOMIC SYSTEM, LIFE CAREER, and THE GHETTO GAME)

CBS Learning Center, 12 Station Dr., Princeton Junction, N.J. 08550. (Games of GITHAKA and THE MARKET PLACE)

High School Geography Project, P. O. Box 1095, Boulder, Colorado 80302. (Games of SECTION and FARMING)

Interact, P. O. Box 262, Lakeside, Calif. 92040.   (Games of DISUNIA, DIVISION, and SUNSHINE)

Science Research Associates, 259 East Erie St., Chicago, Ill. 60611. (Games of ECONOMIC DECISIONS and INTER-NATION SIMULATION)

Scott Foresman & Co., 1900 E. Kale Ave., Glenview, Ill. 60025.   (Game of DANGEROUS PARALLEL)

Project SIMILE, Western Behavioral Sciences Institute, 1150 Silverado Blvd., La Jolla, Calif. 92037.   (Games of CRISIS, NAPOLI, and PLANS)

A comprehensive bibliography for Resource Persons and Organizations, Simulation Games, Films, Books, and Articles and Reports is published in the February, 1969, issue of *Social Education*, "Foreign Policy Association Bibliography on Simulation."   The bibliography is devoted to the social sciences only.

REFERENCES

The following books, pamphlets, and articles provide information on simulation games:

American Behavioral Scientist, October, 1966.   Special section devoted to simulation.

Sarane S. Boocock and E. O. Schild, eds., *Simulation Games in Learning*, Sage Publications, 275 S. Beverley Drive, Beverly Hills, Calif. 90210, $8.50 (1968).

Jack Crawford and Paul A. Twelker, *Instructional Simulation: A Research Development and Dissemination Activity*, Teaching Research, Monmouth, Oregon, $3.00 (1969).

Foreign Policy Association, *Simulation Games for the Social Studies Classroom*, F.P.A., 345 East 46th St., New York 10017, $1.00 (1969).

Instructional Simulation Systems: An Annotated Bibliography, Continuing Education Publications, 100 Waldo Hall, Oregon State University, Corvallis, Oregon 97331, $5.75 (1970).

Social Education, February, 1969. Special section devoted to "Simulation: the Game Explosion."

There are films available, based on games, which will be helpful:

A Bowery Boy Goes to Congress, 16mm, 30 min., sound, b & w, $5.00 rental. The GAME OF LEGISLATURE is used as the basis for this film. (Nova)

Also available from the same source, for the same rental, is a 30-minute film on the PROPAGANDA GAME.

4

DEFINITION

A *motion picture* (also called a movie or film) is a series of still pictures taken in rapid succession usually on 8mm or 16mm film stock, which, when projected through a motion picture projector, give the viewers an illusion of motion.

CHARACTERISTICS

Sound 16mm films are projected at the rate of 24 frames per second, and silent 16mm films are usually projected at 16 frames per second. Sound films use either a magnetic or, more typically, an optical sound track on one edge of the film while the opposite edge contains sprocket holes which permit sprocket wheels on the projector to move the film through the machine.

Motion picture film sizes.

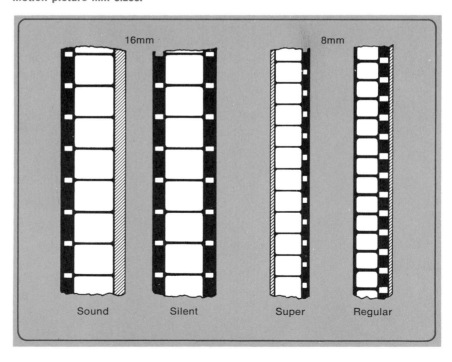

Most 16mm films are stored on reels. The films vary in length from one minute or less (about 40 feet of film), to 50 minutes (about 2000 feet of film). If a 16mm motion picture is more than 50 minutes in length, it is stored on two or more reels. Both silent and sound 8mm films are stored on reels or self-contained cartridges which simplify the threading of the projectors (see illustration below). 8mm cartridge films are exceedingly simple to use, since no threading is required as is the case when films on reels are projected.

Optical sound tracks are printed on the film stock when the picture is processed. Magnetic sound tracks are very similar to audiotapes. The sound is recorded after the processing of the film; it can be erased easily and, as in the case of magnetic tape recordings, new sound can be recorded in place of the old.

There are two types of motion picture projectors: 8mm and 16mm; no projector handles both sizes of film. Silent films can usually be shown on a sound projector (with the amplifier turned off) but 16mm sound films cannot be shown on a silent projector. Although one motion picture projector is basically the same as another in design, threading patterns vary greatly from one manufacturer to another and sometimes from one model to another. Operating instructions come with the projector and there is often a threading diagram permanently mounted on the projector case. Some projectors are self-threading; the motion picture is simply inserted

The 8mm film cartridge requires no threading.

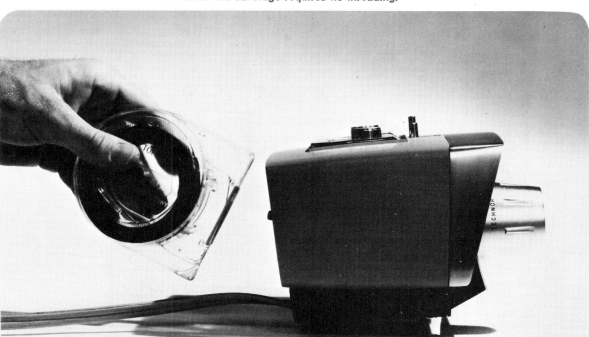

at the beginning of the threading channel and it comes out at the take-up reel. Many of the 8 mm projectors are of the cartridge type. Most projectors require focusing of the lens.

For many years the 16mm film size was virtually the only one used for educational motion pictures. Since 1960, however, more and more educational motion pictures are being produced on 8mm film. Most 8mm motion pictures are permanently stored in cartridges. The film is an endless loop which is never removed from the cartridge except for cleaning or repair. When the teacher or student uses a cartridge film, he merely inserts the cartridge into the projector. He does not touch the film itself; he does not thread the film. Cartridge films are much easier to use than reel-stored films since even a first grade child can learn to operate the projector in as little as five seconds.

The self-threading 16mm projector facilitates the use of film.

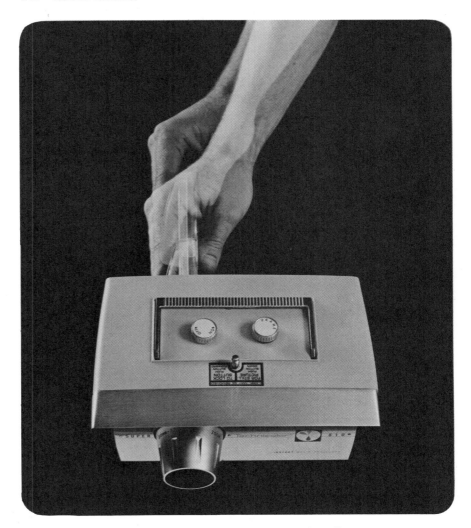

Cartridge films in 8mm formats can be loaded without threading.

Some educators have called the 8mm cartridge film the "paperback" of the film format since it is so readily available, so inexpensive (compared with the more common 16mm films), and so easy to use. 8mm films are now available in both sound and silent formats and can be purchased for as little as $8.00 for silent films and $35.00 for sound. The small size permits individual students or small groups to preview films in a carrel or classroom corner with little worry about special conditions for projection. Students can even take projectors and films home, just as they do library books.

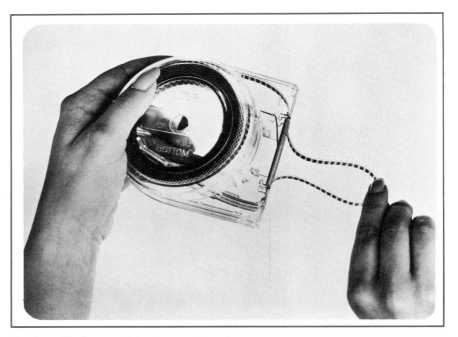

The 8mm film in a cartridge is an endless loop.

Small groups can use the 8mm projector in the classroom without special arrangements.

ADVANTAGES

The advantages of motion pictures stem primarily from their capacity for storage of visual information in an accurate manner and from the fact that teachers can manipulate that visual information to achieve defined objectives. For example:

1. Motion pictures can record events as they happen and make the events available again.

2. Motion pictures can be taken one frame at a time (time-lapse photography). When the film is projected at the normal speed, the action of many weeks can be seen in a matter of seconds. When the growth of a seed or the opening of a flower bud is photographed, several minutes may elapse between the taking of one frame and the next; months of growth can be shown in minutes when such a film is projected.

3. Sometimes we want to reduce rather than increase the speed of an event or process. For example, to record the movement of the vocal cords, a high speed camera may take 4000 pictures a second. When projected at 24 frames per second the "slow motion" permits close study of a process that would otherwise be unobservable to the human eye.

4. Through the process of photomicrography, motion pictures can extend the limits of human vision by combining the characteristics of the microscope with the motion picture camera.

5. By using the one-frame-at-a-time concept, an artist can prepare drawings which are photographed by a motion picture camera to create an animated film. This procedure permits the conceptualization of ideas which do not exist in concrete form, such as visual explanations of jet propulsion or the theory of flight.

6. Motion pictures bring other people and other nations to the screen. One of the early slogans of one film producer was: "Bring the world to the classroom." This is still a valuable contribution of motion pictures.

LIMITATIONS

Most of the limitations are of a technical nature; they are being overcome as films become accessible and equipment becomes easier to operate.

1. Since motion pictures are somewhat expensive (a ten minute color film sells for about $120), it is necessary to purchase prints and place them in libraries which serve a large number of teachers. Since copies are limited, teachers have to request them far in advance. This type of limited access has prevented optimal use of film. Lower costs have made 8mm films more available, thus helping to alleviate this problem.

2. The cumbersome and confusing machine which often faces teachers who try to use films has been a major deterrent to extensive use of the film. The fact that one projector usually has to be shared by

many teachers has also limited film use. Again, simpler projectors, such as the cartridge loading or self-threading units, help to overcome this limitation.

3. Teachers often complain that the available motion pictures are simply not suitable for their subject or grade. Teachers do have to depend upon the products of film producers just as they have to depend upon the textbooks available from book publishers. These materials are not usually made for highly specific purposes. As more films become available, this problem decreases. Teachers now have an ever-increasing choice of film titles on a given topic; new formats, such as the open-ended film, permit teacher and student comments.

SOURCES

The Index to 16mm Educational Films, prepared by the National Information Center for Educational Media, is available from R. R. Bowker Co., 1180 Avenue of the Americas, New York 10036, for $39.50. The *Index* lists films according to subject matter and provides a descriptive alphabetical listing as well. The description includes title, a brief description of the contents, length of the film, indication of color or black and white, the name of the producer, the name of the distributor, and the date of production.

The *Index of 8mm Educational Motion Cartridges*, published by the R. R. Bowker Co., 1180 Avenue of the Americas, New York 10036, lists over 9000 items. It was published in 1969 and sells for $16.00.

The *8mm Film Directory*, published by Comprehensive Service Corp., 250 West 64th St., New York 10023, was published in 1969 and sells for $10.50. Titles are listed by subject matter and are indexed with the Dewey Decimal classification. An alphabetical index of titles and subjects is also included as well as a section on 8mm motion picture equipment.

The *Library of Congress Catalog: Motion Pictures and Filmstrips* began in 1953 and has been cumulative since that date. It includes listing by title and subject of all educational motion pictures and filmstrips released in the United States and Canada and cataloged on the Library of Congress printed cards. Short annotations of each title are provided. Back editions of the listings are available from several sources: 1953–1957 edition ($20.00) and 1958–1962 edition ($40.00) are sold by Rowman and Littlefield, Inc., 84 Fifth Avenue, New York 10011. The 1963, 1964, and 1965 editions ($15.00 each) can be purchased from Gale Research Co., 1400 Book Tower, Detroit, Mich. 48226. The 1966 and 1967 editions ($8.00 each) are sold by the Library of Congress, Card Division, Washington, D.C. 20541. The 1968 edition is available from the same source for $25.00. An alternative source for the 1963–1967 cumulative edition is from the J. W. Edwards Publisher, Inc., Ann Arbor, Mich. 48106.

The *Educators Guide to Free Films*, Educators Progress Service, Randolph, Wisc. 53956, is revised annually and sells for $10.75. The 30th annual edition in 1970 listed 5002 free film titles. These films are primarily sponsored by business and industry, government agencies, and foreign government tourists bureaus. A title and subject index is included.

It is important to note that the *Index to 16mm Educational Films* and the *Library of Congress Catalog* identify only the producer of the film. Only in rare instances does the producer of the film also rent the film to the user. The usual procedure is for the school system or university film library to purchase films from the producers and then make them available to the user through a loan system. Individuals can use these two comprehensive sources to determine whether there is a film in existence on a particular topic. Then the user must go to the catalog of the school system or university film library to see if a particular title is included in the collection that is available.

The *Index to 16mm Educational Films* lists over 4000 producers and distributors of 16mm educational films. It is difficult to single out those who offer the best titles, but it is possible to list those who are the largest producers and therefore cover a wider spectrum of motion picture materials for more subjects than the smaller companies. The quality of the smaller companies' products may surpass those of the larger organizations but the smaller companies do not have the wide selection of titles in their catalogs. Some of the largest producers are:

Bailey-Film Associates, 11559 Santa Monica Blvd., Los Angeles, Calif. 90025

Churchill Films, 662 N. Robertson Blvd., Los Angeles, Calif. 90069

Coronet Films, 65 East South Water St., Chicago, Ill. 60611

Encyclopaedia Britannica Educational Corp., 425 N. Michigan Ave., Chicago, Ill. 60611

International Film Bureau, 332 S. Michigan Ave., Chicago, Ill. 60604

International Film Foundation, 475 Fifth Ave., New York 10017

McGraw-Hill Book Co., Text-Film Division, 330 West 42nd St., New York 10036

REFERENCES

Once sources of films have been identified, it is often helpful to obtain the critical assessment of reviewers.

Film reviews are found in many professional journals, such as *Social Education*, the *Journal of Geography*, and *Science and Children*.

Each month, *Audiovisual Instruction* carries an "Index of Audiovisual Reviews" which offers an excellent reference to sources of reviews for specific film titles.

Film News is devoted primarily to film reviews.

There are two major review services:

Subscriptions to *EFLA Evaluations*, a monthly card service, are available for an annual membership fee of $50.00. The Educational Film Library Association, 250 West 57th St., New York 10019 offers a compilation of its evaluations from 1948 through 1964 for $30.00 in the publication, *Film*

Evaluation Guide. The 1964–1967 Supplement to the *Guide* sells for $12.00. The evaluations provide a complete bibliographic citation plus general and technical ratings, a descriptive annotation, and suggested specific uses, strengths, weaknesses, and overall ratings.

The *Landers Film Reviews* (Bertha Landers, P. O. Box 69760, Los Angeles, Calif. 90069) publishes reviews monthly, except in July and August, for a subscription rate of $33.50 per year. The service began in 1956. Back issues are available (Volumes 6–11 at $27.50 each; Volume 12 and up at $33.50). Each evaluation includes bibliographic information plus descriptive and evaluative reviews of motion pictures produced by over 150 different educational film producers.

The nearest and probably the most available resource for educational motion pictures is the local film library, usually maintained by the audiovisual department of the school system. Catalogs are published and made available to teachers. The film libraries which serve county or regional school systems offer additional resources. Many universities maintain film rental libraries for schools in the state or region. Check all of these sources for motion pictures.

There are a number of audiovisual materials that deal with the value and use of film:

Audiovisual Equipment Operation Series, 27 titles, 8mm film loops, 3–4 min. each, silent, color. Developed for self-instruction in equipment operation with the following 16mm projectors: RCA, Kodak, Graflex, Kalart-Victor, and Bell & Howell. Additional titles deal with splicing and projection practices. (McGraw-Hill)

The 8mm Film in Education: Its Emerging Role, 16mm, 25 min., sound, color. Shows 8mm film being used for diverse educational tasks in such subjects as botany, orchestra direction, preparation of visual materials, lipreading, handwriting, and electrical engineering. (USAC)

Facts About Film, 2nd ed., 16mm, 13 min., sound, color. Basic information about film stock, its maintenance, and repair is shown. Deals with splicing and storage of 16mm sound films. (IFB)

Facts About Projection, 2nd ed., 16mm, 17 min., sound, color. Discusses the need for advanced preparation of the room and equipment prior to a film showing. Demonstrates several methods for improving projection and illustrates operational routines for beginning and ending the showing. (IFB)

Film Tactics, 16mm, 23 min., sound, b & w. Illustrates five essential steps in the effective use of films through a series of experiences in a Navy classroom. The results of poor film use are graphically illustrated in a humorous but provocative ending. (USAC)

Using Motion Film in the Classroom, 8 mm or 16mm, 10 min., sound, color. This film emphasizes a variety of ways a motion picture film can be used in teaching. (EML)

Worth How Many Words, 16mm, 10 min., sound, color. Concerned with the flexibility of film in the learning process. Includes explanations and examples of time-lapse, photomicrography, light, color, and form that are stimulating to the eye. (Kodak)

5

OVERHEAD TRANSPARENCIES

DEFINITIONS

An *overhead transparency* is an image usually 8½″ × 11″ on clear acetate or plastic which has been prepared for use on an overhead projector. An *overhead projector* is a device which throws an image on a screen. It is placed in front of an audience and may be used in a completely lighted or semi-darkened room; it utilizes 3¼″ × 4″, 7″ × 7″, 10″ × 10″, or, most commonly, 8½″ × 11″ transparencies.

CHARACTERISTICS

The lens system of the overhead projector is designed so that the projector can be placed in the front of a room. The projection angle often causes the image to appear in a trapezoid form sometimes called "keystoning" (see illustration). This is corrected by tilting the screen as shown in the accompanying figures. This distortion is not always bothersome and does not measurably change the amount of light on the screen. The projector should be placed as low as possible, as illustrated, so that the body of the

An overhead transparency with an overlay.

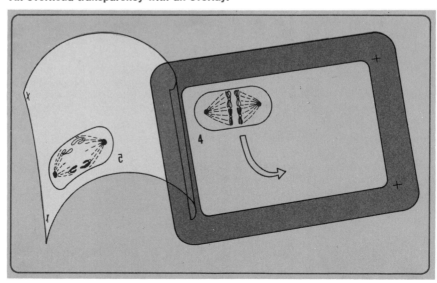

The overhead projector in use.

equipment does not interfere with the line of vision between the students and the screen.

ADVANTAGES

The overhead transparency and projector have become extremely popular since the early 1960's. The cost of the projector has decreased, and the potential for local production of transparencies has increased. In some

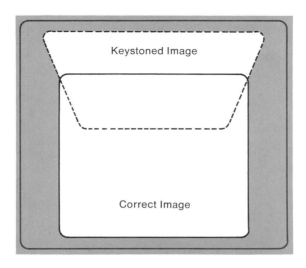

Keystoned Image

Correct Image

Comparison of a correct and a keystoned image.

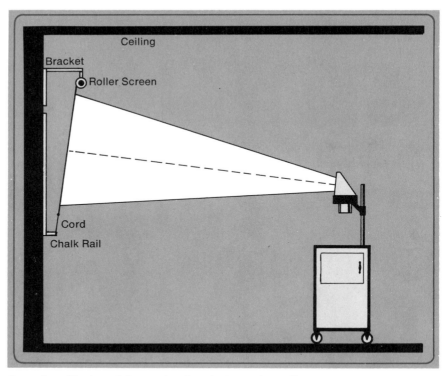

Correct positioning of the overhead projector and a wall screen.

The overhead projector is designed to permit a teacher to maintain eye contact with students.

instructional settings the overhead projector makes an excellent replacement for the chalkboard. There are many advantages to this simple projector and its associated materials.

1.   The equipment is used in the front of the room. The teacher can maintain eye contact with the class while using the equipment.
2.   A bright image can be projected in a fully lighted room. This permits the teacher and learners to see each other.
3.   Materials to be used on the overhead projector are easily produced by the teacher in the local school. The teacher may write on a piece of acetate during the class as he would use the chalkboard. He may use transparencies which have been produced through heat or chemical processes. In either case the transparency is a highly accessible and easily used medium of instruction.

The bright image of an overhead projector allows it to be used in a lighted room.

4. The equipment is simple to operate and has almost no maintenance problems save the occasional replacement of the lamp.

LIMITATIONS

In their enthusiasm for use of the overhead projector, teachers often overlook some of the limitations.

1. Unless the equipment is properly positioned the base and head of the projector may obstruct the students' line of sight. The projector should never be placed on the teacher's desk in the front of the room. A low projector stand or a table with a recessed cut-out is essential.
2. Since the overhead projector becomes such a vital part of the teaching-learning process, it cannot easily be scheduled for use in one classroom one hour and in another the next. Therefore it may be necessary to assign an overhead projector to each room if teach-

Materials for use on the overhead projector can be produced locally.

A low projection stand or a table with a recess offers the best viewing.

ers have extensive needs for this piece of equipment. This may create an economic burden.

SOURCES

There is one reference to commercially prepared transparencies: *Index to Overhead Transparencies*, which covers over 18,000 transparencies (R. R. Bowker Co., 1180 Avenue of the Americas, New York 10036, $22.50). Many individual companies publish a catalog of basic projectuals (overhead transparencies). Some audiovisual producers and book publishers offer transparencies as part of a teaching "package," while others offer transparency "masters" or line drawings from which transparencies can be made locally through a thermal or chemical process. Some of the companies specializing in prepared overhead transparencies and masters are:

DCA Educational Products, Inc., 4865 Stenton Ave., Philadelphia, Pa. 19144

General Aniline & Film Corp., 140 West 51st St., New York 10020

The Instructor Corp., Paoli, Pa. 19301

Keuffel & Esser Co., 300 Adams St., Hoboken, N.J. 07030

Scott Education Division, 104 Lower Westfield Road, Holyoke, Mass. 01040

3M Co., Visual Products Division, 2501 Hudson Road, St. Paul, Minn. 55101

Tweedy Transparencies, 208 Hollywood Ave., East Orange, N.J. 07018

United Transparencies, Inc., P. O. Box 888, Binghamton, N.Y. 13902

Visual Materials, Inc., 2549 Middlefield Rd., Redwood City, Calif. 94063

Visualcraft, Inc., 2737 W. Union St., Blue Island, Ill. 60406

REFERENCES

A collection of commercially prepared transparencies should be augmented by the teacher's personal collection of locally prepared transparencies. These may be hand-drawn or copied from masters or books (with appropriate permission). The techniques are many and varied. For the person who is interested in learning to prepare transparencies, the following booklets and manuals will be useful:

Diazochrome Projectuals for Visual Communications, Tecnifax Corp., 195 Appleton St., Holyoke, Mass. 01040 (1964).

H. C. Hartsell and Wilfred Veenendahl, *Overhead Projection*, Henry Stewart, Buffalo, N.Y. 14205 (1960).

Gaylen B. Kelley and Phillip J. Sleeman, *A Guide to Overhead Projection and the Practical Preparation of Transparencies*, Chart-Pak, Inc., Leeds, Mass. (1967).

Bob T. Mooney, *Student Manual, The Overhead Projection Series*, Educational Media Laboratories, Austin, Texas (1967). Educational Media Laboratories has prepared a comprehensive workshop for the production and use of overhead transparencies in teaching. It is intended for pre-service and in-service teachers. The content is carried in five sound filmstrips *(Using the Overhead Projector, Planning the Projectual, Simple Projectual Production, Advanced Production Techniques,* and *Mounting and Masking Projectuals)*, eighteen illustrative overhead transparencies, and in the instructor and student manuals. For further information, write EML, 4101 South Congress St., Austin, Texas 78745.

Morton J. Schultz, *The Teacher and Overhead Projection*, Prentice-Hall, Inc., Englewood Cliffs, N.J. 07632 (1965).

Richard E. Smith, *The Overhead System: Production Implementation and Utilization*. University of Texas, Visual Instruction Bureau, Austin, Texas 78745 (1966).

Richard P. Weagley, *Teaching with the Overhead Projector*, Instructo Productos Co., Philadelphia, Pa. 19104 (1963).

6

DEFINITIONS

A *phonograph record* (or phonodisc or disc) is a round and flat acetate object which has been molded from a master disc containing an irregular surface which causes sound vibrations that are transferred to the acetate for purposes of reproduction by a needle. The *phonograph* (or record player) is an electronic device that reproduces sound from records.

CHARACTERISTICS

Discs usually come in 7″, 10″, 12″, and 16″ sizes and play at speeds of 16⅔, 33⅓, 45, and 78 rpm (revolutions per minute). The most common sizes and speeds of disc recordings are illustrated here. It is important to

Common sizes and speeds of disc recordings.

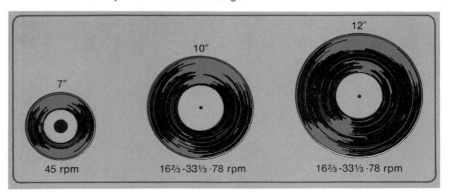

match the correct needle with the correct groove and speed (see illustration). A needle passes over the irregular surface of the grooves in a record. The resulting vibrations are electrically transmitted to an amplifier which converts them to electrical impulses which are in turn fed to a speaker. The speaker converts electrical energy to sound.

A phonograph has two major units: an electronic system and a mechanical system (see illustration). The electrical system contains the pick-up arm, the amplifier, and the speaker. The mechanical system includes the turntable and the motor. The controls most commonly found on the phonograph are: POWER SWITCH (OFF-ON); VOLUME CONTROL; TONE CONTROL; SPEED CONTROL; and VARIABLE SPEED CONTROL.

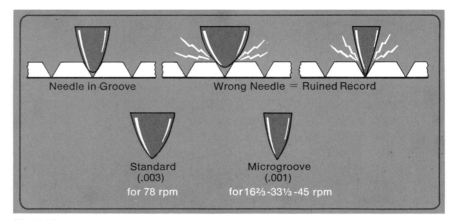

Match the needle with the groove and speed.

Records should receive special care to ensure long life and to preserve quality. Follow these suggestions:

1. Handle records by the outer edges to protect the grooves.
2. Handle the needles with care; be sure the proper needle is being used for the groove of the record; keep the surface of the needle free from the lint which usually accumulates.
3. Keep records in their dust jackets when not in use.
4. Store discs flat or vertically on a shelf away from heat, extreme cold, or dampness.
5. Keep the surface of the record free from dirt and lint which clings to the record due to static electricity. A silicone cloth, available at record stores, is the best cleaning agent.

Basic elements of the record player.

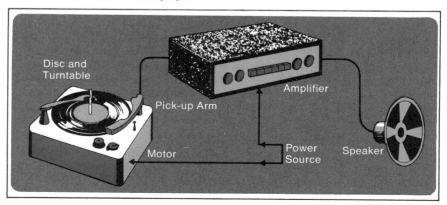

ADVANTAGES

1.   A wide variety of records is available in nearly every subject matter field and at all levels.
2.   Records are inexpensive and readily available. Schools build collections of records, and teachers can acquire personal collections for a very low cost.
3.   Records are easy to store and easy to use. The equipment is more readily available than any other audiovisual device and the operation is simple. Records can be started and stopped at the teacher's discretion.
4.   The wide availability of recordings and equipment means that they can be easily scheduled.

LIMITATIONS

1.   Without proper care, records can be easily damaged.
2.   Usually records cannot be locally produced.

SOURCES

The most comprehensive source of long-playing records, which constitute the bulk of those records used in schools, is the *Schwann LP Record Catalog*. It is published monthly by W. Schwann, Inc., Boston, Mass., and

Sample of the *Audio Cardalog.*

Shaw, George Bernard (1856 — 1950)
MAJOR BARBARA

Synopsis: George Bernard Shaw's play that involves a Salvation Army lass and a munitions manufacturer and points up the moral that the greatest crime is to countenance the continuing existence of poverty. Players include Maggie Smith, Robert Morley, Celia Johnson, Alec McCowen, Warren Mitchell and Gary Bond. A Theatre Recording Society presentation.

Rating and Appraisal: **Excellent** performance and direction of a play that has angered and elated audiences since 1905. The writing is crisp, the acting sharp and delicate as need indicates.

Utilization: The record may be used in school to introduce the dramatic work of the author and to motivate reading of this and other plays. It may be added to loan collections in school, college and public libraries and may be offered in adult education courses as an aspect of modern theatre studies.

Record Label: Caedmon TRS 319 (mono) and TRS 319S (stereo). Four 12 inch 33.3 rpm records with accompanying script and program notes.

1. Title
2. Author
3. Irish Literature

Audio CARDALOG #67096

© *Audio CARDALOG – 1967*

is available at most record dealers. It lists over 35,000 titles; about 500 new titles are added every month. The publisher deletes titles of records which have been discontinued by the producers. The catalog classifies music by artists and composers and carries specialized listings for jazz, folk music, film scores, plays, and spoken voice.

For an evaluation of records, particularly for educational use, *Audio Cardalog*, Box 989, Larchmont, N.Y. 10538, provides 3″ × 5″ cards, each containing an evaluation of a recording, for a $30.00 annual subscription. Back issues are available. From the same source, the *Audio Cardalog Directory of Record Producers* offers a ready reference to producers of educational records.

A general reference to audio materials is the *Educators Guide to Free Tapes, Scripts, and Transcriptions*, from Educators Progress Service, Randolph, Wisconsin 53956. Most of the 392 audio materials listed are sponsored by business, industry, and government agencies. Some are loaned free of charge while others are given to schools for placement in collections.

Local sources for records are numerous, especially in shops devoted to the sale of records and music. Most locally available discs are musical in nature. Other titles have to be ordered from dealers on special order.

7
PICTURES

DEFINITION

A *picture* is a two-dimensional visual representation of persons, places, or things. Most commonly it is a photograph, but it also may be a sketch, a cartoon, a mural, or even a chart, graph or map. Pictures may be used for individual study, for display on bulletin boards and in exhibits, and for projection when groups of students need to look at one picture at the same time.

CHARACTERISTICS

Pictures are usually printed or photographically processed. They vary in size and color. They may be highly representational or abstract. If a picture is desirable for use and it is in a book or pamphlet which is available to an entire class, it probably would be most efficient to ask everyone to turn to the same page at the same time to look at the picture. If, however, only one copy of a picture is available, and group viewing is required, the picture could be projected on a screen:

The easiest method is to place the picture in the opaque projector. The room must be very dark and the screen must be large enough to accommodate the enlarged image. The picture will not be damaged.

The same picture could be copied on 35mm film which would be processed into a 2″ × 2″ slide.

Another option, if the picture is on claybased paper (such as *Life* or *Holiday*), and the picture does not have to be saved, is to "lift" the picture from the paper by the picture transfer process using the rubber cement or a thermal process. The picture is transferred to clear acetate and is used on an overhead projector.

Pictures may be displayed on a bulletin board for individual or small group observation. Bulletin boards in the classroom and in school halls offer display opportunities.

ADVANTAGES

1. Pictures are inexpensive and widely available.
2. They provide common experiences for an entire group.
3. The visual detail makes it possible to study subjects which would otherwise be impossible.
4. Pictures can help to prevent and correct misconceptions.

Pictures can be shown using the opaque projector without damaging the original.

5. Pictures offer a stimulus to further study, reading, and research. Visual evidence is a powerful tool.
6. They help to focus attention and to develop critical judgment.

LIMITATIONS

1. Sizes and distances are often distorted.
2. Lack of color in some pictures limits proper interpretations.
3. Students do not always know how to "read" pictures.
4. Unless each student has a picture or the picture is properly projected, the medium should not be used.

SOURCES

Free and Inexpensive Learning Materials, published by the Division of Surveys and Field Services, George Peabody College for Teachers, Nash-

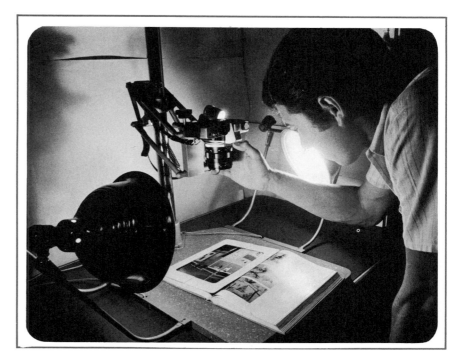

Pictures can be copied using a 35mm camera to produce 2″ X 2″ slides.

Pictures from magazines can be transferred from the printed page to acetate for overhead projection.

ville, Tenn. 37203, contains 258 pages and costs $3.00. The 14th biennial edition (1968) lists over 3500 items which can be obtained from organizations, industries, and government agencies. The entries are classified under 120 subject headings which parallel the units often taught in elementary and secondary schools. A comprehensive index is provided, as well as a table of contents and extensive cross-references.

The *Elementary Teachers Guide to Free Curriculum Materials* is available from Educators Progress Service, Randolph, Wisc. 53956. The 27th annual edition (1970) lists 1641 items available to schools from sponsors in business, industry and government.

Educators Index of Free Materials, Educators Progress Service, Randolph, Wisc. 53956, is in its 27th edition. This card file lists 1762 titles which have been selected on the basis of educational appropriateness, timeliness, format, and content.

A very useful and up-to-date index of primary sources to producers of picture materials is Catherine M. Williams, *Learning From Pictures*, 2nd ed., Department of Audiovisual Instruction, N.E.A., Washington, D.C. (1968), $4.50. A subject index to the primary sources and selected references are also included.

Ruth H. Aubrey's *Selected Free Materials for Classroom Teachers*, Fearon Publishers, 2165 Park Blvd., Palo Alto, Calif. 94306 (1967) $1.75, provides over 570 sources of free classroom materials, chosen, graded, and annotated by a panel of educators. Sources are listed by subject matter and indexed. Items are keyed for appropriate grade levels.

The above references list hundreds of sources of free pictures. There are, however, commercial sources of pictures for specific curricular uses; these are listed below. The costs are generally low, and the picture quality is usually excellent. The collections have been especially designed for classroom use.

Artex Prints, Inc., Westport, Conn. 06880 (Color art reproductions)

Audio-Visual Enterprises, 911 Laguna Road, Pasadena, Calif. 91105 (Color study prints and historical models)

Creative Educational Society, Mankato, Minn. 56001

Curtis Audio Visual Materials, Independence Square, Philadelphia, Pa., 19105

Denoyer-Geppert Co., 5235 Ravenswood Ave., Chicago, Ill. 60640

Documentary Photo Aids, Inc., P.O. Box 2237, Phoenix, Ariz. 85002 (Documentary photos of American history)

Friendship Press, 475 Riverside Dr., New York, N.Y. 10027

C. S. Hammond & Co., Inc., Maplewood, N.J. 07040

Hi-Worth Pictures, P. O. Box 6, Altadena, Calif. 91001

Informative Classroom Picture Publishers, Inc., 31 Ottawa Ave., N.W., Grand Rapids, Mich. 49501

National Geographic Society, School Service Division, 16th and M Sts., N.W., Washington, D.C. 20036

New York Graphic Society Ltd., 140 Greenwich Ave., Greenwich, Conn. 06830 (Fine art reproductions)

A. J. Nystrom & Co., 3333 Elston Ave., Chicago, Ill. 60618

F. A. Owen Publishing Co., Dansville, N.Y. 14437

Perry Pictures, Inc., 42 Dartmouth St., Malden, Mass. 02148

Rand McNally & Co., Box 7600, Chicago, Ill. 60680

Society for Visual Education, Inc., 1345 Diversey Pkwy., Chicago, Ill. 60614

United Nations, Public Inquiries Unit, Dept. of Public Information, New York, New York 10017

W. M. Welch Scientific Co., 1515 Sedgwick St., Chicago, Ill. 60607

Beyond the normal textbook, commercial, and free sources of pictures, there are local and personal resources which should be exploited in the search for pictures. Almost any popular magazine offers excellent pictures, often in color. *Life, Holiday*, and *National Geographic* are especially rich in visual materials. The teacher's personal camera offers an additional source of pictures. Colleagues are often willing to share a collection of pictures, and the local community offers additional possibilities. Chambers of commerce are often good sources of pictorial materials. Historical associations can often give or lend pictures that illustrate the early days in the area. Travel agencies, libraries, commercial artists, photographers, printers, manufacturers, and large retail stores are additional sources.

REFERENCES

There are many good books, pamphlets, and articles available:

Creating Social Studies and Science Bulletin Boards, Standard Oil Company of California, Public Relations Department, 225 Bush St., San Francisco, Calif. 94120.

Fearon Publishers (2165 Park Blvd., Palo Alto, Calif. 94306) have published a series of pamphlets on bulletin boards which offer practical suggestions for the use of pictures:

Marjorie Kelley, *Classroom Tested Bulletin Boards*, 1961.
Thomas Koskey, *Baited Bulletin Boards*, 1954.
Thomas Koskey, *Bulletin Board Idea Sources*, 1963.
Thomas Koskey, *Bulletin Boards for Subject Areas*, 1962.
Doris Ruby, *4–D Bulletin Boards That Teach*, 1960.
Doris and Grant Ruby, *Bulletin Boards for Middle Grades*, 1964.
Matthew F. Vessel and Herbert H. Wong, *Science Bulletin Boards*, 1962.

How to Create Classroom Bulletin Boards, Standard Oil Company of California, Public Relations Dept. (address above).

How to Keep Your Bulletin Board Alive, The Ohio State University, Bureau of Educational Research and Service, Teaching Aids Laboratory, Columbus, Ohio (1958), 15 pp.

Catherine M. Williams, *Learning from Pictures*, 2nd ed., National Education Association, Department of Audiovisual Instruction, Washington, D.C. (1968), 166 pp., $4.50.

The following materials will be helpful in planning for the creative use of pictures:

Better Bulletin Boards, 16mm, 13 min., sound, color and b & w, 1956. Shows materials from which bulletin boards can be constructed, suggests sources for obtaining display materials, illustrates arrangement of materials, and stresses the importance of good selection and design of pictures to attract and hold attention. (Indiana)

Bulletin Boards, An Effective Teaching Device, 16mm, 11 min., sound, color, 1956. Suggests ideas for planning and organizing creatively designed bulletin boards and presents 12 displays arranged by a class. Illustrates class participation in planning and arranging a bulletin board. (Bailey)

How to Keep Your Bulletin Board Alive, 33 frames, color, 1950. Diagnoses faults of bulletin boards in a light and graphic style. Suggests guidelines for captions, illustrations, and text materials to improve layout techniques. (Ohio State)

Mounting Pictures, 58 frames, color, 1956. Describes methods of mounting pictures for a variety of purposes. Describes materials used, steps in mounting, and ways of protecting pictures. (Texas)

Parade of Bulletin Boards, 45 frames, color, 1957. Shows and analyzes 36 classroom bulletin boards through cogent caption comments. (Ohio State)

Study Pictures and Learning, 58 frames, color, 1960. Analyzes purposes governing effective picture study and presents criteria for selecting pictures. (Ohio State)

Teaching with Still Pictures, 53 frames, color, 1958. Applies the findings from experimental research to the use of still pictures in the classroom. (Basic)

8

PROGRAMMED INSTRUCTION

DEFINITION

Programmed instruction is the use of programmed materials (or a program) to achieve educational objectives. Some programs are designed for devices which are commonly referred to as teaching machines. *A teaching machine* is a device that presents a program. Most machines control

A student uses programmed instruction in a teaching machine.

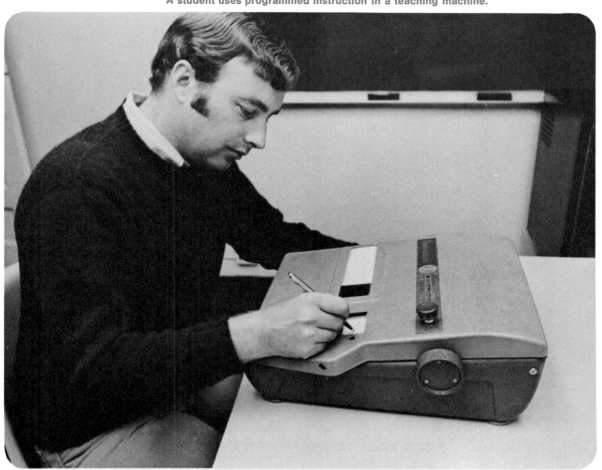

A page from a programmed instruction text for high school geography.

Chesapeake Tidewater	**47** The part of the Atlantic Coastal Plain in Virginia and Maryland is called T _ _ _ _ _ _ _ _ country because the rivers flowing into C _ _ _ _ _ _ _ _ _ Bay are affected by the t _ _ _ s.
Tidewater Chesapeake tides	**48** Parts of D————, M———— and Virginia make-up the Eastern S _ _ _ _.
Delaware Maryland Shore	**49** The first English settlement in North America was near the mouth of the James River. It was called J _ _ _ _ town, and was the first capital of colonial ——————— (colony).
Jamestown **Virginia (Today, Jamestown is a National Historical site. Williamsburg, the second capital of colonial Virginia, is nearby.)**	**50** The wealthy aristocratic land owners of the colonial period lived and had their plantations in Tidewater ——————— and Maryland.
Virginia	**51** Tidewater plantations faced on the rivers and creeks. Plantation owners (had/did not have) boat docks. Ships which carried trade between England and the plantations used the many navigable ——————— and creeks which are tributaries of ——————— Bay.
had rivers Chesapeake	**52** Not far distant from the dock was the plantation owner's mansion. Nearby were the stables, barns, carpenter shop, blacksmith shop and houses of the servants (or slaves) who took care of these activities. Near the fields were the homes of the field-hands. Plantation life (was/was not) largely self-sufficient.

the material to which the student has access at any moment, preventing him from looking ahead or reviewing old items. Many machines contain a response mechanism: a tape on which the student writes, a keyboard, or selection buttons. Some provision is made for knowledge of results, either by revealing the correct answer after the student responds or by advancing to the next item, thereby signaling correct completion of the previous item. However, most programs are in the form of programmed texts. These texts do not differ in outward appearance from conventional workbooks or texts; no equipment is required to use a programmed text.

CHARACTERISTICS

In programmed instruction information is presented; the presentation is controlled, usually by small steps; the presentation stimulus demands an active response by the learner; the student is either told whether his response is correct, or he is permitted to judge whether his response is correct as he compares his with the one given in the program; and there is no established pace at which the learner must move.

ADVANTAGES

Some of the advantages of programmed learning are inherent in the characteristics of the medium, i.e., the individual can move at his own pace; the individual must respond to the stimulus (there is little opportunity for inactivity); and the individual knows immediately whether he is right or wrong. Other advantages include the following:

1. The student follows a logical sequence of thought.
2. By the time the programmed instruction reaches the learner, it has usually been field tested and verified, thus ensuring optimum learning and optimum use of student time.
3. Programmed instruction is especially well-suited to many kinds of learning tasks.
4. A wide variety of media can be employed in presenting stimuli: audiotapes, films, slides, filmstrips, flat pictures, etc.

LIMITATIONS

1. Programmed instruction usually works best with the cognitive learning objectives—those dealing with factual and skill learning. Many teachers question the success of programmed learning since it tends to emphasize content and does not permit feelings or emotions to be used.
2. Some programs, especially those which are organized in a linear fashion, tend to be somewhat dull, especially for brighter students.
3. Programs are difficult to prepare on a local basis. They are time-consuming to write and to field test. If commercial programs are not available, and locally prepared programs cannot be written, the use of PI is not possible.

SOURCES

Carl H. Hendershot's *Programmed Learning: A Bibliography of Programs and Presentation Devices* (Carl H. Hendershot, Bay City, Michigan, 1970) provides a comprehensive reference. This is a loose-leaf catalog of all programs currently available, kept up-to-date by periodical supplements.

Many publishers have entered the programmed instruction area. Some producers of audiovisual materials have generated programs as part of multimedia "packages." Some of the primary sources for programmed instructional materials are:

Addison-Wesley Publishing Co., Reading, Mass. 01867

Doubleday & Company, Inc., 501 Franklin Ave., Garden City, N.Y. 10017

Encyclopaedia Britannica Educational Corp., 425 N. Michigan Ave., Chicago, Ill. 60611

Grolier Incorporated, 845 Third Ave., New York, N.Y. 10022

Harcourt, Brace & Jovanovich, Inc., 757 Third Ave., New York, N.Y. 10017

John Wiley & Sons, Inc., 605 Third Ave., New York, N.Y. 10016

Xerox-Basic Systems, 600 Madison Ave., New York, N.Y. 10022

The only local sources of programmed instructional materials would be those prepared by the individual teacher. To achieve this competency, it would be advisable to take a course at a university in the field of programmed instruction. Consultation of the books listed below offers additional guidance.

REFERENCES

For help in stating instructional objectives, see Robert F. Mager, *Preparing Instructional Objectives*, Fearon Publishers, Palo Alto, Calif. (1962).

For help in writing programmed instruction, see Susan M. Markle, *Good Frames and Bad*, 2nd ed., John Wiley & Sons, New York (1969), and Peter Pipe, *Practical Programming*, Holt, Rinehart and Winston, Inc., 383 Madison Ave., New York 10017 (1966).

For examples of use, see *Four Case Studies of Programmed Instruction*, Fund for the Advancement of Education, New York (1964).

For assistance in the selection of programmed instruction, the Department of Audiovisual Instruction of NEA has available *Selection and Use of Programmed Materials: A Handbook for Teachers*, DAVI, (1964).

The following audiovisual resources are available:

Selection and Use of Programmed Materials, filmstrip, 63 frames, 15 min., sound, 1964. The criteria for selection of programmed instructional materials are presented from the user's point-of-view. (DAVI)

An Example of a Teaching Machine Program, filmstrip, 62 frames, 1960. Presents a complete self-teaching lesson on the reading of the color code on electronic resistors. Permits audience participation while teaching the basic principles of programmed instruction. (Basic)

Teaching Machines, filmstrip, 62 frames, 1960. Presents the basic principles of programmed instruction. Answers questions such as: What are teaching machines? What is a program? What is the educator's role? (Basic)

Teaching Machines and Programmed Learning, 16mm, 28 min., sound, b&w. An orientation to teaching machines and programmed learning for educators. B. F. Skinner, Arthur A. Lumsdaine, and Robert Glaser present theories, materials, and machines related to programmed learning. (USAC)

9

TAPE RECORDINGS

DEFINITION

Magnetic tape is an acetate or plastic ribbon coated on one surface with a layer of magnetizable iron oxide particles (see illustration). The ¼″ width tape is usually employed to record audio messages magnetically for subsequent reproduction.

The *tape recorder*, with which the magnetic tape is used, can record a message and play it back or play back a prerecorded tape. The unit contains recording and playback amplifiers and heads (see illustrations). The heads may be full track, half track, dual track, or quarter track (see illustration).

CHARACTERISTICS

There is a variety of controls on every tape recorder. Some of the most common controls and their functions are listed in the table below.

TAPE RECORDER CONTROLS AND THEIR FUNCTIONS

Controls and Indicators	Function
On-off switch	Controls flow of electric current to the tape recorder
Neutral or stop	Permits motor to keep turning but tape is not in motion
Play or listen	Moves tape forward for listening purposes
Speed selector	Changes speed of tape (usually $1\frac{7}{8}$, $3\frac{3}{4}$, $7\frac{1}{2}$ in./sec)
Fast forward	Moves tape forward at rapid speed
Reverse	Rewinds tape at rapid speed to the beginning
Record	Moves tape forward and activates recording heads; automatically erases any recording on tape
Speaker switch	Turns speaker off during recording operations (done automatically in some machines)
Volume	Controls level of sound being recorded or reproduced
Tone	Determines high or low pitch
Monitor	Indicates volume level (see illustration)
Counter	Indicates number of reel revolutions (see illustration)

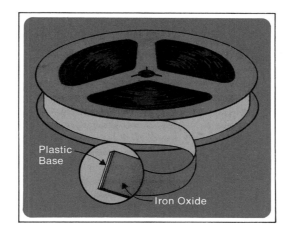

The magnetically coated side of the ¼″ tape is dull; the "shiny" side is the acetate or plastic base.

The process of recording on magnetic tape.

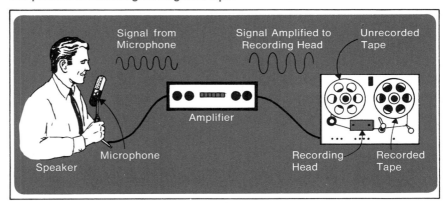

The playback process from magnetic tape.

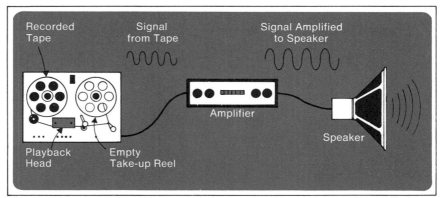

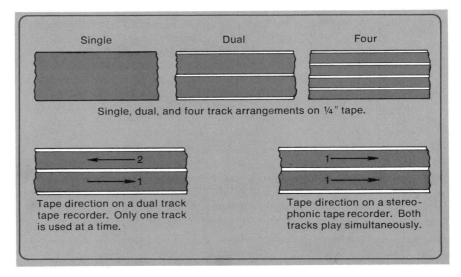

Single, dual, and four track arrangements on ¼" tape.

Tape direction on a dual track tape recorder. Only one track is used at a time.

Tape direction on a stereophonic tape recorder. Both tracks play simultaneously.

Recording formats.

Recording and playing times of tape are governed by reel size, tape thickness, number of tracks used in the tape, and speed selected for recording.

REEL SIZE AND RECORDING TIME (RECORDING ONE DIRECTION)

Reel Size	Tape Length*	3.75 ips	7.50 ips
4 in.	300 ft	15 min	7½ min
5 in.	600 ft	30 min	15 min
7 in.	1200 ft	60 min	30 min

*Length is given for regular type tape. Long play tape will increase recording time. Consult manufacturer's information appearing on the container.

As a general rule, the faster the tape speed, the better the quality of the recording. For example, a tape running at 1⅞ inches per second (ips) or 3¾ ips is adequate for recording speech, but 7½ ips or, better still, 15 ips would be necessary to record music with a high degree of quality. If half track is used, the amount of recording time on the chart can be doubled. With quarter track, it would be four times the time stated. This assumes that the equipment will record and playback on half track or quarter track. It is the machine, not the tape, that determines recording time.

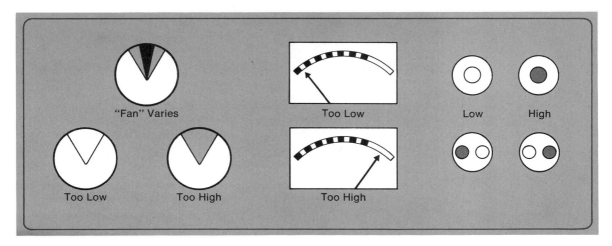

Three types of volume indicators.

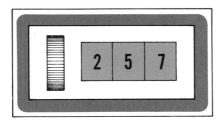

The counter indicates the number of revolutions.

Tape can be used over and over many times. In addition, when a recording is no longer needed, the tape can be used for a new recording because each time a new recording is made, the old recording on the tape is automatically erased. It is difficult to estimate tape life; however, since the magnetic surface usually lasts a very long time, tape recordings rarely "wear out." Tape can break when the equipment is faulty, when the tape is especially dry, or when the tape is suddenly stopped while running at fast forward or rewind speeds. The process for repairing the tapes is simple (see the illustration on the next page). Be sure to use splicing tape especially designed for repairing magnetic tapes, and not ordinary cellophane tape, which could endanger the recording or the playback heads of the recorder.

In an attempt to prevent some of the problems of breakage and mishandling of tapes, the tape cartridge and the cassette were introduced. The continuous loop *cartridge* is one reel of tape with ends joined together to form an endless loop (see illustration). Since there is only one reel, there is no provision for fast forward or rewind. It makes pos-

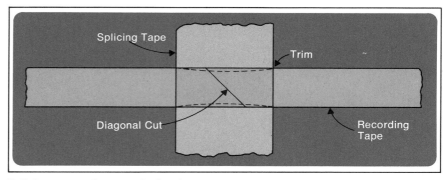

Splicing magnetic tape. 1. Overlap tape and cut diagonally. 2. Align ends with "shiny" side up. 3. Place splicing tape (*not* cellophane tape) over aligned ends. 4. Trim excess tape cutting slightly into recording tape.

sible the repetitive playback of a recorded message without rewinding the tape. The tape is ¼" width moving at 3¾ ips. Four-track and eight-track cartridges are the types usually available.

The *cassette* is an enclosed case which contains two little hubs that permit reel-to-reel recording and playback (see illustration). It differs from the normal reel-to-reel process in that both the tape and the hubs are captive within the cassette housing. Threading is eliminated, and fast forward and rewind functions are possible. Cassette recorders and playback units run at 1⅞ ips and cassettes come in 30-minute to 2-hour units. The tape is 1/7" wide.

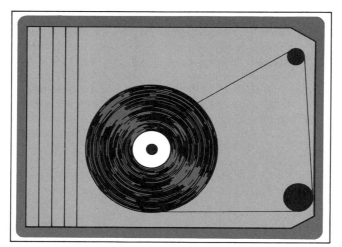

The endless loop cartridge.

The cassette.

ADVANTAGES

The tape recorder has become commonplace equipment in homes, cars, and schools. A unit may cost as little as $10.00 (for battery-powered toy-type units) or as much as several thousands of dollars (for professional equipment). The availability of tape recorders is the first major advantage. Other advantages include:

The battery-powered cassette recorder-playback can be used almost anywhere.

1.   The opportunity to be in two places at one time is possible when a recording can substitute for an individual.
2.   Recording people and events for later use—radio and TV programs, phonograph records, and the work of the students themselves—is possible.
3.   The opportunity to hear one's self is a useful diagnostic tool for helping to improve speech or musical efforts.
4.   The operation of tape recorders is relatively easy. Cartridge and cassette recorders require no threading.

Cassette recorders can provide the sound track for a slide presentation.

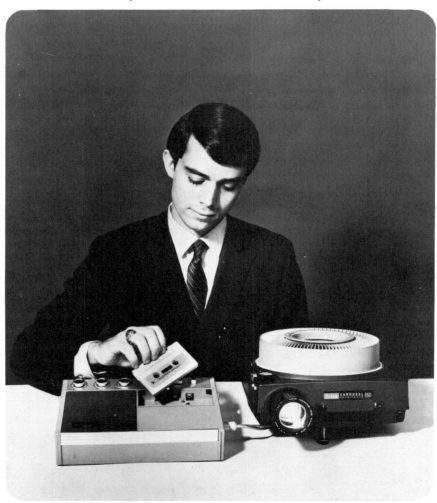

LIMITATIONS

Some people become confused about the operation of equipment which requires several distinct actions before it can be used. Difficulties with equipment operation cause tape to spill off the reel, to break, or to "jam" the machine. Other limitations are:

1.   It is difficult to locate specific recorded items on a magnetic tape; if a recorded message is in the middle of a reel of tape and there is no record of the number of revolutions or no marker on the reel, the search may take a long time.
2.   The great variety of tape speeds and arrangement of tracks (half, quarter, stereo, etc.) may cause some difficulty if a recording is made on one machine and is played back on another which may not have the same features.

SOURCES

There is no comprehensive catalog of tape recordings similar to the Schwann catalog of long playing records. There are, however, several references to educational tapes which should assist the teacher who is attempting to locate tape recordings in specific areas.

The *National Audio Tape Catalog* provides a subject index of tape recordings including more than one hundred subject headings from Aeronautics to Zoology. Types of programs included in the catalog are lecture, discussion, interview, drama, music, instruction, and literature. Titles for all entries are noted, and short annotations are given for each series. More than 5000 titles are listed for use from nursery school to graduate school. One obtains a blank tape and sends it to the National Tape Repository at the University of Colorado. Tapes may be purchased from the N.T.R. The program requested will be dubbed (duplicated) from the master tape in the Center. A small fee is charged for duplication. The *Catalog* is available from the Department of Audiovisual Instruction, National Education Association, 1201 Sixteenth St., N.W., Washington, D.C. 20036, for $3.00.

The 17th Annual Edition (1970) of the *Educators Guide to Free Tapes, Scripts, and Transcriptions* (complete address is given in Media Facts section 6) offers 375 free tape recordings from various sponsored sources.

There are many companies which produce and distribute tapes for educational use. Some of the largest are:

Academic Recording Institute, 4727 Oakshire, Houston, Texas 77027

Associated Educational Materials Co., Inc., P. O. Box 2087, Raleigh, North Carolina 27602

Educational Activities Inc., Box 392, Freeport, N.Y. 11520

EMC Corporation, 180 E. Sixth St., St. Paul, Minn. 55101
Imperial Productions, Inc., 247 W. Court St., Kankakee, Ill. 60901
Spoken Arts, Inc., 59 Locust Ave., New Rochelle, N.Y. 10801
Tapes Unlimited, 13113 Puritan, Detroit, Michigan 48227

Local schools and school districts often develop collections of tape recordings which are made available to all teachers. Copies are usually dubbed from the master in the library collection. Some courses of study, particularly in foreign languages and English language arts, provide series of tapes which are correlated with the printed text materials. Once the school owns the master set, permission is usually granted to make copies as needed.

Many states have established "Tapes for Teaching" libraries. The procedure for using these services, if your state has such a library, is to send a blank tape with a request to dub a copy from the master. Many state education departments have "Tapes for Teaching" libraries. A number of universities also furnish this service.

REFERENCES

A good reference on the tape recorder and the use of tapes in teaching is: *Creative Teaching With Tape*, Revere Mincom Division, 3M Company, 2501 Hudson Road, St. Paul, Minn. 55119 (Free), a collection of case studies about use of audiotape at all levels. Technical information on recording, tape care, and equipment selection is included.

The following audiovisual materials are also useful references:

Behind the Tape—the Teacher, tape, 45 min. Describes the advantages of, and the proper techniques for the use of tape recordings. (3M)

Elementary and Secondary School Demonstration Tape, tape, 15 min. each demonstration. A series of actual classroom examples of tape recording usage at each level with a narrator's "bridge" from segment to segment. (3M)

The Language Laboratory, filmstrip, 52 frames, color, $7.00. Illustrates various language laboratory systems and advantages of each. (Basic)

10

TELEVISION

DEFINITIONS

Television is an electronic system of transmitting still and moving images with accompanying sound over a wire or through space. The system employs equipment that converts light and sound into electrical waves and reconverts them into visible light rays and audible sound. The most common type of transmission is *broadcast* or *open circuit* television where programs are radiated to any viewer within range of the station (see illustration). This is the type of transmission used by commercial and some

A broadcast or open circuit television system.

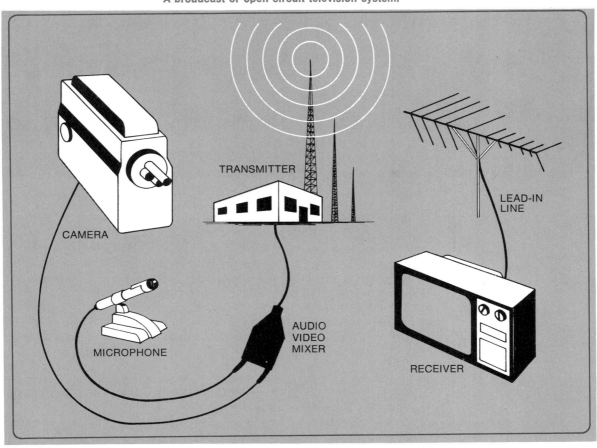

CAMERA

TRANSMITTER

LEAD-IN LINE

MICROPHONE

AUDIO VIDEO MIXER

RECEIVER

educational stations. The other type of system, frequently found in schools and colleges, is the *closed circuit* television system which limits distribution of an image and sound to receivers directly connected to the origination point by coaxial cable or microwave link (see illustration).

A closed circuit television system.

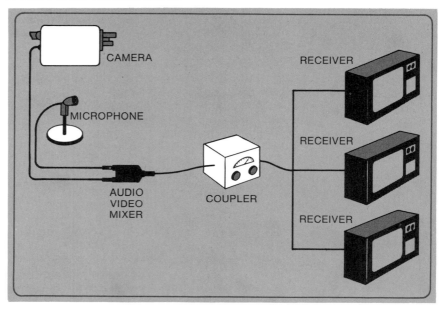

CHARACTERISTICS

There are many books and manuals that cover the technical aspects of television. The outline presented here describes the basic elements of closed circuit and broadcast television systems.

The simple closed circuit system is a good place to start. A vidicon camera with lenses and a television receiver connected to the camera by a wire constitutes a basic system. To add sound, an audio-video mixer (a device which combines the video signal from a TV camera and the audio signal from a microphone and impresses them on a carrier signal for transmission in closed circuit systems) is added. Sometimes a separate sound system consisting of a microphone, amplifier, and speaker can be used. The addition of a videotape recorder permits the recording and instant playback of audio and video images.

Videotape packages are now available as separate systems. These packages include a camera with lenses, a videotape recorder, a television receiver, a microphone, and associated electronic equipment and cables. Prices for the basic system begin at approximately $1000.

When closed circuit systems are extended from one or two locations to many locations on a college campus or in a school system, further modifications of the system must be made. If the closed circuit feature is to remain, the signals have to be carried by coaxial cable (often leased from the telephone company) to each location where TV receivers are installed. Another alternative is the use of low power (2500 megahertz band) transmission or microwave transmission. These wireless systems permit the distribution of four signals simultaneously from point to point on a direct light of sight.

When a broadcast station goes into operation, the entire system is multiplied many-fold. There are cameras and film and tape sources for origination of the programs; there are the audio and the video systems;

A group of fourth level students at Arevalos School in Huntington Beach, California, videotapes a play it has produced. One girl operates a vidicon television camera, and the images picked up are recorded on a videotape recorder at left. The children later view the tape replay and criticize their perfomance before the play is replayed for the entire class.

and there is the transmitter, usually a separate installation with the transmitter tower adjacent. Signals are sent from the transmitter location. Any standard receivers in the broadcasting area are able to pick up the signals.

A further extension of the wireless space-to-space transmission of signals is the use of satellites which pick up signals from one location and send them to distant locations.

ADVANTAGES

Many of the advantages of other audiovisual media also apply to television.

1. It offers a means for providing a common base of experience for all who see a given program at the same time.
2. It brings to the classroom people, places, and events that could not otherwise be seen.
3. Live television—the launching of a space vehicle, the address of the President, or the final game of the World Series—adds the dimension of *immediacy* to events.
4. The preconditionad learner comes to school as a confirmed TV consumer. The use of TV in instruction can capitalize on this acceptance and help him to become a more critical viewer.
5. The reality and concreteness of the visual image are as present in TV as in other audiovisual media.
6. Specialized personnel are often available on TV or videotape. Schools that cannot locate or afford special teachers of elementary foreign languages, for example, can extend the talents of one teacher to many students by television. Very often the teacher who is using TV becomes part of a teaching team which includes the TV teacher, the subject supervisor, and many of the classroom teachers. As teachers use television, many learn new techniques and ideas from the television teacher. This is a major fringe benefit, a type of in-service training.
7. The widespread use of videotape now permits programs to be recorded and used when they are most appropriate. Portable videotape equipment can easily be brought to classrooms and laboratories for recording the performance of individuals or groups; these learners are able to analyze their efforts when the videotape is played back.

LIMITATIONS

1. One of the primary problems of broadcast TV is scheduling. If a teacher does not use a program when it is broadcast (or re-broadcast), it is lost. Consequently, some teachers do not use TV because of timing, or some have used it at inappropriate times simply because it was available and they wanted their students to view the program. The decreasing cost of videotape recorders now permits recording of pertinent programs for playback at an appropriate time.

2. Even on large classroom model TV receivers (21″ and 24″) students may have difficulty in seeing detailed images in large rooms.
3. While there have been genuine attempts to use the visual aspect of the medium, too often instructional TV programs are images of teachers talking. As more teachers gain more experience with the medium and as more is learned about what makes good TV instruction, the quality of programs can be expected to improve.
4. The very familiarity of TV sometimes contributes to habits of inattentiveness and passivity. Students do not know how to learn from TV.

Mentally retarded children at the Johnny Appleseed School in Fort Wayne, Indiana, participate in a recreation period videotaped on a Videotrainer system. Children can look at replays immediately and note how they interact with their peers. The Videotrainer also is an objective indicator of progress the children are making in their school activities.

They often reject it, especially in the secondary schools and colleges, since it appears to be a further step toward depersonalization.

5.   Some teachers perceive TV as a threat, since another teacher is "taking over" when the TV set is on. Some teachers fear that they are being replaced.

SOURCES

Television programs are available from many sources. Current offerings of educational and commercial programs are listed in local papers or the local edition of the *TV Guide*. Programs of special educational value, on both educational and commercial stations, are regularly listed in the *Scholastic Teacher* (50 West 44th Street, New York 10036); *Media and Methods Magazine* (41 East 42nd St., New York 10017); bulletins of the Television Information Bureau (Teacher's Guides to Television, 745 Fifth Ave., New York 10022); and the weekly listings in *Education U.S.A.* (National School Public Relations Assoc., 1201 16th St., N.W., Washington, D.C. 20036; $20 per year for a weekly newsletter).

Programs that have been broadcast by educational television stations, produced for the National Educational Television network, are available from the catalog of *Educational Television Motion Pictures* (NET Film Service, Audio-Visual Center, Indiana University, Bloomington, Ind. 47401). These programs are available in the 16mm film format and on videotape. The National Center for School and College Television (Box A, Bloomington, Ind. 47401) lists complete courses which are available on film and tape.

Programs which have been broadcast on commercial stations are usually assigned to commercial film distributors for rental and sales purposes. It is often necessary to contact the network office to determine which distributor has the "rights" to a specific program. The primary sources for commercial television programs which have educational uses are:

Carousel Films, Inc., 1501 Broadway, New York, N.Y. 10036

Text-Film Dept., McGraw-Hill Book Co., 330 West 42nd St., New York, N.Y. 10036

Modern Learning Aids, 1212 Avenue of the Americas, New York, N.Y. 10036

School and college film libraries often purchase prints of the TV programs from the distributors to rent to local schools. Check local film library catalogs for specific titles.

REFERENCES

For information regarding the technical aspects of television, see Philip Lewis, *Educational Television Guidebook*, McGraw-Hill Book Co., 330 West 42 St., New York 10036 (1961), and *Electrography—Producers Manual*, Magnetic Products Division, 3M Co., St. Paul, Minn. 55101 (1968).

For excellent collections of articles on the use of television in the schools, see Robert M. Diamond, ed., *A Guide to Instructional Television*, McGraw-Hill Book Co., New York (1964), and *Application Bulletins, Vol. 1*, SONY, 47–47 Van Dam St., Long Island City, N.Y. 11101 (1969).

For an analysis of extensive use of TV over a long period of time, see Judith Murphy and Ronald Gross, *Learning By Television*, Fund for the Advancement of Education, 477 Madison Ave., New York 10022 (1966), and *Washington County Closed Circuit Television Report*, Washington County Board of Education, Hagerstown, Maryland 21740 (1963).

Audiovisual materials available on the use of television in the classroom are:

Teaching With Television, filmstrip, 51 frames, color, $6.00. Based on the results of TV research, subjects such as what TV teaching can accomplish, how to use TV in teaching, and how to teach on TV are discussed. (Basic)

Sample programs from NET are available in several "Samplers" from NET Film Service, Audio-Visual Center, Indiana University, Bloomington, Ind. 47401

TV in Your Classroom, filmstrip, 44 frames, color, with 12 min. tape recorded commentary, $15.00. Clarifies the concept of instructional television as a device requiring a cooperative effort. Emphasizes five basic elements of ITV utilization. (Great Plains)

Television Techniques for Teachers, 16mm, 24 min., sound, color, $148.50 (1968). Describes what happens when a teacher suddenly finds himself with a TV set in his classroom and is faced with the myriad problems inherent in such a situation. The teacher educates himself in the use of TV, discovering the many opportunities and pitfalls along the way. (Great Plains)

Demonstration Kits for Utilizing Instructional Television. Each kit contains a 16mm, black and white film approximately 28 min. in length. One teacher's manual contains information for all kits. Each kit may be used individually, but the materials have been designed for use in sequence:

1. *What TV Brings to the Classroom*
2. *Role of the Classroom Teacher*
3. *Preparing the TV Lesson*
4. *Promising Practices*
5. *A Case Study in the Elementary School*
6. *Examples in the Secondary School*

Available for sale or rent from National Association of Educational Broadcasters Teaching Materials Library (NAEB).

SOURCES OF AUDIOVISUAL MATERIALS LISTED IN MEDIA FACTS

Bailey	Bailey-Film Associates, 6509 DeLongpre Ave., Hollywood, Calif. 90028
Basic	Basic Skill Films, 1355 Inverness Drive, Pasadena, Calif. 91103
DAVI	Department of Audiovisual Instruction, National Education Association, 1201 16th St., N.W., Washington, D.C. 20036 (Now the Association for Educational Communications and Technology)
EML	Educational Media Laboratories, 4101 S. Congress Ave., Austin, Texas 78745
GE	General Electric Information Systems-Education, 13430 Black Canyon Highway, Phoenix, Ariz. 85023
Great Plains	Great Plains Instructional Television Library, University of Nebraska, Lincoln, Neb. 68508
IBM	International Business Machines, Armonk, N.Y. 10504
IFB	International Film Bureau, 332 S. Michigan Ave., Chicago, Ill., 60604
Indiana	Indiana University, Audio-Visual Center, Bloomington, Ind. 47401
Kodak	Eastman Kodak Co., Audio-Visual Service, 343 State St., Rochester, N.Y. 14650
McGraw-Hill	McGraw-Hill Films, 330 West 42nd St., New York, N.Y. 10036
Modern	Modern Learning Aids, 1212 Avenue of the Americas, New York, N.Y. 10036
NAEB	National Association of Educational Broadcasters, Teaching Materials Laboratory, Northern Illinois University, DeKalb, Ill. 60115
NFBC	National Film Board of Canada, 680 Fifth Ave., New York, N.Y. 10019
Nova	Academic Games Director, Nova High School, 3600 Southwest 70th Ave., Ft. Lauderdale, Florida 33314
Ohio State	Teaching Aids Laboratory, The Ohio State University, Columbus, Ohio 43210
Rand	The Rand Corporation, 1700 Main St., Santa Monica, Calif. 90406
RCA	RCA Instructional Systems, 530 University Ave., Palo Alto, Calif, 94301
Sterling	Sterling Educational Films, 241 East 34th St., New York, N.Y. 10016
Texas	Visual Instruction Bureau, University of Texas, Austin, Texas 78745
3M	Magnetic Products Division, 3M Co., 2501 Hudson Rd., St. Paul, Minnesota 55119
USAC	National Audiovisual Center, National Archives and Records Service, General Services Administration, Washington, D.C. 20409

MEDIA-SUBJECT AREA MATRIX

HOW TO USE THE MEDIA–SUBJECT AREA MATRIX

General subject area categories are listed across the top; media categories are listed down the left side. To locate an example of the use of a given medium, find the desired category and read across. To locate an example pertinent to a given subject, locate the desired category and read down.

Entries in the columns and rows designate page (by number) and type of objective (by letter).

Key to Letters

A=Affective Objective	M=Motor Objective
C=Constructing Objective	N=Naming Objective
D=Describing Objective	O=Ordering Objective
I=Identifying Objective	U=Unclassified Objective

EXAMPLES

1. I want to find text references to the use of television. I find the appropriate ROW and read across. On page 292 there is a discussion of the use of television to teach something in the category dealing with Language, Grammar, and Speech; the objective, indicated by the "I," is one dealing with Identifying. On page 194 there is a discussion of television as a medium of instruction for a Motor objective in the Spelling and Handwriting category. Reading across this ROW, I see that there are eight additional places in the text where television is discussed.

2. I want to find references to the teaching of Foreign Language. I locate the appropriate COLUMN and read down. On page 106 there is a reference to the use of motion pictures to implement the attainment of an Identifying objective. On page 25 I can find a reference to the use of recordings to implement a Describing objective.

3. I want to find a reference to the use of flat pictures for the teaching of Grammar. At the point of intersection of the appropriate ROW and COLUMN, there is only one entry: on page 167 I can find a reference to a Constructing objective.

	Art	Audiovisual Equipment Operation	Civics	Foreign Language	Geography	Health and Safety	History
Audiotapes and Records; Tape Recorders and Phonographs; Radio		M196	N297	D25 I106	I216	A182, A187 A208-9	N252
Chalkboards			N296				
Demonstrations, Field Trips, Real Things, Community Resources	I97 I104 I150 N213	M315		I98	D293	A184, M194	I106
Diagrams, Charts, Bulletin Boards, Flannel Boards		N114 M196	N297		I94	0149-50 N154, 0154 I155	
Filmstrips and Projectors			N297			A184, A187	I106, N122 I134, N134 D134, I219 N251, D251
Flat Pictures				U299		I104, A182 A187	I106, N122 I134, N134
Games and Simulations							D225
Maps and Globes					D17, I28, I50 N55, N59, N64 I89, I90, I104 N111, N112 N113, N116-18 N131, O155 I290		I116, N116
Models, Mock-ups, Diorama						I45, O153-55 M154, I154 A185, M224	N122
Motion Pictures and Projectors		M196 M298 I316	N297	I106	D226, I292	O154, D154 I155, A182 A184, C208 D221, M224	M122, D131 D132, I134 N134, D134 I165
Opaque Projectors							
Overhead Transparencies and Projectors			N297		I290		N122, I218
Programmed Instruction							
Slides and Projectors	A180-81				I216		I106, N122
Television				I106			
No Specific Medium	N63	U59	D50 O81 D224	U82 I133 N133 D133	C49, I50, N50 N57, D141 I141, C162 M162	O149	O81, D130 O152

Home Economics and Industrial Arts	Language, Grammar, and Speech	Mathematics	Music	Physical Education	Reading and Literature	Science	Social Studies	Spelling and Handwriting
	D17, I292		I105￼C187￼I314	N311	A102, N118-22￼N125, A185￼D293, N311￼D312		D142, A186￼D283	
						N125, O153		
	C167	I80, N80, C81￼I90, N112￼D114, D129￼A187, U209￼C217, I224￼D290		N58￼I193￼M193	N125, I132-33￼N133	I58, I97, I98￼N111, N112￼N113, N124￼D130, N150￼O150, D150￼I169, U209￼U220, U229	A186, D288￼D295	
I104	C167, C168	I140, N140￼D144, O156￼M163, C167￼U211-12			N133, D133￼A177, A181	O63, I97, I98￼I103, N112￼N113, O149￼I169	I96, N113￼D281, D294	
	C168	C163			N123, D133￼D293	D73, I97, I103￼N125, D130￼D270	D142, A179-80￼D283, D294￼D295	
I104	C167	I80, N112￼D290			N111, N125￼D293	I63, I100, N125￼C167, I169￼I281, D299	A186, N299	
	A11	D290				N125, O150￼O156, C167	I95, N95	
	C166	A187, U211-12￼D290	A183	M193￼M309	A102, N125￼D293	D73, I95, I99￼D100, I103￼D129, D122￼D141, I155￼C165, I168￼D269	I142, N142￼D142, A179-80￼A186, D283￼D294, D295	M195
					C165	I169		
	C168, I311￼C316	U211-12	O157	N310	N121, D203￼D311	A15, D73, I97￼N125, D141￼O156, I169￼D269	D294	
M195	C35, D135							C35
M195	C168				A185	D73, I100￼N125, D141	N142, D142￼A186, D295	
M309	I292		M195	M194		D141, D269￼D270	I105	M194
I55￼N115￼O150￼M163	I50, C55￼N59, O150￼I151, N151￼C162, C164￼C166, C314	C49, I61, D80￼O81, N116￼D131, D132￼D133, N140￼D140-41, O150￼O151, I151￼C161, C163￼C164, A178	N114￼O152￼A183	M49￼M64	C50, A101￼D135, A183	O55, O56, I115￼O149, O150￼O152, I152￼A179, N216	C164, A178-79￼D283	